FACILITY PLANNING FOR PHYSICAL EDUCATION, RECREATION, AND ATHLETICS

DAT' 'IE

RICHARD B. FLYNN
Editor and Contributing Author

The Facilities Council
of the
**Association for Research, Administration,
Professional Councils and Societies**
an association of the
**American Alliance for Health,
Physical Education, Recreation and Dance**
1900 Association Drive
Reston, VA 22091

The American Alliance for Health, Physical Education, Recreation and Dance is an educational organization designed to support, encourage, and provide assistance to member groups and their personnel nationwide as they initiate, develop, and conduct programs in health, leisure, and movement-related activities. The Alliance seeks to:

- Encourage, guide, and support professional growth and development in health, leisure, and movement-related programs based on individual needs, interest, and capabilities.
- Communicate the importance of health, leisure, and movement-related activities as they contribute to human well-being.
- Encourage and facilitate research which will enrich health, leisure, and movement-related activities and to disseminate the findings to professionals and the public.
- Develop and evaluate standards and guidelines for personnel and programs in health, leisure, and movement-related activities.
- Coordinate and administer a planned program of professional, public, and government relations that will improve education in areas of health, leisure, and movement-related activities.
- Conduct other activities for the public benefit.

© 1993

**American Alliance for Health,
Physical Education, Recreation and Dance
1900 Association Drive
Reston, VA 22091**

FOREWORD

The American Alliance for Health, Physical Education, Recreation, and Dance has a long history of interest and involvement in facility planning and programming. The material in this text reflects the composite knowledge of many professionals who have contributed to past AAHPERD projects, as well as of those individuals who were solicited to serve as authors, editors, and reviewers for this text.

Richard B. Flynn of the University of Nebraska at Omaha was selected to serve as text editor and contributing author. Flynn, recognized as a leading authority in planning facilities for athletics, physical education, and recreation, has authored a large number of facility-related publications. The chapter authors/editors/reviewers include prominent architects and HPERA professionals with outstanding reputations relative to facility planning.

AAHPERD appreciates the efforts of all those who contributed to this text. We believe it represents one of the most comprehensive resources available on the topic of planning facilities for physical education, recreation, and athletics.

Gilson Brown
Executive Vice President
American Alliance for Health,
Physical Education, Recreation, and Dance

ACKNOWLEDGEMENTS

Appreciation is expressed to the Editorial Board members of ARAPCS for assuming initial responsibility for outlining the content and chapters for the text. While some served as authors/editors for specific chapters in the text, all served as reviewers for assigned chapter drafts.

Dr. Richard B. Flynn, Chair
Dr. Dave Stotlar
Dr. Armond Seidler
Dr. Harvey White
Dr. Raymond Ciszek, AAHPERD Staff Liaison

Thanks also go to Dr. Ted Coates who served as a chapter reviewer.

We are indebted to a number of authoritative sources for permission to reproduce material used in this text:

- The National Collegiate Athletic Association for permission to reproduce drawings from selected 1992 NCAA rule books. It should be noted that these specifications, like others, are subject to annual review and change.

- *Athletic Business* magazine for permission to reprint selected photographs and drawings.

- Selected architectural firms for supplying photographs, line drawings, and other materials.

Special recognition is due those professionals who served as chapter authors/editors: Edsel Buchanan, D.J. Hunsaker, James Karabetsos, Hervey LaVoie, Bradley Macomber, David Miller, Marc Rabinoff, Todd Seidler, Ed Turner, and Harvey White. These individuals worked diligently to present chapter material in an informative and useful manner.

Lastly, the editor wishes to thank and acknowledge Ray Ciszek, Vice President of AAHPERD, for his continued encouragement and support during the preparation of this text.

Richard B. Flynn, Ed.D.
Editor and Contributing Author

TABLE OF CONTENTS

AUTHOR BIOGRAPHIES

Text Editor and Contributing Author

RICHARD B. FLYNN is the Dean of the College of Education, University of Nebraska at Omaha, and served previously as the Director of the School of Health, Physical Education and Recreation at the same institution. He is an internationally recognized authority in the planning, designing and programming of athletic, physical education, and recreation facilities. Dr. Flynn earned his Bachelor's degree from MacMurray College, his Master's from Ohio University, and his Ed.D. from Columbia University.

The Chapter Authors/Editors

EDSEL BUCHANAN is a retired professor and former coordinator of the University of Nebraska at Omaha Recreation and Leisure Studies Program. His primary teaching fields have been administration of health, physical education, and dance; and leadership and programming related to recreation and leisure studies. Dr. Buchanan has held numerous offices in the American Camping Association, AAHPERD, National Intramural-Recreational Sports Association, and has received many awards from local, regional, and national organizations for his service and dedication to the profession.

D.J. HUNSAKER is president of Counsilman/Hunsaker and Associates, Natatorium Planners and Design Consultants in St. Louis, MO. His experience in the arena of recreation and swimming facilities is extensive, having served as past chairman of the Public Pool Division Council of the National Spa and Pool Institute, current member of the Board of Directors of the National Swimming Pool Foundation, past president of the Swim Facility Operators Association of America, and current president of Community Recreation Systems. Mr. Hunsaker is the recipient of three gold medal national awards for design excellence from Swimming Pool Age, NSPI.

JAMES D. KARABETSOS is associate professor and director of campus recreation and the University of Idaho in Moscow, Idaho. He received his Bachelor's and Master's degrees from Northern Michigan University, and his Ed.D. from the University of Northern Colorado. He has taught, coached, and served in sport administrative positions at the interscholastic and intercollegiate levels. His scholarly activities have included publications and presentations in the areas of development of program resources, recreational sports, and sport administration.

HERVEY LAVOIE is principal and president of Ohlson LaVoie Corporation, Architecture and Planning, located in Denver, CO. His firm has developed designs for 112 athletic centers in 24 states, Saudi Arabia, and Japan. Mr. LaVoie's designs have received the Facility of Merit Award from Athletic Business in recognition of an "especially outstanding sports/recreation facility." His degrees in architecture are from the University of Detroit and the University of Colorado, and he is a member of AIA Denver and Colorado.

BRADLEY A. MACOMBER is a Sports Facilities Resource Consultant with two nationally recognized architecture firms. He holds a Bachelor of Science degree in Physical Education and a Bachelor of Architecture degree from Syracuse University. He has served as editor of a number of documents on facilities design for the U.S. Army and Army National Guard, and was consultant to the government of Mexico regarding facilities for the World University Games.

DAVID MILLER is the Sports and Recreation Specialist for Hastings and Chivetta Architects in St. Louis, MO. He holds a Bachelors degree from Western Michigan University, and a Masters degree in Sports and Recreation Administration from Southern Illinois University at Carbondale. Mr. Miller has written many articles for Athletic Business and NIRSA Journal on the topic of sports surfaces and facility design and has worked with many school, university, and community recreation facility projects.

MARC RABINOFF is a professor in the School of Professional Studies, Metropolitan State College, Denver, CO. He holds his Ed.D. from the University of Houston, his Master's degree from the University of Bridgeport, CT., and his Bachelor's degree from Southern Connecticut State College. Dr. Rabinoff has served as a spokesperson for the profession on repeated occasions on national and local radio and television. His areas of expertise include gymnastics, fitness, sports liability, and health clubs. He has published and consulted extensively on risk management.

TODD SEIDLER received his Ph.D. in Sports Administration from the University of New Mexico and is currently the coordinator of the graduate Sports Administration Department at Wayne State University. He is a past chairman of the Council on Facilities and Equipment within the American Alliance for Health, Physical Education, Recreation and Dance and is active as a consultant on facilities for activity. Dr. Seidler presents and publishes frequently in the area of facilities and equipment and often teaches classes on Facility Planning and Design and Facility Management.

ED TURNER received his undergraduate degree from Penn State University and both his Masters and doctorate from the University of Maryland in Physical Education. Dr. Turner is a professor of health, leisure, and exercise science at Appalachian State University in Boone, NC. and has been teaching for 30 years. Past chair of the Facilities Council and a frequent presenter on facility topics, Dr. Turner has been a contributor to earlier editions of this guide.

HARVEY R. WHITE is professor and head of the Department of Health, Physical Education, Recreation and Dance at New Mexico State University in Las Cruces, NM. He received his Bachelor of Science degree from Pembroke State University, his Master of Arts degree from Western Carolina University, and his Ph.D. from the University of New Mexico. He has taught and served as an administrator at kindergarten through university levels. His scholarly interests are in the areas of sport administration (leadership) and facility planning and design.

Chapter 1
FACILITY PLANNING PROCESS: FACTORS TO CONSIDER

by Harvey R. White and James D. Karabetsos

For any new building program to be successful, an immense and exhaustive course of evaluating, priority setting, planning, and estimating is required to address the complex issues inherent with projects of this magnitude. The process is not unlike creating a masterful sculpture or musical composition. Much effort is expended in developing the form or theme of the undertaking - by constantly scrutinizing, revising, refining.

(Joiner, 1991)

INTRODUCTION

Successes or failures in the construction of new or the renovation of old facilities often can be directly attributed to good or poor planning. Errors in fabrication, omission of ancillary features, and miscommunication of needs frequently lead to expensive "change orders" and "cost overruns." These financial debilitants cause needless revenue losses. Even more exacerbating, these errors invariably lead to second-rate results in the construction of the facility which diametrically impair the specific programs for which the facility originally was designed.

Furthermore, the facilities which house the physical education, athletic, and recreation programs to a large extent establish the parameters of program development. With the life span of facilities exceeding 40 to 50 years, effective use of planning techniques will increase both years of usage and the number of users.

HISTORY

In the past, facility planning, as a rule, occurred in a disconnected fashion. Facility administrators, or planning committees, designed their buildings independently of the other agencies within their organizations. This segregation frequently led to vacuous areas of noncoverage or duplication of facilities and programs. These facility planners many times relied solely on hunches and "guesstimates" to design their edifices. Their intuitions and estimates frequently were off-target, and often the facilities they planned did not adequately enhance the programs which were housed within them.

The more conscientious planners of past decades conducted rudimentary surveys to assist with their planning. However, the findings of these surveys on which they predicated their facility designs might not have included input from user groups or program directors. Consequently, this type of "hardline" planning often was received with disgruntled reviews and ambivalent acceptance.

Other types of traditional planning approaches commonly found in past decades included political and "grass roots" planning. In the political planning process, the planner made the facility design decisions to influence certain segments of the population. These "favors" may have resulted in auxiliary benefits to a program but also led to facilities which fell far short of expected standards. The latter strategy, "grass roots" planning, frequently evolved from negotiations with specific segments of the population and led to the selection of specific services or programs for which respective groups lobbied and were not necessarily based on needs assessment findings.

ACCESSIBILITY

Federal, state, and local legislation mandates the provision of certain services to all persons in our society, including individuals with various disabilities. In order for these services to be provided to ALL individuals, architectural barriers must be eliminated. This includes all obstacles which prevent parties from entering the facility or any architectural restraint that hampers moving throughout the building. Accessibility also includes the capability to arrive at the site and requires a physical environment which is designed to enhance usability by individuals who have special needs.

The planning for architectural accessibility is a complex undertaking requiring much conceptual thought, cooperation among facility planners/users, and a positive attitude towards meeting the needs of ALL individuals. Federal health, education, and welfare regulations require that handicapped individuals be consulted when designing public facilities. Supplementally, other good resource groups for facility design include local chapters of national organizations whose primary purpose is to assist individuals who have special needs. A selected list of these organizations is located in the appendix.

Moreover, the standards for designing accessibility are being reviewed and revised constantly; therefore, facility planners must stay informed of changing regulations and assure adherence to current standards in facility design and construction. The specific factors which should be considered in physical education, athletic, and recreation facilities will be discussed in appropriate chapters throughout this book.

PLANNING GUIDELINES

The formulation of requirements is an essential part of facility planning. Regardless of who develops the requirements or how they are developed, they are derived from users, the organizational units, and people who will occupy and use the facility being planned. Accurately defined requirements are essential for effective decisions about leasing, buying, building a new, or modifying an existing building. If requirements are well defined, the resultant solution can achieve a good fit between building and users.

(Bauer, 1986)

The view that users, organizational units, and occupants have primary input into both new construction and/or renovation of existing recreational facilities is the quintessential precept in facility planning. Furthermore, if the data obtained from these principal parties are clearly explained and adequately understood by the designers, the chances of a particular facility meeting the needs of the program constituents is substantially enhanced.

As a result of diminishing financial resources and limited availability of land, effective planning is increasingly important. With input from diverse user groups, plans for facility construction can be realistic and the goal to construct useful, well-designed facilities greatly improved.

The Master Plan (Comprehensive Plan)

To prevent debacles in facility construction because of slipshod planning, today's planners use a well-contemplated, systematized strategy which takes into account the many variables (present and future) which impact the facility. The vehicle is called the Master Plan, or in municipal agencies, the Comprehensive Plan. This Plan is a formal, comprehensive building scheme that identifies the organization's facility needs and establishes the priority in which construction of new or the renovation of existing facilities will occur.

The process of developing a master plan involves a dialog among individuals who have a vested interest in the use of existing and potential facilities. The primary responsibility for developing facility master plans is at the institutional level and involves facility planners, architects, program administrators, community members and engineers. The complexity of developing a master plan is influenced by the size of the institution/agency conducting the planning, human and financial resources available to support the planning process and the master planning skills of individuals involved in the process. An example of the steps that may be followed in the process of developing a master plan for an educational facility is illustrated in Figure 1.1.

The format of master plans may differ among organizations, but basically, they are composed of all the organization's anticipated long- and short-range acquisitions, renovations, and/or constructions. They include all possible community and regional developments, areas which are best suited for future expansion possibilities, predicted demographic shifts, and programmatic need changes. The long-range projection of the Master (or Comprehensive) Plan is usually five or

DEVELOPING A MASTER PLAN

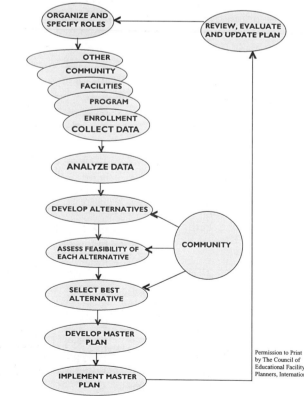

Permission to Print by The Council of Educational Facility Planners, International

Figure 1.1. Developing a Master Plan

ten years, and the short-range projection generally one or two years. In some instances organizations also use long-term forecasts which project a 20- or 25-year outlook (Hamer, 1988). The development and maintenance of a Master Plan is a continuous and ongoing process and is characterized by periods of high active planning. The components of the plan are directed toward the specific planning goals which are identified in the organization's facility development program. (Figure 1.2.)

The components of the Master Plan process that have been presented provide an abstract of transpositions that are to occur at some given point between the present and the future. The general rule when using projections in a Master (Comprehensive) Plan is to forgo conservatism and propose the ultimate in design and imagination. In this way, a state-of-the-art facility is the goal, which allows some latitude for negotiations and cut-backs if future concessions are necessary. Although assurances do not exist, using this progressive approach increases the likelihood that buildings will be well designed and constructed to fulfill the 40- to 50-year life expectancy.

The Master Plan should have as its primary concern the facility requirements and alternatives which are available to accomplish specific goals and objectives of the institution's programs. With a view of what is

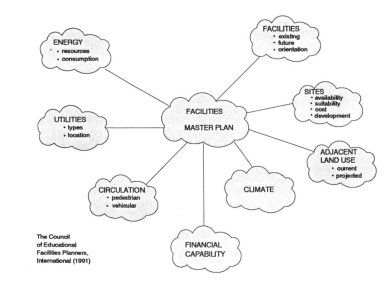

Figure 1.2. Facilities Master Plan

available and what is needed to meet specified goals, facility planners can better understand the sequences which need to take place for alternatives to reach fruition. The Master Plan is paramount in planning, designing, constructing, utilizing, and evaluating quality facility space.

PARTICIPATORY PLANNING

In designing facilities in today's collegiate environment, organizations commonly use a planning approach which attempts to include all persons who are interested in or have a penchant

for physical education, recreation, and athletic (PERA) facility design. The specific thrust varies from one agency to another; (Figure 1.3) that is, community agencies take into account their large, divergent groups, and universities and colleges usually focus on the needs of the educational programs. However, the importance of receiving input from representative user groups is the common thread that is interwoven into the fabric of their approach to facility planning.

A typical participatory, or team planning process, is illustrated in Figure 1.4.

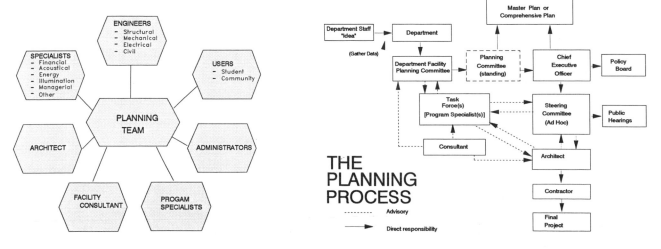

Figure 1.3. Planning Team

Figure 1.4. The Planning Process

Origination of the Idea (Basic Program Level) - The idea typically emanates from individuals intricately involved in the outdated facility and the programs it houses. The idea is discussed carefully and thoroughly, and all facets of the problem are examined judiciously. The accumulation of data justifying the need of the facility is collected and organized in a manner which best supports the proposal. The idea then is carried forward by the originators to the next highest level of authority.

Presenting the Idea to Higher Authority - The personnel conceiving the idea attempt to convince their departmental colleagues of the need for the project, whether it is a new facility or simply remodeling an existing edifice. The amount of support the project engenders at the departmental level plays a crucial, if not vital, part in the project's chances of success. Without support from immediate peers, the project undoubtedly will fail. Therefore, the research findings should be presented in the most effective manner possible, using the presenters' most persuasive techniques with as much empirical data as possible to "sell the project" to their colleagues. The adeptness with which this presentation is achieved and the relevance of the data presented may constitute the deciding factors of whether the idea dies in its conceptual form or is passed on to the next stage for further analysis.

If adequate support is generated, a planning team is selected by the principal administrator of that unit (i.e., department chair, agency head, etc.). The mission of the planning team is to review the initial proposal, modify, and embellish the substance of the report before presenting it to the next highest authority. This embellishment can take the form of an expansive "needs assessment" study, linkage statements with the mission of the organization, figures reflecting a modification or altering programs which reflect the inadequacies of the existing facility, and how the new facilities would enhance the effectiveness of tangential

programs or the organization as a whole. Any other information which would help sell the advantages of investing enormous sums of money for the benefit of a good return on investment could be appropriate to this report.

The single most important requisite when proposing a new or renovating an existing facility is how the project will be funded. Chances that the project will be approved by higher authorities can be enhanced significantly if all available funding sources are researched and a precise funding strategy is developed. This strategy should include a listing of the different funding sources (i.e., governmental grants, private organizations, interested philanthropists, etc.) which are available to support the project or who have expressed a willingness to help provide the necessary funds.

Often the informal "dropping of ideas" or the forwarding of copies of related materials to higher administrative personnel greatly enhances the prospects of the project seeking approval. Therefore, higher authority administrators who possess sympathetic linkages to the project, or who have special interests in the benefits which would be derived from an enhanced program should be identified. The planning team can then make available to these targeted sympathizers all the information possible which would help them make "informed" decisions.

Cooperative Effort to Prepare for Highest Authority - Some colleges/ universities, school systems, and recreation departments require a complex succession of steps to gain project approval, while others have relatively few and simple procedures.

In some organizations (normally the larger ones) there is an intervening step in which a planning committee or board must approve of the proposal before it is passed on to the chief executive officer (C.E.O.). The planning committee usually is composed of high level administrators from inter-departmental agencies who seek answers to ideological questions which reflect

the philosophy of the institution or agency. For this reason the planning committee must revert to the organization's Master Plan when delving into the reasonableness of the facility proposal. The following are examples of the types of questions the planning committee attempts to answer:

- Is it a traditional system, or does it encourage experimentation?

- Are the agencies run independently of other public entities or is cooperation encouraged?

- Is the community able to pay for quality education and programming?

- Is there general support for individual, dual, team, and/or lifetime sports programs?

Answers to these types of questions will help provide a universal consistency to the programs and facilities within the organization and should be dealt with in the Master Plan.

The planning committee may attempt to establish a need by conducting a district-wide (or institution-wide) survey using a validated instrument to authenticate its findings. To further support the need for a new or remodeled facility, comparisons may be made with facility guidelines, facilities at schools offering similar programs, and other important information, i.e., attitudes, interests, desired curricular changes, and the numbers and identity of projected users. If the building project is a "hot issue," that is, faced with much controversy, the deleterious consequences of rejecting the proposal should be identified (i.e., accreditation requirements, liability issues, governmental requirements).

Proposals frequently are shuffled between the department and the planning committee until the proposal is understood clearly, and all areas of concern to the planning committee are addressed. The planning committee then either disapproves the proposal or forwards it to the C.E.O. for review. Frequently, in smaller organizations, the planning committee's responsibilities are assumed by the C.E.O. Consequently, departmental proposals are channeled directly to the C.E.O., and the essential dialogue takes place between this office and the department making the proposal. In either case, the planning committee or the top administrator in the organization should consult the Master Plan to verify that the addition of the new or renovated facility is consistent with the long and short-term plans of the organization.

If the proposal receives approval from the Policy Board, the C.E.O. appoints a steering committee to oversee the building project. This committee is composed of inter-agency representatives, administrators, community representatives, and other individuals who have special interests or proficiencies in facility design or other complementing attributes which would assist with the overall project. A diverse membership promotes better representation which safeguards against biased and ill-conceived design perceptions. However, larger groups are more difficult to assemble, and reaching consensus is often more difficult. Therefore, steering committees usually range in size from no fewer than five and no greater than 10 members.

The steering committee's mission is to develop the procedures for identifying the needs and desires of the constituent groups who are the principal users of the facility. To this end, the steering committee develops a data base of demographic, programmatic, facility design, and financial information, as well as other related data which would have a significant bearing on the new facility. These data frequently are obtained through the use of formal surveys and informal data gathering procedures. In addition, for community facility users, public hearings are held to allow for the airing of support or disapproval by constituencies. This information is used to supplement other needs assessment analyses which have been gathered.

If the building project is to be presented to the public for approval, a public relations (PR) team is appointed. The public relations team first should

Figures 1.5a,b,c. Model and artist's rendering of proposed Miami University Recreational Sports Facility (Courtesy of HOK Sports Facilities Group)

restate and clarify the goals and objectives of the organization so that the public acquires a more definitive understanding of the role of the agency. Then an honest and forthright dissemination of the information on the proposed facility should be carried out by the public relations team, and the needs and value to all potential constituencies who would benefit from the new or renovated facility should be addressed properly.

Establishment of a public relations team and preparation of the

Program Statement for the architect may be started simultaneously if the project is to be presented to the public for approval. Architectural models and artist's renderings of a proposed facility enhance communication between the architect, planning group, potential donors and users. They allow the organization/owner to provide a graphic representation to individuals and groups as support and funds are sought. (Figure 1.5 a,b,c.)

Since the steering committee can often be large and cumbersome, smaller subcommittees or task forces frequently are formed to handle priority areas. All the members of these task force units need not be members of the parent committee, however, the chairperson of each subunit should be a member of the Steering Committee. In this way, a coordinated action between sub-units and the parent committee is facilitated, and a free-flow of information is communicated between task force groups.

Furthermore, since the planning team is composed of individuals directly involved in the programs of the facility, there should also be direct communication between the task force units and the planning team. In this way a sharing of program aims and objectives, data from needs assessments, and other pertinent information relative to the daily operations of the facility can be conveyed easily.

As the task force units examine their assigned priority areas and review the ramifications of the findings, they file a report to their parent group identifying any problem areas which arise and recommending alternative solutions to correct the difficulties. From these alternative solutions the steering committee develops its own alternative solutions and then drafts its "preferred alternatives" which are forwarded to the Policy Board for approval. If their alternatives are rejected they, in turn, revert to the task force subcommittees for further analyses and other recommendations.

Preparing the Program Statement for the Architect - Once a facility project has been approved for detailed planning, a committee needs to be established to accumulate and systemize all information for the architect. The makeup of this committee is predominantly intra-departmental personnel with a member of the highest planning unit in the system, an administrator, and a principal member of the architectural firm to provide direction. The facility consultant, whose responsibilities are defined in

greater detail later in this chapter, should be part of this group.

This committee's role is to gather information from a reasonable sample of user groups and to prepare a final coherent and systematic written report for the architect. This report is called "The Program Statement" and is used by the architect to develop the facility design. To realize an acceptable end product, college and university physical education, athletic, and recreation groups should seek input from program areas such as adaptives, aquatics, team/individual/dual sports, dance, games and outing activities, science, self-testing and combatives, service areas, and team sports. In municipal recreation planning, representation from indoor recreation, outdoor recreation, and therapeutic recreation is germane.

The planning committee works with the architect and makes a majority of the crucial design decisions. This group has the responsibility of reacting to the architect's initial concepts and schematic drawings. It needs to coordinate the planning within the various components of the facility. In addition, it reacts to last minute questions dealing with interpretation, proposal changes, and possible deletions. There should be no changes in plans without first having the input of this committee. When immediate answers are needed, the chairperson of this committee may need to make some of these decisions alone.

A basic administrative principle should be understood clearly by all persons who participate in the planning process. The C.E.O., as the principal administrator of an organization, has the unqualified authority and privilege to intervene in the planning process at any juncture. Some C.E.O.s exercise this right regularly while others prefer to maintain an "at arms length" approach, relying on the system to determine the results. The likelihood of this intervention taking place is predicated on several factors, the most significant being the

management style espoused by the C.E.O.

Renovation, Retrofitting, or Replacing

The practice of buying-using-discarding has become an unacceptable practice today. This not only applies to paper, aluminum cans, and glass, but to facilities as well (CEFP, 1985). Due to the high cost of new construction, upper level administration, whether it be in the private sector, at a university, municipal agency, or in a public school system, has the responsibility of making the wisest use of existing buildings. In meeting this obligation, it is necessary for administrators, with input from knowledgeable resource persons, to consider the feasibility of either renovating or retrofitting an existing building, or of constructing a new facility.

By definition, the renovation of an existing facility is the rehabilitation of the physical features of that building, including the rearrangement of spaces within the structure. Retrofitting, on the other hand, is the addition of new systems, items, features, materials, and/ or equipment to a facility which were not installed at the time the building was constructed. These changes may be minor, or they could be significant to the point of changing the primary function of the facility. (Figure 1.6.)

To accurately ascertain whether renovation, retrofitting, or new construction is the most prudent alternative, administrators have a myriad of factors to consider. One of the more important is the effect that the construction process has relative to ongoing programs. Consideration must be given to program modifications and adaptions that may occur during the construction process. A close scrutiny of the advantages and disadvantages of both the present and the possibility of a new building should be undertaken. The following is an adequate representation of the factors to consider:

Figure 1.6. The upper section of an old gymnasium was remodeled into squash and racquetball courts in the Physical Education, Recreation and Intramural Facility at the University of Hartford.

Cost Considerations

A. What is the cost of new construction to provide comparable space?

B. What is the cost of construction needed to bring the existing facility up to compliance with safety codes/accessibility?

C. Does the cost of renovation or retrofitting exceed 50 percent of the cost of new construction?

D. Will the increased cost of maintaining an older building justify renovation instead of constructing a new facility?

E. Could the existing facility be sold or leased to a private entity to help defray the cost of new construction?

F. If the amount of construction time becomes critical, which method, renovation or new construction, could be completed in the least amount of time?

Site Considerations

A. Is a site available, and how effectively does the site meet the agency's immediate and long-range goals?

B. Is the location of the present structure easily accessible?

C. Is the parking adequate at the present site?

D. How efficient is the sewer and storm water control?

E. How is the soil-bearing performance of the present site?

F. What is the general condition of the grounds?

G. Is there sufficient area for all program activities?

H. Are vehicular drives well located for safe ingress and egress?

I. Are the existing utilities on or near the site adequate to provide the needed services?

Architectural and Structural Considerations

A certified architect and engineer should be sought to determine the following structural factors:

A. Is the present facility aesthetically appealing and structurally sound?

B. Does the existing facility meet current and long-range program goals and, if not, would renovation or retrofitting realistically elevate the facility to acceptable standards?

C. What is the availability of utilities?

D. How energy efficient is the present facility? Does it meet all updated energy codes?

E. Are there signs of deterioration of footings, foundations, or piers?

F. Are structural members adequate and in serviceable conditions?

G. Is the exterior masonry sound? Are there structural cracks, water damage, or defective mortar?

H. What is the condition of the roof and roofing surfaces, roof drains, and skylights?

I. What is the condition of flashing, gutters, and downspouts?

J. What are the conditions of doors and windows?

K. What are the conditions of door hardware and panic devices?

L. What are the locations, numbers, types, and condition of plumbing fixtures?

M. What is the condition and capacity of the present water supply, sewage lines, and drainage systems?

N. Is the present HVAC System adequate and energy efficient? Does it meet updated codes?

O. What is the condition and adequacy of lighting and power distribution systems?

P. Do the existing light fixtures provide adequate illumination in all areas?

Q. Are stairways, circulation patterns, and exits safe and adequate in number?

R. What is the present condition of fire alarms and inter-communication systems?

Educational Considerations

A. Is the building now meeting the agency's program?

B. What is the current inventory of rooms and their sizes?

C. Are laboratories adequately served by all required utilities?

D. Is the library adequate to house the required book collection and to provide media and related services?

E. Are food service facilities adequate to meet present and projected needs?

F. Are physical education, recreation, and athletic areas usable or capable of being retrofitted if required?

Community Considerations

A. Will the renovation of the building be consistent with present zoning requirements and policies?

B. What are the plans for the area served by the program as projected by city or area planning agencies?

C. Is the building on or eligible for placement on the National Register of Historic Places?

D. Will a new facility constitute a political problem with businesses in the private sector?

Before deciding on the wisdom of renovation, retrofitting, remodeling, or replacing, factors concerning the existing and proposed facilities should be evaluated in detail, both individually and collectively. It also would be beneficial for administrators to project a reasonable life expectancy of the facility, taking into account factors such as:

- increased or decreased populations served by the programs within the facility,

- growth and development of areas surrounding the facility, and

- the potential reorganization, community re-zoning, or consolidation of schools in the district.

A decision on whether renovation or retrofitting is advantageous over new construction then should be rendered, based on a composite of all the factors. (Figure 1.7)

THE PROGRAM STATEMENT - A Written Report

The Program Statement is a written report describing for the architect the program concepts and objectives, organizational structure and function, interrelationships of education, recreation and athletic activities, and the proposed future use of the facility. This report describes the program's resources which the proposed facility must sustain and the types and amount of spaces which will best conform to

program requirements. Also known as "The Building Program" or "The Educational Specifications," this document communicates the needs of the organization's programs to the architect and the steering committee. As a consequence, it is an extremely valuable document that serves as a tie-in between the program and technical facility requirements (CEFP, 1991).

The initial step in developing the program statement is establishing goals and objectives to be achieved in each functional area of the programs. Goals are defined as desirable conditions sought, and objectives are defined as specific ends to be achieved in each of the programs.

The next step is to conceptualize the program(s) that are necessary to achieve the desired goals/objectives. Data to be included in the Building Program Statement are depicted in Figure 1.8.

It is essential that the document be written in a clear, concise manner reflecting an optimal as well as minimal level of the program(s) to be offered. The Building Program Statement typically will be the result of a critical evaluation of the current programs determining whether the new programs should be emphasized, if old ones should be eliminated, or if old and new programs should be combined. All facility needs should be considered, both indoor and outdoor, and the location of buildings should be addressed in the report alluding to its importance on programming.

To assure that the Building Program Statement reflects the professional opinion of all members of the Planning Team (intra-departmental personnel, administrators, facility consultant), a rough draft copy should be circulated to all contributors for their review and comments prior to sending the statement to the architect. From this draft a final copy is developed and presented to the steering committee and project architect.

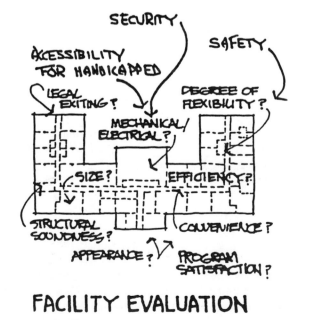

FACILITY EVALUATION

Figure 1.7. Facility Evaluation (Permission to print by the Council of Educational Facility Planners, International)

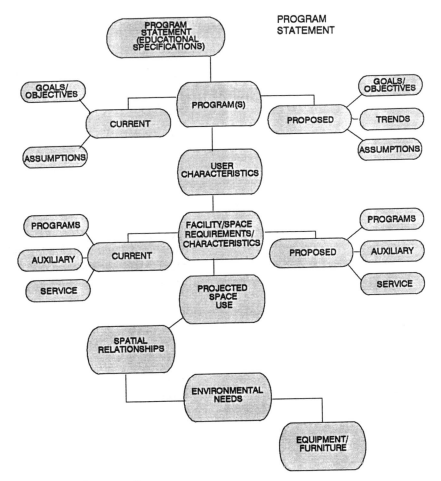

PROGRAM STATEMENT

Figure 1.8. Program Statement Components

A sample Building Program Statement outline follows.

Part I. Objectives of the Programs
A. Instructional (Professional and Service)
B. Recreational Sports
C. Adapted
D. Athletics (Interscholastic and Intercollegiate)
E. Club Sports
F. Community/School Programs
G. Others

Part II. Basic Assumptions to be Addressed
A. Facilities will provide for a broad program of instruction, adapted activities, intramural sports, athletics, club sports, and others.
B. Demographics of the population who will use the facility.
C. Existing facilities will be programmed for use.
D. Basic design considerations - "What's most important?"
E. Facility expansion possibilities will be provided for in the planning.
F. Outdoor facilities should be located adjacent to the indoor facilities.
G. Consideration will be given to the administrative and staff needs.
H. Existing problems
I. Others

Part III. Trends Affecting Planning
A. A re-emphasis of providing ALL programs for the handicapped
B. The club sports movement
C. The Community Education, or "Lighted School" program
D. The surge of new non-competitive activities being added to the curriculum
E. Expanding intramural sports and athletic programs
F. Sharing certain facilities by boys and men and girls and women (athletic training rooms and equipment rooms)
G. Coeducational programming
H. Emphasis on individual exercise programs
I. The weight training movement
J. Federal and state legislation (PL 94-142, PL 503)
K. Systems approach in design and construction
L. New products
M. Others

Part IV. Explanation of Current and Proposed Programming
A. Instructional
B. Intramural sports
C. Athletics
D. Club sports
E. Adaptive programs
F. Community/school
G. Recreational programs
H. A priority listing of programs
I. Others

Part V. Preliminary Data Relative to the Proposed New Facilities
A. The existing indoor facilities, square footage broken down by area (i.e., equipment, storage, training room, etc.)
B. A priority listing for the proposed new indoor facilities and the function of each
C. The existing outdoor facilities broken down by area (i.e., football field, track, etc.)
D. A priority listing for the proposed outdoor facilities and the function of each

E. The community facilities being used as resource or adjunct facility areas for present programs (i.e., golf courses, trap range, rifle range, bowling alleys)

F. Others

Part VI. Space Needs and Allocation in the Proposed New Facilities
A. Main gymnasium
B. Spectator seating
C. Lobby or concourse
D. Administrative offices
E. Faculty offices
F. Conference rooms
G. Laboratory/classrooms
H. Other considerations (wall clocks, acoustical treatment of certain areas, mechanical, etc.)

Part VII. Purposes and Uses of Auxiliary Space Areas
A. Exercise/therapy
B. Multi-purpose gym
C. Golf area
D. Archery area
E. Wrestling gym
F. Main dance studio
G. Street shoe usage room
H. Handball/racquetball courts
I. Squash courts
J. Others

Part VIII. Service Facilities
A. Locker rooms
B. Shower rooms
C. Toweling areas
D. Toilets for locker area
E. Equipment and supply storage areas
F. Custodial storage areas
G. Athletic training rooms
H. Laundry
I. Others

Part IX. Projected use of Present Facilities

Part X. Spatial Relationships (relationship of areas to each other)

Part XI. Environmental Necessities

Part XII. Equipment/Furniture List (all movable and fixed items identified in the document)

PLANNING PROFESSIONALS

Participatory facility planning requires the expertise and cooperation of all individuals involved in the planning process. All participants are important to the process; however, their levels of involvement vary during the different phases of planning based on the need for their services. The expertise of instructors, administrators, facility users, custodians, engineers (mechanical, structural, electrical, civil), program specialists, facility consultants, and architects usually will be needed during the planning of most projects. Input into the Program Statement is normally coordinated through one of the program specialists, facility consultant, or architect. The roles of these three professionals are identified in the material that follows; however, it should be noted that the services provided by all professionals are based on the client's needs and included in the contractual agreement (CEFP, 1991).

Program Specialist

The role of the specialist in facility planning is of general importance. The program specialist normally is an individual who is actively engaged in the use of the facility which is being investigated. The program specialist should be an individual who is knowledgeable about the uses and problems of the facility so that contributions made by this individual in developing the Program Statement are both accurate and realistic.

Examples of the type of input the program specialist offers include the following:

- determines the number of activity stations needed to serve the instructional, intramural, recreation, athletic, club, and adaptive programs,

- helps in the selection of materials (i.e., hardwood, maple floors and/or synthetic floors, lighting requirements, acoustical treatments, and maintenance problems), (Figure 1.9)

In addition, other typical functions of the program specialist include:

- Informs all appropriate persons and the general public about the

Figure 1.9. The program specialist assists in the selection of materials. Lakewood (OH) High School Natatorium--Materials used on the exterior include brick, synthetic stucco, translucent fiberglass paneling, metal roofing, anodized aluminum, and glass.

program purposes, needs for the facilities and explains the facility plans.

- Ascertains the various sizes of teams, classes, and groups which will use the facilities and knows the requirements of their activities and the implications they present in facility design.

- Explores the multiple-purpose uses which are made possible with the new/expanded facilities.

- Assists in establishing a priority list of program needs (i.e., staff agrees that tennis should be taught in the instructional program, introduced as an intramural sports activity, and added as an inter-agency sport. If this is a high priority program, the building of a suitable teaching area would be a high facility priority).

- Monitors trends which are relevant to facility planning (i.e., synthetic surfaces, all weather tracks, coed athletic training rooms, coed and senior citizen classes, programs for the handicapped, total community use of recreational facilities, and rapid development of sports clubs are trends which may be considered in developing program statements).

- Identifies, studies, and recommends desired traffic patterns for various individuals and groups, including spectators.

- Identifies, studies and recommends proper space relationships for various indoor and outdoor facilities. Within the locker room complex, the laundry space, equipment storage space (both in and out of season), equipment issue area, athletic training area, and sauna may be arranged so that coed use is feasible. Duplication of personnel and equipment can be avoided by dual usage.

- Points out errors of design, space relationship, traffic patterns, safety, supervision, isolation, assessibility, flexibility, departmentalization, validity, and aesthetics.

- Provides the architect and planning committee with examples of facilities that meet desired needs. If the sites are too distant for visitation, slides or pictures may be taken as illustrations for the architect and planning committee. Points out areas that represent quality as well as those that represent minimal quantitative standards.

- Points out the special considerations necessary to allow handicapped persons full use of facilities.

The program specialist may be assisted by a facility consultant in identifying specific material needs, dimensions, space relationships, innovations, and other pertinent information.

Facility Consultant

A facility consultant is frequently a professional in the field who is either employed by another organization or is self-employed in the facility consulting business. This individual usually has had experience with facility planning and is familiar with recently constructed facilities in the country. The consultant is up-to-date with the latest innovations in facility design, construction materials, building concepts, and general programming. In many instances this professional should know the location of some recent renovation or construction projects and would be a good reference to the planning committee when hiring an architect.

An outside consultant assists the planning committee in developing alternatives and establishing priorities in its building project. As an objective expert, the consultant normally is looked upon as an influential person who can exert considerable influence in persuasion, which often may lead to the deciding factor on items in "hot" debate.

A facility consultant may assist in selecting an architect and may serve as a liaison between the architect and the steering committee. The consultant's role becomes more critical when the architect lacks professional orientation which may result in difficulty relating to individuals in a specific pro-fession. For this reason, and for the previous stated functions which often fall upon the shoulders of the facility consultant, the selection of this person is of significant importance in constructing a functional facility.

Architect

The central and most critical member in the facility planning and design process is the architect. Since the architect's role is of paramount importance, a great deal of thought and discussion should be centered on the firm and/or individual selected. Factors to consider when selecting an architect are the firm's knowledge and experience, the project architect's job related experience, and the project architect's interpersonal skills and ability to establish rapport with other members of the planning team. Ideally, the entire steering committee should participate in the selection of the architect.

There are three basic methods for selecting an architect:

1) The architect may be appointed by the State Building Commission;

2) The architect may be selected by a direct appointment;

3) The architect may be selected through competition from a group of prospective architects.

Most states have laws that require that the architect selected be licensed to practice architecture in a state where the facility is to be erected. The American Institute of Architects can be helpful in providing information relative to the certified individuals in a given geographic area. The selected architect should possess an impeccable reputation in the field, be able to furnish references of previous clients, and show proof to the steering committee of completed projects which are similar in nature and design to the proposed project.

There is a decided advantage in selecting an architectural firm which is in close proximity to the construction site. Besides the political benefits of this selection, the close proximity to the construction site allows for frequent visitations to the site and provides a greater safeguard against the possibility of major errors. In recent years it has been common for local architects to enlist the assistance of larger national firms specializing in sports related facilities. With supervision as an integral function of the architect's responsibilities, the selection of an individual whose management skills are well honed is preferred.

A common practice used to select architects is to request proposals (RFP) from qualified firms stating the specifications needed. The RFP is developed reflecting facility needs specified by the Program Statement. The RFP is submitted to the planning committee which uses the proposal when selecting the architect for the project.

The architect's responsibilities are numerous and vital, and may include, but are not limited to, the following:

In regard to **Pre-Design Planning**:

a) Program representatives identify the facility and equipment needs of all user groups of the facility. A differentiation of the critical from less acute needs will greatly assist the architect's efforts.

b) The architect develops a written ledger of requirements and explains the architectural possibilities and limitations.

c) The architect develops a time schedule for each stage of the project.

d) The architect turns the Program Statement into an architectural or building program.

In regard to **Schematic Design** the architect:

a) Translates the written program into a graphic representation of a building plan.

b) Designs and presents plans regarding space relations of various functions and accessibility to the facility for different functions. Shows how the facility will satisfy the needs as identified in the pre-design conference.

c) Studies the site, its topography, its relationship to the community and to traffic patterns, and the availability of utilities. Determines how the site might be developed.

d) Determines what types of buildings are most appropriate for the site and the program.

e) Reviews applicable codes and laws to determine their effect on the design.

f) Conducts preliminary cost studies of the project.

g) Provides opportunities for thorough analyses and discussions of strengths and weaknesses of plans and reaches decisions with programmers on how well the facility satisfies the requirements of the program.

h) Presents the approved schematic design for acceptance.

In regard to **Design Development,** the architect:

a) Develops the general design of the facility once approval from highest authority is secured.

b) Prepares sketches of elevations and models to establish the visual character of the project. (Figure 1.10)

c) Determines building materials and outlines their specifications along with the utilitarian value, aesthetic qualities, and mechanical and electrical systems.

d) Makes equipment and furniture arrangements which conform to the project specifications.

e) Develops detailed cost estimate and final plans for the steering committee and proper authorities to review and approve.

In regard to **Construction Documents,** the architect:

a) Prepares complete working drawings and construction specifications.

b) Reviews and updates earlier cost estimates.

In regard to **Bidding,** the architect:

a) Assists the client in obtaining bids and awarding contracts.

b) Determines with the client how the project will be bid and the contractors who will be qualified to bid.

c) Answers questions for bidders and clarifies any aspects of the construction documents.

d) Provides copies of specifications, documents, and drawings for contractors, owners, and others who may need them.

e) Assists client in preparation of the construction contract.

During the **Construction Phase,** the architect:

Figure 1.10. Architects develop models to depict the proposed facility. (Courtesy of Ohlson LaVoie Corporation)

a) Meets with the client and contractor to outline the project and discuss operating procedures.

b) Issues bulletins and change orders to accomplish changes requested by the client or required by field conditions.

c) Visits the site frequently to monitor progress of work.

d) Interprets requirements of the contract when questions are raised.

e) Rejects work which fails to meet requirements.

f) Establishes the date of "Substantial Completion" and the date of "Final Completion."

Additional Services

There are a number of additional services the architect may perform as required or as requested by the client. These services require prior authorization from the client, and the architect usually is paid for them, in addition to the basic fee. Some of these services are:

- makes measured drawings of existing construction when required for planning additions or alterations,

- revises previously approved drawings, specifications, or other documents to accomplish changes not originally initiated by the architect,

- prepares change orders and supporting data where the change in basic fee is not commensurate with the services required,

- prepares documents for alternate bids requested by the client,

- provides detailed estimates of construction costs,

- provides consultation and professional services concerning replacement of work damaged by fire or other causes during construction,

- provides interior design work or other services required in connection with selection of furniture or furnishings, and

- provides services as an expert court witness.

SUMMARY

Poor facility planning often leads to needless expense and frequently produces inadequate results. Therefore, the importance of a properly planned building approach cannot be overemphasized.

An organization's approach to facility planning can be enhanced immeasurably with the use of a Master Plan (Comprehensive Plan). This invaluable planning guide helps avoid communication failure and provides all persons, from high level administrators to program directors, with a "beacon" around which present and future building strategies can be focused.

The participatory planning process is based on the precept that all individuals who have an interest can give input into the design of a facility. The participatory process begins with the "idea" and, after consulting with program professionals, is taken to the next higher authority (usually the department administrator) for backing and embellishment. If approved, the proposal, along with documented support, is advanced to the planning team or committee (larger organizations) or directly to the C.E.O. (smaller organizations) for endorsement. The C.E.O., after consulting the Master Plan, and upon receiving approval from the Policy Board, appoints a steering committee to oversee the project. The steering committee then becomes the principal decision-maker in the construction project.

The steering committee selects the project's architect and functions as a data gathering body which makes judgments on problems that arise in the construction phase. The committee also may choose the facility consultants and program specialists who advise the committee (and project architect) on specifics in their respective areas of expertise.

If the endeavor is politically controversial, requiring special funding, or if a special need for public support is perceived, the steering committee has the option to hold public hearings. The committee appoints a public relations committee which informs the public of the project particulars, answers questions, and facilitates all group discussions.

The steering committee remains involved with the project until the facility is completed. During the later stages of the construction phase, the primary responsibilities of the committee are to advise the architect on design problems which arise and to inform the C.E.O. of the progress of the project.

A Program Statement is a written report developed to assist the project architect in designing the facility. Inasmuch as this document becomes the primary guide by which the architect bases his/her drawings, it is paramount that input into this document is provided by representatives of all program areas.

The decision to renovate an existing facility or to build a new facility must be addressed by upper level administrators (normally the C.E.O.) early in the planning process. With input from structural engineers and architects, many considerations (i.e., cost, site, structural, educational, and community) must be contemplated before deciding upon the feasibility of new construction. Only after all information is considered is a decision rendered as to which type of project would be the most cost effective, while yielding the most favorable results.

The project architect is the central figure in the construction process. Because of the prominence of the architect's role, a great deal of thought should be given to the selection of this individual. The architectural firm's reputation, location, and previous experience should be considered and the request for proposal ("RFP") process is recommended. The architect then works with the steering committee, consultants, and specialists to design the facility. In return for the agreed upon fee, the architect is responsible for a number of specified items. Additional services can be rendered. However, additional financial compensation generally is expected in return.

Planning for a facility is the most important step in the entire building process. It is initiated with the inception of the "idea" based on a proposed set of actions by which the program goals/objectives can be achieved and terminated with the final "signing-off" of the completed facility. If properly managed, the planning phase can be the driving force towards completion of a magnificent and functional athletic, physical education, and/or recreational facility. (Figure 1.11)

REFERENCES

Bauer, Robert L. 1986. *Facilities Planning*, New York: Amacom, American Management Association.

Council of Educational Facility Planners (CEFP), International. 1985. *Guide for Planning Educational Facilities*. Columbus, OH.

Dahnke, H., Jones, D., Mason, T., & Romney, L. 1971. *Higher Education Planning and Management Manuals*. Boulder, CO: Western Interstate Commission for Higher Education and American Association of Collegiate Registrars and Admissions Officers.

Flynn, Richard B. (Ed.). 1985. *Planning Facilities for Athletics, Physical Education, and Recreation*, The Athletic Institute and American Alliance for Health, Physical Education, Recreation and Dance.

Flynn, Richard B. June, 1981. The Team Approach to Facility Planning, *Athletic Purchasing and Facilities*, pp. 12-26.

Hamer, Jeffrey M. 1988. *Facility Management Systems*, New York: van Nostrand Reinhold Company.

Joiner, David. May, 1991. The Process: Programming, Design and Construction. *The Pressbox.*

Figure 1.11. A completed facility is the result of cooperative and careful planning. Student Activity Center, Central Michigan University. (Photo by Balthazar Korab, Ltd., courtesy of TMP Associates, Inc.)

ABOUT THE AUTHORS:
Harvey R. White is professor and head of the Department of Health, Physical Education, Recreation and Dance at New Mexico State University in Las Cruces, New Mexico.

James D. Karabetsos is associate professor and director of campus recreation at the University of Idaho in Moscow, Idaho.

Chapter 2
INDOOR FACILITIES
by Ed Turner

Included in this chapter is information on physical education, athletic, and recreational indoor facilities for college/university, elementary school, and secondary school levels. Factors common to all levels are discussed first, along with college/university indoor areas. Specific information is provided on the special design needs of elementary and secondary schools' indoor spaces, along with a comprehensive checklist on general indoor facility features to aid in planning.

SITE SELECTION

Site selection either can help keep costs down, or it can escalate costs phenomenally. A first and paramount consideration in site selection is to be concerned with what is below ground level at the site. Placing the building in an area with large quantities of underground rock will be costly because rock needs to be drilled and blasted and is time consuming to remove. A site with little or no underground rock encropments will be much less costly to excavate.

Underground water also may create delays in construction since it must be dealt with as foundations are dug and poured. Dealing with this water is costly in time, labor, and materials so it would be best to select a site with little or no underground water. Even when construction with underground water problems is completed, there is a good chance this water will be an unending nightmare in the facility for the duration of its existence. Constant water seepage into below ground portions of the building and continuous use of sump pumps are additional cost factors. All possible site areas always should be tested for underlaying rock and water problems.

In selecting a building site, one also needs to look above ground. Try not to select a hilly or mountainous area to build the facility because excavation costs will be high. Usually it is much cheaper to excavate level or nearly level ground than it is to excavate hills, mountains, or rolling terrain.

Another important above ground consideration in site selection is existing water runoff and flood plains. Placing a building in a flood plain is not allowed by most zoning codes. However, if no zoning or little zoning is prevalent, for example in a very rural area, one needs to pay particular attention to nearby streams and rivers. These sometimes small streams and rivers may swell to immense proportions and flood their banks during the rainy seasons and during heavy downpours. If the newly constructed facility is in the flood plain, the overflow waters may flow directly into the facility. When building, stay away from flood plain areas. Check topographic maps and check with local inhabitants as to which direction waters flow during flood stages. If the facility must be constructed near or on a flood plain, the use of pilings can keep the building above water and therefore keep the water out of the facility.

Another water problem to be avoided in site selection is runoff water from nearby hillsides and slopes that could be funneled to the building site and thus cause water drainage problems in the facility. Along with this, the location of springs and other underground water sources need to be planned for. Some springs are considered to be wet weather springs and flow only during moist seasons. These ''wet'' weather spring areas need to be determined and planned for so that the facility can be built around them, not over them.

Two other factors that need to be considered in site selection are prevailing winds and natural barriers. In selecting the building site, plan to utilize natural barriers such as berms, hills, and wooded areas to control prevailing winds in order to reduce facility heating and cooling costs.

Still another consideration for building site selection is planning to utilize natural energy. This may take two totally different forms. The first is to plan for solar energy either in an active form or a passive nature. The facility may not be in an extremely sunny environment, yet passive solar energy might heat the hot water, creating a good yearly operational savings. Total solar energy can heat and cool the facility at a very reasonable initial cost of installing the basic solar energy system. With the use of solar energy in mind, the layout, direction, and axis of the building will need to be properly planned for to take full advantage of existing sun rays.

The other natural phenomena to consider in site selection is to investigate deep underground pools of geothermally heated water called aquifers. If one can tap into these subterranean heated pools of water, much of the facility's hot water and possibly the total heating and cooling of the building can be done with this energy. Several schools have made use of aquifers with good success.

Planning for a new facility site selection also should take into consideration other existing sport and recreational facilities. Rather than building duplicate facilities such as locker rooms, shower rooms, storage areas and the like, connect the new building with the old facilities and jointly use existing areas. This can be a real cost reducer and therefore can add new usable square footage within the new complex. Buildings may be attached directly or may utilize above ground enclosed corridors, underground tunnels, or enclosed sky walks. Parking is another important "shared space." If there is ample existing parking near current facilities, make use of it and save the cost of developing new parking areas at the new building site.

Access needs to be considered in building site selection. Access in site selection takes two forms. The planner needs to consider access for construction. If the site has close and easy access for development and construction via existing roads, it will save money. Along with this concept, if building and materials must be hauled into difficult access areas, it takes a much longer time to have the materials on site. And in this case, the old adage "time is money" is very appropriate. The placement of the new building in relation to the existing infrastructure is important. If existing infrastructures must be extended over long distances, costs will be very high. Site selection "in close" many times saves much money in relation to new utility installation.

Site selection must be planned for public and user access. Utilizing existing roads rather than constructing new thoroughfares is important in site selection. If a selected site needs new roads, attempt to keep the new roads as short as possible in order to save costs.

Developmental constraints in site selection are important both politically and legally. Restrictive zoning, easements, covenants, and other possible legal constraints all need to be investigated before site selection is confirmed. Community resistance can be a major developmental constraint. Physical education, recreation, and athletic complexes are large facilities

and can create many problems for nearby residents of the community. This potentially volatile situation may be lessened by involving the community in the site selection process and having the general public be knowledgeable as to the reasons and justifications for site selection.

PEDESTRIAN TRAFFIC CIRCULATION

Building location is a most important consideration in traffic circulation and control. A careful study of the relationship of the proposed structure to student housing, academic buildings, classrooms, and the community will provide valuable information relative to placement of primary and secondary entrances and exits.

The foremost purposes of planning for traffic circulation and control include:

- minimizing congestion in corridors, stairwells, locker rooms and spectator areas,

- minimizing the disturbance of students and staff in offices, classrooms, and study rooms,

- providing for ease of building supervision and separation of various units where necessary,

- enhancing efficient and safe movement, both during normal use and during emergency times, and

- providing for future building expansion.

Special circulation problems created by intramural, recreation, and spectator programs should be included in the traffic control study. The placement of service, activity, instructional, and spectator areas should provide for efficient means of supervising those using the facilities.

Area Relationships

The relationship of activity areas, instructional areas, and service areas to the placement and size of corridors,

lobbies, stairs, and doors needs careful consideration. Spectator spaces should be separated from the swimming pool and pool deck areas, gymnasium floor, and other activity areas. Entrances to the seating area should be direct from the outdoors or from corridors or foyers without requiring travel through locker rooms or across pool decks or gymnasiums. It also is important that traffic to and from the locker room not cross the gymnasium floor.

The individual components of the locker room areas should permit entrance to, and exit from, each area without cross traffic in wet and dry areas. The location of restrooms in relation to the swimming pool and to outside facilities should be given careful consideration, especially with reference to public use.

Multi-level structures need relationship planning both horizontally and vertically. Classrooms and office relationships with activity areas need to be planned carefully for traffic flow, acoustics, safety, and security.

Units within the building which require truck delivery service should be grouped to reduce the number of delivery points. Delivery of supplies should be planned so there is no traffic or delivery through locker rooms or across gymnasium floors. A loading dock is desirable. In multi-storied structures, elevators should be provided.

Corridors, Foyers and Lobbies

In large buildings, athletic and instructional units should be accessible from at least two passageways leading from the principle classroom areas to prevent traffic congestion during change of periods.

Provision needs to be made for heavy traffic from the dressing rooms or the locker suites to playfields. The designated corridor widths should be clear of all obstructions, including the swing of locker and room doors. All equipment, such as heating units, drinking fountains, fire extinguishers, and telephones, should be recessed.

Each corridor should terminate at an exit or stairway leading directly to a point of exit.

Public rooms, including gymnasiums used for large public groups, should be designed with entrance foyers. The size of the foyer will depend on the seating capacity. The planning of this area should include consideration for ticket sales, concessions, public telephones, and an information desk, designed for both personnel and a 24-hour computer monitor service. The foyer should be accessible to public toilets for men and women. Often, it is advisable to provide cut-off gates or lockable doors, so it will not be necessary to supervise the entire building when specific areas are not in use. Try to keep foyers and lobbies as open as possible to aid in security. Corridors should be as short and straight as possible. Bends and corners in corridors hinder supervision and make maintenance more difficult. The size of all three of these areas will be dictated by the square footage of the facility, the number of users, and local, state, and federal guidelines.

Stairways, Ramps and Elevators

Buildings of two or more stories should have no fewer than two stairways located at the extremes. All stairways should be of fire-resistant construction, and all main stairways should lead directly to grade exits. Two-lane stairways are recommended, and they should have a clear width to conform with the local fire code.

Stairways should be divided into runs of not more than 16, nor fewer than three risers. Risers should not exceed 6 1/2 inches, and treads should be at least 10 1/2 inches measured from riser to riser. The rounded nosings of all treads and landings should have nonslip, flush surfaces. Abrupt over-landing nosing should not be used.

Adequate stair aisles must be provided for all bleachers of more than three rows, whether movable or fixed.

Circular or winding stairways should be avoided. Any curved stairway creates a safety hazard with steps being narrow on one side and normal on the other side. Nonslip ramps are desirable to compensate for minor differences in levels in floors and to accommodate the special needs of the handicapped. Ramps make traffic flow easier, but they utilize more space than stairs. Where ramps are employed, the height-length ratio and width must meet or surpass federal handicapped guidelines. Changes in ramp direction (turns) must be planned carefully for wheelchair users so as to provide enough space to easily turn a wheelchair.

Elevators must be provided in any structure of more than one floor. This is necessary first for the handicapped individual, and second for moving heavy objects and equipment from floor to floor. The size and number of elevators will be determined by local, state, and federal guidelines. All stairways, ramps, and elevators should have minimum maintenance handrails, newel posts, floor surfaces, and baseboards. The use of polished aluminum or stainless steel for handrails and posts and a dark baseboard at least four inches high is recommended to keep maintenance to a minimum in these high traffic areas.

Access-Egress, Doors

Exits should be located so at least one exit, or stairway leading to an exit, will be within 100 feet of a doorway of every room designed for occupancy. Every floor should have at least two exits, remote from one another, and additional exits as prescribed by the National Fire Protection Association formula in the Building Exits Code. Exits should be located for convenience as well as for safety. It is important that the number of exits and their locations be properly related to the seating capacity and the space in the gymnasium, swimming pool, or other gallery areas.

All doors should open outward, with the entire door swinging free of the door opening (side hinges). Double exterior doors either should not have a center mullion or be provided with a removable center mullion so that each door will operate independently and allow large equipment and wheelchairs to pass through. Every room should be provided with exits as prescribed by the Building Exits Code, and all outside doors should be equipped with panic hardware.

The doors to rooms where combustible material is kept should be constructed in accordance with Fire Underwriters' specifications. Exterior doors and all doors in damp areas, such as the swimming pool area, laundry rooms, shower rooms, whirlpool, jacuzzi, sauna, and steam rooms should be heavy-duty and moisture-resistant.

If exterior doors cannot be recessed, they should be protected against the weather by projections, overhangs, or soffits. The overhangs must be large enough to afford protection. Outside entrances should be provided with mud and dirt grates or mats for cleaning the mud and dirt from shoes. One method which has proved satisfactory is the use of a grate-covered recess about six feet deep and the width of the door opening, placed so persons entering the building must walk across it with both feet. Consideration should be given to the size of the openings in the grate to prevent accidents to persons wearing high-heeled shoes. Rough textured porous synthetic mats also have been effective in removing debris at entrances/exits.

While minimum widths of corridors, stairways, and exits are determined by local codes, these areas should be considered in the light of maximum use of the building's facilities. Stairways and exits are most important in preventing traffic congestion and should, in most cases, be wider than code requirements.

It also is important to plan for immediate adjacent traffic flow on the outside of the building. Internal traffic flow might be well planned, but if all traffic comes to a standstill as users disembark the building, a flow and safety problem still exists. Therefore, it is important to plan for adequate adjacent perimeter walkways, ramps, stairs, and hard surfaced areas to allow pedestrian traffic to disburse quickly.

Internal traffic circulation should be planned to move pedestrians through the shortest, quickest, and safest route. Major circulation patterns need to be planned around existing office and classroom space for both acoustical and security reasons. Most doors open outward into hallways, so high pedestrian traffic hallways need to be planned with this in mind. Internal doors need to be wide enough to pass large equipment and wheelchairs. Double doors, to rooms where large gymnastic type equipment is utilized, should not have a center mullion.

Thresholds should not be placed in any internal doorways so as not to impede wheelchairs, wheeled carts, and floor cleaning.

All doors should have low maintenance push plates and kickplates attached securely to them. These plates should be placed at the spots where most hands and feet will hit the door. All access areas must be equipped with ample locks and security systems to prevent vandalism and theft.

TEACHING STATIONS

The unit of primary importance is the room or space where teaching occurs. All other parts of the school plant are, in a real sense, secondary. In physical education the determination of the number and character of the teaching stations is basic to the planning process.

The term "teaching station" is used to identify any room or space where one teacher can instruct or supervise the learning experience of a class or group of students. For instance, a gymnasium would constitute a teaching station and if divided, could provide two or more teaching stations.

Swimming pools, auxiliary physical education teaching stations, and dance rooms are examples of other kinds of teaching stations. More than one class can meet in an activity space at a time. For example, a diving class and a beginning swimming class may meet simultaneously, utilizing opposite ends of the aquatics area, and thus affording two teaching stations in the pool area. The number of students accommodated by a teaching station is controlled by the nature of the specific activity as well as the size of the facility.

Institutions will vary as to the timing of peak load and consequently, as to when the required number of teaching stations is needed. Colleges and universities with a large professional preparation program and/or a required program for the general student body usually will have the greatest need during the regular instructional hours. Other schools may find the greatest need for different teaching stations during the after-school hours when athletic teams are practicing or when an extensive intramural program is in operation. Schools in a climate which has a long cold season will have a greater need for extensive indoor facilities.

The number of teaching stations required is dictated by enrollment, policies pertaining to instructional physical education, average class size, diversity of program, number of periods in the school day, and other uses of the facilities. Folding partitions and dropnets can be used effectively for flexibility and to increase the number of teaching stations within a given area.

Planners should be aware that indoor facilities for physical education, athletics, and recreation are difficult and costly to expand at some future date. The ultimate enrollment potential should be researched by the school planner. The anticipated enrollment five to 10 years after completion of construction should serve as a basis for determining the required number of original teaching stations. Long-range planning is imperative to provide for

the logical and most economical expansion. The initial design should make provisions for the anticipated construction.

Two aspects of activity-oriented teaching stations need special mention. Planned storage is a must for each teaching station. There should be no need to carry heavy, cumbersome equipment or a large number of items to class each day. Well planned built-in storage areas will vary in size and location within the teaching station depending on the activity, the numbers of students, the type of instruction, and the type of equipment utilized in the class. All storage areas should be well secured. Lastly, in our high tech, computerized, audio-visual world, each teaching station should have a planned, built-in video system with at least one wall or ceiling mounted camera, a tape deck, and a 25-inch color monitor. Videotaping students while performing activity and allowing them to view themselves should be standard procedure for all classes. Ample security and protection should be provided for this equipment. There should be no new facility or renovated facility for activity use where the instructor needs to constantly move and carry audio-visual equipment for class use. The cost factor for built-in videotaping is negligible in comparison to other building costs.

SURFACE MATERIALS

The selection of indoor surface materials becomes complicated because indoor facilities may be subject to multi-use and they must meet minimum standards in terms of acoustical and light-reflecting properties. Geographic location and the availability of certain surface materials are factors to be considered as to costs of various surfaces.

Figure 2.1 is a guide to suggested indoor surface materials for certain spaces in the activity complex. Other specific sport activity surfaces will be discussed under that specific activity.

Figure 2.1. Suggested Indoor Surface Materials

ROOMS	FLOORS						LOWER WALLS								UPPER WALLS						CEILINGS			
	Carpeting	Synthetics	Cement, asphalt, rubber, & nonabrasl., linoleum	Maple hard	Terrazzo, abrasive	Tile, ceramic	Brick	Brick, glazed	Cinder Block	Concrete	Plaster	Tile, ceramic	Wood Panel	Moistureproof	Brick	Brick, glazed	Cinder Block	Plaster	Acoustic	Moisture-resistant	Concrete or Structure Tile	Plaster	Tile, acoustic	Moisture-resistant
Apparatus Storage Room			1	2			1				2	1	C											
Classrooms		2		1							2	1			2			2	1		C	C	1	
Clubroom		2		1							2	1			2			2	1		C	C	1	
Corrective Room	1			2					2	1					2		2	2	1	2				1
Custodial Supply Room			1			2																		
Dance Studio				1																	C	C	1	
Drying Room (equip.)			1		2	2	1	2	1	1						1		1						
Gymnasium	1			1					2	1					2	2	2	1	2	*	C	C	1	
Health-Service Unit		1		1							2	1			2			2	1				1	
Laundry Room			2			1	2	1	2	2			1	C	*					*			*	*
Locker Rooms		3		3	2	1		1	2	2	3	1			*	1		1	2			C		1
Natatorium		2				1	2	1	3	2			1		*	2	2	1		*	*	C	1	*
Offices	1		3		2				2			1	1			2	1						1	
Recreation Room		2		1			2		2		1	1			2			1	2	*		C	1	
Shower Rooms			3		2	1		1		2	1				*	2	1	2	2				1	*
Special-activity Room		2		1					2			1	1			1	1					C	1	
Team Room	1		3		2	1	2	1	2	2	3	1			*	1		1	2			C	1	
Toilet Room			3	-	2	1		1	2	2	2	1			*	1		1	1				1	
Toweling-Drying Room			3		2	1		1		2	1				*	2	1	2	2		*		1	*

Note: The numbers in the Table indicate first, second, and third choices. "C" indicates the material as being contrary to good practice. An * indicates desirable quality.

Floors

The activity within a given teaching station should dictate choice of the floor surface. Unfortunately, many teaching stations are utilized for many activities. This multi-use application, along with cost factors, also must play a large role in floor surface selection. Just as important as the before-mentioned selection factors is the safety component that a specific floor surface affords to its users. Longevity, along with daily and long-term maintenance costs, also must be investigated as one makes the final decision on floor surfaces.

At least three distinct types of floor surfacing are required in facilities described in this chapter. Floors in service areas such as locker rooms, shower rooms, toweling rooms, and toilet rooms require a surface impervious to moisture. In general, gymnasiums and other activity areas require either a hardwood or a resilient synthetic material. Classrooms, corridors, offices, and like areas may be grouped together for common surfacing.

Special activity areas require different treatments. For example, a dance gymnasium that is used for instruction in modern dance should have a finished treatment which will allow the dancers to slide or glide across the floor. In other areas, such as basketball courts, the finish should be of a nonslip nature.

Flexibility, durability, and cost are three criteria that have been instrumental in seeing synthetic surfaces challenge hardwood floors for installation in activity areas. Synthetics take the form of synthetic grass surfaces or as smooth or roughed non-grass surfaces. The most popular synthetic surfacing materials can be classed into two types: plasticized polyvinyl chlorides (PVCs) and polyurethanes. The PVCs are primarily prefabricated, while the polyurethanes are either poured in place or are produced in factory prefabricated sheets which are adhered on the site. In general, the polyurethanes possess most of the desirable characteristics sought in a floor surface.

In general in the past, classrooms, corridors, and offices have been satisfactorily surfaced with some type of tile, such as asphalt, vinyl, vinyl asbestos, rubber, or linoleum. Consideration now should be given to utilizing carpet and other synthetic surfaces in offices, classrooms, hallways, and other appropriate areas. Hard maple floors are the most expensive to install initially, yet over a long time span, the square footage cost is less than most synthetic surfaces. Indoor-outdoor carpet is the cheapest floor surface of the four, compared over the long time frame.

It must be understood that there are many different types or "systems" of hard maple floors, and the cost varies from system to system. Costs also vary with synthetic surfaces and carpets, depending on the materials that form the body of the surface and the actual thickness of the surface. Thicker synthetic surfaces may give more resilience and absorb more shock, but they are more expensive.

Walls and Ceilings

In addition to isolating and dividing specific areas, walls should serve as barriers to sound, light, heat, and moisture. In selecting wall surfacing, considerations should be given to the acoustical properties of the material. In general, moisture-resistant walls with good acoustical properties are recommended. Many teaching stations employ smooth surfaced glazed block or a similar smooth surface on walls up to eight feet to ten feet high. A smooth surface is important as it is easy to clean and stays cleaner than a rough surface. A smooth wall surface also does less damage to various athletic balls that strike it. And, a smooth sur- face is safer than a rough surface in that a student sliding against the smooth wall would have fewer abrasions compared to sliding against a rough wall.

Walls also are important aspects of many teaching stations and must be planned appropriately. Walls are utilized as rebound areas; large equipment is mounted to walls, and they are utilized in fitness testing and measurement. When designing a rebound wall, one must consider activities such as tennis, volleyball, and soccer. Large wall-mounted equipment such as a speed bag, high bar, or squat rack require structurally reinforced walls where this equipment is mounted. Vertical jump boards and peg boards need walls planned for open space as well as structural reinforcement.

Acoustical treatment on walls should be high enough so that it will not impede utilizing the wall space and so that it will not be constantly damaged by users and objects. There is a trend to utilize colors, murals, and graphics on many wall surfaces. This can brighten your teaching station and make the environment more aesthetically pleasing. Pastel colors seem to work the best in most teaching areas. One also might consider the psychological value of color schemes. Red-orange spectrum colors denote a psychological warmth and might be utilized in cold climates. Blue-green color spectrums denote a psychological cool color, and thus might be appropriately utilized in a hot climate. (Figure 2.2)

In locker rooms, shower rooms, and toilet rooms, where high humidity often is present, it is important to select wall surfacing that is moisture-resistant and has good acoustical properties. Walls serving as barriers between toilet rooms, handball courts, squash courts,

and other areas where noise is a problem should have a minimum of sound transmission.

Roof design, type of activity, and local building codes should determine the ceiling construction. Ceilings should be insulated to prevent condensation and should be painted to provide pleasing aesthetics and to enhance light reflection. Bright white ceilings are not recommended in areas where white shuttlecocks and white volleyballs might be used. It is very difficult to visually follow a white object on a white surface. A light color is recommended for ceilings, and an off-white seems to work well.

In any teaching station that is designed to house activities that need high ceiling space, the lowest suspended object, distance-wise from floor to ceiling, should be a minimum of 24 feet. This is particularly true for today's style of play in volleyball and badminton.

Acoustical ceiling materials are desirable in instructional and activity areas. Dropped ceiling panels susceptible to damage by objects or individuals will require considerable maintenance. Since most acoustical materials are soft, they need to be placed out of range of hard hit or kicked balls. In some low ceiling activity areas,

dropped ceilings can be equipped with spring loaded clips which always bring the acoustical panel back into its space even after it has been jostled. False ceilings with catwalks above them have been effectively designed to permit maintenance and repair of lighting and ventilating systems.

ACOUSTIC AND SOUND CONTROL

Because of the amount of noise and sound that emanates from the activities in physical education and sports, acoustics and sound are of paramount importance in building design. Acoustical treatments must both enhance sound so that we can hear easily, and absorb sound. Background noise, basically unwanted sound that originates either in the teaching station itself or intrudes from another area, must be controlled. Internal background noise might consist of "squeaking" chairs sliding on a floor, reverberation or "echoing" of sound, and reflective sound. All sound travels spherically. When a space is to be acoustically treated, walls, ceilings, floors, and other surfaces within that space must be considered for appropriate materials.

Figure 2.2. Wall graphics assist in giving color to large areas, such as in this gymnastic room.

Hard surfaces reflect sound and produce excessive unwanted reflection and reverberations. For example, a plaster wall reflects about 97 percent of sound, whereas a soft surface may reflect only 5 to 10 percent of sound. Thus, the space may be "noisy." Soft or absorbable surfaces turn the sound into another form of energy and can produce areas that are too "dead." Therefore, most areas must have some materials with sound-absorbing qualities in order to balance the sonic environment for good hearing conditions.

Internal Treatments

An acoustical engineer should be consulted when dealing with the absorption and reflection qualities of all surfaces within a facility. There are four common modes of internal acoustical treatment of spaces. The use of walls and other barriers is one method of controlling sound. Air space itself is an acoustical treatment. The larger the space, and therefore the further sound travels, the more it is absorbed. The use of soft acoustical materials on various surfaces is a major means of sound control. Acoustical clouds suspended over large open arenas is still another means of controlling sound.

External Treatments

External background noise or unwanted sound from outside the teaching space also must be planned for acoustically.

Unwanted sound or noise may be transmitted into the room by means of ventilating ducts, pipes, and spaces around pipe sleeves. The transmission of sound through ducts can be reduced by the use of baffles, or by lining the ducts with sound-absorbent, fire-resistant materials. The ducts also may be connected with canvas to interrupt the transmission through the metal in the ducts. Pipes can be covered with pipe covering, and spaces in the pipe sleeves can be filled.

Sound also can be transmitted through the walls, floors, and ceilings. This can be reduced to a desirable minimum by the proper structural design and materials. In conventional wall construction, alternate studs can support the sides of the wall in such a manner that there is no through connection from one wall surface to another. This sometimes is known as double-wall construction. The space inside the walls can be filled with sound-absorbing material to further decrease sound transmission. Sometimes three or four inches of sand inside the walls at the baseboard will cut down the transmission appreciably. Likewise, sound absorption blankets laid over the partitions in suspended ceiling construction frequently can reduce the sound from one room to another.

Machinery vibration or impact sounds can be reduced by use of the proper floor covering and/or by installing the machinery on floating or resilient mountings. "Sound locks," such as double walls or doors, are needed between noisy areas and adjoining quiet areas. Improper location of doors and windows can create noise problems.

It is imperative to consider the location of the facility itself and also to consider the placement of internal areas of the facility for sound control. Placing physical education and sport facilities in a semi-isolated area of a school helps control acoustics. This same theory needs to be applied internally within the sports facility. The placement of "noisy" areas such as weight training areas, aerobic areas, locker rooms, swimming pools, gymnasiums, and spectator areas must be planned for in relation to quiet areas such as classrooms and offices. It is not good acoustical planning to have a weight room above or next to a classroom.

Care must be taken in the maintenance of acoustical materials. Oil base paint reduces the sound-absorbent qualities of most materials. Surface treatment for different acoustical materials will vary. The most common treatment of acoustical-fiber tile is a light brush coat of waterbase paint. Most acoustical materials lose their efficiency after several applications of paint.

Exterior Treatments

Sometimes the exterior of a space or building must be acoustically treated. If a gym is located on the landing flight path of a local airport, or if it is located next to a fairly steep grade on a major truck thoroughfare, exterior acoustical treatment might be needed. Utilize the same acoustical principles as inside, with an exterior twist. Keep hard surfaces such as paved areas and parking lots, to a minimum. Use shrubbery, trees, and grass wherever possible. Walls, solid fences, berms, and water are all good exterior acoustical items.

It is important to plan for acoustics and sound control in a variety of ways. Think spherical, think internal, think external and think exterior in order to best acoustically treat a facility.

ILLUMINATION

Illumination is supplying or brightening an area with light. Illumination is measured by the footcandle. Brightness is the luminous intensity of any surface and is measured by the footlambert. Glare, which is an important consideration in physical education and sport facilities, is nothing more than excessive high brightness.

In addition to the amount of light in any given area, the quality of light is of equal importance. Providing efficient illumination is complicated and challenging, and the services of an illuminating engineer are recommended in order to obtain maximum lighting efficiency. Gymnasiums, classrooms, corridors, and other specific areas have distinct and different lighting requirements. Planning for electric illumination requires that each area be considered relative to specific use.

Measurements of Light

The footcandle is a measurement of light intensity at a given point. Light intensity, measured in footcandles, is one vital factor in eye comfort and seeing efficiency, but intensity must be considered in relation to the brightness balance of all light sources and reflective surfaces within the visual field.

The reflection factor is the percentage of light falling on a surface which is reflected by that surface. In order to maintain a brightness balance with a quantity and quality of light for good seeing, all surfaces within a room should be relatively light, with a matte rather than a glossy finish.

The footlambert is the product of the illumination in footcandles and the reflection factor of the surface. For

Area	Footcandles on Tasks	Area	Footcandles on Tasks
Adapted physical education gymnasium....	50	Squash	70^2
Auditorium		Tennis	70^2
Assembly only	15	Volleyball	50
Exhibitions	30-50	Weight-exercise room	50
Social activities.	5-15	Wrestling and personal-defense room....	50
Classrooms		Games room	70
Laboratories	100	Ice rink.	100^3
Lecture rooms		Library	
Audience area.	70	Study and notes	70
Demonstration area	150	Ordinary reading	50-70
Study halls.	70	Lounges	
Corridors and stairways	20	General	50
Dance studio.	$5-50^3$	Reading books, magazines, newspapers ...	50-70
Field houses	80	Offices	
First-aid rooms		Accounting, auditing, tabulating, bookkeeping, business-machine operation.	150
General	50	Regular Office work, active filing, index references, mail sorting.	100
Examining table	125	Reading and transcribing handwriting in ink or medium pencil on good-quality paper, intermittent filing	70
Gymnasiums			
Exhibitions	50^2		
General exercise and recreation.	35		
Dances.	$5-50^3$	Reading high-contrast or well-printed material not involving critical or prolonged seeing, conferring and interviewing.	50
Locker and shower rooms.	30	Parking areas.	1
Gymnastics	50	Storerooms	
Archery		Inactive	10
Shooting tee	50	Active	
Target area	70	Rough bulky	15
Badminton.	50^2	Medium	30
Basketball	80^2	Fine	60
Deck tennis.	50	Swimming pools	
Fencing	70^2	General and overhead	50
Handball	70^2	Underwater[4]	
Paddle tennis.	70^2	Toilets and washrooms	30
Rifle range			
Point area	50		
Target area	70		
Rowing practice area.	50		

These standards have been developed by a panel of experts on facilities for health, physical education, and recreation after careful consideration of the activities involved. In all instances, the standards in this table are equal to, or exceed, the standards which have been recommended by the Illumination Engineering Society, American Institute of Architects, and National Council On Schoolhouse Construction.

[2] Care must be taken to achieve a brightness blance and to eliminate extremes of brightness and glare.
[3] Should be equipped with rheostats.
[4] Must be balanced with overhead lighting and should provide 100 lamp lumens per square foot of pool surface.

Courtesy of Illuminating Engineering Society of North America

Figure 2.3. Levels of Illumination Currently Recommended for Specific Indoor Areas

example, 40 footcandles striking a surface with a reflection factor of 50 percent would produce a brightness of 20 footlamberts (40 by .50 = 20). These brightnesses are necessary when computing brightness differences in order to achieve a balanced visual field. Figure 2.3 gives a relative indication as to a comparison of illuminations for specific indoor spaces.

Basic Lighting Considerations

Lights in high ceiling activity space need to be a minimum of 24 feet from the floor surface. In areas where balls are hit, kicked, or thrown, lights need a shock absorption system. In this system, when an object hits the light the impact is partially absorbed by springs, swinging of the light, or shock absorbers. Lights need to be covered with transparent polycarbonate sheeting for protection from airborne balls. The lighting system must be accessible for maintenance, especially for bulb replacement. Plans need to be made in advance as to how bulbs will be replaced. Catwalks, poles, hydraulic hoists, and crawl spaces all give good access to lights. The central light switch box should be located at a major entrance area, and all teaching stations should be equipped with individual light switches. Lights need to be arranged so as not to provide direct or reflected glare, and they should not allow shadows to exist. Special attention needs to be paid to light switches in wet areas and lights in swimming pools. Perimeter lighting of the pool deck is best for ease of maintenance and bulb replacement.

Indirect lighting, or beaming the light upward to reflect off the ceiling, creates a very clean and pleasant form of light arrangement in almost any indoor space. Vapor-proof lighting units are recommended for damp areas such as toilets, showers, the dressing-locker suite, and the swimming pool. Locker room lights should be spaced to light the areas between lockers. (Figure 2.4)

Figure 2.4. Example of indirect lighting in an open aerobics area (photo by Lee Bloom)

Windows

Windows allow natural light into a facility, and this is aesthetically very pleasing. The major problem with windows is that it is very difficult to control the glare that they allow to enter. Avoid windows in any activity area where visual acuity is an important commodity for both learning activity skills and safety. Windows break easily. Windows also can create a security problem. Windows are highly recommended for offices, classrooms, conference rooms, weight rooms, lobbies, and foyers. Skylights may be utilized in any of these areas also. The largest problem with skylights is leakage and glare. Windows also have been a source of severe heat loss or cold gain. The insulation capacity of some newer style windows has been increased to nearly equal walls.

Types of Lighting

Incandescent, fluorescent, mercury-vapor, metal halide, quartz and sodium-vapor lighting systems are used most commonly in gymnasium buildings. The incandescent light is instantaneous, burns without sound, and is not affected by the number of times the light is turned on or off. Incandescent lights and fixtures are considerably cheaper in

initial cost, are easier to change, and the lamp, within limits, may be varied in size within a given fixture.

Incandescent fixtures, however, have excessively high spot brightness and give off considerable heat, a problem when high levels of illumination are necessary.

Fluorescent lamps have the advantage of long life and give at least two- and one-half times the amount of light that incandescent lamps give for the same amount of current used. They frequently are used in old buildings to raise the illumination level without the installation of new wiring.

Mercury-vapor lighting is expensive in terms of initial installation. The overall cost of mercury-vapor lighting, however, is cheaper than incandescent lighting. The primary objection to mercury-vapor lighting is the bluish color. However, when incandescent lighting is used in addition to mercury-vapor, a highly satisfactory lighting system results.

Metal halide lights do not last as long as mercury-vapor lights but give a better light output and operate more efficiently. Metal halide lights do not have the bluish tint of mercury-vapor lights. Quartz lights and high pressure sodium lights are outdoor lights. It has been only over the past few years that these lights have been utilized indoors.

Quartz lights are not much different than incandescent lights, except they have a slight bronze color and are slightly more efficient. High pressure sodium lights might well be the indoor activity light of the future. They have long life expectancy; they are highly efficient and give the best light output of all the lights mentioned. The only problem with high pressure sodium lights is the yellow-bronze hue associated with them. Figure 2.5 shows comparisons of our typical lighting system.

Supplementary Lighting

It is advisable to provide supplementary lighting on such areas as those containing goals or targets, and to place dimmers on the lighting in spectator areas. Supplementary light sources should be shielded from the eyes of participants and spectators in order to provide the proper brightness balance.

Night lights which burn continually are recommended for gymnasiums, swimming pools, handball courts, squash courts, and other indoor activity areas. Lobbies, corridors, and some classrooms also should be equipped with night lights. These lights are extremely important for safety and security purposes and should have separate controls.

Provisions for outside lighting should be considered. Exit lights must follow the prescribed codes of the local community and the state. Electrically illuminated exit lights, clearly showing the direction of exit to the exterior, should be provided over all exit doors from gymnasiums, combined auditorium-gymnasiums, multi-purpose rooms, and other rooms used for assembly purposes; over all exit doors from the building, and at the head and foot of exit stairways. All exit lighting should be on special circuits.

Emergency (white) lighting systems should be provided for exits (including exterior open spaces to which the exits lead) in gymnasiums, multi-purpose rooms, and other places of assembly or large group activity. This lighting should be on a special emergency circuit. All controls should be located so as to be under the supervision of authorized persons, and all other aspects of the installation should meet the specifications prescribed by the Underwriters Laboratories, the Building Exits Code, and state and local fire laws and regulations. The reader is referred to the Illuminating Engineering Society of North America for further guidance regarding lighting.

CLIMATE CONTROL

Planning for climate control is really planning for an optimal thermal environment. An optimal thermal environment provides conditions which make it possible to dissipate body heat in the most effortless manner. In other words, a climate that allows for maximum human efficiency is the goal. There are four factors that, when combined, give an optimal thermal environment:

- radiant temperature where surface and air temperatures are balanced,
- air temperature between 64° and 72° F,
- humidity between 40 and 60 percent, and
- a constant air movement of 20 to 40 lineal feet/per/min at a sitting height.

In order to achieve optimal thermal environment, the following items and concepts must be planned for in depth. Windows can be thermal nightmares with drafts, leaks, and sunshine. Heat loads produced by lights must be factored into the calculations. Heat loads produced by bodies must be considered, especially highly active bodies and a large number of bodies, such as spectators. Zone thermal controls should be installed so that individual spaces can be self-controlled. Air diffusers on duct work must spread air adequately through the open space of the room, not just directly down on the surface below the diffuser. And with special consideration for physical education and athletic facilities, adequate drying, air exchange, and ventilation must be present to control odor and humidity.

Heating, Air Conditioning, and Ventilation

The engineering design of heating, air conditioning, and ventilating systems should be based on the technical data and procedures of the American Society of Heating and Ventilating Engineers. The selection of the type of heating, air conditioning, and ventilating systems should be made with special consideration for:

- economy of operation
- flexibility of control
- quietness of operation
- capacity to provide desirable thermal conditions.

The design and location of all climate control equipment should provide for possible future additions.

Since the number of occupants in any given area of the building will vary, special consideration should be given to providing variable controls to supply the proper amount of fresh air and total circulation for maximum occupancy in any one area. Specially designed equipment and controls are necessary to ensure that climate control in some major areas can be regulated and operated independently of the rest of the facility.

All three mechanical systems -- heating, ventilating, and air conditioning -- are interrelated and should be planned together. The services of a competent mechanical engineer should be obtained, not only for design, but also for making inspections during construction and for giving operating instruction to the service department.

Some problems involved in the installation of heating, ventilating, and air conditioning systems include:

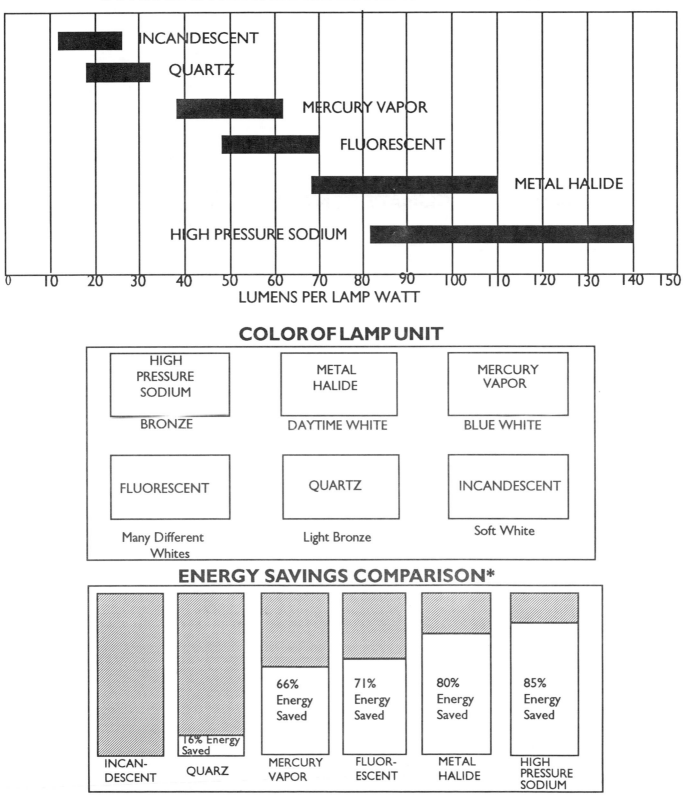

Figure 2.5. Technical Lamp Information

- maintaining a minimum noise level,

- maintaining separate temperature control for laboratory areas,

- insulating all steam, hot water, and cold water pipes and marking them with a color code,

- exhausting dry air through the locker rooms and damp air from the shower room to the outside,

- providing a minimum of four changes of air per hour without drafts,

- installing locking type thermostats in all areas, with guards wherever they may be subject to damage,

- placing the thermostats for highest efficiency,

- zoning the areas for night and recreational use,

- eliminating drafts on spectators and participants.

Total Energy Concept

Total energy is when a school installs its own electric generating system, then captures the system's "waste heat" and converts this waste product into steam or hot water and uses this byproduct for heating, air conditioning, and hot water. In order for the total energy concept to be feasible, four factors must exist:

- there needs to be a high and constant electric power demand for extended portions of the day and over most of the year,

- the school must use air conditioning in the summer and heat in the winter,

- the gas and fossil fuel rates must be low in order to compete with electric rates, and

- the school must be able to pay a two to five percent increase in the initial building cost.

If all four criteria can be met, thousands of dollars a year can be saved, and the initial building differential cost can be recouped within a three- to eight-year period of time.

ELECTRICAL SYSTEMS, SECURITY AND APPLIED HIGH TECHNOLOGIES

Electrical systems in facilities are more important than ever. More electronic equipment is being utilized in both classrooms and in activity areas. Computer laboratories, computerized equipment, and personal office computers are dependent on the electrical system of a facility. Security is of major concern in the design of any facility because of both the expense of the facility itself and the cost of the equipment housed within. The security and safety of participants has become a major concern of facility administrators. Many new electronic visions have been utilized in facility design outside the realm of physical education and athletic facilities. It is the intent now to provide information on these new systems so that they might be utilized in sports facilities.

Electrical Systems

All electrical service, wiring, and connections should be installed in accordance with the requirements of the National Electric Code of the National Board of Fire Underwriters, and of state and local building codes and fire regulations.

The capacity of each individual electrical system should be determined accurately for the obvious reasons of safety and economy. Full consideration should be given to present and future program plans when designing the electrical systems. The increasing use of electrically-operated equipment, higher standards of illumination, and special audio-visual equipment should be anticipated.

Electrical Service Controls

The entrance for electrical service should be installed to ensure the safety of the students and building personnel. When practical, it should be located at the side or rear of the building and away from heavy traffic or play areas.

Main service panels with main service switches, meters, and main light and power panels should be located so as to prevent entrance by anyone except those authorized.

Secondary control panels should be placed for the convenient use of individuals who open or close the facilities during hours of darkness or outside of regular hours. Electric lighting and power should be fully available to all athletic, physical education, and recreation facilities during hours when the main offices and classrooms may be closed.

The main distribution panel, all secondary panels, and all circuits should be protected by automatic circuit breakers. A number of spare circuits should be provided in panels for future use. Secondary panels, located in corridors, halls, and similar places, should be of the flush-front type provided with locks.

Wiring for program-signal systems and communications should not be in the regular service conduits. Switches in instructional rooms should be arranged so that lights adjacent to the interior wall may be controlled independently of the lights adjacent to the exterior wall. Consideration should be given for placing light switches at the height convenient for wheelchair users.

Stairway and corridor lighting should be on separate circuits. Three-way switches should be provided at the foot and head of stairs, near each end of corridors, and near doorways of large classrooms, activity rooms, or gymnasiums. This will permit control of the lights from two or more points. Switches should be located on the open side of entrances to all spaces in the building. Switches also should be provided in projection booths to control the lights in the rooms used for spectator activities. Remote control switches should have pilot lights.

Services for Appliances and Other Electrical Equipment

There are many needs for electrical wiring and connections which require careful analysis and planning. The following will illustrate:

- basic construction: motors to operate folding partitions, blowers for heaters and ventilating ducts, exhaust fans in gymnasium ceilings or walls,

- custodial and maintenance services: receptacles for floor cleaning equipment and power tools,

- dressing locker rooms: wiring for hair and hand driers and electric shavers,

- lounges, kitchenettes, snack bars, and concessions: outlets for refrigerators, water or soft drink coolers, electric stoves, blenders, mixers, coffee urns, and hot plates,

- office suites: wiring for individual air conditioners, business machines, floor fans, and other mechanical and electrical equipment,

- laundry rooms: wiring for washers, driers, and irons,

- pools: provision for underwater vacuum cleaners, pumps, and special lighting,

- gymnasiums: provision for special lighting effects, spotlights, and rheostats or controls to lower the illumination for certain activities,

- health suites: receptacles and provision for audiometers vision-testing equipment, floor fans, and air conditioning units, and

- computerization: provisions for classrooms, offices, laboratories, and personal use hookups.

Fire and Smoke Alarm Systems

Electrical fire alarm systems should be separate and distinct from all program-signal or other signal systems, and should be designed to permit operation from convenient locations in corridors and from areas of unusual fire hazard. All fire alarm and smoke alarm systems should meet the specifications prescribed by the Underwriters Laboratories and by state and local fire laws and regulations.

Program-Signal System

Gymnasium buildings can be wired for a signal system operated by a master clock or push buttons from the main administrative offices. Secondary controls may be placed in other administrative units of the facility.

Program-signals should be independent of the fire alarm system and should not be used as a fire alarm system.

Program signals usually include:

- buzzers or chimes in the classrooms,

- bells in corridors, pool, gymnasiums, fields, and dressing-locker suites, and

- large gongs on the outside of the building.

In many instances, signals placed strategically in corridors rather than in individual classrooms are adequate. Electric clocks should be included in all indoor areas in the program-signal system.

Security Concepts

The athletic and physical education complex presents a unique security problem. The facilities and the programs attract large numbers of individuals who move at all times during the day and week and through many areas in different directions.

It is reasonable to believe that all students and visitors who come to the building have a distinct purpose in coming and should be welcome. This is the type of building which people enter through many outside doors and disperse to offices, classrooms, dressing rooms, activity areas, and spectator galleries. There should be some plan for pedestrian control and for the handling of visitors.

Security is accomplished in two ways:

- constructing the facilities according to a plan which allows for maximum security,

- adopting an administrative plan for the direction and control of all persons using the building.

The physical layout will facilitate security but will not guarantee it. A good administrative plan will help. However, a good administrative plan cannot completely accomplish effective security if the physical layout does not lend itself to the attainment of such security.

Security Features of Construction

Entrance doors constitute the first barriers against illegal intrusion. Open and descending stairways, walled entries, and deep-set entrances should be avoided. The points of entrance to buildings should be well lighted from dusk until dawn. The corners of buildings should have floodlights which light the face of the structure. So-called "vandal lights" should be installed and protected to make them vandal-proof.

Corridors which are continuous and straight, providing unbroken vision, add qualities of safety and security to the building, its contents, and its users. Corridors are best lined up with entrance doors, providing a commanding view of the doorway from the corridor, and of the corridor from the entrance door. There should be an attempt to avoid angular corridors and to eliminate niches or cubbyholes.

The use of night lighting within the building and at its entrances will assist in protection against vandalism and other forms of undesirable conduct. Night lighting will require separate wiring and switches in order to maintain a desirable amount of illumination. Switches for such lighting should be key-controlled to prevent their use by unauthorized individuals. A building chart for day and night "on" and "off" lights should be developed. There should be additional directions for "on" and "off" at every switch, and such directions should be changed according to need. A key-station system for night-watch checking is desirable.

Keep ground level windows to a minimum, and keep window ledges small on higher windows. Covered walkways should not adjoin the building since walking on the top of the "cover" can give access to the second floor of the building. Protrusions from the external building walls should be kept to a minimum. This includes lights, ledges, and metal fasteners.

Security of the Building

Securing the building and its component rooms against illegal entry is the first and most logical consideration in terms of building protection. Good door framing, substantial doors, and heavy-duty hardware and locks hold up against wear and abuse. In their long life and securing qualities, they constitute a reasonable investment. In reducing replacement costs for materials and labor, the installation of good hardware is economical in the long run.

To reduce loss through breakage and theft, the additional security factor of quality hardware should never be overlooked at any cost.

A lock-and-key system, developed with the help of experts in the field of building administration, usually will result in a plan which considers some of the following features:
- a building master plan, including a lock-and-key system,
- lock-tumbler adjustments so that an area may have its own control and authorization,
- area division (vertical division) by responsibility or usage for key assignment, "level" division (horizontal division) for key assignment, or a combination of both vertical and horizontal divisions, and
- a policy of not lending keys is recommended.
The person to whom the key is assigned signs a pledge for no lending. The keys for the facilities should be identified by a distinguishing mark, and a policy should be established with key duplicators in the areas that they will refuse to duplicate keys carrying such identifying marks.

Security and Safety of Participants

Security and safety suggestions related to the use of specific facilities ordinarily found in a gymnasium structure include:
- All swimming pool doors are to be locked unless unlocked by a person authorized to do so. When a door is unlocked for a purpose, the individual unlocking the door is responsible for the accomplishment of that purpose. Outdoor and some indoor pools may be connected with a sonar detection system or a sound amplification system which will announce illegal use or entry. The signal can go to one or several strategic control points. Swimming pools normally should be keyed differently than other areas in the structure.
- In a gymnastics room and in weight rooms, the room or certain pieces of equipment must be locked except when an instructor is directly in charge. Providing storage areas sufficiently large to store all equipment for this activity is recommended. If possible, a separate room, secure from students and faculty, is most desirable.
- In viewing balconies, stairs should have handrails and lights at the sides, or luminous reflector material on the edges. Bleacher seats should have aisles and exits to allow rapid clearing other than to the playing floor.
- Activity room floors should be free of objects or floor plates which set up above the floor level.
- Shower room and dressing room floors should be kept free of objects and obstructions which may cause foot injury.
- Shower rooms should be equipped with towel bars to aid in safety of those individuals using the facility. Hot water available through shower heads should have a maximum temperature of 120°F.
- Areas of vigorous activity in which combative or competitive sports take place should have floor and/or wall covering to protect the participants. No specifications of classifications are given here, but every consideration is urged, and every precaution should be taken.
- Doors to steam rooms and dry-heat rooms should be capable of being locked from the outside when the room is unsupervised. The door should have an instruction plate by the door lock, bearing directions to those who have a key to unlock the door. Steam room controls should be set not to exceed a maximum room temperature of 130°F. This control should be tamper-proof. The steam room should have a bar latch of the panic type (noncorrosive hardware) to make exit readily possible under any conditions, even if the door should be locked from the outside.
- Dressing room entrances should be away from the main traffic and in the area where only participants go to change clothes. Toilet rooms should be away from direct view of the lobby, and yet be in service corridors rather than in isolated parts of the building.
- Stairs should be well lighted. In some cases, the edges of stairs should be marked. Objects in the building that need to be identified for safety or position may need to be color coded or marked in some manner. In basement passageways and around motors and equipment, it is important to mark corners, low pipes or beams, and safety zone areas. On main floors, it is desirable to mark fire alarms and extinguishers, some traffic lanes, and first aid boxes, and to indicate service and toilet areas with their appropriate service designations by door labeling or signs at door top height. Designation of objects can be accomplished by painting the objects or zones according to a color code.

Applied High Technologies

Facility planners need to incorporate the newest electronic technologies in building design. Rheostats that either manually or automatically dim or turn lights off can save both utility and labor costs. Sensors that can detect room use, temperature changes, and smoke can aid in utility savings, security, and early fire detection. These sensors not only report the information to a central security area, but they can be programmed to automatically close doors and secure corridors and rooms.

An example of an annunciator system for security is where outside doors or other doors of importance, such as swimming pool doors, may be connected to an electrically controlled system. Any door can be connected in or out of the annunciator by a lock-controlled switch at the door or a switch at the annunciator. Thus, a door tampered with or illegally opened after the annunciator is set for the "on" position will direct a warning signal. The annunciator may be developed to work by a light on a control box, the sound at a control box, an alarm sound of general broadcast in the building, or an alarm system with signals directed to the campus security office. The nature of the annunciator response should be determined by whether it is wished to quietly apprehend unauthorized persons or if it is desired to deter them or frighten them away.

A variety of trends in lighting systems has developed in conventional structures. One system utilizes primarily skylights and is supplemented with conventional artificial light. In such a system, a light sensor assesses the light level coming through the skylight in the working area just above the floor. At this point, the sensor signals that information to the artificial light system to shine from 0 percent to 100 percent of the wattage capacity, depending upon how much light is coming through the skylights. The sensor in this system can raise or lower the intensity of the artificial light to an acceptable and predetermined candle power dependent on the activity. Installation of a skylight plus a light sensor system will add additional construction costs, but this installation will reward the institution with energy conservation and cost saving.

In addition, consider that without the utilization of a light sensor system, a facility's lights would be required to be on full-time whenever the building was occupied. Also, a high percentage of the total kilowatt hours used in a facility is designed conventionally for artificial lighting. A skylight and light sensor system will accrue a significant savings in energy cost. Artificial lights also generate considerable heat, and by reducing the amount of artificial light (heat), a skylight and light sensor system would have a significant impact on saving air conditioning costs by one-half and lighting costs by one-third.

For instructional purposes, all facilities should be wired and cabled for computerization and satellite/cable television reception. Any room or teaching station that might utilize computerization or television hookup needs to be wired for such. All teaching stations, including classrooms and activity areas, should have built-in video cameras, tape decks, and 25-inch color monitors. The cameras should be mounted out of reach on a wall or ceiling and protected from being hit with objects. The monitor and the video deck should be mounted flush into the walls and covered by secured doors. The camera should be operable, automatically, from the monitor deck location. All students and all classes should have easy access to being videotaped as an instructional tool. All facilities also should be equipped with at least one large screen television set for instructional purposes.

COLLEGE/ UNIVERSITY INDOOR ACTIVITY AREAS

Over the past decade there has been a major philosophical change in physical education, athletic, and recreational facilities. Before this time most facilities had been multi-use facilities, shared by each of the areas of physical education, athletics, and recreation. This philosophy of sharing still exists along with the newer philosophy of constructing a specific type of building for each area. With this philosophy a college or university would have separate buildings for physical education, athletics, and recreation.

The major accomplishment of constructing a facility for one major need or area is that one does not have to compromise as one must do in a combined or shared facility. This means then that buildings will meet the needs of the users more accurately. The major problem with separate facilities is the cost factor. Separate facilities for physical education, athletics, and recreation mean much higher costs. With today's economic downturn, it might be very difficult to raise enough funds to construct separate facilities. When facilities are shared there must be trade-offs. The more the facility is utilized by different segments of the college/university community, the more trade-offs one must make. A facility designed to meet the needs of physical education and athletics will make fewer concessions in design than a facility that contains both of these areas plus a recreational component. Because of fund limitations, shared facilities seem to be likely during the 1990s. As one plans and designs a college/university facility, one must decide which building philosophy, shared or specific, will be utilized.

Another factor that must be considered is whether the local community will be utilizing the college/ university facility. If the college/

university is community oriented, then community utilization must be planned for in the facility design. With the aforementioned considerations in mind, this chapter will give information pertaining to multi-use or shared facilities.

Space requirements of various programs of institutions of higher learning have caused those responsible for Master Plan development to request standards for facilities in terms of square feet per student. Standards in these terms are meaningful to campus planners, since relating standards to predicted enrollment results in assured space for all disciplines involved.

The following standards are recommended for consideration by those involved in planning college and university facilities for physical education, intramural sports, inter-collegiate athletics, and recreation. It has been estimated by intramural leaders that the extent of participation in physical recreation by graduate students is 25 percent of that of undergraduates. Consequently, it is suggested that planners add 25 percent of the graduate enrollment when computing space needs for recreational areas.

Teaching Stations

The space requirements are 8.5 to 9.5 square feet per student (total undergraduate enrollment). They include: gym floors, mat areas, swimming pools, courts, and the like (adjacent to lockers and showers and within 10-minute walking distance of academic classrooms).

Indoor Space

A breakdown of indoor space would include:

- large gymnasium areas with relatively high ceilings (minimum 24 feet) for basketball, badminton, gymnastics, apparatus, volleyball and the like (approximately 55 percent of indoor space),

- activity areas with relatively low ceilings (minimum 12 feet) for combatives, therapeutic exercises, dancing, weight lifting and the like (approximately 30 percent of indoor space),

- swimming and diving pools (approximately 15 percent of indoor space),

- racquetball/handball or squash courts (not included in percent breakdown, however it has been recommended that one such court is needed for 800 undergraduate students).

Investigation indicates that a reasonable standard for determining the space needed for lockers, showers, toweling rooms, equipment storage, supply rooms, and offices associated with indoor space is a square footage equaling approximately 40 to 45 percent of the play or activity area in a gymnasium facility. As an example of how this figure may be used, assume that a building is being planned to provide 100,000 square feet of activity space. In other words, the square footage of the swimming pool surface and deck and of all gymnasium floors, including high and low ceiling areas, equals 100,000 square feet. The space needed for ancillary areas would be in the neighborhood of 40,000 square feet.

All other space in a building, including hallways, stairways, wall thicknesses, lobbies, public toilets, bleachers for public use, custodial space, and space needed for service conduits of all types, is spoken of by many architects as "tare." By adding tare, ancillary, and net space, a rough estimate of the gross footage of a building plan can be computed. This figure is helpful in preliminary discussion of costs involved.

Other considerations with regard to indoor space include enrollment relationships and peak load after-school hours.

Enrollment Relationships

When standards in terms of square feet

per student are used as guides in college or university planning, it is natural to ask where the computation begins. At what point, from 10 students up, do the standards become meaningful? Obviously, for a college of 200 students, nine square feet per student of indoor area for sports and athletics would be woefully inadequate. It would not even provide one basketball court.

A university or college meeting the space standards for 1,500 students represents the minimum physical recreation space needs of any collegiate institution. As a college or university increases in size, these standards are applicable regardless of enrollment.

Gymnasiums (Main Area)

The type and size of gymnasium facilities needed for a given college or university will depend upon many factors, including the anticipated enrollment. A gymnasium building planned to serve 2,000 students will, obviously, be considerably smaller than, and different in design and construction, from a facility planned for a university of 10,000 or more students. If a college or university has a definite enrollment ceiling, the building may be planned for this enrollment. If the enrollment ceiling is indefinite, however, the structure should be planned so additions to the buildings are feasible. Universities of 15,000 or more students may find it desirable to build more than one gymnasium structure, each servicing an area of the campus.

Another factor that will affect the type of building constructed is the philosophy of the administration concerning athletics and physical education. Many questions need to be answered before planning begins:

- What will be the priority for usage, among athletics, physical education, and recreation?

- Will all students be required to take physical education for one, two, three, or four years?

- Will the required program

provide the students with a variety of opportunities to develop sport skills?

- Is teacher education in physical education to be part of the program?

- What responsibility does the college or university take for the physical education, recreation, and fitness of its faculty?

- Will research in physical education, health, and recreation be an important aspect of the program?

- What will be done to provide facilities for an expanded program of campus recreation (including intramurals)?

Size, Shape, and Location

The basic shape of most physical education, athletic, and recreation facilities has been rectangular. This shape is dictated by designing a facility around an intercollegiate basketball court. The rectangular configuration is fine if the intercollegiate basketball court is the most important aspect of the facility. Rectangular and square spaces also are easier to plan for than other shaped spaces. If the facility is to serve major needs other than basketball, the college/university should investigate other shapes and configurations in the planning process. Elliptical, round, hexagonal, and multi-sided facilities might be appropriate. These designs take careful planning in making sure all curved and odd shaped areas and rooms are making maximum use of existing space. Main gyms do not have to be rectangular, but rectangular facilities make it easier to plan for maximum space utilization.

Perimeter space at activity areas needs careful attention during the planning process. Clear thoroughfares need to be provided around the activity floor space. Traffic should not have to walk through activity areas, around equipment, or walk under nets. Perimeter space also must be provided for the safety of the activity participants. Seating and other obstacles such as pillars and walls should be set back from the playing area. For most activities, a 15-foot perimeter space provides adequate safety as long as objects are not "stored" in this perimeter space.

The open gym concept is an idea that should be considered in planning. Rather than having many teaching stations enclosed in individual rooms, have them be a part of an open gym concept. The utilization of dividing nets, different elevations, clear polycarbonate sheeting, and partial walls can separate areas and yet give an open atmosphere to the gym.

Indoor facilities for sports and athletics should be planned so that all activity areas will be available to both men and women. Good planning will permit easy access to all areas from both men's and women's locker rooms. This type of planning permits the flexibility necessary for efficient utilization and control.

Roll-away or folding bleachers should be considered in order to use the available space efficiently. Most colleges and universities can neither afford to invest large sums of money nor give large areas of space to permanent seating that is used only a few times each year.

The traffic patterns for a building should be studied carefully. Lockers, showers, and toweling rooms should be centrally located in the building so they may serve all activity areas. Easy access should be provided from the locker room to the playing fields adjacent to the building.

If physical education and athletic facilities are used by all the students, the gymnasium facility should be located conveniently near the academic buildings and student housing. Buildings used only for intramural and intercollegiate activities may be located farther from classrooms and housing. This is especially true if the activities promoted in these buildings are scheduled. If the building is to be used for unscheduled participation of students, however, the amount of use will vary inversely with the distance from housing and other campus buildings.

Floors, Walls, and Ceilings

There are many types of floor surfaces that can be used successfully on the main gym floor. The surface should be dictated by the needs of the users. Hardwood or synthetic floors can be utilized. Hardwood floors allow for more sliding than do synthetic floors. So if the activities on the floor involve much sliding activity, a wood floor would be a better choice. Wood floors can be designed a number of ways including sleeper systems, subfloor systems, channel systems, cushioned systems, and spring systems. The more materials and labor needed to install the floor, the more the cost. Safety should be the paramount concern, but cost will need to be weighed heavily.

Wood floors, depending on their suspension system, can have "dead spots" in them. Synthetic floors do not have "dead spots" and give better acoustical treatment to your facility than wood floors. Synthetic floors normally are softer than wood floors.

Upkeep of all gym floors is a never ending and costly endeavor. Rubberized synthetic floors have a larger maintenance cost than wood floors and "carpet like" synthetic floors take less money for maintenance than wood floors. All gymnasium floors take constant maintenance in order to keep a good looking and durable surface.

It would be desirable to inquire about other facilities similar to the one you are designing to find out which floors lend themselves best to which activities. Communicate with maintenance personnel, instructors, and students since you will obtain a different perspective of floor suitability from each group. All floors expand and contract to some degree. An expansion space of two inches is recommended around the perimeter of your floor.

If floor plates are to be installed, they should withstand 5,000 pounds of pull. Floor plates should be covered and flush for both safety and ease of maintenance. Electrical outlets should be provided on the gym floor, and they should be covered and flush with the floor surface.

Diagrams for volleyball and basketball follow. Dimensions should be confirmed with the appropriate associations prior to finalizing building plans. (Figures 2.6, 2.7)

Walls in the main gym should be smooth to a minimum eight-foot height and should be planned for padding in any area where facility users might run into the wall. Electrical outlets should be provided in the walls at 50-foot intervals. Some flat wall space should be provided for teaching and rebound space. Acoustical treatment, pastel colors, and structural reinforcement at stress points must be considered.

The ceiling should be a minimum of 24 feet high to the lowest obstacle. An off-white color usually is appropriate for the ceiling. Clear span design without substructure girders and minimum support pillars should be investigated for viewing, aesthetics, safety, and more open, usable space. If equipment is to be mounted or stored in the ceiling area, structural reinforcement is necessary at those sites.

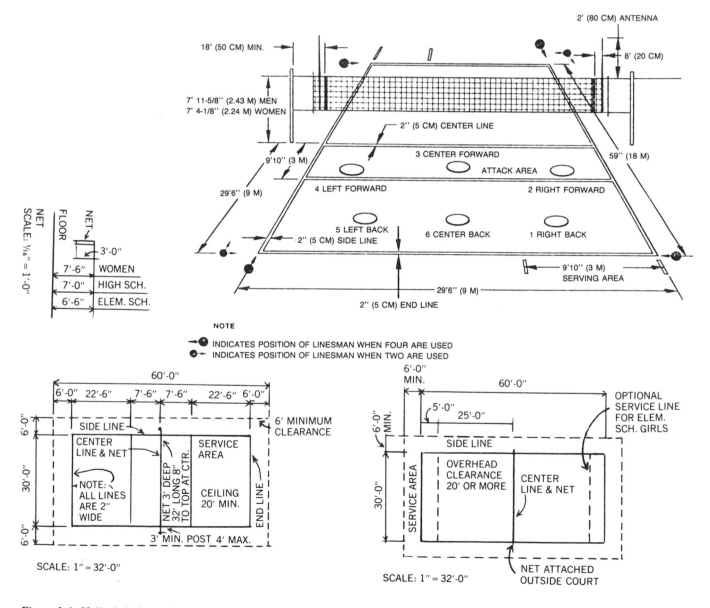

Figure 2.6. Volleyball Court Dimensions

THE THREE-POINT FIELD GOAL LINE

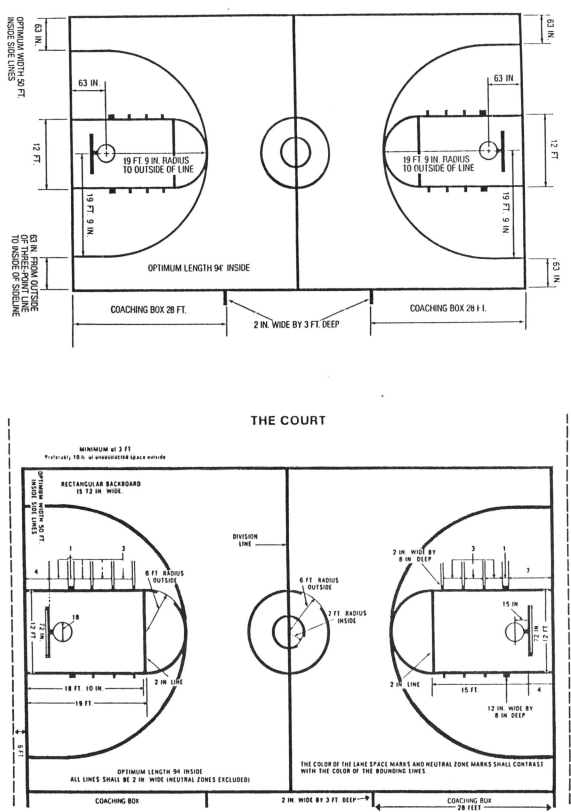

Figure 2.7. Basketball Court and Three Point Field Goal Line (1992 NCAA Basketball Men's and Women's Rules and Interpretations)

Seating and Storage

If the gymnasium is to be used for intercollegiate athletics, seating must be provided for spectators (three square feet per person). Portable folding bleachers, which can be easily moved, are recommended for seating. In larger institutions, it may be necessary to install roll-away bleacher seats in the balcony, which, when combined with the bleachers on the main floor, will provide the required number of seats. Seating should be modular and planned for all sports, not just basketball. Seating arrangements need to be different for wrestling, gymnastics, volleyball, and other indoor sports.

Plans need to be made for the seating of timekeepers, scorers, announcers, and other officials. This seating arrangement will vary from sport to sport. None of this seating and/or tables should be in the 15-foot perimeter space. Press boxes and media boxes need to be provided for television coverage, videotaping and other media, teaching, and coaching uses.

Permanent seating with backs and arm rests certainly is desirable for spectators. The problem with this type of seating is the cost per seat and the cost for the space these seats take up. Telescoping bleachers take up much less space when folded up and cost much less than permanent seats. A combination of telescoping permanent seating is now available, but again this is much more costly than bleachers that fold up.

Storage space many times is not planned for carefully and is added as an afterthought in facility design. Because of the uniqueness of a sports related activity center, the nature of the equipment, and the coming of high technology electronic equipment, storage areas must be planned carefully as to location, size, and number.

Storage rooms for equipment and supplies should be carefully planned and functionally located. These rooms should be of three types:

- central receiving storage rooms, to which all equipment and supplies are delivered and which should be accessible by truck,

- utility teaching station storage rooms adjacent to gymnasiums so bulky and small equipment may easily be moved to the floor and back to storage, and

- supply rooms with an attendant's window opening to the locker rooms.

Off-season storage rooms are critically needed. The type of equipment to be moved and stored will define the dimensions of the room and size of the doors needed. Reserve storage also should be provided.

All storage rooms need to be accessible and functional. Size, height, and width of rooms is important. Door openings must be large enough to allow the appropriate equipment to pass through easily. There should be no thresholds on the floor, and the floor surface needs to be compatible with the equipment that will be moved over it. Storage shelves, bins, and racks must be planned for small equipment housing. Storage areas need ventilation and should be cool. All storage areas should be built flush with existing walls and should be planned for good security.

Partitions

In some situations it is applicable to divide large gymnasium type areas with partitions. Two basic partition concepts may be employed. Folding panel partitions give maximum isolation to the divided areas. The panels are usually four feet wide and three inches thick for acoustical purposes. The partition is mounted on a ceiling height track and also may have its base tracked. The problem with a track on the floor is that it may collect debris, and it also may not be totally flush with the floor surface. Having the floor track does give more stability to the partition when it is fully open. The panels should be covered with a vinyl type surface for ease of

maintenance, and kick plates should be provided to a height of three feet on both sides of the partition. The partition should be of heavy-duty construction so that it may be used for rebounding drills. The folding partition is motorized and usually key-operated. Ample doors need to be included in the partition in order not to congest traffic flow. A minimum of two doors per partition is recommended. These folding partitions can divide a large area into two, three or even up to six smaller individual teaching areas.

The other form of partition is dividing nets. The nets may be all mesh, or the bottom section may be closed to give better visual isolation. These nets are suspended from the ceiling area and can divide large spaces into many configurations. The nets usually are nylon, vinyl, or polyester fabric. The nets, like the folding partitions, should be motorized and key-operated. Dropnets may be permanently installed to separate areas such as basketball courts that are surrounded by a running track. If permanent net dividers are utilized, a small space should be left between the bottom of the divider and the floor so that a floor broom can pass under this area for ease of cleaning. The following figure shows the use of dropnets in a gymnasium. (Figure 8)

With either type of partition, color schemes should be planned carefully to add aesthetic qualities to the gymnasium. The solid folding partitions are more expensive than the net type dividers. When employing a partition of any type, perimeter safety and access space must be planned for carefully.

Water Fountains

A minimum of one water fountain should be located in, or adjacent to, each teaching station. Large space areas such as a main gym may need more than one fountain. All fountains should be refrigerated and inset flush with wall surfaces. Fountain surfaces that will

Figure 2.8. Use of dropnets in a gymnasium (Photo by Lee Bloom)

have constant wear from hand placement should be made of a maintenance-free material. Refrigerated fountains must have an electrical hookup built into its site location.

Water fountains may be placed in the gym area or in adjacent areas. If they are in the gym itself, water on the floor can be a problem. Having the fountain located in an adjacent hall gives less visual control over the users. If the fountain is placed in the teaching area, make sure it is not located in a high speed traffic area such as behind the end lines of the basketball court directly behind the backboard. In multi-level gymnasiums, water fountains should be available on all levels.

Electrical Considerations

Electrical outlets should be provided approximately every 50 feet in a gymnasium, both on the floors and on the walls. They all should be flush with their mounted surface, and they should be covered. Electrical outlets need careful planning for video usage, computerization, security, and maintenance purposes. Consideration for electronic fitness equipment, scoreboards, backstops, and for

broadcasting must be taken into account when wiring plans are designed for the facility. As previously mentioned, pre-planned design of video cameras, decks, and monitor stations should be included in all teaching stations throughout the facility. Wiring consideration for cable hookups, computer hookups and F.M. broadcasting throughout the facility needs careful planning.

Scoreboards must be planned for electrically and visually. All wires running to scoreboards, whether floor, ceiling, or wall- mounted, should be built-in. There may need to be multiple sites planned for scorers and officials for different sports such as wrestling, basketball, and gymnastics.

Scoreboards should be multi-sport oriented so that one basic scoreboard will meet the school's total scoring needs. Scoreboards must be visible from all areas of the facility by both sport participants and spectators.

Backboards and Standards

Most gymnasiums will house basketball courts, volleyball courts, and badminton courts. Backboards for basketball can be mounted on the wall, ceiling, or floor. Backboards also may be

permanent or moveable. For the most advantageous utilization of space, moveable backboards are best. If the backboards are wall and/or ceiling-mounted, a cable hoist system works nicely to maneuver the backboards out of the way of other activities. The cable hoist system should be motorized and key-operated. If floor- mounted backboards are needed, they should be telescoping, hydraulically or electronically operated, and be located far enough from the end lines so as not to be a safety factor. The bases of the floor backboards must be padded. Storage areas for floor- mounted, moveable backboards need to be built adjacent to their use area. All backboards should be glass, even though other materials may be utilized. Users prefer glass. For the college game, the only acceptable backboard is a rectangle six feet (1.83 m) wide by four feet (1.23 m) high. The bottom edge of the board must be padded. The upper edge of the basket rings must be 10 feet (3.05 m) above the floor. Floor-mounted, moveable backboards are the most expensive. Glass is more expensive than wood, plastic, or metal.

Standards or net poles for badminton, volleyball, and indoor tennis should be carefully considered during the planning phases of the facility design. Net poles can be free standing or attached to the floor. The standard method of attaching net poles is to utilize conventional floor plate systems. This system is still adequate, but the newest system innovation is telescoping standards that fold directly into the floor itself so no moving of poles or storage of poles is needed. These poles may be activated manually or electronically. When one plans for standards, plans also must be made for cable guy supports in order to totally stabilize the standards. These cables will need fasteners in either the floors and/or walls. If standard floor-mounted net poles are utilized, adjacent storage space to house the nets and poles needs consideration. Perimeter access space should not be intruded upon by nets or poles.

Weight Lifting/Training Areas

The design of this space will be dictated partially by the number of weight machines, free weights, and types of training done in the room. A weight area would be designed differently for power-lifting activities as compared to weight-training activities. An attempt will be made to include all aspects of weight-training and lifting in the design analysis in this section. If a weight area is designed for one primary use, that major use purpose would influence the planning. For example, a total free-weight area would be designed differently than an all machine-weight area. (Figure 2.9.)

Size, Safety, Shape, and Aesthetics

With the increased interest in weight use and weight-training, the weight area should be as large as possible. The minimum size should be 3,000 square feet (approximately 67-by-45 feet) but many facilities contain several times that amount depending upon student enrollment. Safety should be one of the major concerns in the design of a weight area. The more free weights within a given area, the more the safety factor must be considered. Ample space must be provided for individual free weight lifting areas, machine lifting areas, and traffic flow areas. Ample space must be provided so that individuals are not lifting free weights over or above other lifters. Each machine may require a different amount of square footage and must be planned for accordingly. Pedestrian traffic flow areas must be planned for both into and within the weight area. An individual should be able to walk through various portions of the weight area without impeding either free or machine lifting.

Safety must be planned for in accordance with the type of user, type of instruction, and type of weights employed. The weight area must be able to be secured at any given time. If the weight area is a room, this is a

Figure 2.9. Weight training room in University of Virginia athletic training facility (Photo by Alan Karchmer, courtesy of HOK Sports Facilities Group)

simple matter of locking the doors. However, if the weight area is a space within an open concept facility, perimeter roping or chaining with visual security needs careful planning.

The shape of the weight area conventionally has been rectangular. Any shape may be appropriate depending on the use of the area. Square, round, elliptical, and many-sided areas have been utilized successfully. Aesthetics is an important consideration in weight areas. The use of colors in floors, walls, ceilings, and machines and weights should be considered. Lighting, both indirect and natural, can be employed successfully. Because of the heavy use of weight areas, maintenance concepts need careful thought.

Equipment and Storage

Most weight areas today will include a combination of free and machine weights. Free weight lifting must be designed to absorb the impact of dropped and rolling weights. Mirrors should be attached above the height of the largest diameter weight plate to avoid breakage. Platforms or pre-stressed floor areas for "Olympic" type of weight lifting should be built-in. Storage racks should be

provided for all free weights to aid in cleaning the area. If all racks are labeled, it will make the weight inventory easier. Machine weights need to be selected carefully for specific use, lack of breakdowns, ease of maintenance, and digital computerization. Electrical outlets need to be planned in conjunction with these electronic machines. Some machines, such as stationary bicycles and step climbers, might be located better near the weight area but not in it. Then these machines could be used by participants even if the weight area is closed. A storage area for maintenance equipment, spare parts, and tools is needed in the weight machine area. (Figure 2.10.)

Floors, Walls, and Ceilings

There are many surfaces that can be used, with good results on weight area floors. Specific rubberized floor surfaces work well. Indoor/outdoor carpeting is good if it can be vacuumed daily and steam cleaned monthly. The ability to withstand high impact and provide cushioning and acoustical properties should all be considered in floor surface selection. If stretching and other weight activities are to be

Figure 2.10. Storage of weights (Photo by Alan Karchmer, courtesy of HOK Sports Facilities Group)

done on the floor, soft cushioning must be considered.

Walls should employ color, and be pre-stressed for anchoring racks and machines. Full length mirrors should be provided on a minimum of two adjacent walls. Mirrors are an integral part of the design of a successful weight area. Wall-to-wall mirrors work well.

Ceilings should be a minimum of 12 feet high for a weight area. Higher ceilings give more of an open concept and should be planned for if an open concept is utilized. Ceiling mirrors should be planned for in certain portions of the weight room. In particular, ceiling mirrors should be provided for bench pressing activities.

Acoustics and Ventilation

Free weights and many weight machines are noisy when used. Acoustical treatment should be planned for walls, ceiling, floor, and machines. The weight area is housed best on the ground or basement level of the facility in an attempt not to have other areas of the facility under the weight area. Bodies produce much heat and odor in weight areas, thus good ventilation is important. Air conditioning and the use of floor,

ceiling, and wall fans can all be utilized. Large screened windows on opposite sides of the weight area also can help in obtaining good air flow.

Technological Additives

Color-coded floor surface is a good concept to designate lifting and traffic flow areas for weight areas. All weight areas should have both radio and audio built-in tape equipment. Video equip-

ment, including cameras, monitors, and tape decks, also should be built into weight areas. A large screen television should be planned for video playback and video music. Three-sided mirrors, similar to those in clothing stores, should be provided for some free weight lifting activities. Mirrors, factory mounted on weight machines, give an added incentive to users. Both regular and electronic signage indicating rules and safety features should be built into the initial design of the weight area.

Aerobics/Fitness

The trend with aerobics is to have an area that is just for aerobics. Some schools include exercise machines in this area. These machines have been discussed previously. With the popularity of aerobic fitness, the size of this activity space has grown. Similar to the weight area, a minimum of 3,000 square feet is recommended. The aerobics area may be any shape with rectangular and semi-curved spaces being utilized to a large degree. Aerobic areas should use color on the floor and wall areas. Indirect lighting adds a good aesthetic factor in this area. (Figure 2.11.)

Padded synthetic and hardwood floor surfaces are recommended. Both of these surfaces work well, but

Figure 2.11. Arizona State University aerobics area (Photo by Larry Smith)

both need to be specifically designed for aerobic use. If hardwood is employed, it must be more resilient than the normal gymnasium floor. The type of aerobic programs, either high or low impact, also will influence floor selection. Walls should be fully mirrored on at least a minimum of two adjacent sides. Ventilation must be planned carefully since there may be very large numbers of active aerobic participants in a relatively small space. High volume music and instructor commands indicate the need for good acoustical treatment on wall surfaces, ceiling, and possibly on the floor surface.

A storage area designed for aerobic equipment should be in the area. This storage area should be planned for a large number of individual aerobic mats, individual aerobic steps or platforms, individual aerobic stretch exercisers, and individual dumbbells of light weight. The storage area also should house a library of both video and audio tapes. A maintenance storage area also should be included in the aerobic space. Water access should be provided in this room for wet mopping and disinfecting matted floors.

Each aerobic area should be equipped with radio/audio tape capabilities, cable television connectors, and built-in video camera, monitor, and tape deck. It is recommended to install at least one large screen television (72 inches or more). Lighting in the aerobics area can be controlled rheostatically by utilizing dimmer switches and can be color controlled with both red and blue spectrums to give a psychological cool or hot environment when deemed needed.

Dance Facilities and Equipment

The essential dance facilities and equipment should be supplied in sufficient quantity and quality to provide for all dance activities in the required and elective curriculum and in the extracurricular program. Particular attention should be given to adequate provisions for the program of professional preparation (both the teaching program and the performance program) and to dance performance and observation.

Provision should be made to include the following units if the dance facility is to be comprehensive:
- locker/dressing rooms
- shower area
- toilets
- restrooms (remote from toilets and showers)
- public lavatories
- therapy room
- storage spaces
- construction rooms for costumes, props and sets, and music (composing and recording)
- custodial space
- office space
- laundry and cleaning facilities
- box office
- parking area

Total facilities should be determined according to the amount of emphasis placed on various aspects of the dance curriculum. Considerations should include space needed for classes, individual work, extracurricular activities, and concert practice. Based on the design of the dance curriculum, facilities should be considered in terms of teaching space, practice space, and choreography, rehearsal space, performance space, research space, auxiliary space and equipment, and classroom space. At least two distinct areas should be provided, one area for modern dance and ballet and one area for folk and social dance.

Modern Dance and Ballet Area

A minimum of 100 square feet per person is recommended. An area of 3,000 square feet will accommodate 30 students. If an area is to serve as an informal theater and instructional area, it should be between 4,800 and 5,000 square feet to accommodate both the class and the needs of the theater section.

A ceiling height of 24 feet is recommended for all dance areas. Full height is essential for large dance areas (over 2,400 square feet), and 16 feet is the minimum height for small dance areas.

Dance activities require air space between floor and foundation, as well as "floating" floors for resiliency. Floors should be of hardwood, such as maple of random lengths, and tongue-and-groove. They should be laid with the grain going in one direction. The floors should not be slippery, and they should be constructed for easy cleaning.

The finish should provide a smooth surface upon which dancers can glide with bare feet or soft sandals. Tung oil is considered by most to be a satisfactory finish; an alternative might be several coats of wood sealer.

Walls should be smooth and easily maintained. Consideration should be given to having one unobstructed wall of neutral background for filming purposes. To support ballet barres, stress factors for the walls should be considered. Thin walls are inadequate.

Incandescent light is preferable to fluorescent light. Lights that also serve as house lights during performances should be controlled from wall switches, as well as from the light control board.

Consideration should be given to natural lighting. Large windows contribute to an aesthetically and psychologically desirable atmosphere. To avoid direct sunlight, the best location for windows is the north wall. Windows should be curtained so the studio can be darkened for film showing and studio performances. When total construction necessitates no windows, the aesthetics may be improved by the use of color on the walls.

Storage space for sound equipment should be adjacent to the dance area and should be locked. Storage rooms should have double doors and a flush threshold for easy movement of such large equipment as a piano. Built-in storage space for records, sound and video equipment, tapes, and musical instruments should be provided. An area in the storage room where instructors can listen to records and view tapes is highly desirable. This area should have adequate acoustics, ventilation, and electrical outlets.

Heavy-duty wiring is essential for all dance facilities. Wiring should be capable of supporting a portable light board as well as phonographs, additional speakers, tape recorders, projectors, and other video equipment. Wall outlets should be convenient to all areas. Television conduits should be installed when the building is constructed.

Temperature should be maintained at 65 to 68 degrees. The air should be well circulated, and consideration should be given to the use of natural air. Mechanisms for heating and circulating air should be as nearly silent as possible to avoid interfering with the quality of sound and its reception.

Planning for a dance facility should include consideration of accessories. Leaf-fold mirrors, which can be folded for protection or curtained during performances, may be installed along two adjoining walls so that movement can be analyzed from two directions. Wall mirrors should be installed flush with the wall and raised 12 to 18 inches from the floor.

Ballet barres should be smooth in texture and made of wood, stainless steel, or aluminum. The minimum length to accommodate one dancer is five feet. Barres from 42 to 48 inches in height may be installed permanently; they should extend six to eight inches from the wall. If necessary, barres may be placed in front of mirrors. In such instances, it may be necessary to use pipes for the barres. The barre supports may be screwed into recessed floor sockets just in front of the mirror, thus facilitating the removal of the barre and supports when not needed.

Custom-made percussion cabinets mounted on rollers are a fine accessory. They may have a carpeted top surface, slide-out drawers lined with felt for small instruments, and larger partitions to accommodate cymbals and drums. Heavy sound equipment should be built-in or placed on stands of table height equipped with rollers for ease of transportation. Because moving affects the tuning of a piano, this instrument should be placed on an inside wall where it will not be subjected to extreme heat or cold, and it should be protected by a suitable cover and lock. If it is to be moved frequently, the piano should be placed on a heavy-duty dolly.

Chalkboards and bulletin boards are useful accessories. A glass-enclosed exhibit case for photographs, costumes, costume plates, manuscripts, and other items may be installed near the dance area.

Folk and Social Dance Area

An area of 5,400 square feet (54 by 100 feet is suggested) will accommodate a class of approximately 60 students. Dance areas generally are rectangular with a length-width ratio of approximately three to two (e.g., 90 by 60 feet). Ceiling height should be in proportion to the size of the room, but never lower than 12 feet. An outside entrance into a main corridor of the building will provide for traffic flow for the relatively large groups using the area.

Floors as specified for ballet and modern dance are necessary. An epoxy finish will enable the use of street shoes without damage to the floor. Specifications for lighting, ventilation, acoustics, sound equipment, storage space, wiring, and temperature control should follow those for ballet and modern dance facilities. Racks for coats and books should be installed either within the dance area or along the outside corridor wall. Bulletin boards, chalkboards, and display cases are highly desirable.

Gymnastics

In addition to the main gymnasium where gymnastic meets, exhibitions, and other competitions are held before a viewing public, a separate gymnasium should be provided for the permanent installation and storage of apparatus and equipment and for instruction in gymnastics. The dimensions of this gymnasium should be determined by space requirements needed to accommodate the apparatus and equipment to be installed, by space needs for performance in gymnastics, and by total school enrollment and interest in gymnastics. Ideally, if spectators are to be accommodated, the size of this gymnasium should be 120 by 90 feet, with a minimum ceiling height of 24 feet. This height permits a clearance of 22 feet for the rope climb and is ideal for hanging the various mechanical systems used in gymnastics. Some have found it desirable to install tracks on the ceiling supports to make it possible to use trolleys for moving equipment and for attaching safety belts used in the instruction of tumbling and vaulting.

Floor plates for attaching equipment should be recessed and flush with the floor. It may be necessary to reinforce the floor to install floor plates where tension is unusually severe. Wall boards should be installed securely to the wall when equipment is attached to it. Apparatus suspended from the ceiling should be securely attached to metal supports.

The ceiling should be treated acoustically. Lights should be shielded. Doors should be constructed without a threshold and wide enough to accommodate the movement of equipment to other areas. The facility should be air conditioned in accordance with standard specifications. Wall construction should be of the same materials as recommended for other gymnasiums.

A common failure in planning is to overlook the need for adequately and conveniently placed storage space for gymnastic equipment. If frequent use of this equipment is expected, transportation carts and dollies should be provided. Specifications on size and installation of the various pieces of apparatus and equipment may be obtained from the manufacturer. Ideally, the gymnasium for gymnastics should be equipped with the following types of items: side horse, horizontal bar, long horse, parallel bars, bucks, bats, still rings, uneven parallel bars, balance beam, and other special apparatus.

A gymnastic landing pit, 10 feet wide, 20 feet long, and 30 inches deep, filled with sponge rubber -- for use with parallel bars, horizontal bar, still rings, and uneven parallel bars -- is a desirable feature.

Racquetball/Handball/Squash Courts

Suggestions for court construction are the same for both racquetball and handball. The recommended four-wall court is 40 feet long and 20 feet wide, with a front wall and ceiling height of 20 feet, and a back wall at least 12 feet high.

When more than a single battery of courts is to be constructed, the batteries should be arranged so the back walls of each battery are separated by a corridor approximately 10 feet wide and eight feet high. Courts should be located in the same proximity of the facility rather than being spread out. This aids in quality instructional time. A corridor located immediately above and at least 12 feet high may serve an instructor or be used as a spectator galley. Corridors and galleries should be illuminated with indirect light. The minimum number of courts should be dictated by maximum class size and total student enrollment. Normally no fewer than six to eight courts are

recommended which can adequately handle 15 to 20 students at a time.

Walls, Floors, and Ceilings

Walls may be constructed of hard plaster, Portland cement, wood, laminated panels, or tempered glass. Laminated panels and tempered glass are recommended most. The panels are four-by-eight feet particle board or resin-impregnated kraft papers covered with a melamine sheet. The panels come in different thicknesses from 13/16 inches to 1 1/8 inches. The thicker the panel, the truer the rebound action of the ball. The thicker panel also is more expensive. The panels have a high life expectancy and are maintained easily. Glass walls of one-half inch thick tempered, heat-soaked glass are ideal, but expensive. It is recommended that all courts have the minimum of glass back walls, and one court should have an additional glass side wall. This will give good instructional and spectator viewing. The use of an open or glass enclosed viewing balcony/gallery in the back wall above the 12-foot height also is good for instructional and spectator viewing.

(Figure 2.12.) If glass walls are utilized, spectator and instructional viewing areas should be planned for carefully. These areas usually are stepped and carpeted, with risers along either side wall or back wall of the court. A built-in, two-way audio system should be utilized for this court. Carpet color should not be totally dark and, particularly not blue, since player ball visibility through the glass walls is obscured with dark colors as a background.

Floors should be hardwood, as in standard gymnasium construction. Court line markings should be a lighter color, rather than a dark color like blue or black. Again this helps the participants' visual acuity in following a dark ball across lighter lines. The first 12 feet of the ceiling, from the front wall, should be void of any heat or ventilating ducts. This portion of the ceiling must be hard and compatible to the wall surfaces for ball rebounding. Lighting and any other fixtures in the ceiling must be totally flush. The rear eight feet of the ceiling is not as crucial since this part of the ceiling is used very seldom in play.

All doors should be of standard size located in the center of the back

Figure 2.12. Glass fronted racquetball courts provide for easy viewing at the University of Arizona.

wall. All doors and door hardware should be flush. Glass doors work well. Doors should open out from the court, and there should be no door thresholds. Storage boxes may be built into side walls near the back wall of each court to house valuables and extra balls. These must be flush with wall surfaces. One court should have a clear glass square in the front wall with rear access for a video camera hook up. This panel is usually small, two-by-two feet, and close to the floor level. Storage areas for students' coats, books, and other equipment should be provided in an area near the courts. Storage for racquetball racquets, handball gloves, and squash racquets, eye guards, and balls should be provided securely near the court area.

Lighting, Acoustics, and Ventilation

As mentioned before, all lighting must be flush with the ceiling. Lights should illuminate all portions of the court equally; therefore they should be spread throughout the ceiling. Shadows and low-light areas are not acceptable in these courts. Light accessibility for changing bulbs must be planned carefully. Since there are normally a battery of courts, the changing of light bulbs is magnified by the number of courts in which one must utilize a bulb changing system. Each court should be controlled by one light switch. This switch may be in a master control panel, by each court's door, or built into the door's closing mechanism.

A recommended method of turning the lights on and off in handball and squash courts is to install switches that are activated by the opening or closing of the door to the court. When the door is opened, the lights will turn off automatically, leaving only the night light to burn continuously. When the door is closed, lights in the court will turn on. Usually, a two to three-minute delay occurs prior to the lights going off after the door has been opened. This

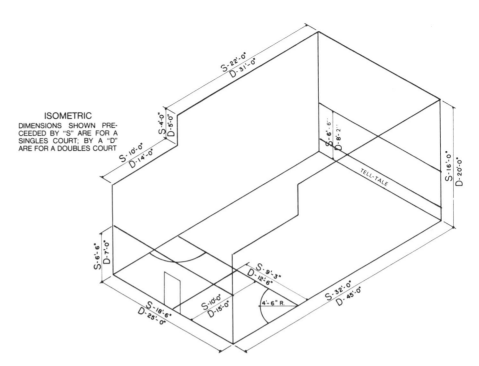

Figure 2.13. Squash Court Dimensions

prevents a disruption of lighting during the brief time it takes for players to exchange the court. This system eliminates the possibility of the lights being left on when the courts are not in use. This system cannot be utilized with a metal halide lighting system.

However, the lights, when turned off, will come on instantaneously when new players enter the court and close the door. With this system, warning lights can be located outside each court to indicate when a court is in use. A relatively new concept utilizes an annunciator (an electrically controlled signal board) to indicate to the building reservation/control center which courts are occupied at any one time. Lights on the signal board are activated by the "trip" switch on each door as it opens or closes.

Court walls are hard surfaces, and much sound is reverberated in the courts. Acoustical treatment is important within the walls (except for glass) and in the rear eight feet of the ceiling. This is minimal acoustical treatment, but is very important and should be considered in each court.

Ventilation may be provided by air conditioning or forced air. The ventilation of each court is very important so that moisture does not build on wall surfaces. Moisture on wall surfaces makes the courts unplayable. Ample air circulation and dehumidifying the air are major concerns in the ventilation of the courts. It also is suggested that courts not be built underground with walls exposed to external moisture. It is very easy for moisture and/or condensation to intrude to the interior wall surfaces of the courts. If courts must be built underground, extra waterproofing needs to be completed in this portion of the facility.

In some instances these courts are utilized for other activities such as volleyball, fitness activities, and rebounding areas. If the courts are utilized for other activities, these activities must be planned for carefully. Walls may need supports; lights might need to take greater impact, and ceilings may need added strength in order to house these other activities successfully.

Squash is very popular in some localities, and the number of courts should be determined by local interest. A singles court is 18.6 feet wide by 32 feet long and 16 feet high. A doubles court is 25 feet wide by 45 feet long and 20 feet high. (Figure 2.13.)

It is possible to install movable metal "telltales" across the front of handball/racquetball courts so they can be used for squash instruction purposes. However, the courts are racquetball size, not squash size. The floors, walls, ceilings, lighting, heating, and ventilation of squash courts are similar to those of four-wall racquetball/handball courts.

Wrestling/Martial Arts

This area is designed for wrestling and martial arts activities. The room should be rectangular in shape, at least 50 by 100 feet, and should be of sufficient size to accommodate two square mats, each measuring a minimum of 42 by 42 feet. The mats should have 10-foot practice rings consisting of three rows of six circles to each row, for a total of 18 practice rings. A satisfactory standard is 10 by 10 feet or 100-square-feet per student during peak usage, based on 40 to 45 students per class. The floor area not covered by the regulation mats should be covered with carpet for classroom instructional type atmosphere. The ceiling should be of acoustic material and should be a minimum of 12 feet high. (Figure 2.14.)

The floor of the wrestling room should be constructed of or covered with resilient material to prolong the life of the mats. These materials may be rubberlock products, other newly dev-

eloped resilient materials, or wood. Concrete is not recommended. The walls should be covered with mats up to a six-foot height. Adequate lighting, heating, and forced ventilation are essential in this room. If intercollegiate wrestling is planned, this room needs individual controls for heat. Coaches tend to prefer warm wrestling rooms. A refrigerated water fountain, flush with the wall, should be in the room. A blackboard, bulletin board, and scale should be available. An electric scoreboard wall clock should be attached to the wall. A sound system should be present, with a wall pulley machine and a takedown machine included as basic equipment.

Safety, Maintenance, and Storage

Safety is of paramount importance in a matted space. Having all areas of the activity space matted is important. There should be no protruding objects, doorways, or furniture in this matted space. Support columns should not be present in this space. It also is important to provide daily cleaning and disinfecting of the mats. With this in mind, a maintenance storage area needs to be in or adjacent to the matted room. This area must have running water, a trough, and be large enough for mopping, cleaning, and disinfecting equipment. Built-in storage also is important for wrestling headgear, video cameras, monitors, tape decks, and martial arts equipment.

Fencing

Fencing often is included in the instructional, recreational, and intercollegiate programs for both men and women. The field of play is a piste, or more commonly referred to as a "strip" in the United States.

A room 55 feet by 90 feet allows for four fencing strips 40 feet long and six feet wide, with 15 feet between strips. These strips may be used for informal competition and instruction. Intercollegiate competition, however, requires a 52-foot length of floor area, with a minimum of 18 feet between the strips.

For instructional purposes, the strip may be painted on a nonslip hardwood floor or synthetic surface, or a rubber runner of correct measurements may be laid on the floor and removed when not in use. For the electric foil and epee, a metallic piste must cover the entire length of the strip, including the extensions.

Electrical outlets and jacks should be placed at the rear of the tournament strips to provide power for the electrical equipment. If permanently affixed wall scoreboards are provided, portable score boxes are unnecessary. Brackets or eyebolts for mounting fencing targets should either be recessed flush with the wall or placed above the seven-foot level.

The fencing area should be a well-lighted room with a minimum ceiling height of 12 feet. The installation of rollaway bleachers for spectators may necessitate raising the ceiling height, and it also may require an increased capacity ventilating system.

A secured, built-in, equipment room should be located adjacent to the fencing room and should be large enough to store the weapons and protective equipment used by classes. This storage space also should house a built-in video camera, monitor, and tape deck. One hundred-square-feet is the minimal space required for storage and to accommodate a small cabinet work

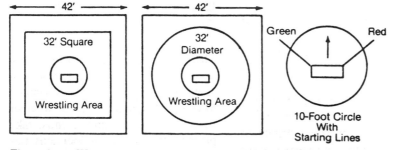

Figure 2.14. Wrestling area configurations (1992 NCAA Wrestling Rules and Interpretations)

counter for the repair of equipment. Portable strips will require additional space.

Archery

Instructional and recreational groups need an indoor archery area suitable for practice during inclement weather.

An area 78 feet long is adequate for official ranges of 10, 15, and 20 yards for indoor archery. The 78 feet includes three feet for the target, 60 feet for the range, and a 15-foot width is required for 24 students. This area will accommodate six 48-inch targets set 10 feet apart on centers, or 12 five-foot lanes for indoor targets. A minimum ceiling height of 15 feet should be provided between the shooting line and targets.

The floor in the archery area will receive hard usage from street shoes and flying arrows. A hardwood, tongue-and-groove floor, with boards running the length of the shooting area, is preferred. A durable synthetic surface may be considered as a viable alternative.

The location of structural features in the archery room should be given careful attention. Obstructions ahead of the shooting line, such as supporting pillars and overhead lights in a low ceiling, should be recessed or otherwise protected from flying arrows. The area behind the target should be covered with a backdrop to protect the wall and prevent arrow breakage. A large heavy run, or a commercially available nylon net which arrows cannot penetrate, may be used. All doors and windows in the area should be located behind the shooting line. The same is true for tackboards and chalkboards.

Targets may be affixed to the backstop or placed on easels in front of it. A variety of targets are available, including straw, double-curl excelsior, and styrofoam with composition centers. The target should be constructed and placed so as to allow an arrow to penetrate at least 20 inches without striking any obstruction that would damage it.

Figure 2.15. A golf-fencing-archery room was included in the HPER Building at the University of Nebraska at Omaha. Archery targets are mounted directly on a horizontally flattened cardboard box wall.

A low-cost innovative back stop has been designed using flattened cardboard boxes piled from floor to ceiling covering an entire wall. Targets are simply pinned to the cardboard, and the arrows penetrate the cardboard six to 15 inches.

In a multi-purpose room, target holders should be mounted on wheels or set in floor plates. The plates should be flush with the floor when the target holder is removed. The backdrop behind the targets would be pulled to the side or rolled overhead when not in use.

Storage space for targets and other equipment should be adjacent to the range. Their size and location will be determined by the type of targets used. Racks for hanging bows and shelves for storing arrows should be included in a storage area behind the shooting line. This location enables a student to replace or exchange equipment while other students continue to shoot. The video camera, monitor, and tape deck also should be housed in this area.

The feasibility of installing automated lanes should be considered seriously. Several types of commercial lanes are available. Automated lanes have lane dividers at the shooting line and an automatic warning system to halt shooting in the event a person steps in front of the shooting line. Electric

target returns bring the targets to the shooting line so arrows can be removed, and the targets can be adjusted for different shooting distances without altering the shooting line.

Both fencing and archery are unique in that actual weapons are being employed in the activities. Because of this, safety of both the participants and passers-by must be planned carefully. For the participants, there should be no objects to stumble over or objects that an arrow might hit and therefore rebound to the shooting line. Both areas should be isolated from casual passers-by either by being placed in an isolated portion of the facility or by being secured by walls, doors, and ceiling. Arrows, in particular, can travel a great distance and still do damage. Therefore, both of these spaces must somehow be self-contained. (Figure 2.15.)

Golf, Tennis, Riflery, and Climbing

There may be a need for some facility design to include outdoor activities in an indoor space. This may be attributed to curricular decisions and/or weather factors. Careful planning must take place when bringing outdoor activities indoors.

Figure 2.16. Commercially produced golf training devices aid players in refining their stroke technique.

Indoor Golf Practice Area- Provisions can be made to accommodate golf instruction and practice indoors. Balls may be hit into a large durable nylon net or canvas placed several yards in front of the hitting positions. Driving cages also may be used. Hitting positions may be established by placement of practice mats available from golf supply houses. (Figures 2.16, 2.17.)

In addition, commercial golf systems now are available that complement any instructional/ recreational program. These computerized programs actually simulate outdoor golf with video and audio components. The users actually take the needed shots from the tee, to the fairway, to the green in this one location. All shots are computer measured as to distance and direction to afford accurate game-like situations. It usually is economical and efficient to consider designing this area to accommodate other activities when not used for golf (i.e., archery, fencing, etc.).

Indoor Tennis Facilities- Tennis can be played indoors on any firm surface of sufficient size for a tennis court, espec-

ially where court markings and a net are provided. Sometimes tennis court markings are placed on the general use gymnasium floor, and provisions are made for temporary placement of net posts, or the net is attached to rings inserted in the wall. Another teaching aid is simply a solid color contrasting line painted at net height on a flat wall

of the gymnasium which provides a rebound surface for practicing one's strokes. Portable tennis courts also might be used in the gymnasium or field house.

The composition of a synthetic surface can be altered to offset the bounce of the tennis ball. A surface constructed for playing basketball usually proves to be too fast for tennis competition, but will suffice for beginning instruction.

A few colleges have constructed a special indoor facility specifically for tennis. If this is done, the facility should include a minimum of four courts, along with a tennis drill area. Such a facility would enable 16 students to play tennis, while other students use the tennis drill area. This approach would demand frequent rotation of students.

If the courts are in a separate building, it should be located convenient to locker rooms. Consideration also should be given to a covered passageway between the gymnasium and the tennis building.

Indoor Rifle Range- A rifle range can be used for class instruction, competitive shooting, and recreation for both men and women. On campuses where a

Figure 2.17. Nets are pulled out for easy conversion to golf practice and fencing lanes are painted on the synthetic floor.

range within the athletic and physical education complex is not deemed feasible, the ROTC units might be contacted for possible collaboration in constructing and financing a range.

A room 75 feet by 42 feet will accommodate eight firing points, or a class of 24 students. At least eight firing points are recommended on the basis of one point for every three members of a class. The National Rifle Association standard shooting distance for rifles is 50 feet, measured from the firing line to the target. The bulletstop should be six to 10 feet beyond the target. The space varies with the type of installation.

A minimum of 15 feet is required behind the firing line for mats, scoring tables, rifle racks, and walking space. The ceiling should be eight feet high in front of the firing points. This ceiling height reduces the amount of wall space that must be covered behind the backdrop, and facilitates the installation of target carriers. Each firing point should be at least 5 1/2 feet wide. Safety features and acoustical treatment are two very important planning considerations.

For specifications on construction of indoor rifle ranges, write to the National Rifle Association of America, 1600 Rhode Island Avenue, N.W., Washington, D.C. 20036.

Indoor Climbing Walls- There is a great interest in many outdoor pursuits such as hiking, camping, and climbing. In many instances a campus is not located near the outdoor areas that afford the environment needed to reach these skills. Indoor climbing walls have been designed to teach both technical climbing skills and rappelling.

Like all facilities, the design of the climbing wall is paramount. Careful planning must be completed as to size, price range, placement, weight bearing factors, and visual appeal of the climbing wall. Because of the inherent danger in climbing, the wall must be placed in an area with total security. Consideration must be given to whether the wall will be free standing or attached

Figure 2.18. Artist's rendering of rock climbing wall designed for University of Miami (Sneary, 1992, courtesy of HOK Sports Facilities Group)

to the facility structure itself. Walls may be small (6 feet by 12 feet) or they can be large (30 feet by 80 feet). Structural integrity of both the wall and the facility itself for support of the wall weight is important to consider.

Walls should be designed for a wide skill variation from beginning to advanced levels. Some walls come equipped with moveable hand and foot holds and easily can have their routes changed. It is highly recommended to consult an indoor climbing wall specialist to design the wall itself and the climbing routes on the wall. Most indoor climbing wall companies provide such expertise. (Figure 2.18.)

There are panel wall systems, molded and shell systems, wall tiles, and vertical gravity-operated treadmill design climbing walls. The importance of safe design cannot be overly emphasized. The attachment of the panels and tiles must be engineered for stress and support. Stress and support for both the panels, rock and tile, and the live and dead load weight of the climbers all must be considered. Load bearing, impact strength, durability, and flammability must be considered in indoor climbing wall plans. Most indoor climbing walls are made of plywood,

and/or synthetic, rock-like polymer concrete. Walls may be relatively flat, bulbous, contoured, and be designed to be high or low. Walls can be designed to be natural in appearance or futuristically sculptured. Costs vary as to type of wall system and size of the facility. Careful planning as to the needs of the users and safety and security of the climbing wall is most important.

Storage areas must be provided for ropes, harnesses, helmets, and other climbing equipment. Careful belay systems planning must take place from both upper and ground levels of the climbing wall. The climbing wall must meet all local building codes. Indoor rock climbing walls are utilized for instruction, therefore configuration of the wall must aid in instructional viewing and auditory command.

Multi-purpose/Auxiliary Gym Areas

These activity spaces serve a variety of program needs. They are back-up teaching stations for both scheduled and nonscheduled classes and activities. These spaces can be either high ceiling or low ceiling. Low ceiling, auxiliary spaces should be a minimum of 70 feet by 90 feet and can be surfaced with either hardwood or synthetics, depending on the types of activities to be held in the room. High ceiling multi-purpose space should be a minimum of 90 feet by 120 feet. If this space is to be utilized primarily for sliding activities, a hardwood floor would be appropriate. This space is large enough for basketball, volleyball, badminton, and other standard indoor activities. It also is large enough to be utilized by outdoor activities during inclement weather. Indoor activity facilities can be designed without multi-purpose/auxiliary gym areas and still can be excellent facilities. These additional spaces give flexibility and increased latitude in planning curricular and non-curricular activities, as well as serving as quality inclement weather activity space. (Figures 2.19, 2.20, 2.21.)

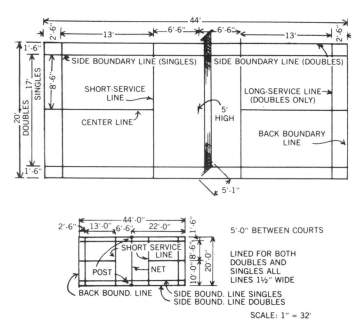

Figure 2.19. Badminton Court Dimensions

Activity	Play Area in Feet	Safety Space in Feet*	Total Area in Feet	Minimum Ceiling Height
Archery	5x60	15e	5x75	12
Badminton	20x44	6s, 8e	32x60	24
Basketball				
Jr. High instructional	42x74	6s, 8e		24
Jr. High interscholastic	50x84	6s, 8e		
Sr. High interscholastic	50x84	6s, 8e	62x100	
Sr. High instructional	45x74	6s, 8e	57x90	
Neighborhood E. Sch.	42x74	6s, 8e	54x90	
Community Junior H.S.	50x84	6s, 8e	62x100	
Community Senior H.S.	50x84	6s, 8e	62x100	
Competitive - College & University	50x94	6s, 8e	62x110	
Boccie	18x62	3s, 9e	24x80	
Fencing, competitive	6x46	9s, 6e	18x52	
instructional	4x30	4s, 6e	12x42	12
Handball	20x40			
				20
Racquetball	20x40			
				20
Rifle (one pt.)	5x50	6 to 20e	5x70 min.	12
Shuffleboard	6x52	6s,2e	18x56	
				12
Squash	18.5x32			16
				24
Tennis				
Deck (doubles)	18x40	4s, 5e	26x50	
Hand	16x40	4½s, 10e	25x60	
Lawn (singles)	27x78	12s, 21e	51x120	
(doubles)	36x78	12s, 21e	60x120	
Paddle (singles)	16x44	6s, 8e	28x60	
(doubles)	20x44	6s, 8e	32x60	
Table (playing area)			9x31	
				24
Volleyball				
Competitive and adult	30x60	6s, 6e	42x72	
Junior High	30x50	6s, 6e	42x62	
Wrestling (competitive)	24x24	5s, 5e	36x36	

*Safety space at the side of an area is indicated by a number followed by "e" for end and "s" for side.

Figure 2.20. Space Needed for Selected Indoor Activities

Multipurpose use of a gymnasium, for meetings for example, may require special sound system considerations. The University of Nebraska-Kearney's new Cushing HPER facility makes use of 96 speakers wired to an elaborate sound system to accommodate large group sessions. (Figure 2.22.)

Indoor Tracks

With the increased popularity for fitness and exercise, short mention will be made concerning recreational tracks. These tracks should be designed to be as long as possible with as few curves as possible. The track should be surfaced with a synthetic rubberized material that provides good cushioning. Cushioning on these indoor tracks is very important since the track is provided for recreational runners of all ages and all skill levels. A minimum of five to six lanes should be provided. Depending on the size and curvature of the track, consideration should be given to banking the turns. (Figure 2.23.)

Indoor tracks may be on the main level of the facility, or they may be elevated approximately 12 feet above

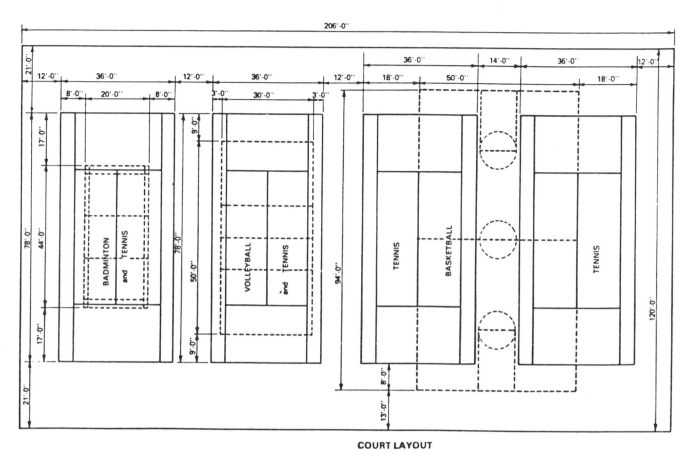

COURT LAYOUT

Figure 2.21. Combination Court Layout

the main floor. If the track is elevated, it should not interfere with other main floor activities. Elevated tracks need a combination barrier/railing system running around the inside perimeter of the track for safety. If the track is on the main level, it may be segregated from other floor activities by utilizing dropnets. An area for user storage of books, warmups, jackets, and towels should be provided adjacent to the track. Large faced, large numeral, 60-minute, sweep second-hand clocks should be provided throughout the track area, and a recessed, refrigerated water fountain also should be provided. An electronic light system built flush into the floor of the track has been used successfully. The lights are timed and come on in sequence so that a runner keeps pace with the next light as it comes on. The timing can be changed for slow and fast paces, and there is little upkeep or cost with this system after initial installation.

Research Areas

Research facilities to support physical education, health, athletics, and recre-

ation are becoming increasingly important in colleges and universities. A majority of the research conducted by physical education professionals

Figure 2.22. Alternate use of a multipurpose gymnasium area at the University of Nebraska-Kearny

Figure 2.23. Indoor jogging track
(Photo by Lee Bloom)

requires laboratory settings with special equipment.

It is impossible to list all the tools that any individual investigator will need to use in research. A lab's design often is dictated by the type of equipment to be used in it.

Despite the wide diversity in research tools, there are some facilities and equipment commonly used in laboratories for research in athletics, physical education, health, and recreation. Some general considerations and some specific types of research facilities now in use or projected for the future follow.

The nature of the educational institution and its objectives and function will determine in large measure the type, number, size, and relative importance of research and teaching laboratories for athletics, physical education, health, and recreation. In junior colleges, or in four-year institutions in which only service courses are offered, sophisticated research laboratories will seldom, if ever, be required. However, laboratory experience may be desirable as a part of a course, and some testing equipment

may be required for use in the gymnasium or on the playing field. Furthermore, there are liberal arts colleges and other research-oriented institutions whose undergraduate curriculum requires that the student have research experience. In such institutions, it is not unreasonable to provide limited research facilities and supervision of selected research activities.

In colleges and universities offering professional preparation in physical education or recreation, and especially in those with a graduate curriculum in these areas, there is a greater need for the development of research and teaching laboratories. Such facilities are required not only to provide experience and training for students, but also to attract and retain capable research scholars.

Separate teaching laboratories should be provided to handle laboratory sections of various courses. The same teaching laboratory cannot be used for some of the laboratory sessions in a variety of courses, including tests and measurements, physiology of exercise, and biomechanics. At least one such teaching laboratory should be available, equipped with stationary lab tables containing gas, water, and electricity. Hoods for the Bunsen burner, cabinets for storing small pieces of equipment, and a connecting supply room also are essential. Closed-circuit television receivers are desirable. The laboratory can be designed to accommodate equipment used in conducting experiments with animals and human beings.

Frequently, the teaching laboratory can be equipped with durable, inexpensive, and easily serviced apparatus where students can carry on experiments individually or in small groups. While such equipment may not provide the degree of precision expected from sophisticated research apparatus, it generally is accurate enough to present desirable principles. A space of approximately 1,200 square feet, with a 12-foot ceiling, will accommodate a class of 20 students.

It is likely that laboratory

experiences will replace and/or supplement some of the course lectures, particularly at the graduate level. This will increase the need for teaching labs as well as research labs. Graduate students should have considerable laboratory experience before they embark on collecting data for a doctoral dissertation.

Several forces are acting to accentuate the role of the research investigator in colleges and universities. The availability of funds, greater specialization, increased research encouragement from the administration, and competition for university faculty have had a positive influence on the place of research. The recent interest within the fields of health education, physical education, and recreation in developing a body of knowledge, and the development and expansion of graduate programs in these fields, also has created a greater demand for research facilities and trained investigators.

A sizeable proportion of some faculties now are doing research, sometimes with several faculty members sharing a common interest or specialty. Provisions must be made for this increased interest and emphasis. (Figure 2.24.)

Joint appointments, in which a faculty member holds an appointment in more than one department, are increasing in number in the fields of physical education, health, and recreation. Provisions should be made for some faculty members to do research in other departments, and conversely, members of other departments may be expected to use some of the physical education, health, and recreation research facilities.

A related development is the organization in many large universities of centers or institutes for research that cut across departmental lines. There are a number of advantages to such organizational setups, including interdisciplinary work and the sharing of elaborate facilities and expensive apparatus. In the planning of research facilities for physical education, health, and recreation, the existing as well as the proposed relationships on the campus should be investigated.

Research Equipment Purchasing- The manufacture and sale of research equipment has become a very competitive business. As a result, there frequently is a wide range of the same kind of equipment available under different brand names. Before purchasing large expensive units, it is worth the time and effort to investigate carefully the variety of equipment on the market. The annual meetings of professional societies generally include exhibits by manufacturers of research equipment appropriate to the particular area of investigation. Consultation with a colleague in the same field who has used the equipment is a good idea before a purchase is made.

In considering particular pieces of equipment, the following determination should be made:

- if students or trained researchers are to use the equipment,
- initial and annual servicing cost,
- if the equipment is electronically compatible with other equipment now in use or contemplated (often it is more economical to purchase units that match others from the same company so that the responsibility for servicing them rests with one company),
- what power supply is needed,
- ease with which the instrument may be calibrated and if other equipment is needed for the calibration,
- portability of the equipment,
- what service the company is willing to provide and where the service centers are located, and

- noise, vibration, and heat generated by the equipment.

Unbiased answers to these and other questions sometimes can be found best by having discussions with other researchers who have used such installations.

Measurement and Evaluation Laboratories- Much of the so-called practical or applied research will be conducted in the gymnasium, swimming pool, and other indoor and outdoor activity areas. This means that in order to utilize measurement and evaluation equipment effectively, the regular activity areas must be planned and constructed in such a manner as to facilitate the conduct of research. For example, many skill tests are administered with the use of some type of wall volley as a part of a battery to measure skill in a certain activity. Therefore, it is important to construct the walls of a gymnasium so that present tests, as well as those developed in the future, may be utilized.

Consideration should be given to the attachment of special equipment to walls and ceilings, such as jump boards, ropes, and strength-measuring devices. Grids could be painted on the walls of the gymnasium, as well as on the wall of a diving well in the swimming pool, in order to measure distance and height when analyzing movement.

A great deal of the research equipment needs to be portable so that it can be moved to the action areas. This means that proper electrical outlets and suitable acoustic treatment of these areas must be planned in advance.

These laboratories will contain the equipment that will be used at the elementary, junior high, and senior high school levels. Physical education teachers at these levels should be encouraged to make use of some of this equipment on the job.

Within this lab area should be at least 10 personal computer terminals with hard drives. This laboratory should be the department's main data acquisition area. Plotters, laser printers, and a mini-main frame server should be

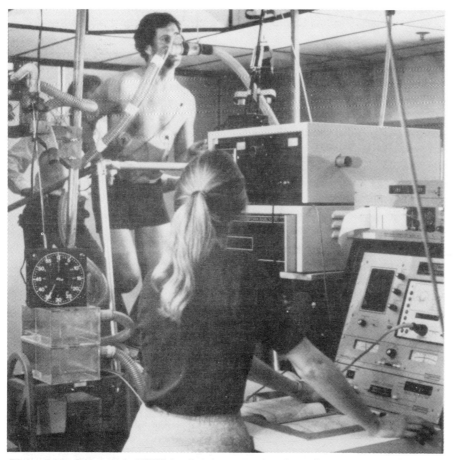

Figure 2.24. Research in HPER has become more popular and sophisticated, thus careful consideration must be given to the planning of laboratories.

available to all users. This computer area needs to be isolated from areas where objects might be thrown, kicked, hit, or rebound. All tests and measurement labs need to have a computer area. These areas should be both applied and research oriented.

Biomechanics Laboratories- There are many areas in the field of biomechanics in which research may be conducted. The type of research may range from cinematography to human engineering. If there is a physiology of exercise laboratory available, experimentation may take place in which the equipment from this laboratory is used either jointly with the exercise physiologist or separately by the kinesiology researcher.

In cinematographic research (especially time lapse and high speed), a room 30 by 30 feet, with a ceiling height of at least 24 feet, is a necessity. High speed cameras whose frame rates vary from 64 to several thousand frames per second are useful. Special film readers and projectors should be provided in order that accurate measurements may be made. Mirrors may be used to reflect images. (Figure 2.25.)

Equipment typical of the type used in this kind of laboratory includes:
- movement developing camera,
- 35mm SLR camera,
- high speed motion picture camera (motor-driven; 50 to 500 frames per second),
- stroboscopic equipment (including single and multi-flash units with strobolume and strobotac parts),
- force-measuring devices (including individual strain gauges and multi-dimensional force plates),
- videotape recorder with two channels and playback capacity,
- oscilloscope,
- electronic counters,
- amplifiers compatible with measuring and recording devices,
- metal storage cabinets (approximately 18 inches deep by 36 inches wide) with locks,

Figure 2.25. Biomechanics laboratory (Photo by Lee Bloom)

- six personal computers with hard drives,
- digitizing systems, both two and three dimensional,
- minimum 52-inch diagonal size large screen monitor television.

Special simulated game areas may be constructed so that a true picture of a performer in action may be studied. A miniature running track may be developed, as well as other similar replicas of playing areas. Nets and other devices may need to be used to catch objects or to prevent them from traversing the customary distance. Adjacent to these areas should be a video center with non-glossy and dark background walls that can be used for videography. All portions of the biomechanics lab should be housed in an area between 3,000- and 4,000-square-feet in size.

Physiology of Exercise Laboratory- This laboratory should be a minimum of 65 feet by 65 feet or about 4,000-square-feet in size.

The most popular methods of standardizing exercise in human beings are:

- by means of a motor-driven treadmill, bicycle, or other ergometer,
- step tests of various kinds.

The exercise room should be large enough to accommodate all the needed equipment. There should be space for several technicians as well as for scientific instruments.

Since some noise and vibration results when the treadmill is operating -- and some treadmills are quite heavy -- it is preferable to locate this room on the ground floor, with provisions for reducing noise. The treadmill should be installed in a pit (and even on a pad to help reduce further noise), if possible, with space in the pit for servicing. (Figure 2.26.)

The room should be air conditioned, with control over temperature within a plus-or-minus 1 1/2° F and control over humidity of plus-or-minus five percent. Electric current (110v and 220v) should be supplied through numerous outlets. A large thermopane observation window also should be installed.

A room 20 by 25 feet with a ceiling height of 12 feet to allow for walking, running, or riding a bicycle up

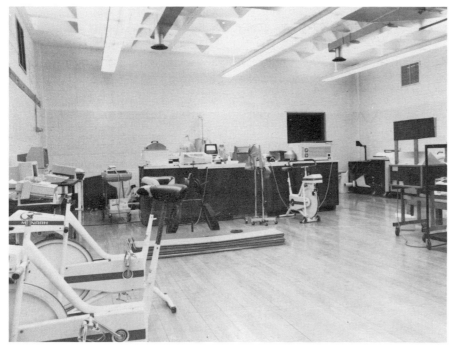

Figure 2.26. Exercise physiology laboratory (Photo by Lee Bloom)

a grade on the treadmill, is generally sufficient. If the treadmill is not installed in a pit, the ceiling may have to be higher. It usually is desirable to have connecting cables, including voice communication, to a space adjoining the exercise room so desirable data can be recorded outside the room. An alternate method of constructing a platform surrounding the treadmill may be more practical. The types of equipment found in the exercise room, in addition to exercising apparatus, might include the following:

- multi-channel recorder
- tape recorder (multi-channel)
- gas meters
- cot
- spirometer
- telemetering apparatus
- electronic gas analyzers
- Douglas or meteorological bags
- barometer
- thermocouples
- submersion tank
- six computer terminals
- vertec apparatus for vertical jump measurement
- two metabolic carts

- reaction timers interfaced with computers
- two spectrophotometers for chemical analysis
- refrigerated blood centrifuge
- large freezer with a -80°F capacity
- large refrigerator
- glucose/lactate analyzer.

In many departments, additional major facilities may be required. Because research in exercise physiology is closely related to research in environmental physiology and nutrition, the following facilities may be needed:

- barometric chamber (with space for controlled exercise)
- hot room (with space for controlled exercise)
- cold room (with space for controlled exercise)
- diet kitchen
- flow-through water tank for studying energy metabolism during swimming and rowing
- isotope storage, handling, and counting equipment.

In addition, animal exercise and housing rooms may be considered.

All exercise physiology labs should have built-in video stations with mounted camera, monitor, and tape deck as mentioned previously for all teaching stations.

Wellness Areas- Many colleges and universities are providing wellness programs to faculty, staff, administration, and their families. In the past many of these programs were a part of the physiology of exercise labs. The trend now is for the wellness area to have a separate lab space. Currently wellness areas share other activity-oriented space such as tracks, pools, aerobic areas, and weight areas with physical education, recreation, and athletics. Because of the expense of duplicating these activity areas, future wellness areas need to be planned in conjunction with and in close proximity to the track, weight and aerobic areas, and the pool.

When indoor tracks, weight areas, swimming pools, and aerobic areas are designed, the wellness area staff should be available to share in the plans. Ideally, all four of the aforementioned areas and the wellness lab and office area should be in close proximity to each other.

The wellness lab area should consist of the following items:

- a treadmill with EKG hookups for stress testing
- bicycle ergometer interfaced with a computer
- cholesterol centrifuge
- blood analyzer
- refrigerator
- freezer with -80°F capacity
- scales, skinfold calipers, and blood pressure measuring equipment
- two computer terminals.

The wellness area should have access to a two-to-four-lane track for walking and jogging, five bicycle ergometers, five rowing machines, five stair climbing machines, and free and machine weights. There should be a wellness classroom specifically located adjacent to the lab area. Four to five offices need to be provided for the staff for a waiting area and for conferences. Ample storage must be provided in all areas of the wellness center for audio-visual materials, educational materials, and models. A demonstration kitchen including a microwave, stove, and refrigerator should be an integral part of the wellness area. The kitchen is utilized to teach proper cooking and eating habits. Correct nutrition and dietary habits also can be promoted through use of the demonstration kitchen. Cardiac rehabilitation programs could be a part of the wellness center. If this is true, additional space is required, and plans should address the needs of the cardiac rehab patient. Locker and shower rooms also must be easily accessible to the wellness area.

Motor Learning and Sport Psychology Laboratories- Much of the research equipment found in measurement, biomechanics, and exercise physiology labs can be used interchangeably among these labs. Much of this equipment also may be utilized in the motor learning lab. The motor learning/sport psychology lab should be a minimum of 2,000 square feet with a 12-foot ceiling.

The arrangement of the equipment in the room will depend on the research underway at the moment. In any event, the electrical devices used should not be moved constantly, or they will become unusable.

Some equipment that might be included in a laboratory for research in motor learning and psychology of sports includes:
- audio and video amplifiers
- biofeedback machines
- reaction timers
- anticipation timers
- stabilometer
- pursuit rotor
- accelerometer
- videographic digitizing system
- multi-channel recorders
- clocks
- muscle stimulators
- electronic counters
- telemetry units.

This lab also should be designed for isolated areas so that specialized research may take place without interfering with other use of the lab or vice versa. Areas for learning novel tasks such as juggling and the use of mazes should be included in the plans. Acoustical treatment of this lab is very important.

Pedagogy Laboratory- A lab to study the science of teaching should be established with a minimum size of 2,000 to 3,000 square feet. This lab should be equipped with one-way viewing areas, videographic equipment, and areas for activity and theory classroom environments. The activity area may need a 24-foot high ceiling. Storage areas and racks should be constructed to house both activity and pen/pencil equipment. Lighting should be rheostatically controlled.

Other Laboratory Considerations- Although there is a need for individual research laboratories, some facilities lend themselves to shared use. A workshop supervised by a capable machinist or other skilled worker is an essential ancillary facility in institutions where considerable research is being conducted. If the research productivity of the physical education, health, and recreation unit is sufficiently great, there is justification for housing and supporting this type of ancillary facility in this unit. If, however, research and laboratory teaching is done on a smaller scale, the facility may be shared by other units in the college or university, or such services may be purchased as needed.

If a workshop is planned, 110v and 220v electric current with good ground connections should be made available. Oversized doors should be provided, as well as a good ventilation system so that sawdust and other pollutants will not become a hazard or annoyance. Cupboards with locks should be in ample supply to store hand tools to prevent their being stolen or misplaced. Since considerable noise

may be generated, the workshop should be isolated from other facilities where quiet work is being done. There should be a minimum of 80 footcandles of light on the task being performed. The room should be at least 500 to 600 square feet in size, with a ceiling height of 12 feet.

The dark room, for obvious reasons, should not have an outside wall with a window. Therefore, good forced ventilation is essential. The room should be provided with running water, sinks, ample wall cupboards, and a generous supply of duplex electrical outlets (110v). The recommended room size is 225-square-feet or more, with a 12-foot ceiling.

A number of researchers and teachers have need for graphic services in preparing materials for publication, for presentation at meetings, and for instruction. Camera equipment that can produce a two-by-two inch slide and overhead transparencies in a matter of minutes at little cost should be provided. Duplicating equipment also may be housed in this facility.

If the needs of the department are sufficiently large, a full-time or part-time employee may be required to prepare graphic materials. A room used for this purpose should be well lighted (a minimum of 80 footcandles is recommended) and should have large wall cupboards for storing drafting and some camera equipment. A room with a minimum of 400-square-feet and a 10-foot ceiling height will provide sufficient space for the usual requirements of this facility.

Individual offices for the various faculty members and graduate students involved in research should be convenient to the various laboratories. The installation of one or more rooms to be used for quiet work (e.g., calculating, reading, and writing) is helpful. These office spaces must provide isolation for the faculty member/technician, yet they must be an integral part of laboratory planning. They need to be located in the lab, or immediately adjacent to the lab, with direct access to the lab.

In planning research facilities, serious thought should be given to the development of a mobile laboratory. The trend to eliminate laboratory schools makes the consideration of a mobile laboratory more urgent.

Trailers, campers, trucks, and other vehicles -- even railroad cars -- have been converted into mobile laboratories. Often the use of a field generator is necessary to provide current for operating mobile laboratory equipment. It is surprising how much equipment can be installed compactly in a mobile facility. These mobile labs can take on many forms, from exercise science labs to pedagogy labs.

Classrooms

Classrooms should be designed in accordance with the use of the room. Some classrooms should be science-oriented with lab tables, water, sinks, and built-in desk storage areas. Classrooms for large lecture sections and classrooms for small discussion classes should be planned carefully and early in the facility design. The size and shape of the classroom will vary as to its function. Large lecture rooms may have permanently affixed disks and chairs arranged in an amphitheater pattern. Small discussion classrooms will have moveable desks and chairs

and can take any shape and/or size. (Figures 2.27a,b.)

The teaching styles of the faculty who will be utilizing the classroom must be considered in designing the classrooms. Faculty should be consulted on all phases of classroom planning. Floors, walls, and ceilings will be dictated by the type of instruction utilized in the classroom space. Carpeted floors, moveable walls, one-way viewing areas, and high/low ceiling heights need careful consideration in classroom design.

Storage areas such as showcases, shelves, and closets also need careful attention in classroom design. All audio-visual equipment should be built-in to each classroom so that this equipment can remain stationary for most of its use. Each classroom should be equipped with a mounted camera, videotape deck and a 25-inch colored television monitor. The monitor and deck should be built-in flush with the wall and be secured by a door. Some storage areas will need to be secured, while others will be exposed areas.

Acoustical treatment should be done for the total classroom environment. Within the classroom, treatment of the floor, walls, ceiling, and desks should be considered. External acoustical treatment for the walls and the actual placement of the classroom in relation to "activity noise spaces"

requires careful planning. Ample electrical outlets, cable and computer hookups, energy-saving devices, and security for all classrooms also should be planned carefully.

The aesthetical environment of a classroom can make a huge difference on the amount of learning that may take place in any given space. Windows should be planned for all classrooms, and glare factors should be planned for carefully. Curtains, blinds, and other coverings for windows should be considered in the design of each individual classroom. Utilizing pastel colors, controlling unwanted sound, and using the latest technology in teaching devices all aid in the learning of the student. Desks that serve the needs of the user are important. The desks should fit the size of the student and be designed for the type of learning that is to take place in that classroom.

The design of the classroom as to air circulation, heat, and air conditioning is important. The design also should be considered to keep maintenance of the classroom to a minimum. Mar-proof and easy-to-clean surfaces should be included whenever possible. Bulletin boards, display areas, and blackboards should all meet the criteria of being useable, practical, and easily maintained. Blackboards or grease boards that comprise whole walls

Figures 2.27a and 2.27b: A variety of classrooms should be planned for the different classes to be accommodated within a comprehensive HPER facility.

from the floor to a seven-foot height give maximum board usage.

Faculty Offices

Faculty office space should be designed to meet the needs of its users. Minimum size should be 120-square-feet. If possible, all offices should have windows to the outside that can be opened. Blinds, curtains, or other coverings for windows should be provided. All offices should contain shelving for books, periodicals, and papers. Carpeted floors and the use of pastel colors on the walls give a pleasant aesthetic appearance to faculty offices. (Figure 2.28.)

Secured storage areas in the form of file cabinets, lockers, or closets should be standard in faculty offices. The office should have ample electrical outlets on both the floor and walls. Telephone jacks should be located conveniently in the office space. Bulletin board and grease board space should be provided for each office. All faculty offices should be wired for cable television and for computerization. Space should be provided for a personal computer, monitor, and printer in each office. If internal windows are provided to the office area or corridor, appropriate closures/coverings need to be provided for these windows.

Offices must be secured, private, and be located in close relationship to meeting rooms, secretarial areas, and work rooms. The administrator's office should be large enough to hold small meetings within the office itself. A conference type table should be provided for this purpose. Air circulation, air conditioning, and heating along with illumination should be planned carefully in all offices. Space within all offices should be arranged for individual conferences, with both students and colleagues. Comfortable chairs, privacy, good acoustics, and a pleasant environment are all important aspects in office planning.

Figure 2.28. Faculty offices are a necessary part of collegiate facilities in which research is conducted and classes are taught. (Photo by Lee Bloom)

Consoles, Checkouts, and Concession Areas

Whether the facility is athletic, academic, or recreational in nature will dictate its needs for design in consoles, checkouts, and concessions. Many recreational facilities are designed so one or two individuals at a centrally-located counter or console can admin-istratively man the building. The console should be placed near the main entrance in order to have admittance control. It also must be located in such a position so that the worker(s) has visual acuity over most of the facility. The console also should be the exit station for facility users. (Figure 2.29.)

Elevating or raising the console can be advantageous for open vision

Figure 2.29. A view from the console in an open facility (Photo by Lee Bloom)

Figure 2.30. Concession areas can be incorporated in the lobby design--State College Area (PA) High School.

throughout the facility. The console should be equipped with storage areas, computer terminal, telephone, and master controls for lighting and audio throughout the facility. The console should be large enough for two individuals and should be provided with counter space. A circular or elliptical console area works nicely. The console is basically the center of the operation of the facility. The checking out of equipment also may be done at the console.

If equipment checkout is not desired in the console area, a main equipment checkout/storage area needs to be provided. This area must be located centrally to all activity areas within the facility, and it must be secured. A counter area must be provided, along with adequate storage racks, bins, and shelves for sign-out equipment. The room should be well ventilated, cool, and dry. The storage area should be wired for a telephone and a personal computer hookup. A permanent screen, electronic board, or display board should be located at this area. This board will highlight announcements and rules concerning equipment, facilities, and current events on a daily basis.

If the facility is spectator-oriented, then concessions need careful planning. Concession areas should be built flush with existing walls. Numbers will be dictated by the size of the facility and the number of spectators serviced. Planning for adequate concession areas is important. Counter space must be provided, and menu boards placed to be seen easily. Concession stands must be planned for beverages, hot and cold food, and general merchandise sales. Methods of cash distribution must be planned. The use of cash registers, till boxes, or computer posts needs careful planning in each concession area. The number of personnel utilized in each concession area also must be carefully planned. (Figure 2.30.)

Adequate electrical outlets, sinks, and drains must be provided in the concession area. Concession areas should be designed with minimum maintenance and must be able to be secured. Location of concession area sales lines should not impede other interior traffic flow in the lobby or foyer areas. Specific storage needs for each concession area should be considered.

SPECIAL CONSIDERATIONS FOR ELEMENTARY SCHOOL FACILITIES

Most all the guidelines previously given for college and university facilities are applicable to the elementary school. Some modifications may be made as to size, space requirements, and special need facilities. The information in this section gives specific insights for the special needs of elementary indoor activity areas.

The elementary school physical education program centers around the teaching of fundamental movement patterns, rhythmics or dance, games and sports, gymnastic activities, and aquatics. The design and scope of physical education facilities should reflect the activities included in the elementary physical education curriculum.

A major consideration fundamental to the planning of an elementary school indoor activity area is the anticipated use by the community. More and more community use of these facilities is expected in future years.

Several of the standard planning principles apply particularly to the elementary facility. Such planning principles would include:
- establishing priority use for the facility
- giving basic consideration to the primary age group using the facility
- allowing for use by physically and mentally impaired children
- designing for the participants ahead of the spectators
- remembering considerations for maintenance of the facilities.

Elementary schools often are more compact than other schools, and it is desirable to have the activity area apart from the classrooms to reduce noise disturbance. With the increasing use of such facilities by the community, consideration must be given to accessibility from the parking areas. In addition, it should be adjacent to the outdoor play fields. This allows for easier storage of equipment and increases the efficiency of the area to be used as a neighborhood playground in the summer months.

Physical Education Teaching Stations

Elementary school physical education classes may be organized by a number of methods. The average class size usually is based on the number of pupils in the classroom unit. Because of differences in pupil maturation, physical education periods generally vary from 20 minutes for kindergarten and first grade to 45 minutes for fifth and sixth grades, with the school average (for computation purposes) being 30 minutes per class.

The formula for computing the number of teaching stations needed for physical education in an elementary school is as follows:

Minimum Number of Teaching Stations
=
Number of Classrooms of Students
x
Number of Physical Education periods per week per class (Total number of Physical Education class periods in a school week).

Examples:

- Number of classrooms of students -- school contains grades K to 6, three classrooms for each grade level, or a total of 21 classroom units
- Number of physical education periods per week per class -- one period per class for physical education each school day during the week equals five periods per week
- Total number of physical education class periods in school week -- there are five instructional hours in the school day, and the length of a physical education period is 30 minutes;

thus, a total of 10 30-minute periods each school day may be scheduled for physical education, or a total of 50 periods for the five-day school week.

The teaching station needs would be calculated as follows:

- Minimum number of teaching stations equals 21 classroom units times five periods per day, 50 periods per week, equals 105 divided by 50, equals 2.1.

In the above situation, if one classroom section was dropped each week (bringing the total to 20) then the need would be 2.0 teaching stations. Therefore, to achieve the requirement for physical education, five periods per week in the school used as an example, it would necessitate employing two physical education teachers each hour of the day.

In many school systems the above situation would be too idealistic. More likely only one physical education instructor would be available (either a specialist, or the classroom teacher, or a paraprofessional in collaboration with one of the other two). This then would drop the number of sessions per week for each classroom unit from five to an average of 2.5. One teaching station would handle this setup.

If only one teaching station can be provided in the elementary school, then preferably it would be a gymnasium. Despite the fact that some other type of auxiliary station might prove superior for instruction in the lower grades, the elementary gymnasium remains the preferred facility because of its heavy use by both the upper grades and the community. If the school system and the community were in need of an indoor swimming pool, this would be the choice for a second teaching station.

Gymnasium

In planning the elementary school gymnasium, a minimum of 100- square-feet per pupil and a total of at least 4,860 square feet is recommended. Spectator

seating (if provided) and storage rooms require additional space. Many of the general considerations recommended for secondary school gymnasiums also apply to elementary school facilities.

The specific dimensions of the gymnasium should provide for a basketball court of 42 by 74 feet, with a minimum safety space of six feet around the perimeter. An area of 54 by 90 feet (4,860 square feet) would be adequate. The ceiling should be at least 22-feet high. This space is adequate for activities normally included in the elementary school program and will serve the community recreational program. The gymnasium will be of a larger size if the decision is made to use it as a multiple teaching facility and include a folding partition or dropnets as part of the design.

Auxiliary Teaching Stations

If a second indoor physical education teaching area is built, it should be an auxiliary instruction room. The auxiliary teaching station is most practical when the main gymnasium cannot fulfill all of the school's needs for teaching stations.

At least 60-square-feet per primary pupil, with a total minimum of 1,800 square feet of space, is suggested for this unit. A ceiling height of 18 feet in the clear is preferred, although lower ceilings may be used. One wall should be free of obstruction to be used for target and ball games or throwing practice. A smooth masonry wall will provide an adequate rebounding surface. If included, windows should be of breakproof glass or be protected by a shield or grill and located high enough to not restrict activities.

The auxiliary unit should be planned to accommodate limited apparatus and tumbling activities, games of low organization, rhythmic activities, movement exploration, and other activities for the primary grades. Often a 25-foot circle for circle games is located at one end of this room, allowing for permanent or semi-permanent equipment at the other end. The equipment could include such items as climbing ropes and poles, ladders, mats, stall bars, rings, large wooden boxes, horizontal bars, and peg boards. These should be located so as not to interfere with other activities or so they may be moved easily out of the way. A storage room for equipment and supplies should be included. A section of wall can be equipped with hangers for mat storage.

Electrical outlets are required for the use of sound equipment. This room will, for the most part, be used by the lower grades and should be accessible to those classrooms. If the area is to serve the after-school recreational program for pupils or community groups, toilet facilities should be accessible.

Shower and Dressing Rooms

Although it has been standard practice not to include shower, locker, and dressing room facilities in the elementary school, such facilities are essential if the gymnasium is to be used for intramural/inter-school competition and community usage. The size, number of lockers, showers, and toilet facilities will be dependent on the extent of usage. If swimming pools are added as part of the school community complex, such facilities are a must. Provision for outdoor restrooms is desirable if the general public is involved.

SPECIAL CONSIDERATIONS FOR SECONDARY SCHOOL INDOOR ACTIVITY AREAS

Indoor activity areas for secondary schools, similar to the elementary school, can follow most of the college/ university guidelines with some modifications. Those special needs for secondary schools are now presented.

Teaching Stations

The type and number of indoor teaching stations for a secondary school depends on the number of students and the specific program of physical education and related activities. In all situations, a gymnasium is required. By determining the number of teaching stations essential for the formal program of instruction, planners will have a basis for calculating other needs.

The minimum numerical requirement is identified by the following formula:

$$\text{Minimum Number of Teaching Stations} = \frac{700 \text{ Students} \times 5 \text{ classes/week}}{30 \text{ students/class} \times 30 \text{ Periods/Week}}$$

$$= \frac{3500}{900} = 3.9$$

The fraction is rounded to the next highest number, making four teaching stations the minimum requirement. This number also would afford some flexibility of class scheduling.

In computing teaching station requirements for the secondary school, the desired class size must not be set so low as to require an impossible number of teachers and facilities, nor should it be so high that effectiveness is impaired. An average class size of 30 with daily instruction is recommended. However, if the physical education classes meet only two periods per week, the total number of class periods per week in the formula must be adjusted accordingly.

The next step for planners is to determine the degree to which the number of teaching stations for the program of instruction will meet the needs for voluntary recreation, extramural and intramural activities, and interscholastic athletics for girls and boys, as well as the possible use of facilities by the community. The needs

must be based upon the season of the year representing the greatest demand for facilities.

The following guide can be used to determine the number of teaching stations needed for activities other than the formal program of instruction in physical education:

Minimum number of teaching stations, or fractions thereof, needed for interscholastic team practice at peak load
plus
Minimum number of teaching stations, or fractions thereof, needed for intramural and extramural activities
plus
Minimum number of teaching stations, or fractions thereof, needed for student recreation
plus
Minimum number of teaching stations, or fractions thereof, needed for community recreation
equals
The total number of teaching stations needed for any specific after-school period.

Note: Physical education facilities for the middle school should follow the standards for secondary schools.

To illustrate, assume a school has two interscholastic squads, an intramural program, a voluntary recreation group, and no community recreational use of facilities immediately after school during a specific season. The total needs are as follows:

Required teaching stations
equals
2 interscholastic
plus
1 intramural
plus
1 voluntary recreation
equals
4 stations

The need for four teaching stations for the after-school program then must be compared to the number necessary for the formal program of instruction in physical education. If the after-school needs exceed those for the regular periods of instruction, additional teaching stations should be provided. Careful administrative scheduling results in maximum utilization of facilities.

Types of Teaching Stations

A wide variety of teaching stations is possible, depending on the number of different activities that would be included appropriately in the physical education program. Among the possible types of indoor teaching stations that might be included are gymnasiums, rhythm rooms, rooms for gymnastics, adapted physical education room, weight rooms, wrestling rooms, classrooms, swimming pools, archery ranges, rifle ranges, and racquetball courts.

The problem for some schools is not lack of an adequate number of teaching stations, but rather lack of facilities to accommodate the desired variety of activities. For a secondary school with 360 students, a divisible gymnasium will create an adequate number of teaching stations for the program of instruction in physical education, but may not meet the peak load requirement for after-school activities. The facility must be planned and designed to serve all program needs as adequately as possible.

Whenever a school's teaching requirements are such that a basic gymnasium is inadequate, planners should consider special purpose stations, such as an auxiliary physical education teaching station, a natatorium, or a dance studio.

Gymnasium

The building or portion of the school that houses the gymnasium should be easily accessible from classrooms, parking areas, and the outdoor activity area. This also makes possible the use of the facility after school hours or during weekends or holidays without having to open other sections of the school.

For general purposes, allow a minimum of 125-square-feet of usable activity space for each individual in a physical education class at peak load. The space requirements and dimensions of a gymnasium floor are influenced significantly by the official rules governing court games, particularly interscholastic basketball and the extent of spectator seating. The minimum dimensions required in a gymnasium for basketball, however, should be expanded, if necessary, to accommodate other activities. In some instances, an entire gymnasium is not required for an activity. Folding, soundproof partitions can be used to divide the area and provide two or more teaching stations.

Spectator Seating

The extent of the demand for spectator seating depends upon each school and the community it serves. Modern design uses power-driven folding or roll-away bleachers which require little permanent space. If possible, the outer surface of folding bleachers should create a flat, wall-like surface so it may be used for ball rebounding.

The width of each seating space should not be less than 18 inches. Roll-away bleachers most commonly allow 22-inch depths for seats. The number of rows available in roll-away bleachers varies, with 23 rows the maximum for standard equipment. In some instances, bleachers with 30 rows can be obtained by special order. Planners should investigate local and state codes.

Balconies can be used to increase the total seating capacity beyond the maximum permitted at floor level. The space at both levels should be considered as activity areas when the bleachers are closed. It may be desirable, in some instances, to provide less than maximum seating at floor level so a balcony will be wide enough to serve as a teaching station for specific activities. Balcony bleachers can be installed to telescope from the back to the front so that in the closed position they stand erect, creating a divider wall at the edge of the balcony. This arrangement affords partial isolation of the teaching station and enhances the safety of participants.

Auxiliary Gymnasium

Depending on the demands placed on a facility for classes, after-school athletics, intramurals, and student and faculty recreation, more than one gymnasium may be necessary. Careful program scheduling will determine what is best in each situation. However, most schools need at least one auxiliary gym. Room dimensions should be based on the anticipated uses with special attention to the need to accommodate standard-size wrestling mats.

The other type of auxiliary gymnasium closely resembles the main gym, except there is little or no need for spectator seating, and the floor dimensions may be smaller. A 75-by-90 foot gym will house two volleyball courts, three badminton courts, three one wall handball courts, and space for some gymnastic equipment.

The auxiliary gyms can serve a variety of other activities in the instructional, intramural, recreational, or interscholastic program, which cannot all be accommodated after school in the main gymnasium. Some auxiliary gyms are large enough to be divided into two teaching stations. The characteristics of these facilities are similar to those in the gymnasium. A less expensive type may have a ceiling as low as 12 feet. Such activities as wrestling, tumbling, calisthenics, self-defense, and fencing may be conducted in such a room.

Dance Area

Few secondary schools have specialized facilities for dance. There is some indication, however, that specialized concentration (dance, sports, aquatics, gymnastics) in teacher preparation is beginning to alter this pattern, particularly in suburban areas and in certain consolidated school districts. As these programs begin to establish their value, obtaining facilities may be easier.

A minimum dance facility will provide:
- 100-square-feet per student, one dimension to exceed 60 feet
- full length mirrors at a corner for analysis of skill from two directions
- a speaker system designed to distribute sound evenly throughout the room
- a control system for record players and microphones
- practice barres on one wall at heights of 34 inches and 42 inches

The floor for modern dance should be of hard northern maple which has been sealed and then buffed with fine abrasive.

Portable percussion racks made in an industrial arts department can solve the problems of storage and efficient class and program use. Portable mirrors, six feet tall and eight feet wide, can be mounted 18 inches from the floor on rollers and moved into the dance area if wall-mounted mirrors are not feasible. Portable ballet barres of lightweight aluminum are desirable when unobstructed wall space is at a premium.

Adaptive rooms, gymnastic rooms, weight training rooms, or recreational game rooms may have dance space. Careful pre-planning of new facilities suggests the possibility of combining two or more of these.

CHECKLIST FOR PLANNING AND DESIGNING INDOOR ACTIVITY AREAS

A checklist has been prepared to aid those responsible for planning facilities for athletics, physical education, health and recreation. The application of this checklist may prevent unfortunate and costly errors.

GENERAL

_____ 1. A clear-cut statement has been prepared on the nature and scope of the program, and the special requirements for space, equipment, fixtures, and facilities have been dictated by the activities to be conducted.

_____ 2. The facility has been planned to meet the total requirements of the program, as well as the special needs of those who are to be served.

_____ 3. The plans and specifications have been checked by all governmental agencies (city, county, and state) whose approval is required by law.

_____ 4. Plans for areas and facilities conform to state and local regulations and to accepted standards and practices.

_____ 5. The areas and facilities planned make possible the programs that serve the interests and needs of all the people.

_____ 6. Every available source of property or funds has been explored, evaluated, and utilized whenever appropriate.

_____ 7. All interested persons and organizations concerned with the facility have had an opportunity to share in its planning (professional educators, users, consultants, administrators, engineers, architects, program specialists, building managers, and builder) - a team approach.

_____ 8. The facility will fulfill the maximum demands of the program. The program has not been curtailed to fit the facility.

_____ 9. The facility has been functionally planned to meet the present and anticipated needs of specific programs, situations, and publics.

_____ 10. Future additions are included in present plans to permit economy of construction.

_____ 11. All classrooms and offices are isolated from background noise.

_____ 12. Ample numbers and sized storage areas are built-in flush with walls at all teaching stations.

_____ 13. No center mullions or thresholds are on storage room doorways.

_____ 14. All passageways are free of obstructions; fixtures are recessed.

_____ 15. Storage areas are well ventilated, dry, and cool.

_____ 16. Buildings, specific areas, and facilities are clearly identified.

_____ 17. Locker rooms are arranged for ease of supervision.

_____ 18. Offices, teaching stations, and service facilities are properly interrelated.

_____ 19. Special needs of the physically handicapped are met, including a ramp into the building at a major entrance.

_____ 20. All "dead space" is used.

_____ 21. The building is compatible in design and comparable in quality and accommodation to other campus structures.

_____ 22. Storage rooms are accessible to the play area.

_____ 23. Workrooms, conference rooms, and staff and administrative offices are interrelated.

_____ 24. Shower and dressing facilities are provided for professional staff members and are conveniently located.

_____ 25. Thought and attention has been given to making facilities and equipment as durable and vandal-proof as possible.

_____ 26. Low-cost maintenance features have been considered.

_____ 27. This facility is a part of a well-integrated Master Plan.

_____ 28. All areas, courts, facilities, equipment, climate control, security, etc., conform rigidly to detailed standards and specifications.

_____ 29. Shelves are recessed and mirrors and supplies are in appropriate places in restrooms and dressing rooms.

_____ 30. Dressing space between locker rows is adjusted to the size and age of students.

_____ 31. Drinking fountains are placed conveniently in locker room areas or immediately adjacent areas.

_____ 32. Special attention is given to provision for locking service windows and counter, supply bins, carts, shelves, and racks.

_____ 33. Provision is made for repair, maintenance, replacement, and off-season storage of equipment and uniforms.

_____ 34. A well-defined program for laundering and cleaning towels, uniforms, and equipment is included in the plan.

_____ 35. Noncorrosive metal is used in dressing, drying, and shower areas, except for enameled lockers.

_____ 36. Antipanic hardware is used where required by fire regulations.

_____ 37. Properly placed house bibbs and drains are sufficient in size and quantity to permit flushing the entire area with a water hose.

_____ 38. A water-resistant, covered base is used under the locker base and floor mat and where floor and wall join.

_____ 39. Chalkboards and/or tackboards with map tracks are located in appropriate places in dressing rooms, hallways, and classrooms.

_____ 40. Book shelves are provided in toilet areas.

_____ 41. Space and equipment are planned in accordance with the types and number of enrollees.

_____ 42. Basement rooms undesirable for dressing, drying, and showering, are not planned for those purposes.

_____ 43. Spectator seating (permanent) in areas that are basically instructional is kept at a minimum. Rollaway bleachers are used primarily. Balcony seating is considered as a possibility.

_____ 44. Well-lighted and effectively displayed trophy cases enhance the interest and beauty of the lobby.

_____ 45. The space under the stairs is used for storage.

_____ 46. Department heads' offices are located near the central administrative office which includes a well-planned conference room.

_____ 47. Workrooms are located near the central office and serve as a repository for departmental materials and records.

_____ 48. Conference area includes a cloak room, lavatory, and toilet.

_____ 49. In addition to regular secretarial offices established in the central and department chairmen's offices, a special room to house a secretarial pool for staff members is provided.

_____ 50. Staff dressing facilities are provided. These facilities also may serve game officials.

_____ 51. The community and/or neighborhood has a "round table" for planning.

_____ 52. All those (persons and agencies) who should be a party to planning and development are invited and actively engaged in the planning process.

_____ 53. Space and area relationships are important. They have been considered carefully.

_____ 54. Both long-range and immediate plans have been made.

_____ 55. The body comfort of the child, a major factor in securing maximum learning, has been considered in the plans.

_____ 56. Plans for quiet areas have been made.

_____ 57. In the planning, consideration has been given to the need for adequate recreational areas and facilities, both near and distant from the homes of people.

_____ 58. Consoles for security, information, and checkout have been ideally located.

_____ 59. Every effort has been exercised to eliminate hazards.

_____ 60. The installation of low-hanging door closers, light fixtures, signs, and other objects in traffic areas has been avoided.

_____ 61. Warning signals - both visible and audible - are included in the plans.

_____ 62. Ramps have a slope equal to or greater than a one-foot rise in 12-feet.

_____ 63. Minimum landings for ramps are five-by-five feet, extend at least one foot beyond the swinging arc of a door, have at least a six-foot clearance at the bottom, and have level platforms at 30-foot intervals on every turn.

_____ 64. Adequate locker and dressing spaces are provided.

_____ 65. The design of dressing, drying, and shower areas reduces foot traffic to a minimum and establishes clean, dry aisles for bare feet.

_____ 66. Teaching stations are related properly to service facilities.

_____ 67. Toilet facilities are adequate in number. They are located to serve all groups for which provisions are made.

_____ 68. Mail services, outgoing and incoming, are included in the plans.

_____ 69. Hallways, ramps, doorways, and elevators are designed to permit equipment to be moved easily and quickly.

_____ 70. A keying design suited to administrative and instructional needs is planned.

_____ 71. Toilets used by large groups have circulating (in and out) entrances and exits.

_____ 72. All surfaces in racquetball, handball, and squash courts are flush.

_____ 73. At least one racquetball, handball, or squash court has a tempered glass back and side wall.

_____ 74. All vents in racquetball, handball, and squash courts are located in the back one-third of the ceiling.

_____ 75. Standard size doors are utilized on racquetball, handball, and squash courts.

_____ 76. All aspects of safety are planned carefully for the weight areas.

_____ 77. Racks are provided for all lose plates, dumbbells, and barbells in weight areas.

_____ 78. Special attention is paid to acoustical treatment in weight areas.

_____ 79. Ample walk areas for traffic flow are planned around lifting areas in weight rooms.

_____ 80. Concession areas are planned for and built flush with existing walls.

_____ 81. Adequate numbers of concession areas are planned.

_____ 82. Concession stand cash handling methods have been planned carefully.

_____ 83. Storage and maintenance has been planned for concession areas.

_____ 84. Classrooms are planned by instructors, students, and maintenance staff.

_____ 85. Classrooms are planned for the numbers of users and the styles of teaching to be utilized in the room.

_____ 86. Careful attention has been paid to storage areas in classrooms.

_____ 87. Faculty offices should be private and secured.

_____ 88. Storage areas and windows are planned in faculty offices.

_____ 89. Laboratories need to be planned for both teaching and research utilization.

_____ 90. Ample space and subdivisions within laboratories are planned carefully.

CLIMATE CONTROL

_____ 1. Provision is made throughout the building for climate control - heating, ventilating, and refrigerated cooling.

_____ 2. Special ventilation is provided for locker, dressing, shower, drying, and toilet rooms.

_____ 3. Heating plans permit both area and individual room control.

_____ 4. Research areas where small animals are kept and where chemicals are used have been provided with special ventilating equipment.

_____ 5. The heating and ventilating of the wrestling gymnasium has been given special attention.

_____ 6. All air diffusers adequately diffuse the air.

_____ 7. Storage area ventilation is planned carefully.

_____ 8. Humidity and ventilation are balanced properly in racquetball, handball, and squash courts.

_____ 9. Thermostats are located out of the general users' reach and/or are secured.

_____ 10. The total energy concept has been investigated.

ELECTRICAL

_____ 1. Shielded, vapor-proof lights are used in moisture-prevalent areas.

_____ 2. Lights in strategic areas are key-controlled.

_____ 3. Lighting intensity conforms to approved standards.

_____ 4. Adequate numbers of electrical outlets are placed strategically.

_____ 5. Gymnasium and auditorium lights are controlled by dimmer units.

_____ 6. Locker room lights are mounted above the space between lockers.

_____ 7. Natural light is controlled properly for purposes of visual aids and to avoid glare.

_____ 8. Electrical outlet plates are installed three feet above the floor unless special use dictates other locations.

_____ 9. Controls for light switches and projection equipment are located suitably and are interrelated.

_____ 10. All lights are shielded. Special protection is provided in gymnasium, court areas, and shower rooms.

_____ 11. All lights must be easily accessible for maintenance.

_____ 12. The use of metal halide and high pressure sodium lighting has been investigated.

_____ 13. All areas have been wired for television cable and computer hookups.

_____ 14. Indirect lighting has been utilized wherever possible.

_____ 15. All teaching areas are equipped with a mounted camera, 25-foot color monitor, and tape deck securely built-in flush with the existing walls.

WALLS

_____ 1. Movable and folding partitions are power-operated and controlled by keyed switches.

_____ 2. Wall plates are located where needed and are attached firmly.

_____ 3. Hooks and rings for nets are placed (and recessed in walls) according to court locations and net heights.

_____ 4. Materials that clean easily and are impervious to moisture are used where moisture is prevalent.

_____ 5. Shower heads are placed at different heights; four feet (elementary) to seven feet (university) for each school level.

_____ 6. Protective matting is placed permanently on the walls in the wrestling room, at the ends of basketball courts, and in other areas where such protection is needed.

_____ 7. Adequate numbers of drinking fountains are provided. They are properly placed (recessed in wall).

_____ 8. The lower eight feet of wall surface in activity areas is glazed and planned for ease of maintenance.

_____ 9. All corners in locker rooms are rounded.

_____ 10. At least two adjacent walls in dance and weight areas should have full length mirrors.

_____ 11. Walls should be treated acoustically 15 feet and above.

_____ 12. Walls are reinforced structurally where equipment is to be mounted.

_____ 13. Flat wall space is planned for rebounding areas.

_____ 14. Walls should be flat with no juts or extruding columns.

_____ 15. Pastel colors are utilized on the walls.

_____ 16. Windows should be kept to a minimum in activity areas.

CEILINGS

_____ 1. Overhead support apparatus is secured to beams that are engineered to withstand stress.

_____ 2. The ceiling height is adequate for the activities to be housed.

_____ 3. Acoustical materials impervious to moisture are used in moisture-prevalent areas.

_____ 4. Skylights in gymnasiums, being impractical, are seldom used because of problems in waterproofing roofs and of controlling sun rays.

_____ 5. All ceilings except those in storage areas are acoustically treated with sound-absorbent materials.

_____ 6. Ceilings should be painted an off-white.

FLOORS

_____ 1. Floor plates are placed where needed and are flush-mounted.

_____ 2. Floor design and materials conform to recommended standards and specifications.

_____ 3. Lines and markings are painted in floors before sealing is completed (when synthetic tape is not used).

_____ 4. A cove base (around lockers and where wall and floor meet) of the same water-resistant material that is used on floors is found in all dressing and shower rooms.

_____ 5. Abrasive, nonskid, slip-resistant flooring that is impervious to moisture is provided on all areas where water is used (laundry, swimming pools, shower, dressing, and drying rooms).

_____ 6. Floor drains are located properly, and the slope of the floor is adequate for rapid drainage.

_____ 7. Hardwood floors are utilized in racquetball, handball, and squash courts.

_____ 8. Maintenance storage is located in areas with synthetic floors.

_____ 9. Floors should be treated acoustically when possible.

_____ 10. Hardwood floors should be utilized in dance areas.

REFERENCES

Departments of the Army, Navy, and Air Force. _Planning and Design of Outdoor Sports Facilities_, Washington, D.C., 1975.

Flynn, Richard B. (Ed.) 1985. _Planning Facilities for Athletics, Physical Education and Recreation_, The Athletic Institute and American Alliance for Health, Physical Education, Recreation and Dance.

Flynn, Richard B. 1990. "Sports Surfaces." In Morris B. Mellion, M.D.; W. Michael Walsh, M.D.; and Guy L. Shelton, P.T., A.T.C. (eds). _The Team Physician's Handbook_, Philadelphia, PA: Hanley and Belfus, pp. 47-58.

Flynn, Richard B. December, 1982. "People Traffic, Security and Emergency Precautions," _Proceedings from Athletic Purchasing and Facilities National Conference._

NCAA Guides. Overland Park, KS: National Collegiate Athletic Association.

ABOUT THE AUTHOR:
Ed Turner is a professor of health, leisure and exercise science at Appalachian State University in Boone, N.C.

Chapter 3
OUTDOOR FACILITIES
by Bradley A. Macomber

INTRODUCTION

The awareness and interest of the general public in the benefits of a balanced life style, as well as an enhanced quality of life, has placed an increasing emphasis on the type, quantity, and availability of outdoor facilities. The increased need for facilities has created pressures on regional agencies and local communities to re-evaluate existing facilities and consider construction of new facilities. Factors such as an increasing number of people becoming involved in activities and an increasing number of people available to participate in programs are considered primary reasons for over use of the existing facilities. These concerns, combined with the availability of space, the demand for space to accommodate buildings, the diversity of programs being offered, and the escalating costs for property, have contributed to a shortage of outdoor facilities.

Once these shortcomings have been acknowledged, an improved situation can be planned. Existing facilities and programs will be utilized as a basis for future facilities and as an inspiration for significant changes and development.

Chapter 3 introduces the subject of outdoor facilities for athletics, physical education, and recreation. The chapter describes in narrative and graphic form the concepts that will be helpful to clients, users, and design professionals in understanding the programming, planning, design, and installation of outdoor facilities. These resources will help the team communicate more effectively to develop solutions to problems. The

contents provide a basis of knowledge on the subject of outdoor facilities:

- Facility Evaluation
- Site Plan Development
- Support Facilities
- Surfaces
- Lighting Design
- Court Sports
- Diamond Fields
- Sport Fields
- Track & Field Events
- References
- Planning Checklist

Considerations

Although there may be numerous issues that come to mind as one reads this chapter, there are several important considerations that the reader must focus on:

- Since no one entity of the Project Team, which includes the owner, the user, and the designer, is more important than the other with respect to the roles each plays on the team, they will be referred to collectively as the "Team" throughout the chapter.

- For each situation there is a wide range of variables and alternatives to be identified, researched, and analyzed at each level of the process prior to developing a viable solution. Therefore, it stands to reason that this chapter may be biased in certain areas based on the author's experience or personal preference.

- Although this chapter may imply a process for addressing issues, there is no singular means required for approaching or resolving issues within the design process. Each Project Team will develop characteristics and patterns

of operations intrinsic to the particular problem and Project Team.

- The Team must realize that information is the most important resource. Since the space available in this chapter limits the amount of information to be presented, the Team must attempt to gather project-specific as well as new information in order to address common problems and present innovative solutions.

FACILITY EVALUATION

Master Plan

Development of a Master Plan is usually one of the first steps taken in the planning process. A Master Plan which contains documentation to support planning, development, and administration based on the available and projected resources, programs, and facilities, serves as guide for the future. The Master Plan process, which is discussed in Chapter 1, may be applied to any size site or regional area. Since the Master Plan will be discussed in another section of the book, this chapter will address only specific aspects of a Master Plan which relate to outdoor facilities.

Programming

Outdoor facilities should be planned to accommodate an activity or activities which best meet program as well as site limitations. The particular activity(s) selected for incorporation, based on the facility Master Plan, generally is determined by program needs, group interest, and the quantity of participants to be accommodated. In addition, each activity may be prioritized as to the benefits the program and its participants receive.

The following attributes may be helpful in determining the site locations and relative positions best suited to a specific activity:

- Flexibility addresses the capability of an activity area or site to being used for different activities;

- Seasonal usage refers to synchronizing the activity with weather elements and seasonal changes;

- Progression relates to those provisions made for normal increases in skill levels through the facilities offered.

Based on these premises, the following factors should be considered strongly during the planning process:

- number of participants for any single space and for a total area within a given time span

- number of spectators for any single space and for the total area

- movement patterns of participants, support services, and spectators

- interrelationships between curricular, extra-curricular, and community activities

- priority ranking of each space with respect to an activity

- equipment necessary for each activity, as well as the equipment required for operations and maintenance of the facility

- environmental conditions and influences on the space

- projected use for space based on a Master Plan

- possible changes in the programs and activities based on trends.

Although the areas around educational facilities generally are dedicated to the physical education, athletic, and recreation programs, they also can serve to support other community activities and programs. Teams should consider combining educational facilities with other community uses, such as recreation centers, armories, fitness centers, parks,

and recreation, to meet program needs of varying use groups when addressing critical issues regarding land-use planning. Spaces such as these offer the Team an opportunity to construct unique environments with spaces that offer varying and creative experiences, in addition to satisfying programmed activity needs. Wherever possible, care should be exercised to avoid sites which may restrict design options and future program goals. (Figure 3.1.)

Site Analysis

A site analysis involves the preparation of a survey to inventory, classify, and prioritize the natural characteristics on an existing or proposed site.

These characteristics which influence site usage can be identified as the physical size of the site, the topography of the site, the composition of the surface and underlying layers of earth, surrounding vegetation, surface and subsurface hydrology, and climate.

The physical size of the site required to accommodate a program will depend on the type of activity(s) planned for the site. Likewise, the site may dictate what activity(s) may be used in this location. Some sites offer an adjacent area ideally suited for expansion of facilities. However, the Team should exercise caution and thoroughly investigate all surroundings of the site to include potential areas for acquisition and expansion. Portions of the site may require extensive work or may not be available for future use. Considerable costs may be expended to alleviate or mitigate the site problems.

The topography of the site (elevations, slopes, orientation, and irregularities in the surface) will be very important in determining the cost of renovation and/or construction. Costs associated with development of the site and providing accessibility for vehicles and pedestrians must be considered. Where the availability of sites for outdoor facilities is minimal, extensive site improvements may be required in order to accommodate the program.

The composition of the surface and subsurface soils may affect the engineering design and construction techniques required to install outdoor facilities. Excavation of rock or replacement of swampy areas will increase drastically the cost of preparing the site for activity areas.

The surrounding vegetation can affect the microclimate in the area. Properly selected as well as strategically-placed vegetation can contribute to reducing surface temperatures, retaining water, and minimizing the effects of winds on the area.

Hydrology refers to the movement of surface as well as subsurface water in the area. Established patterns of water movement may affect the positioning of activities or require alternative methods to control water distribution on and around the activity area. Diverting surface water or draining subsurface water from the site may require extensive engineering design and construction techniques which could increase significantly costs of site preparation.

Although climate is a characteristic which may be geographically site-specific and not capable of being changed by artificial methods, its influences can be dealt with by other means. The Team must recognize the regional affects on the site, and plan the site activities accordingly. Factors such as orientation, temperature, precipitation, wind, and snowfall can affect the activity program. In most cases, scheduling of activities has been the most effective method used to overcome climatic influences.

Other factors, in addition to those listed above, also may affect the Team's plans for use of a site. These factors, although not as important to the activity use of the site, may affect the type of functions or limit portions of the site to a specific activity. Factors such as the historical significance, a habitat for endangered species, and land use policies require serious consideration prior to deciding to invest valuable time and funding for a particular site.

PLANNING CHECKLIST

The following is an abbreviated list of items to be considered during the planning process:

CIRCULATION

- **Types**: Vehicle (cars, trucks, buses, maintenance, etc.); pedestrians (handicapped, different teams); participants (different teams, players, coaches, officials, etc.); main entry; secondary entries; control and security points, etc.
- **Roadway**: Type of vehicles (trucks, cars, buses, etc); quantity of traffic (conduct survey); type of roadway system (single or two directional); roadway width (vehicle size and number of lanes); surface systems (materials); protection devices (bollards, guard rails, etc); etc.
- **Parking**: Type of vehicles (trucks, cars, buses, etc.); quantity of vehicles; sizes (length and width) of vehicles; drainage (surface or subsurface, water collection/detention areas); snow removal (storage areas); protection devices (bollards, guard rails, tire bumpers, etc.)
- **Walkways**: Type of use (pedestrian and/or vehicle); walkway widths; surface system (materials); elevation changes (walks, ramps, stairs and lifts); railings.

ACTIVITY AREAS

- **Landscaping**: Type of surfaces (grass, etc.); type of plantings (ground cover, shrubs, plantings, etc.); etc.
- **Game Standards**: Applicable Association regulations for each sport; etc.
- **Activity Configuration**: Areas (separate or combined activity); orientation; flexibility; etc.
- **Surfaces**: Type (natural, synthetic, or combination); grading and drainage (surface and subsurface); etc.

SPORTS AREAS

- **Diamonds**: Type of sport(s); type (game and/or practice); size; quantity; etc.
- **Courts**: Type of sport(s); type (game and/or practice); size; quantity; etc.
- **Fields**: Type of sport(s); type (game and/or practice); size; quantity; etc.
- **Ranges**: Type of sport(s); type (game and/or practice); size; quantity; etc.

STRUCTURES

- **Tickets**: Type (fixed or portable); surfaces for portable types (pads); utilities; quantity of units (location on site); etc.
- **Security**: Type (fixed or portable); surfaces for portable types (pads); utilities; quantity of units (location on site).
- **Medical Treatment**: Type (fixed portable); surfaces for portable types (pads); utilities; quantity of units (location on the site); etc.
- **Storage**: Type (fixed or portable); Surfaces for portable types (pads); utilities; quantity of units (location on site); type of storage (equipment and tools); etc.
- **Communications**: Type (fixed or portable); utilities (supplemental); quantity of units (location on site); type of systems; etc.
- **Concessions**: Type (fixed or portable - owner or vendor-supplied); surfaces for portable types (tent pads, trailer pads, etc.); utilities; quantity of units (location on the site); etc.
- **Seating**: Type (standing and/or seats); persons (spectators, teams, officials, etc); natural (berms, sloped areas, etc.); artificial (prefabricated bleachers, type of seat, guard rails, etc.); etc.

SIGNAGE

- **Vehicle**: Type (direction, information, safety, etc.); etc.
- **Pedestrian**: Type (direction, information, safety, etc.); etc.
- **Activity**: (by sport, area, etc.); etc.
- **Scoreboard**: activity (single or combined use); type (manual or electronic); size; etc.

BARRIERS

- **Vehicle**: Type (sound, visual, safety, etc.); natural (plantings, berms, depressed areas, etc.); artificial (walls, fencing, railings, etc.);
- **Person**: Type (sound, visual, safety, etc.); natural (plantings, berms, depressed areas, etc.) artificial (walls, fencing, railings, etc.) etc.
- **Security**: Type (gates, juxtaposition, or open); etc.

UTILITIES

- **Power**: Site lighting (pedestrian and vehicle); activity lighting; structures (tickets, security, storage, communications, concessions, etc.); etc.
- **Water**: Irrigation; sanitary; drinking fountains (hot and cold), etc.
- **Sanitary**: Type of units (fixed or portable); etc.
- **Storm Drainage**: Type (surface and subsurface); etc.
- **Communications**: Scoreboards; team sidelines to observation booth; public address for game; telephones for public and private use; broadcasting for television and radio; portable communications for security personnel; emergency; etc.

Figure 3.1. Planning Checklist

PLANNING

There are basically two approaches to planning outdoor facilities:

1. **Site Design**: Select a site and determine what activities, based on a prioritized program, might be physically configured on the site; or determine that:

- Site area may not accommodate a full program;

- Site may not be of sufficient size to accommodate sports which require a larger area;

- Program may be fragmented due to program located in multiple areas;

- Additional costs may be realized due to travels, etc.

2. **Program Design**: Establish a fixed program, and determine the amount of space required to meet the program, thereby establishing the size of the site required. This approach is preferred since program needs are realized. It also consolidates programs and maintenance.

In either case, the planning process should contain similar planning strategies:

- Accessibility: Consider accessibility to the site as well as the activity areas to support spectator and maintenance requirements.

- Isolation: Activity areas should be isolated from persistent and unnecessary distractions. Conversely, activities should be located so that the activity and its associated functions do not interfere with or influence other activities.

- Integration: Activity areas should be integrated into the natural as well as the built environment. Proper planning will assure strategic placement of activities, skill levels, and support facilities.

- Adaptability: A site planned for outdoor activities should express a sense of permanence while containing sufficient space to maintain flexibility of use. Multiple activities may be planned for single areas if usage changes required for the season and the surface

will accept the level of play. The arrangement of activities should allow for minor changes in placement and size. Alterations to accommodate change should be implemented with an economy of efforts and funds.

- Expandability: Plans for long-term efficient use of facilities should be contained in the Master Plan. This plan should anticipate changes in the existing landscape as a result of program needs, future growth, and changes in trends.

Site Planning Evaluation

Prior to searching for a new site, the Team first must evaluate the efficiency of the existing facilities, with respect to the current as well as the proposed usage. Too often the existing facilities have been modified, rearranged, or increased without forethought. Therefore, a study can be a means of identifying a requirement to renovate existing facilities or construct new facilities on another site. Spaces allocated to discontinued programs should be reassigned to new programs. It would be unwise to save space for programs which may be resurrected at some unknown time in the future. As a result of this simple exercise, sufficient space may exist to accommodate the proposed programs.

When it has been determined that additional space will be required to accommodate expanded or new activities, it is important to identify and evaluate different sites since each site may present a unique characteristic or potential for future development. Generally, undeveloped existing sites present the most potential for cost savings since funds do not have to be expended for property. However, sites are becoming more difficult to find in the built-up areas of the country. In these areas, one must resort to creative measures, such as combining agencies (education, government, and recreation facilities), using uncommon space (rooftops), or dedicating portions of

developments or commercial properties to sports and recreation programs.

Regulations

Prior to planning and developing layout of a site, one should obtain the latest edition of the official rules for each activity to be located on the site. For example, the rule books of the National Collegiate Athletic Association (see appendix for address) are very useful. The rule books will provide information on the size and layout options of the area required for each skill level. Verification of facilities through the use of rule books is critical since sports improperly laid out may not be acceptable for competition. This could prove very embarrassing if activities could not be accommodated in the space and could be extremely costly to replace. Generally, dimensions not indicated in the rule books are considered optional and left up to designer discretion. However, official organizations will assist in making decisions and will offer recommendations.

Landscape Design

The role of the landscape architect is invaluable when it comes to laying out the site, improving the playing conditions, enhancing the surrounding areas, and providing an environment for enjoyment of the activity. In addition to providing an overall concept plan for the site, the landscape architect will coordinate various activity areas, circulation, support facilities, materials, plantings, and other site amenities.

Layout Process

The process of defining activity space requirements begins with a study of scheduled activities, utilization of spaces, and arrangement of activity elements. These programming requirements, coupled with support facilities and intra-circulation, dictate the final layout. The process of determining an efficient layout generally starts with determining the size of activities based on literature from recognized athletic associations. Templates for each activity are created to the scale of the site plan and arranged according to the specific requirements of each sport. The arrangement of several activities on one space is considered efficient use, such as a particular space accommodating football, soccer, and lacrosse. Several complete layouts may be required to produce a final layout which responds to the needs of the user. After all requirements have been satisfied, a compete layout will be produced for review with the client. (Figure 3.2.)

Orientation

Orientation of activities with respect to the sun angle and wind direction are of primary concern, first for participants and then for the viewer. The primary direction of play should be oriented slightly perpendicular to the late afternoon or early morning sun angles. The orientation of the activity playing surface should be based on the position of the sun at mid-season. Sports which have irregularly configured fields and multiple viewing points, such as baseball and softball, should be oriented to protect the players in positions which present the most hazardous conditions. This would be the batter, the pitcher, and the catcher. In this particular case, the axis of orientation should be through the home plate-to-second base position in relation to the north to northeast compass points. This position also protects the first baseman who receives many throws from the direction of the late afternoon sun. Rectilinear fields and courts are oriented along the long axis of the playing area and are aligned with a north-south axis.

Topography

Topography, which is the representation of surface features on a map, may

influence the arrangement and configuration of the activities planned for the site. Features such as steep slopes, depressions, or streams may prevent efficient use of the site. Wherever possible, relatively flat or gentle sloping surfaces should be selected for development. When these conditions are not available, one must include a cost contingency in the project for adjustment of physical features.

Drainage

Surface as well as subsurface drainage for the movement of water must be considered on each site. Although we generally are concerned about the removal of water from the playing surface, water can affect the substrata or underlying layers in such a manner as to undermine an activity area if certain precautions are not taken. Where necessary, on-site collection basins have been provided as a means of managing water movement.

Circulation

Circulation relates to the categories of movement by pedestrians or vehicles onto and around the site. Each category may be reflected in sub-categories such as participants (players, cheerleaders, coaches, referees, etc), maintenance (buildings and grounds), vendors (concessions), and spectators.

Although each of these sub-categories is influenced by both pedestrian and vehicular movements, it may or may not interact. Obviously, each type must be separated from the other to minimize conflict and the potential for injuries. The frequency of use and interaction between categories will depend on the configuration of outdoor facilities. Therefore, careful attention must be paid to circulation.

Accessibility

Accessibility refers to providing means for persons who have disabilities to

attend activities. Recent federal legislation, ''Americans with Disabilities Act,'' requires that certain areas be made accessible. One should realize that removing barriers is a benefit to all who use the facility.

Barriers

Barriers fulfill many requirements associated with recreation and sports facilities. Barriers may be selected for one or more of the following reasons, however, each factor should be considered in the selection of the barrier. Barriers may secure an area, provide safety, isolate an area, enclose an area, separate activities, abate noise, control environmental factors such as wind and sun, aesthetics, control accessibility (for pedestrians as well as vehicles), protect participants and spectators, and protect property.

Environmental Concerns

The proximity of sound or noise to the site should be taken into account during site visits. Sounds generated off-site may inhibit instruction as well as play. Conversely, the site should not be located so that it will interfere with instruction or other activities. The air quality at the site should be tested to insure pollutants are not contaminating the area. Soil and subsoil conditions should be tested for presence of contaminants.

Vandalism

Each aspect of the design should be reviewed to determine the likelihood of vandalism:
- Materials should be selected which will allow for easy cleaning of surface subject to graffiti.
- Protective covers should be placed on glass areas and light fixtures where required.
- Access to areas should be restricted.
- Fencing should be placed

GENERAL ACTIVITY SPACE REQUIREMENTS				
ACTIVITY		**DIMENSIONS PLAY AREA**	**DIMENSIONS TOTAL**	**AREA SQFT**
Archery	Min	50'x300'	110'x40'	44,000
Badminton	Singles	17'x44'	27'x54'	1,458
	Doubles	20'x44'	30'x54'	1,620
Baseball	Official	350'x350'	400'x400'	160,000
	Pony	250'x250'	300'x300'	90,000
	Little League	200'x200'	250'x250'	62,500
Basketball	Official	50'x94'	62'x114'	7,068
	High School	50'x84'	62'x104'	6,448
	Recreation	40'x70'	52'x90'	4,680
Croquet		35'x70'	45'x80'	3,600
Deck Tennis	Singles	12'x40'	20'x50'	1,000
	Doubles	18'x40'	26'x50'	1,300
Field Hockey		180'x300'	200'x320'	64,000
Football		160'x360'	180'x380'	68,400
Lacrosse	Men - Min	160'x330'	180'x350'	63,000
	- Max	180'x330'	200'x350'	70,000
Lacrosse	Women - Min	150'x360'	170'x380'	64.600
	- Max	150'x420'	170'x440'	74,800
Soccer	Men - Min	195'x330'	115'x350'	40,250
	- Max	225'x360'	245'x380'	93,100
Soccer	Women - Min	120'x240'	140'x260'	36,400
	- Max	180'x300'	200'x320'	64,000
Softball	Fast Pitch	225'x225'	250'x250'	62,500
	Slow Pitch - M	275'x275'	295'x295'	87,025
	- W	250'x250'	270'x270'	72,900
Tennis	Singles	27'x78'	51'x120'	6,120
	Doubles	36'x78'	60'x120'	7,200
Volleyball		30'x60'	50'x80'	4,000

* Refer to recent regulations for changes.
**The area above does not include space for support facilities.

Figure 3.2. General Activity Space Requirements

around fields to prevent access by vehicles.

- Adequate lighting may assist in discouraging crime.

Risk Management

The time to implement a risk management program is during the planning stages of the project. This action is a wise first step in controlling insurance costs, future operating and maintenance costs associated with removing hazardous conditions, and the potential costs stemming from litigation of potential hazardous conditions and situations. Although one is not able to remove all hazards, the number of potentially serious conditions will be reduced significantly due to the Team's efforts. The following suggestions provide a basis for a risk management program:

- Insure sufficient space is provided between activity areas.
- Provide sufficient space or physical barriers between activity areas.
- Avoid constructing areas where persons can hide.
- Provide adequate lighting for all pedestrian areas and roadways.
- Avoid crisscrossing vehicular and pedestrian paths whenever possible.

- Provide barriers around or between the activity area and hazards, such as railroad tracks, roadways, or bodies of water.

- Isolate activity areas for different age groups.
- Provide supervisors in areas where existing deficiencies cannot be corrected.
- Post rules and regulations in close proximity to the activity. Information may be required in various languages to accommodate area ethnic groups.
- Conduct frequent inspections of the fixed and movable equipment, lighting, and surfaces.
- Review each activity for hazards associated with that particular sport.

See Chapter 8 for a more comprehensive discussion of risk management.

DEVELOPMENTAL SITE PLAN

The efficiency of existing facilities or of proposed facilities may be reviewed in a simple format known as a developmental site plan.

This is a form of map or plan for the site with components arranged to show existing or proposed conditions. Documentation of existing conditions permit a constructive evaluation of the existing facilities with respect to future needs, while a map of proposed facilities allows for definition of future program alternatives. In either case, the plan becomes one means of looking at basic planning as a whole through a relationship of various elements that include circulation, activities, structures, and others. Although the site plan is not a substitute for a Master Plan, it may be a simple, valuable tool that may be used as a planning guide. Additional benefits of such a guide may be its use as a device for prioritizing program elements or phasing implementation of programs and construction. (Figure 3.3.)

The work involved in the preparation of a developmental site plan requires a thorough understanding of the site and its surroundings. This task generally requires a review of supporting documentation (Master Plan, programming documents, sports regulations, and interviews with user groups, etc.), technical documentation (topographic surveys, property records, utility surveys, borings of subsurface conditions, etc.), and field inspection of the site and its adjacent areas of influence.

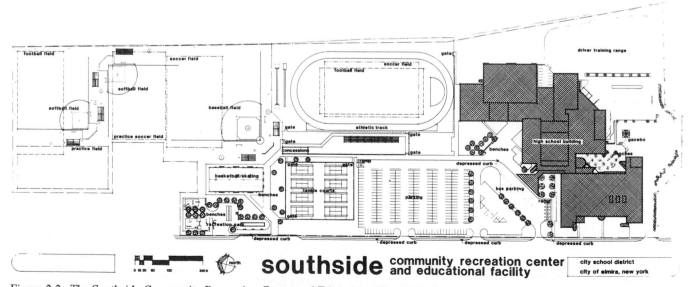

Figure 3.3. The Southside Community Recreation Center and Educational Facility in Elmira, New York is a good example of a comprehensive athletic complex to serve both the high school and the community.

Common steps in the preparation of a developmental site plan are:

1. Identify the uses intended for a site.

2. Identify combined activities.

3. Produce an orderly arrangement of activities to define the size of the site.

4. Locate the site. This step may have been performed previously. Therefore, the Team may be required to tailor the program to the site.

5. Verify the size of the site based on previous plans.

6. Make adjustments in the plan to conform to the site conditions.

Developmental Site Plan Format

The developmental site plan should respond to the programming documents through the use of a simple format which contains:

1. Vicinity site plan, prepared on a small scale, to encompass all adjacent properties and uses which would influence the use of the spaces.

2. Site plan, prepared on a large scale, to define the "footprint" of all activities and associated space requirements planned for the site. The larger scale provides a clear understanding of the site constraints with respect to the program. The plan should convey as much information as necessary to identify usage, availability, and quality of facilities:

- primary and secondary program requirements
- type of activities planned
- time of year relative to the type of activities planned (spaces should service multiple sports and seasons of the year whenever possible)
- type of activity uses and the surfaces required for each activity
- maximum flexibility, whether an existing or new site (alternatives to site utilization, joint-use facilities between agencies or municipalities).

3. Outline of proposals for new construction which define relative costs for the work anticipated.

4. Design guidelines which identify standards for activities, construction, and quality control.

In many instances, facilities have been constructed without the benefit of a planned program for development. Too often the lack of prior planning is evident in existing facilities. The absence of a formal plan as a guide to others has led to fragmented and inefficient use of land. Therefore, it is in the interest of the Team to document ideas through the use of a developmental site plan which will establish a format for rational land use planning.

SUPPORT FACILITIES

Structures

Tickets: Ticket purchasing facilities, whether open or partially enclosed, are a necessity for control of receipts and tickets. Space should be large enough to accommodate a minimum of two persons and have a transparent opening, a deal shelf, and drawers for storage of tickets, programs, and daily receipts. The booth should be lockable from the inside to prevent unwanted access. The amount of security construction should be based on the attendance. A portable booth may be more economical since it may be moved to different fields for use.

Security: Separate permanent facilities for security generally are not required for most activity events since security operations may be performed by roving patrols with communication devices and vehicles. This mobile concept of providing security is considered the norm to accommodate the intermittent use of activity events. Where security facilities are necessary, portable type command posts are desirable.

Medical Facilities: Separate permanent facilities for medical treatment generally are not required for most activity events. Portable facilities such as tents may be warranted for large

events, while mobile vehicle type units will suffice for other events.

Storage: Permanent buildings or portable buildings should be provided for storage of activity equipment. Separate buildings should be provided for field maintenance equipment. Lists of all sport and maintenance equipment, such as hand tools, motorized equipment, layout templates, etc. to be stored in the structures should be developed to assure proper sizing of the buildings. Fenced areas may be provided to store large pieces of activity equipment, such as goals.

Communications: Structures should be provided for members of the media. Whenever possible, these structures should be elevated to provide a clear view of the activity area. The size of the building(s) will depend on the number of local media that generally attends activity events.

Concessions: An area convenient to the activity area should be designated for positioning various types of concessions, such as food and programs. Fixed or portable structures and or parking pads for mobile vendor units should be considered in the design of this area.

Seating: The placement of fixed type seating should be a primary consideration with respect to the type of sport(s) the seating will service. Ideally, a seating area should accommodate as many sports as possible due to the costs associated with the installation. Although seating generally is thought to be used for athletic events, other activities such as physical education and athletic instruction, field day events, concerts, and graduation should be considered as alternate uses.

Seating areas for events may be constructed using natural features or prefabricated components (bleachers or grandstands). Providing a sloped area or incorporating seating tiers into the side of berms are inexpensive means of accommodating seating. However, they take up valuable land area. Prefabricated bleachers may be purchased as fixed or portable units. Fixed bleachers require foundations, similar to building structures, to accommodate a greater number of persons, while the portable bleachers may be placed in various locations but will accommodate a minimal number of persons. Aluminum or reinforced plastic type seats will reduce maintenance costs associated with repair of seats (rotted wood or corroded metals). Seating areas should be elevated above the playing surface to permit a clear view of the playing area. Where the distance from a seat to an adjacent surface or ground is greater that 30 inches, guard rails should be provided for the safety of spectators.

Roadways

Site Access: The design of roadway systems and access to the site generally is provided by civil engineers who determine requirements based on the capacity and use of the site. Therefore, it is necessary that the Team provide accurate and appropriate site planning information to the local planners so that sufficient access is available for the site.

Activity Area Access: The design of circulation within the confines of the site generally is provided by the landscape architect or civil engineer. The Team should provide information and comments on positioning of structures and the accessibility route.

Guidelines
- Vehicle access routes to the activity areas should be as inconspicuous as possible.
- Use walkways for vehicle access to activity areas to minimize the amount of space dedicated to circulation.
- The amount of access will determine whether asphalt is required.

Parking

The design and arrangement of parking accommodations is provided by the landscape architect or civil engineer. The Team should provide comments relative to the desirable location of

various facets of the design, that is, there may be a more desirable location for visiting team parking than that suggested by the professional.

Guidelines
- Allocation of space for off-street parking of automobiles and buses is a major consideration in the design. Proximity of parking to the activity area(s) is critical to persons who attend events. In fact, distance may inhibit attendance when insufficient space or improper locations are planned.
- Where the outdoor complex contains many activity areas, several locations of parking should be planned near the the highest concentration of users. This concept will permit a more environmentally-sensitive response to the usual "sea of automobiles" by dispersing the parking areas.
- Parking areas should be properly delineated for each type of parking. Buses should be located in separate area where the riders may enter and exit the area without crossing automobile traffic.

Walkways

Walkways generally are designed by a civil engineer for public areas and by the landscape architect or civil engineer for site-specific areas. Walkways generally are arranged by the landscape architect. The Team should be available to provide information about the numbers and common access routes of people attending.

Guidelines
- Walkways should be used for pedestrian as well as maintenance vehicles whenever possible to reduce hard surface areas.
- Walkways should be provided from all known public access points to the area, as well as to all activity areas on the site.
- Walkways should be sized to accommodate the volume of pedestrians anticipated to attend activity events. Worn grass adjacent to walkways is indicative of undersized walkways.

- Worn grass areas indicate preferred pedestrian passageways.

Signage

The intent of signage is to make traveling, whether by foot or vehicle, more efficient through information and directional signage. Signs for the site may be designed by the site architect or the landscape architect. Signage associated with traffic generally is specified by the civil or transportation engineers, based on standard guidelines.

Guidelines
- The type, size, style, and color of lettering and signage should be coordinated throughout the facility.
- The size of lettering should be sufficient to be read from an intended distance.
- Traffic and parking signage should be coordinated with Department of Transportation guidelines.

Lighting

Site: Lighting for roadways, walkways, and general illumination should be designed by an engineer. Fixture types generally are selected by the landscape architect.

Activity: Lighting for activities should be designed by lighting consultants to insure appropriate coverage. Refer to the separate section on Lighting Design Guidelines in this chapter.

Guidelines
- Lighting should be planned to minimize the amount of "spill light" which enters onto adjacent properties.

Barriers

Plantings are effective barriers. Trees, depending upon the type selected, may form a barrier which is both aesthetic and functional. This barrier is not readily available since it take several years for trees to mature. Shrubs may present a viable seasonal screen. However, plantings provide more of a visually aesthetic barrier than other methods. Plantings may be vulnerable to vandalism by vehicles or persons.

Berms actually are earthen mounds strategically positioned to provide a wind break, a seating area, or a visual barrier. Unfortunately, this barrier may require a great deal of space, thereby reducing the area available for other sports.

Depressed areas, such as streams and ponds that are designed to convey or hold water, may be used as physical barriers. Access should be controlled where deep water is present. These areas may be hazardous to the safety of young children attending activities and should be guarded with a safety barrier.

Large stones or low masonry walls provide an excellent barrier against vehicle access to an area, as well as enhance the environmental quality of the site.

Guidelines

- Characteristics of quality barrier design are stability, durability, economy of maintenance, attractiveness, and effectiveness.

- There are numerous means of achieving the design requirements. Combining two or more types of barriers may provide an interesting environmental concept for the site.

- Minimize concealed spaces which could foster crime.

Fencing

Fencing is made of different types of material such as wood, plastic, and metal which may be available in various styles. Chain-link type, metal fencing made of steel, galvanized steel, and aluminum is generally the fencing of choice. Plastic colored coatings may be added to the fence to extend its life and afford color. In addition to the above, colored slats (wood, plastic, or metal) may be inserted between the links to further limit visibility and add color to the barrier.

Guidelines

- Its appeal is that it requires a minimal amount of space. This characteristic is valuable since space is generally at a premium.

- Fencing may be connected to other forms of barriers.

- The structure of the fence may be used for attachment of accessories such as rebound walls for tennis (providing that the fence supports have been designed to accommodate the wind loads).

Utilities

Each type of utility generally is designed by an engineer with a discipline in that particular specialty. The engineers will need information from the Team in order to size each utility. The Team may be required to provide such information as capacities, frequency and types of use, and other parameters related to each utility.

Electrical: Power service should be considered for each structure and activity area on the site. The primary distribution to the activity area should be sized to accommodate relative future needs, such as installation of lighting for activities. Lighting of activity areas should be considered where funds are available to provide flexibility in programming.

Water: Water connections should be considered for irrigation of fields, personal consumption, sanitation, and food preparation. Where funding is available, installation of an automatic sprinkler system should be considered to minimize the maintenance effort. Frost protection for water connections is a must in the northern regions.

Sanitation: The availability of sanitary facilities for spectators and participants should be considered a requirement. Portable units (contracted through a local service company) or permanent structures may be furnished. Portable units have grown in popularity in recent years over permanent structures due, in part, to reduced maintenance required by the owner and increased cleanliness of the units. Hand washing facilities should be provided for portable as well as permanent facilities. It appears that vandalism is not as prevalent in portable facilities as in permanent facilities.

Storm Drainage: The means and methods of collecting surface and subsurface water should be included in the planning process. The Team should be briefed thoroughly on how drainage will be handled at the site, as well as how it may affect the availability of facilities and the play of the game. Manholes and catch basins should be located outside the immediate playing area to prevent interference with play.

Communications: Communications systems to be considered are:

- Public Address System: Input and output connections located strategically to provide full coverage of the activity area, including the playing field, seating area, and the concessions area,

- Record Score: Communications connections between the scoreboard and the official scorer's box,

- Official Communications: Communications between officials on the field and the scorebox may be required,

- Regional Broadcasting: Input and output connections between the media box and the mobile communications vehicle for local radio and television,

- Team Coordination: Team communications sets for each team between the coaches and the observation box,

- Emergency: Communications for emergency response,

- Telephone: Telephone for public use is desirable,

- Security: Portable phones.

SURFACES

There is no one surface which will meet satisfactorily the needs of all outdoor activities. Each activity has its own unique characteristics, which help to define the appropriate qualities of the surface and the system. Qualities such as durability, stain resistance, appearance, resiliency, longevity, initial cost, operation and maintenance cost, extended seasonal usage, etc. become the basis for making decisions. Where possible, those systems are selected which contain qualities desirable to several activities so that a "multiplicity of use" may be scheduled for one activity area.

The following paragraphs will address different types of materials and their desirable uses. However, before there is discussion of materials and their uses, there must be an understanding of how different materials are combined to form a "system."

The "System"

The process of selecting surfaces for any activity should begin with the definition of the total "system" components. The system is defined as a multi-layered, multi-component product designed to act as a whole. The composition of the system is made up of materials, the assemblies, and the method of installation to achieve a desired performance. Each component and its placement within the system becomes interdependent upon one another.

Because of the complexity of the systems and the advances in technology, selecting the appropriate system continues to confront sports professionals. Too often, high quality products are included in a substandard system. This combination leads most certainly to premature failure of the system. Generally, the high quality product is included in the surface component instead of the base. Unfortunately, when the base fails, the entire system fails and must be replaced. Conversely, quality base systems may last indefinitely while the surface changes several times. Therefore, it appears to be a wise decision to invest in a sound foundation and avoid costly renovations.

The factors which individually or collectively contribute to the failure of the system are:
- poor system design
- poor product or component selection
- improper system selection for a particular activity
- poor installation techniques
- improper maintenance of the surface and/or system
- inadequate maintenance of the surface and/or system
- abuse of the surface or system
- control of vegetation under the system.

With the understanding of the "system," we can begin to review materials, components, and subsystems.

Soils

Soils, in their natural and exposed conditions, generally are not conducive to use as a surface for most outdoor activities. However, the basic characteristics of a soil may be changed by the addition of various components to modify the properties of the soil and create favorable playing conditions. Caution must be exercised when modifying soils so as not to create conditions which minimize other attributes of the soil and produce a condition which is detrimental to its use for an activity. For example, the addition of asphalt, calcium chloride, or cement may stabilize the soil and reduce erosion, but these products may increase the hardness of the surface and reduce the resiliency. The addition of sand increases the porosity of the soil while reducing erosion, but adds an abrasive element to the surface. These alternatives, as well as others, must be analyzed carefully with respect to each activity.

Advantages: Repairs are relatively inexpensive but frequent. Products are found throughout the country. Surface gives under horizontal pressure. Relatively uniform bounce where fine aggregate is used to stabilize the surface.

Disadvantages: Continued daily maintenance increases operating and maintenance expenses. Surface is highly susceptible to damage. Surface requires substantial time to dry after a rain shower. Subject to area erosion as a result of activity play, water, and wind.

Turf

Natural grass has been in use for centuries and continues to be preferred as the surface for use on activity fields. Its inherent attributes of attractiveness, resiliency, and nonabrasiveness make it adaptable to all activities.

The system components generally consist of a subbase founded on existing soil, a rootzone layer, and a surface layer. The subsurface drainage system usually is contained within the subbase layer and existing soil.

Advanced systems, such as "Prescription Athletic Turf" (PAT) or the "Cambridge System" have devised means to control the environmental conditions of natural turf surfaces. The technologically-advanced PAT system contains many engineering features that automatically irrigate the field, mechanically drain water from the surface, and maintain the ground temperature well above freezing by heat of the ground. Each of these techniques is meant to control the natural playing surface conditions and extend the use of the field.

Advantages: The color and grooming of the turf is aesthetically pleasing. Provides a great resilience and acts as a natural cushion. Superior footing. Clean surface and dust free. Cooler surface temperature. Surface dissipates light to minimize glare. Acceptable surface for many activities.

Disadvantages: The nature of the system requires higher operating and maintenance costs. A perfect surface condition is required to provide a uniform bounce. Surface is slippery when damp or wet. Slow drying after showers. Objects and clothing may be discolored when in contact with the surface. Surface does not withstand high concentration of activity (areas turn to soil). Although it still is possible to install water distribution systems to irrigate the field or heating systems to thaw out the frozen area, these alternatives present a costly option. Sod must be made available to repair portions of the field, or play will be affected by the conditions of the field. The desirable attributes of natural grass are lost when frost and water penetrate the playing surface. The speed at which the ball travels is slowed somewhat by the irregularities in the depth and density of the turf. It is harder to predict the hop of a ground ball due to the slight unevenness of the field. Low spots are screened from view by the density of the turf.

Critical factors in maintaining the natural turf field.

- Drainage: surface grading and subsurface drainage should be combined to minimize the negative effect on turf growth

- Soil: type of soil to support the turf

- Turf: wear resistant and uniform footing. Consult local Cooperative Extension Bureau for appropriate types

- Irrigation: through surface or subsurface systems

- Maintenance: mowing, weed control, pest control, fertilizing, and aerating

- Scheduling: field use should be regulated to allow turf to recover

- Positioning: field sports should be shifted from time to time to allow areas to recover, such as around goals.

Aggregates

Aggregates, such as gravel, graded stone, cinders, etc. are used as materials for drainage and base layers for various systems. Aggregate may be combined with soils to provide wearing surfaces for some activities. Aggregates also are used commonly for light traffic roadways and walkways.

Advantages: Low initial cost. Generally very porous, but depend on the composition. Excellent as base for other systems.

Disadvantages: Aggregate requires constant maintenance. Aggregate may be used as weapons to assault people or for vandalism.

Masonry

Masonry products, such as brick, concrete masonry units, and stone, are used for walkways, light traffic roadways, retaining walls, and buildings. The system generally consists of a base over which sand is laid to receive the masonry product. Light traffic roadways may require the addition of a concrete base to support the increased loads associated with vehicles.

Advantages: A brick surface is a very durable, all-weather type surface. The system may be usable shortly after showers if properly pitched for drainage. Relatively low maintenance except for occasional surface cleaning. Brick and stone chips may be used as components of other systems, such as concrete to provide durability. Brick is available in a variety of colors and textures.

Disadvantages: The cost of brick and the required labor for its installation generally is very high, compared to other systems. The surface is harder on a player's lower torso (other surfaces may be placed over the brick to create a less hard system). The joints between bricks, whether mortar-filled or flush, may require replacement of chipped brick and pointing of mortar. Elevated brick edges present a tripping obstacle to users.

Concrete

Concrete products, such as poured-in-place concrete (reinforced, where required), post-tension concrete, pre-cast concrete, or concrete-stone composition panels may be used as walkways, roadways, retaining walls, and buildings. The on-grade system generally requires placement of the concrete over an aggregate base.

Advantages: A concrete surface is an extremely durable, all-weather type surface. The system will be usable shortly after rain showers if properly pitched for drainage. Excellent base or subbase for other systems, such as asphalt or brick. Relatively low maintenance except for occasional surface cleaning. Resists major cracking. The concrete units are available in a variety of colors and textures.

Disadvantages: The cost of the concrete and its installation is higher than other systems. The surface generally is harder on the player's lower torso (other surfaces may be placed over the concrete to create a less hard system).

Asphalt

Asphalt products, such as Penetration-Macadam, asphalt/concrete mixes (hot and cold laid), and a variety of layered systems may be use for walkways, roadways, and courts. The layering, as well as the components within the systems, may be changed to provide a more resilient or more durable system. The system usually requires placement of the asphalt over an aggregate base. The attributes of the system may increase when colored coatings are applied to the surface.

Advantages: An asphalt surface is a very durable, all-weather surface. The system will be usable shortly after rain showers if properly pitched for drainage. Excellent base for other systems. Relatively low maintenance except for occasional surface cleaning.

Disadvantages: The cost of the system varies depending upon the system components. Systems may be complex, requiring a skilled installer. The surface may cause unusually premature wear on footwear. The system is more susceptible to seasonal changes of heat and freeze/thaw than concrete, and cracks may develop. The surface is harder on the player's lower torso (other surfaces may be placed over asphalt to create a less hard system). The surface will require periodic treatment with coatings.

Synthetic Surface

Synthetic surfaces include monolithic poured-in-place, pre-manufactured sheet goods, and interlocking modular tiles consisting of chemical and natural substances. Products, such as rubber granules, may be added to the chemical composition to provide a nonslip surface. The system generally consists of a subbase course of aggregate; a base course of aggregate, asphalt, or concrete, and the manufactured system components. These surfaces are used for courts, tracks, and some field events.

Advantages: Greater degree of player comfort, especially with cushioned systems. Uniform bounce. Ability to resurface existing deteriorated activity areas without repairing the existing area. Ease of maintenance. Built-in drainage through system tiles or joints. Durable and interchangeable pieces with modular system. The color and dimension of prefabricated units is controlled under shop conditions, permitting a more uniform color match in the field.

Disadvantages: Requires specialized knowledge and training to install. High traffic areas, such as the inside lane of a track, will deteriorate due to excessive wear from track spikes. Monolithic poured-in-place systems vary in thickness and color with each installation due to custom mixing and installation which are performed at the site. Seams between sheet goods may separate under extreme changes in temperature.

Synthetic Turf Surface

The synthetic turf system is used to replaced those areas generally covered by natural turf. The system components generally consist of a gravel subbase

founded on existing soil, a subsurface drainage combined within the existing soil and the subbase, a layer of permeable material (usually asphalt), a cushioning pad (with perforations to allow water to pass through the layer), and the surface turf layer. Synthetic turf is not recommended for use on fields where track and field events will be held.

Advantages: Permits continued use of the surface for numerous activities on a continued basis. Recent system changes provide more responsiveness to the movement of the player. Occasional inspection of seams and cleaning is required. The speed of an object on the surface is higher than grass. Bounce is uniform but higher than on grass.

Disadvantages: Initial cost. Seams between carpet pieces are the weakest points of the system and require the most inspection and repair (sewn seams require less attention to maintenance than seams connected by adhesive). Degradation of fibers exposed to ultraviolet light. Periodic cleaning of the surface. Surface is slightly harder than grass.

Critical Factors in maintaining the Synthetic Turf Field:

- Replacement of the resilient shock pad is necessary after several years of use.

- Seams require most repair. In the order of best to least, the sewed and glued seams are best, followed by sewed, and finally glued. Glued seams are subject to dimensional instability due to temperature changes.

- Periodic sweeping of the system is required.

- Adhesion of the system should be checked frequently.

- Sand-filled turf system requires redistribution of the sand to remain effective.

Synthetic "Sand-filled" Turf

The synthetic sand-filled turf system differs from the synthetic turf system in that the number of strands of fiber have

been reduced considerably and the voids filled with sand. This change was made to increase the maneuverability of players while reducing the potential for injury.

Advantages: Sand-filled system reduces friction between player's equipment, shoes, and playing surface. Helps support the synthetic strands in the upright position while protecting the turf from ultraviolet degradation. Porous system permits usage shortly after rain showers.

Disadvantages: Sand-filled system requires occasional brushing of sand to maintain uniformity of depth over the entire surface. The redistribution of sand during the activity may influence play or the bounce of the ball. Fibers may be crushed and require replacement if sand is not distributed evenly to assist in support of the fibers. (Figure 3.4.)

LIGHTING DESIGN

When the program demand for outdoor facilities exceeds the availability of facilities, the installation of lighting appears to be one alternative to extend the use of existing facilities to accommodate program needs.

The task of designing lighting for outdoor facilities presents the Team and design professional with unique problems in that:

- Large outdoor areas require high levels of illumination.

- The transition between areas of different light intensity must be relatively even.

- Light is projected significant distances from light fixtures positioned around the perimeter.

Classification

Recent advances in the engineering and technology of lighting design for outdoor facilities have changed the way illumination is applied for various activities. Current practices associate

SURFACE SELECTION PROCESS

A systematic approach must be followed to conduct a search to determine the appropriate surface. The following guidelines will assist in the decision-making process:

1. **Definition**: Define the characteristics required to meet specified needs. These characteristics should be material, system, and activity-specific, such as, the effects of sunlight on synthetic materials, the internal filtration of water through the system, or the bounce of a ball on the surface, respectively. This task may seem research-intensive, but it usually isn't since many of these questions already have been addressed by the manufacturers in their literature.

2. **Solicitation**: Don't allow a cost limitation to prevent review of all available systems. Request information from as many manufacturers as possible to obtain literature. The information contained in the literature will provide you with a broad knowledge of different systems, a basis to compare systems, and instill a curiosity to question system design. Project costs as well as material estimates should be obtained. References, list of installers, and locations of systems should be furnished with the literature.

3. **Comparison**: Review and compare each system after receiving the manufacturers' literature. Categorize the information by type and desirable qualities, such as natural versus synthetic or resiliency, etc. A table of desirable attributes is most helpful in comparing the systems.

4. **Visitation**: After the type of products has been narrowed to a few systems, the sports professional should plan to visit various sites to inspect the products, as well as discuss the performance and maintenance factors with the users.

5. **Selection**: Select a system based on research to this point. Although this may be the system eventually purchased, other factors still have to be considered and may influence the final selection

6. **Quality**: Defining the quality of a system may become difficult since several systems may be very close in design. Quality refers to the materials as well the installation of the system.

7. **Manufacturers**: What type of reputation does the manufacturer have? Ask for references, but don't be surprised if they give the manufacturer and the installer high marks. Some manufacturers have provided products to clients at reduced rates in exchange for their marketing assistance. How many years has the manufacturer been in business? What type of technical support is available through the manufacturer and the local representative? Ask for information regarding the manufacturer's method of monitoring quality control in the plant as well as in the field.

8. **Installer**: The installer should be recommended by the manufacturer to be assured that the installer is familiar with the products and installation. The installer should be asked questions similar to those asked of the manufacturer.

9. **Maintenance**: Since maintenance can be a considerable portion of the operating budget, it is important to define the extent of the system. Questions, such as these will help with planning: What type of maintenance is required? What is the frequency of each type of maintenance?

10. **Initial Cost**: What is the "total" initial cost of the system? Ask if two systems are considered the same, then why is one system more costly than the other? It may be that the quality of the materials or the system or both are

the reason for the cost reduction. In some instances, the product name will increase the cost of the system, or hidden costs will be identified by the low bidder after the work has been awarded.

11. **Life Cycle Cost (LCC)**: This a comparative analysis of each type of surface which considers the initial cost, the operation and maintenance cost, and the replacement cost, if necessary, during an established time period. The figures generated from the analysis provide the anticipated total costs. Generally, the more expensive systems (initial cost) will be comparable to the less expensive systems when all factors are considered.

12. **Bidding**: When the owner is required to conduct competitive bidding for products or services, attention should be directed to the written specifications, to insure that the products and methods of installation are clearly and accurately described. Too often the specifications make assumptions which permit systems of lesser quality to be considered as equals and therefore acceptable.

13. **Installation/Installer**: Up until this point, the owner has had control over the selection process. However, this phase is where additional expertise will be required. It is in the owner's interest to require the manufacturer to perform periodic on-site supervision of the installer to insure compliance with the manufacturers' specifications.

Figure 3.4. Surface Selection Process

the play and level of facilities for each activity to a "skill level." In simple terms, the illumination level increases as the level of play and number of spectators increase.

Illumination criteria is grouped into four classes based on facility types and illumination classes. For example, Class I lighting is associated with the highest levels of play and facilities, while Class IV lighting reflects the lowest levels of play and facilities. Of course, facility levels may be included in other classes, based on the anticipated levels of illumination required.

Classification Index

- Class I accommodates competitive play before 5,000 to 200,000 spectators at international, national, professional, college, semi-professional and sports club levels
- Class II accommodates competitive play before 4,000 to 6,000 spectators at college, semi-professional, sports clubs, amateur leagues, and high schools.
- Class III accommodates competitive play, without special provisions for spectators, at amateur leagues, high schools, training facilities and elementary schools.
- Class IV accommodates non-competitive social and recreation play at training facilities, elementary schools, recreational events, and social events.

Sport Groupings

For the purposes of providing illumination at outdoor facilities, sports and recreational activities have been classified further by the position of the playing object(s). The position of the object may be divided into aerial sports or ground level sports. Each group is categorized further as multi-directional or uni-directional.

Aerial Sports: Aerial sports may be identified as activities in which the position of the object is viewed in varying levels above the playing surface.

Multi-directional aerial sports, such as badminton, basketball, baseball, football, handball, squash, tennis, and volleyball require viewing from multiple positions as well as multiple angles. Illumination is required over the entire playing area. Locating the lighting fixture is crucial to controlling direct glare.

Uni-directional aerial sports, such as the golf driving range, ski jumping, and skeet and trap shooting, require viewing of the aerial object from one location on the ground.

Ground level sports: ground level sports may be identified as activities in which the position of the object is viewed within a zone a few feet above the playing surface.

Multi-directional ground level sports, such as ice hockey, skating, field hockey, swimming, boxing, and wrestling require viewing of an object from multiple positions, normally looking down, horizontally, and occasionally upward.

Uni-directional ground level sports, such as archery, bowling, shooting, and skiing require general illumination with light focused on the end vertical target.

Design Standards

The design of lighting systems usually is based on the information contained in *Sports Lighting, Recommended Practice for Sports and Recreational Area Lighting,* published by the Illuminating Engineering Society of North America (IESNA). Based on this information, manufacturers of lighting systems have prepared standard lighting layouts for various types of sports and recreation activities. These layouts can be applied readily to standard activity configurations, as well as modified by the use of computers to meet requirements. Many manufacturers provide brochures which contain information on lighting systems explained in lay person terms.

Light Sources

The type of lighting lamps available for use in outdoor facilities generally is limited to three types of high intensity discharge (HID) light sources: metal halide, high pressure sodium, and mercury. Incandescent and fluorescent fixtures generally are not used due to higher operating costs. Metal halide lamps, because of their directed concentration of light, make it easier to control and focus the light on the playing area, thereby reducing the per-square-foot cost of light on the playing area. The high pressure sodium (HPS) lamp generates more light, however, the focus of the light distributes the light over a larger area which increases the per-square-foot cost of the lighted area. The following table (Figure 3.5) is a simplified form of comparing qualities of various light sources. One should not rely on tables or the written word to define light characteristics. The Team should visit various facilities to observe the quality of lighting.

Illumination Levels

The days of applying one or two illumination levels over the entire playing field have been put aside for the more specific science of distributing light as required for play. The level of light for each sport is based on a number of factors which include:

- the type of sport with respect to the speed of play and the size of playing objects
- the skill level of the players
- the size of the playing area
- the number of spectators and their distance from the playing area
- broadcasting requirements, which generally will require higher levels of illumination
- general aesthetics.

For these reasons, it would be impractical to reproduce the illumination requirements for each sport in such a publication as this. Therefore, the Team should review (IESNA)

	Lumen Output Per Lamp	Efficacy	Life Expectancy	Color Acceptability	Degree of Light Control	Maintenance of Lumen Output
INCANDESCENT	FAIR	LOW	LOW	HIGH	HIGH	GOOD
TUNGSTEN HALOGEN	FAIR	LOW	LOW	HIGH	HIGH	HIGH
MERCURY	GOOD	FAIR	HIGH	LOW	GOOD	GOOD
PHOSPHOR MERCURY	GOOD	FAIR	HIGH	FAIR TO GOOD	FAIR	FAIR
METAL HALIDE	HIGH	GOOD	FAIR	GOOD TO HIGH	GOOD	FAIR
HIGH-PRESSURE SODIUM	HIGH	HIGH	FAIR	FAIR	GOOD	GOOD
40-WATT FLUORESCENT	LOW	GOOD	GOOD	GOOD TO HIGH	LOW	GOOD
HIGH-OUTPUT FLUORESCENT	FAIR	GOOD	GOOD	GOOD TO HIGH	LOW	GOOD
1500-MA FLUORESCENT	GOOD	GOOD	FAIR	GOOD TO HIGH	LOW	FAIR

There are four ratings for each characteristic—high, good, fair, and low.

Figure 3.5. Comparative Characteristics of Light Sources for General Lighting Purposes

Publication RP-6-8 of the Illuminating Engineering Society of North America for more specific information regarding sports lighting for particular activities.

Supports

The support structure and its components consist of a luminary assembly and a vertical support assembly such as a pole or grille. The luminary assembly consists of a lamp, reflector, ballast mounting, crossarm, and crossarm connector. The function of the support is to maintain the luminary assemblies at the appropriate height and position required to achieve optimum aiming angles. Supports generally are made of wood, concrete, or metal (steel or aluminum alloy). While the metal and concrete supports are more expensive than wood, they provide a more stable aiming position and a longer life than wood supports, which may decay and twist or warp.

Service

In addition to the initial cost of the system, one should review the amount of scheduled maintenance that can be expected with each manufacturer's system. Variables, such as life of luminaries, the number of luminaries, the quality of the assembly, control of the system, etc., can increase the work load for the maintenance staff, as well increase operating expenses. The number of circuits for lighting should be diversified to the maximum extent practical to avoid a complete failure of the lighting system during events.

Particular attention should be paid to the illumination levels expressed in initial and maintained footcandles since these factors have an impact on the initial and operating cost of the system. While initial levels are associated with the initial phase of use, the maintained levels are those levels that one can expect over the life of the lighting system.

Design Standards

The design of lighting systems usually is founded on information contained in *Sports Lighting, Recommended Practice for Sports and Recreational Area Lighting*, published by the Illuminating Engineering Society of North America (IESNA). Based on this information, manufacturers of lighting systems have prepared standard lighting layouts for various types of sports and recreation activities. These layouts may be applied to standard activity configurations, as well as modified by the use of computers to meet requirements. Many manufacturers provide brochures which contain general information on lighting systems explained in lay person terms.

Bidding Standards

The scope of work should be defined properly through the use of contract documents. Specifications and drawings define all components of the lighting system to insure that all contractors are submitting bids based on established criteria. Without these performance standards, bidders may misinterpret the scope of the project, which could result in substandard substitutions, incomplete scope assignments, and higher priced bids.

Role of the Sports Professional

Since the design of the illumination system is produced by a professional engineer with the assistance of computer-aided design programs and manufacturer's information, the role of the Team should be focused on relating and interpreting the requirements of each sport.

One possible method of viewing certain conditions on the playing area would be the use of a three-dimensional modeling of the playing area. With the aid of this computer design tool, one can simulate positions on a playing area to understand the effects of various levels of lighting.

The Team should be prepared to define requirements such as the speed of sports, purpose of play, skill level of players, spectator capacity, and broadcasting so the design professional may determine the appropriate illumination levels required for each activity. When more than one activity or event will be scheduled for the playing area, the Team will have to determine which activity illumination level takes precedence over the other.

Vandalism and Risk Management Considerations

- protective covers for light fixtures where fixtures are vulnerable to vandalism
- installing protective devices to prevent debris from falling or provide fenced area below the fixture
- limit access to the lighting fixtures to maintenance personnel only

- ground level access to power should be through a secure device
- compile a list of unacceptable conditions.

COURT SPORTS

Area

Generally the size of courts will be constructed in accordance with a governing authority, such as the NCAA. The diagrams included within this text are recommended only, the reader is advised to check with the appropriate organization for official specifications. There are instances when the size of the court may be modified to accommodate age groups or recreation programs. The designer should coordinate this information with the user group. Where space or funds are at a premium, one should consider multiple use of court areas. However, multiple court design requires careful planning of programs and scheduling of activities to insure areas are being used in the most efficient manner.

Orientation

Courts should be oriented so that the direction of play is in a north-south direction, that is, the goals should be on a north-south axis for basketball while the base lines for tennis, as well as other courts, should be perpendicular to the north-south axis.

Court Markings

The size, configuration, and color of the courts lines should be in accordance with the governing association requirements when courts are to be used for tournaments. When the purpose of the courts is defined for recreation only, these parameters may be modified to meet the recreation concepts. For instance, recreation basketball may require only the perimeter lines, foul line, foul lane, and the half court line for basketball. Special symbols or logos

will increase the cost of the court markings.

Where a playing surface is to be used for two or more court games, the designer must pay attention to the size and color of lines for each sport. Too many lines on the playing surface may create a maze of lines which may be confusing to the players. Generally, the sport played the most will have the more predominate line size and color.

Color of Markings

The color of markings should contrast with the color of the playing surface. The higher the contrast, that is, light to dark, the more visible the line. Avoid using a mixture of pastel colors with white on multiple court surfaces. The pastel colors may appear white in intense sunlight. The finish of the markings should be matte to minimize the amount of shiny or reflective surfaces.

Drainage

The court area should be constructed on a porous base elevated above the surrounding terrain to minimize the likelihood of surface water collecting on the court or in the base. Perimeter surface drainage collectors should be provided to direct water away from the areas.

Since drainage of the court takes precedence over the levelness of the court, each court surface should be constructed to drain from (1) side-to-side, (2) end-to-end, or (3) corner-to-corner. Sloping should be from the center to the sides.

Risk Management

In an effort to minimize liability for injuries, the following recommendations should be considered in the design of court areas:
- Provide sufficient space between courts, at the sides and at the ends. Ideally, a 10-foot-wide safety zone should be provided.

- Posts supporting basketball backstops should be a minimum of four feet from the basketball court baseline and extend four feet into the court.

- Posts supporting basketball backstops should have absorbent material.

- Provide protective padding on the bottom of the backstop.

- Provide a break-away rim.

- Install benches at the perimeter, rather than at the sidelines, to remove obstacles from the playing area.

- Install drinking fountains and any other service facilities on the exterior of the area.

- Where courts are closer than recommended, provide barriers between the courts.

- Drains should be located outside the playing area or between courts when absolutely necessary.

Basketball

Court Dimensions: The court dimensions for basketball generally are determined by age group and the program (competition or recreation). The size of courts for recreational and non-competitive programs should be determined by the user group.

Backboards and Goals: There are two popular types of basketball backboard shapes. These shapes are rectangular and fan-shaped. Although the four-by-six foot rectangular type backboard is preferred over the standard fan-shaped backboard for playable surface area, it does cost slightly more. Backboards are available in wood, metal, fiberglass, and glass. Metal or fiberglass appears to withstand the environment and vandalism best in an exterior environment.

A regulation basketball rim with the break-away option is preferred for goals. Although the nylon or chain nets may be attached to the goal, the latter provides more durability and less maintenance.

Practice Walls: Practice walls may be constructed as part of the perimeter enclosure or as a separate area. Separate areas are desirable when funding and land are critical factors.

Outdoor Handball

Outdoor handball is played by two or four players in a one- or three-wall configuration, respectively. Courts generally are constructed in multiple back-to-back configurations (common front wall). The horizontal playing surface is made of concrete or asphalt concrete (with surface coating). The walls must be constructed with materials which will withstand wind loads and weathering. Cast-in-place concrete or pre-cast concrete is the preferred material. The courts should be pitched toward the rear of the court. Pitching the court to the sides or front wall may create difficulty in play or in drainage of water. The slope should be a minimum of one inch in 10 feet.

Shuffleboard

A level, highly polished playing surface, oriented on the north-south axis, is essential for play. A well-graded soil base course should be incorporated to facilitate subsurface drainage and minimize heaving due to frost. The surface should be poured as one monolithic surface to prevent irregularities in the playing surface. Backstops may be installed, however caution must be taken to design the backstops of materials which will absorb the force of the playing object, thereby preventing it from rebounding into the playing area. Seating generally is located at the sides of the courts.

Tennis

The United States Tennis Association (USTA) is one organization that has compiled extensive information regarding the planning, design, and construction of tennis facilities. The extent of services, publications, and consultants that this organization provides makes it difficult to address any single facet of the subject. Therefore, the subject of tennis facilities generally will be addressed as it relates to other facilities.

Practice Walls: Practice walls may be constructed as part of the perimeter enclosure or as a separate area. Separate areas are desirable when funding and land are critical factors.

Wind Screens: Wind screens provide a uniform colored background for identification of the ball during play and help reduce the effect of wind across the playing area. Wind screens should extend from the playing surface to 10 feet. (See Figures 3.6 and 3.7.)

DIAMOND FIELDS

General

The term "diamond fields" is associated with the sports played on an irregular shaped playing field, such as baseball and softball.

Area

The size of the playing area required for positioning of diamonds is based on the various skill levels.

Orientation

The diamond may be positioned in any orientation, provided that the user understands the limitation of each orientation. Ideally, the diamond axis, formed by a line between home plate and second base, should be positioned between south-southwest and north-northeast. The playing positions most affected by the sun angle are the batter, the pitcher, and the first baseman, in that order. Other orientations may limit the use of the field during the daylight hours due to a conflict between the sun position and the views on the field. (Figure 3.8.)

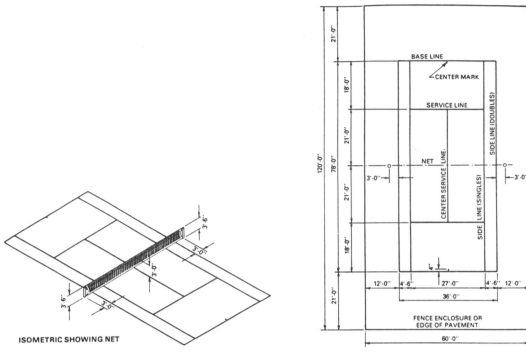

ISOMETRIC SHOWING NET

COURT LAYOUT

TENNIS

Figure 3.6. Tennis Court and Net

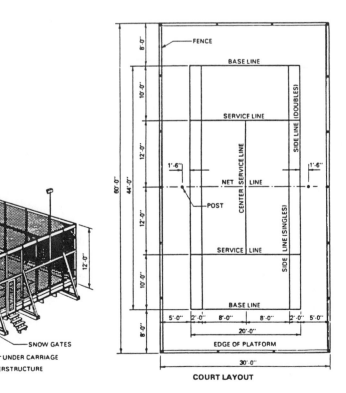

LIGHTS

PIER

TENSION FENCING

SNOW GATES

UNDER CARRIAGE

SUPERSTRUCTURE

ISOMETRIC SHOWING FENCE (TYPICAL WOOD CONSTRUCTION)

COURT LAYOUT

Figure 3.7. Platform Tennis

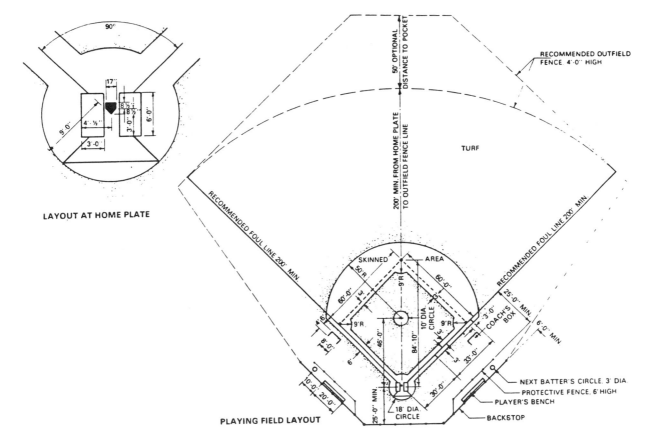

LAYOUT AT HOME PLATE

PLAYING FIELD LAYOUT

RECOMMENDED OUTFIELD FENCE 4'-0" HIGH

TURF

50' OPTIONAL DISTANCE TO POCKET

200' MIN. FROM HOME PLATE TO OUTFIELD FENCE LINE

RECOMMENDED FOUL LINE 200' MIN.

RECOMMENDED FOUL LINE 200' MIN.

SKINNED AREA

COACH'S BOX

NEXT BATTER'S CIRCLE, 3' DIA
PROTECTIVE FENCE, 6' HIGH
PLAYER'S BENCH
BACKSTOP

LITTLE LEAGUE BASEBALL

Figure 3.8. Little League Baseball Field

Risk Management

- Provide sufficient depth on the warning tracks at the perimeter of the field and the outfield to allow time for players to react to a potential impact with a barrier.

- Use break-away bases to minimize limb injuries.

- Construct team areas at grade. Depressed areas present hazards, such as an elevation change using steps.

- Provide protection of players in adjacent areas, such as the on-deck circle, team area, pitcher's area, batting cage, etc. through the use of fencing.

- Place display or advertising signage outside the playing area. Signage hung on walls inside the playing area at low levels presents potential hazards to players.

- Construct barriers to contain play within a designated area, especially where the playing area is limited. Players may run into the roads or other obstacles.

- The top and bottom fence wires should be bent over onto themselves to prevent puncture injuries.

- Posts or projections on fences should be covered.

Surfaces

The area planned for the playing field should be as near to level as possible. Importation of fill should be considered strongly to attain a level playing area. Sloped fields can present an unfair advantage to the offense or defense, depending on the layout.

Turf Areas

Soil Areas: Areas usually designed for soil are the pitcher's mound area, home plate area, baselines (inclu-ding the extended area beyond the baselines between the three bases), warning tracks, on-deck circles, and coaches' boxes. In some areas of the country, the whole infield is constructed of soil which can mean a faster play for the ball. The width of the warning track should be based on the perimeter location and the skill level of the players to provide sufficient time for the player to react when entering this area.

Drainage: The surface of the field should be sloped from a variety of points toward the exterior of the field to remove water from the playing area. The outfield should be sloped toward the outfield and the sidelines, while the infield should be sloped toward the baselines. Where the slope creates a significant elevation between the infield and the outfield, drainage tile may be installed at strategic locations or throughout the field to reduce the slope or to create a level field, respectively.

Team Areas, Dugouts: The traditional dugout, which usually is sunk into the ground, is a costly means of providing a team area. In addition to problems with removing water (drains become clogged due to maintenance), the perimeter steps and curb present obstacles to the players and remove valuable space for team use. An on-grade enclosure, a fence with a wind screen and weatherproof roof, offer protection from the elements while focusing the players' thoughts on the game. Openings should be provided at each end for access to the field. The end closest to home plate should provide access to the field through an adjacent "on-deck area." An enclosed on-deck area is advisable for all skill levels and a necessity for the lower skill levels to protect inexperienced players. Storage containers for player's gloves, bats, etc. should be incorporated into the layout.

Fencing: The fence behind the plate should be at least 20 feet in height. A fence of at least four feet in height may be used around the sides of the field, except where spectators may be affected by direct-hit foul balls. In this case, the fence should be of sufficient height to prevent line drives from entering into the stands. The outfield fence should be a minimum of eight feet in height. Fence posts should be positioned on the outside of the fence. Where the possibility exists of contact with a post, such as in the outfield, the posts should be covered with padding to protect the players. Openings in the fence should be made by gates or off-set fence posts.

Backstops: The purpose of the backstop is to contain the ball within play. Secondary to this is the protection of the spectators. Backstops generally are constructed of wire fencing and posts extending between 20 feet and 30 feet above the ground. Backstops are constructed in a variety of configurations, ranging from semi-circular to angular. The design of the backstop should be given serious thought. Too often the fencing extends over the plate and the area behind the

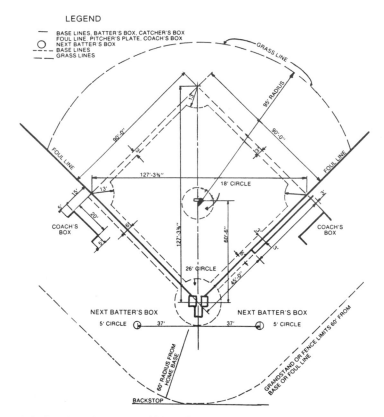

Figure 3.9. Baseball Field (1992 NCAA Baseball Rules)

plate creating a canopy which can limit the play of the catcher. If a sloped canopy is required for structural integrity between offset posts, then the canopy projection into the playing area should be the minimum necessary to provide support.

Distractions: To minimize distractions for the pitcher, a single-colored wind screen should be placed on the fence behind the catcher. This screen provides a distraction-free, uniform, visual background surface for the pitcher and may minimize the possibility of wild pitches. A similar wind screen should be placed on the center field fence to provide the catcher with a uniform visual background for picking up the baseball thrown by the pitcher.

Scoreboards: Scoreboards for baseball should be positioned so that they may be seen by both players and spectators. Generally a location just outside the center field fence is considered most advantageous. Posi-

tions along the sidelines may be screened from view of players and spectators. Scoreboards should contain the following information as a minimum: names of teams playing, runs obtained in each inning for each team, inning number, number of outs per inning, and total runs. Operation is electronic or through manual replacement of cards.

Pitching Area: A practice pitching area should be provided behind each team area. This area should be positioned outside the playing area and enclosed with a fence at least six feet in height to contain pitches.

Batting Area: Consideration should be given to constructing an enclosed cage for batting practice. This permits batting practice to be conducted while the field is being used by other players or other activities. The small investment in fencing will increase the flexibility of the facility. As a minimum, a small cage should be provided where batters may practice with the batting tee. The ideal is a full length, enclosed batting cage. Enclosing the area is to protect people outside the cage, protect the batter from stray balls thrown from outside the cage, and contain baseballs. The length of the cage will depend upon the skill level to use the cage. The width and the height each should be 16 feet. A small shed might be considered to house a batting machine if one is available. The shed, if attached to the cage, should be located to the side and open into the space. A uniform background behind the machine may be unwise since this will give the batter a false security in identifying the baseball.

SPORTS FIELDS

General

The term ''sports fields'' is associated with sports played on a rectilinear playing field, such as football, soccer, field hockey, lacrosse, etc. (Figures 3.10, 3.11, 3.12, 3.13.)

Area

The area required for each type of activity is based on such factors as the level of play and the category of play, that is, competitive or recreational.

Orientation

Sports fields should be oriented so that the direction of play is in the north-south direction, that is, the goals should be perpendicular to the north-south axis.

Risk Management

- Goal posts should be covered with tear-resistant protective padding to a height of eight feet.
- Components of the irrigation system should be located below ground level and extend upward to water the playing surface area. Protective covers should be placed over the area when the system is not in use. Whenever possible, the heads should be placed outside the primary playing surface area and

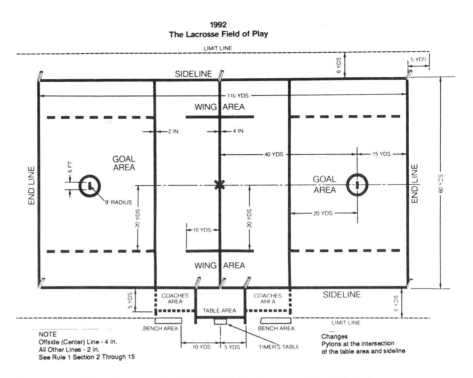

Figure 3.10. Men's Lacrosse Field (1992 NCAA Lacrosse, Men's Rules)

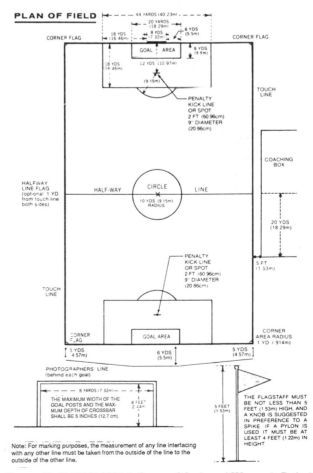

Figure 3.11. Soccer Field (1991 NCAA Soccer, Men's and Women's Rules)

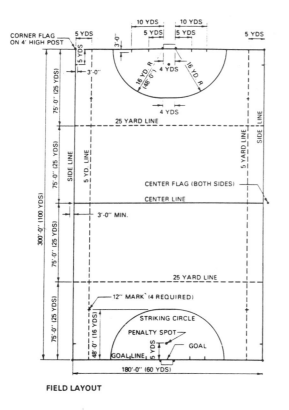

FIELD LAYOUT

FIELD HOCKEY

Figure 3.12. Field Hockey

supplemental irrigation systems should be used in areas where the underground system cannot water.

- Corner post supports should be imbedded below the playing surface. Posts should have the capability to bend over when contact is made by the player.

- Goals (lacrosse and soccer) should have the ability to "break-away" from the underground field support in the event of a collision.

TRACK & FIELD EVENTS

General

The planning and design of facilities for track and field events generally is based on two concepts: a separate, independent facility or a combined multi-sport facility. The decision to choose one concept over the other depends on several considerations regarding funding, availability of space for all

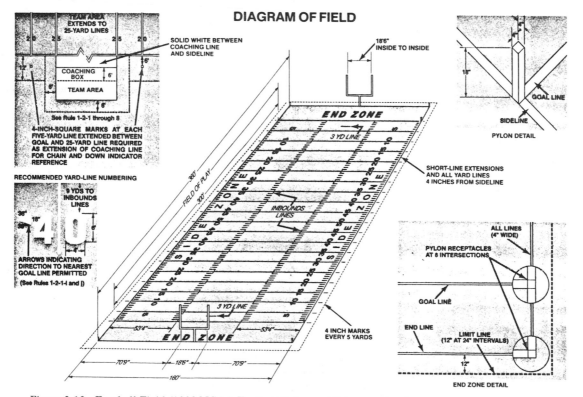

DIAGRAM OF FIELD

Figure 3.13. Football Field (1992 NCAA Football Rules and Interpretations)

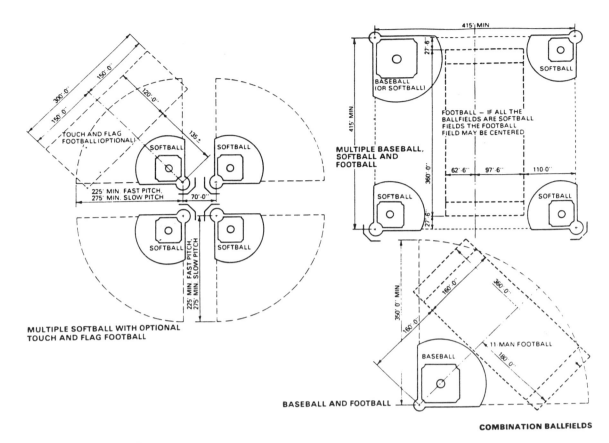

Figure 3.14. Combination Ball Fields

sporting events, space for spectators, and type of surface materials selected. The field events include the steeplechase, the high jump, the pole vault, the long jump, the triple jump, the shot put, the hammer throw, the discus throw, and the javelin. (Figures 3.15, 3.16, 3.17.)

The Independent Facility

Characteristics of the independent facility:

- requires duplication of space for the event areas as well as spectator areas
- single sport use
- maintenance work load presumably will double
- infield may be used for other sports as a practice or alternate game area

The Combined Multi-Sport Facility

Characteristics of the multi-sport facility:

- may pose scheduling problems between sports using the area for practice as well as games
- may require more maintenance attention than normal since the load usage has increased
- where synthetic turf is used on the infield, an additional area will be required for field events, such as javelin and hammer.

Layout - Orientation

The arrangement of track and field events is an exercise in efficient use of space as well as creative programming of activities. The field events generally take place within a turf-covered area (infield) surrounded by a track used for running events. Generally, the infield area is large enough to include one or more field sports.

The track and field events are oriented along the long axis of the track in a north-south direction to minimize the effects of the sun on the activities. The straight portion of the track used for sprint running should be located on the west side of the track, along with spectator seating. This position will minimize the effect on the participants, as well as eliminate spectators' viewing into the low-angle sunlight. Where funding is available, straight track portions and dual-oriented field events may be included to take advantage of seasonal changes of the wind. The area approximately eight feet to 10 feet inside the track should remain open for participant stretching/warm-up and coaching.

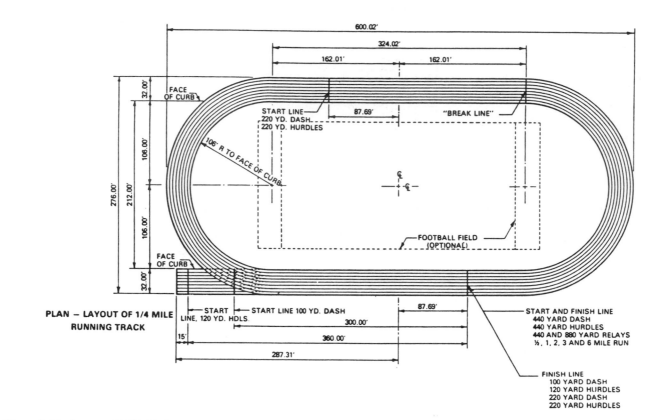

PLAN — LAYOUT OF 1/4 MILE RUNNING TRACK

Figure 3.15. Layout of 1/4 Mile Running Track

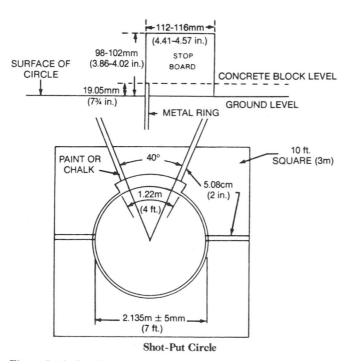

Shot-Put Circle

Figure 3.16. Shot Put Circle (1992 NCAA Track & Field/Cross Country Men's and Women's Rules)

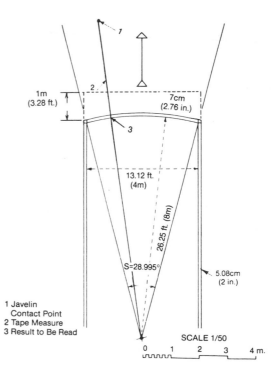

1 Javelin
  Contact Point
2 Tape Measure
3 Result to Be Read

Javelin Throwing Area

Figure 3.17. Javelin Throwing Area (1992 NCAA Track & Field/Cross Country Men's and Women's Rules)

Surfaces

The track surface and surfaces for certain field events may consist of an aggregate composition, natural turf, or synthetic material. Surfaces for landing pits should consist of sand or a sand/composition mixture. Surfaces for throwing circles should consist of concrete.

Drainage

The track should pitch toward the infield area. Drains should be located approximately eight feet to 10 feet inside the track. These drains also may be used to collect water from the infield area. Each approach area should be pitched to drain surface water adequately. The landing pits for the long jump and the triple jump should have separate subsurface drainage systems to remove water. Where curbs are provided on the inside of the track, they should have openings for passage of surface water to drains.

Markings

Markings for the track and field events should be located by survey. The layout should be certified by the installing engineer in accordance with current regulations.

Steeplechase

The water obstacle may be located on the inside (with banked track) or outside of the track surface. An additional running surface must be provided for the approach to and departure from the water jump. The track curb must be removable in this area if the water obstacle is located on the inside of the track.

Pole Vault

The orientation of the runway and pit should be such that the prevailing winds are at the vaulter's back.

Jumping Events

The orientation of the runway and pit should put the prevailing winds at the jumper's back or side. The top elevation of the sand in the pits shall be at the same elevation of the take-off board. Leveling boards (screeds) should be incorporated.

Throwing Circles

The throwing circle should have a slip-resistant surface.

REFERENCES

Berg, Rick. November,1990. "Getting on the Tight Track." *Athletic Business*, pp. 63-67.

Berg, Rick. May, 1990. "Turf Enough For Everyone." *Athletic Business*, pp. 63-66.

DeChiara, J. and Callendar, J.H. 1990. *Time Saver Standards for Building Types.* New York: McGraw-Hill.

Departments of the Army, Navy, and Air Force. March, 1981. *Installation Design.* Army Technical Manual TM 5-803.5.

Departments of the Army, Navy, and Air Force. October, 1975. *Planning and Design of Outdoor Sports Facilities.* Army Technical Manual (TM) 5-803-10.

Flynn, Richard B. (Ed.). 1985. *Planning Facilities for Athletics, Physical Education and Recreation,* The Athletic Institute and American Alliance for Health, Physical Education, Recreation and Dance.

Flynn, Richard B. 1990. ''Sports Surfaces.'' In Morris B. Mellion, M.D.; W. Michael Walsh, M.D.; and Guy L. Shelton, P.T., A.T.C. (Eds.). *The Team Physician's Handbook,* Philadelphia, PA: Hanley and Belfus, pp. 47-58.

Frier, John P.March,1990. "Outdoor Lighting Beams Ahead." *Athletic Business*, pp. 41-47.

Frier, John P. September, 1989. "Selecting Proper Sports Light- ing." *American School & University,* pp. 37-39

Gold, Seymour M. 1980. *Recreation Planning and Design.* New York: McGraw-Hill.

Illuminating Engineering Society of North America. 1988. *Sports Light: Recommended Practice for Sports and Recreation Area Lighting.* New York: IES.

Johnston, Robert J. November, 1991. "Surface Tension." *Athletic Business*, pp. 59-61.

Jones, Tilford C. April, 1990. "Choosing Court Colors." *Athletic Business*, pp. 60-61.

Kelsey, Craig and Gray, Howard (1986). *Feasibility Study Process for Parks and Recreation.* Reston, VA: American Alliance for Health, Physical Recreation, and Dance.

Moon, Douglas V. May, 1987. "1 Lighted Field = 2 Unlighted Fields Plus Cost Savings." *Athletic Business*, pp. 40-46.

MUSCO-Sports Lighting 1982, rev. 1990. *Guidelines for Recreation and Athletic Field Lighting.* MUSCO Lighting, Inc.

MUSCO-Sports Lighting 1990. *Facts of Lighting.* MUSCO Lighting, Inc.

NCAA Guides. Overland Park, KS: National Collegiate Athletic Assoc.

Penman, Kenneth A. 1977. *Planning Physical Education and Athletic Facilities in Schools.* New York: Wiley.

United States Tennis Association. 1990-1991. *Tennis Courts.* Lynn, MA: H.O. Zimman.

ABOUT THE AUTHOR: Bradley A. Macomber is a Sports Facilities Resource Consultant with two nationally recognized architecture firms.

Chapter 4
SWIMMING POOLS AND NATATORIA

by D.J. Hunsaker

The purpose of this chapter is to review current trends in swimming pools and natatoria.

The field of aquatics has experienced a broad and comprehensive transition since the early 1980s. From the standpoint of professional programming, activities have been developed for all age groups with attendance increasing mostly among seniors, followed closely by preschoolers. Through the entire age span, North Americans have found aquatic activity in outdoor and indoor swimming facilities to provide entertainment, education, and skill enhancement.

Until the 1970s, swimming/diving activities almost always took place in a rectangular swimming pool which was shallow at one end and deep at the other. The introduction of the wave pool at Point Mallard, Alabama in the late 1960s demonstrated the opportunity to have more fun and excitement in a man-made swimming tank that was filled with filtered and hygienically clean water. This new approach led to successive facilities in the commercial sector which are called water parks. As private capital underwrote these projects, public agencies at the municipal and county level began to experiment with non-rectangular pools which featured zero entry water areas, waterslides, and children's water play

Figures 4.1a and 4.1b. Children enjoying leisure pool activities (Courtesy of Counsilman/Hunsaker & Associates)

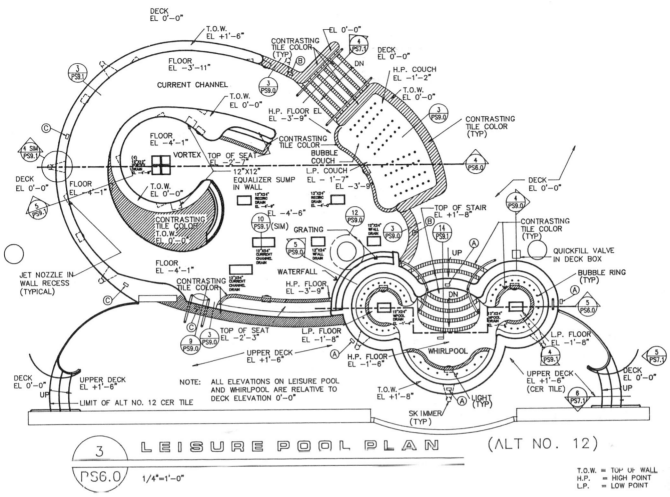

Figure 4.2. Leisure pool plan (Courtesy of Counsilman/Hunsaker and Associates)

areas. While most of these initiatives with moving water have been cautious, the trend in public aquatic recreation definitely is moving toward the design philosophy which is accepted on a broad front in western Europe, Canada, and Japan.

AQUATIC CENTER TRENDS

Leisure Pool Features

Leisure pool features include water falls, fountains, whirlpools, current channels, lazy rivers, and participatory water play apparatus. They must be designed carefully, considering first costs, operating costs, life cycle costs, and long-term popularity. (Figures 4.1a and b.)

Falling water can be a dramatic focal point in a natatorium or an outdoor aquatic center. An indoor facility must be designed with acoustical treatment to reduce the reverberation time of the splash noise. An indoor facility also must be designed to minimize atomization of water. Falling water is different from the misting of sprays. The latter will increase the humidity in the space and increase the water vapor inhaled by people in the natatorium.

Current channels, lazy rivers, and water slides must be designed for safety and economy of operation. Since many states do not have regulations that specifically address these new concepts in aquatic recreation features, designers must work with jurisdictional officials to develop systems, designs, and configurations that reflect the philoso-

phy of the agency. Computer technology is a cost effective component of water features when used to activate and deactivate motors. The motors control the water pumps in an economical sequence which varies at different times of the day, week, and season. (Figure 4.2.)

Water slides offer many options for the leisure pool designer. Most installations are engineered by manufacturers based upon the design developed by the architect. The resulting protocol is essentially design/build and allows the configuration to be developed by the organization that is most knowledgeable about this very specialized equipment. In so doing, the manufacturer/designer/constructor accepts the liability for the product.

Figure 4.3. Water slides are becoming a common feature.

With few exceptions, the water slide industry produces only fiberglass flumes. The slides can be open or totally enclosed as a tube. Each year more elaborate designs are produced for large and small venues. (Figure 4.3.)

Current channels and lazy rivers can be designed in a variety of ways. The difference between the two concepts is the velocity of the current and the length of the channel. The lazy river is usually a closed loop that allows the participant to float continuously at a slow speed, where the current channel is a part of the leisure pool that provides a relatively short flume with a much faster current.

Therapy Pools and Whirlpool Spas

Another new type of pool that is appearing with frequency in North Am-erica is the therapy pool. These pools are being included in the construction of new wellness and fitness centers, many of which are being developed by hospitals. The therapy pool usually features an access ramp, recessed stairs, underwater benches, a deep water area, and hydraulic lifts or movable floors for the non-ambulatory. These pools can be a part of an out-patient facility that specializes in treatment for temporary disabilities, i.e., post-surgical, post-injury or post-trauma, cardiac, etc. Other pools are located in rehabilitation centers for in-patients with permanent disabilities, i.e., paraplegia, quadriplegia, stroke, multiple sclerosis, etc. Such pools also are in health care facilities that specialize in the treatment and/or care of the physically and mentally disturbed. In many cases the therapy pools are designed for and serve a variety of user groups. (Figure 4.4.)

The whirlpool spa has become a standard water feature in many natatoria at municipal, college, and university sites. However, the spa seldom is seen in high school natatoria. Spas also are popular in health clubs and wellness centers. Their appeal is wide among frequent users of a recreation and fitness center. (Figure 4.5.)

Pools and Natatoria

Many new public and semi-public pools are being built in North America because of a demand by communities and their residents. While most new facilities are the conventional outdoor competition pools, the free form leisure pools (with or without waves) are gaining support from the park and recreation professional.

Figure 4.4. Tulane University--Sports medicine/hydrotherapy area (Photo by David Richmond)

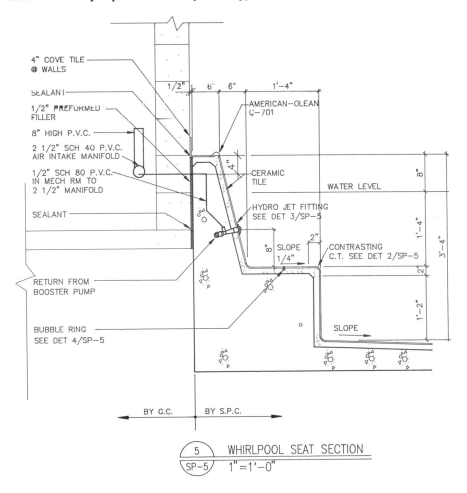

4" COVE TILE
@ WALLS

SEALANT

1/2" PREFORMED
FILLER

8" HIGH P.V.C.

2 1/2" SCH 40 P.V.C.
AIR INTAKE MANIFOLD

1/2" SCH 80 P.V.C.
IN MECH RM TO
2 1/2" MANIFOLD

SEALANT

RETURN FROM
BOOSTER PUMP

BUBBLE RING
SEE DET 4/SP-5

AMERICAN-OLEAN
C-701

CERAMIC
TILE

WATER LEVEL

HYDRO JET FITTING
SEE DET 3/SP-5

SLOPE
1/4"

CONTRASTING
C.T. SEE DET 2/SP-5

1/2"   6"   6"   1'-4"

4"

8"

8"   SLOPE
        2"

1'-4"   3'-4"

2"

1'-2"

SLOPE

BY G.C.   BY S.P.C.

5
SP-5   WHIRLPOOL SEAT SECTION
        1"=1'-0"

Indoor natatoria are being built increasingly also. These facilities are being created frequently in Canada with its colder climates, as well as throughout the United States. The reasons are several. The year-round benefits are being recognized along with the justification of higher capital costs for the 12-month programs they provide. Other indoor aquatic centers are being constructed at educational institutions to meet an expanding demand on the campus; and to meet the competition from other schools, colleges, and universities, which are targeting the same prospective student. (Figure 4.6.)

These indoor facilities, along with others in health clubs, wellness centers, the YMCA, and the JCCA, etc. are providing the opportunity for their respective populations to recreate and develop skills that will enhance the aquatic experience throughout a life-

time. ''Moms and Tots'' programs introduce infants to the water in the most secure environment, i.e., in the mother's (or father's) arms. Preschoolers also have the opportunity to learn to swim and be water safe in a way that provides the foundation for lifelong participation in water sports. Competitive swimming and diving is usually the next plateau that the young person will master, although many youngsters find their enjoyment in unstructured recreation swimming. Other skills are learned in the aquatic centers. These include advanced swimming techniques, lifesaving, lifeguarding, and scuba. Many of these skills will carry over into family pastimes and fitness regimens. The latter usually takes form as fitness lap swimming on a year-round basis.

Regardless of the reason for creating a new swim center,

a definite protocol should be followed to produce the most efficient, cost effective, and programmable facility. This chapter describes this necessary procedure and discipline for creating the facility that will best meet the owner's needs.

NEEDS ANALYSIS

While many people believe that the first step is to select an architect, there really are two essential tasks that should be executed before an architect is asked to design a building. The first is to analyze the needs of the organization/owner; the second is to develop a design program for the facility. This analysis of needs is executed by identifying the current users, potential users, and future users. A description of the activities that these users will want is supplemented by a list of activities and programs that the organ-

Figure 4.6. An indoor aquatic center   (Courtesy of Counsilman/Hunsaker and Associates)

ization/owner's aquatic staff believes is warranted for the activity program in the new facility.

The analysis of the community's needs is more than a simple list. The data also must show the time and space requirements for the various activities proposed. This allocation of time and space will reveal potential priorities and demands.

The first step toward the objective is to develop an in-depth understanding of deficiencies in the existing aquatic program and the potential for meeting future demand. This can be carried out best by an individual or individuals with experience in this important phase. It is at this time that some organizations/owner groups seek the assistance of a design and planning consultant to help them develop the information needed to take the correct and necessary steps toward a commitment to such a complex.

The first phase of the needs analysis is a meeting with the staff and the administration, followed by meetings with user groups. As a means of developing an understanding of the true core needs of the community, interviews are conducted, public meetings are held, and existing data are reviewed, including previous programs and previous efforts. Finally, a consensus must be developed among the various parties interested in the project.

Once the needs have been established and agreed to by all parties, the next step is to develop a design program. The design program is an outline of the features that must be provided in the aquatic center and a designation of the area required for each feature. This process includes not only the natatorium but also the necessary support spaces for the aquatic center.

Once the spaces have been identified and have been given surface area values, it then is possible to develop an estimate of the construction cost. This is done by identifying the square footage involved, estimating a cost per square foot by using a conventional formula, comparing the industry average for recent construction, comparing this information to similar projects in like construction market areas, and adding an escalation factor to reflect the time frame between completed projects and the date of the bidding for the proposed project.

As these numbers are developed, it is essential that a distinction is made between construction costs and project costs. This is an area that often is misunderstood, and construction costs are emphasized when, in reality, the total project cost must be determined. A project cost includes the hard cost of construction, plus all of the soft costs of loose equipment, administration, and design required for the end product.

Once the project cost has been established and confirmed, it is necessary to move on to the source of financing. This source may be a capital fund drive, the state legislature (university and college), a bond issue, certificates of participation, a capital expansion budget, donations, a build/lease back, or a combination of the above.

After the source of funding has been identified and a commitment received, the next step is to select an architectural team. There is a protocol which should be followed in this phase of the project. The first step is to develop a request for qualifications, which is a formal communication in letter form that is sent to a number of architectural firms. A formal advertisement also is placed in the newspaper. The respective firms will determine whether they wish to be considered for such a project. If they do, they will submit by a specified date a package which will reflect information about their selected team, as well as past history and experience with projects of all types including, presumably, those similar to the proposed project.

These submittals will be reviewed, and a selection committee will choose a limited number for an interview. The interview of the respective architectural teams will be scheduled for a specific period of time, and the firms will be given a format for their presentation which usually includes 60 to 75 percent of the time for a formal presentation and 40 to 25 percent of the time for answering questions by the interview committee.

The interview process should follow a certain format, and the interview committee should be experienced or at least prepared for a methodical evaluation of the different teams. The important issue is to create a structure whereby all teams are given the same opportunity and benefit relative to presentation time and question- and-answer opportunities.

In addition to the interview, it is suggested that the background and experience of the respective teams be researched with former clients.

The final step is to select the architectural team and to sign agreements between the owner and the architectural firm that will lead the team throughout the project. This firm usually is identified as the project architect or architect of record.

What are the tasks and scope of services of the chosen architectural team? At this point an owner's steering committee should be formed, which is made up of individuals representing the users, the administration, the staff, and the owner's project manager. Together this group must be qualified to make decisions as the process moves forward.

PROGRAMMING

Much of this work was done when the design program was developed prior to determining funding needs. At this time the owner and the architect will confirm the design program surface area needs and requirements developed in the design program stage. The construction cost estimate will be reviewed and confirmed or changed by the project architect. As a result there will be a confirmation of the project cost estimate at this time.

An aquatic center or a community center featuring a natatorium is a very complex building. It is helpful if the organization/owner's steering committee understands the situation and the necessary design process. By comparison, a more simple building is an office building which basically repeats floor plans floor to floor, and which has very few special use areas in the building. The next level of complexity may be a school which still features a lot of redundancy in the classroom requirements with several special areas such as a gymnasium, auditorium, lunch room, etc. The next level of complexity is the special use building which describes a community center or an aquatic center. In this type of building there is very little redundancy, and the entire facility is unique unto itself. As a result, the design time is much greater than, for example, the office building. The square foot cost usually is higher because of the special features and characteristics that the building must provide.

Once the design program and corresponding budget estimate is confirmed, the architect will develop a series of bubble diagrams and adjacency priorities. This information will be discussed with the steering committee and a consensus reached.

The next step is to develop a schematic floor plan which will reflect the data developed in the step above. It is at this point that floor plans, access points, and general operating efficiency will be developed.

As the above issues are resolved, the schematic plans and elevations (single line drawings) will be developed. The schematics will be reviewed by the steering committee, and after discussions and contributions by all members, a consensus will be arrived at, resulting in an approved set of schematics. At this point it may be necessary for the architect to create a study model. Some architectural teams prefer the use of the models as a means of evaluating and studying the total building, both inside and outside. Once

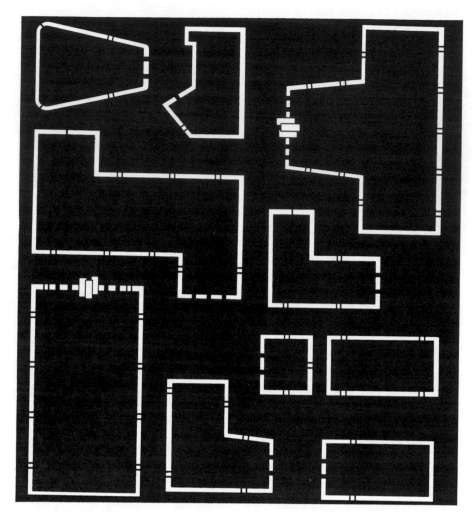

Figure 4.7. Some typical pool shapes.

the model has been approved, an estimate of construction costs will again be developed.

If the project is on course with budget and program, the design development stage will begin, and more detailed drawings will be created at this time. Outline specifications also will be developed by the architect and the various consultants on the design team. These will be reviewed by the steering committee. The outline specifications and design development drawings will be used to provide an update of estimated construction costs. (A constant monitoring of construction cost estimates is necessary to keep the project in line with the budget.)

At this time the steering committee will be required to work closely with the architect until the design development drawings and outline specifications are approved.

Once the design development stage has been completed, the next phase is creation of the construction documents, i.e., drawings, specifications, and general conditions.

When the construction documents are approximately 50 percent completed, a review should occur again with the various consultants and the steering committee. This is an effective point to estimate again the construction costs and see if there is any necessity for a mid-course correction. When the construction documents reach 90 to 100

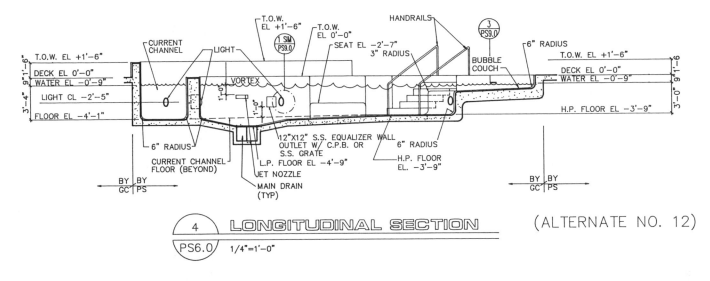

Figure 4.8. Longitudinal section of a pool (Courtesy of Counsilman/Hunsaker and Associates)

percent completion, they should be reviewed again by the respective consultants and the owner's steering committee. If all team members are in agreement and there are no omissions or errors, the architect will assist the owner in advertising for bids.

When the bids are opened one of three things will occur:

- The project will be under budget, and the design team will proceed or add any add alternates that may have been called out in the construction documents.

- The budget will be the same as the accepted bid, and the project will proceed into the next stage.

- The low bid will be over budget, and deduct alternates will be deleted.

In the event there is a significant over-budget situation, even after deduct alternates, a common process is to submit the overall design for value engineering and develop a priority of deletions. This sometimes is done in concert with the low bid contractor.

When the construction contract has been signed between the owner and the general contractor, the project then moves into the construction phase. At this time it also should be noted that there is an alternative to a general contractor protocol and that is the use, by the owner, of a construction management firm. In construction management, an experienced management team serves as a contract manager for the owner, in which case the construction management firm is paid a fee for its expertise. As the owner's agent, the construction management company negotiates directly with the respective subcontractors. While a relatively new concept, the construction management approach does offer some benefits in certain types of projects.

WHAT HAPPENS DURING THE CONSTRUCTION OF THE NATATORIUM?

Site Situations: Ideally the site for an aquatic center is level with good quality soil. Many times, however, the site is not level and there are subsoil problems, i.e., rock, high water table, undesirable types of soil, cuts and fill, compaction, removal and replacement with engineered fill.

Design Options: A swimming pool and/or natatorium may feature several below grade designs. One is a full basement, another is a tunnel around the pool shell, a third is a pool shell backfilled with no below grade space, and a fourth is a combination of any/or all of the above.

Benefits and Disadvantages of Basements

Benefits: The basement can provide a storage area, equipment area, piping and plenum location, access for maintenance repair, and no hydrostatic pressure on the pool shell. (The problem of hydrostatic pressure under a swimming pool is significant. If there is a high water table, and no means have been created for relieving this pressure, it is possible that the swimming pool can float out of the ground at a time when it is empty, due to construction or maintenance. For this reason, special considerations must be made and appropriate designs engineered.)

Disadvantages: The below grade space creates greater costs, delivery problems for mechanical equipment used in the below grade areas, remote chemical rooms relative to the filter equipment, and sometimes access problems for maintenance personnel.

Swimming Pools and Natatoria   97

Swimming Pool Shell Construction

Cast-in-place concrete--

Advantages: The structure can be built above grade or surrounded by a tunnel/basement, and there is no backfill required. It can be included in the conventional concrete work by the concrete contractor. It is advantageous for tile and a paint finish.

Disadvantages: It is costly to create in a free form configuration; water stop and honeycombing leaks are possible, and the wall-to-floor cove is more costly to build as compared to pneumatically applied concrete.

Pneumatically applied concrete swimming pool shells--

Benefits: It is relatively economical pool shell construction when the pool walls are constructed against a soil embankment or cut. Irregular shapes can be constructed efficiently and at a relatively low cost compared to cast-in-place. The wall-to-floor cove is simple and effective. Monolithic pneumatically applied concrete construction has advantages over the cast components in a cast-in-place pool which depend upon water stop at joints. It is compatible with tile and marble plaster adhesion.

Disadvantages: It is costly and difficult to build a pneumatically applied pool with no earth cavity. The necessary forms needed for this type of construction erode the cost benefit of the process. Sometimes it is difficult to apply tile to the swimming pool interior. When painting is required, a multi-step preparation procedure is necessary. Often times it is difficult to find experienced and qualified contractors in a local bidding market.

Structural Features In the Natatorium

The first choice is structural steel with concrete and masonry walls, plus a concrete roof system.

Because of cost, most natatorium roof structures are made of mild steel beams, joists, and trusses. When these steel components are used, they must be coated with highly effective, long-life coating systems. The roof and ceiling systems must be designed carefully to withstand corrosion created by condensation.

Wood roof structures are effective if humidity is controlled and air circulation in the space is properly engineered.

A concrete roof structure has many advantages over steel and wood. It is non-corrosive and durable. Its cost, however, is greater than the other two lighter weight options.

Fenestration: Skylights or top lighting are advantageous for location of a natural light source and control of reflective glare on the water. The relation of fenestration to spectator areas, lifeguard locations, and teaching stations is important. Wall and room penetrations for skylights, exhaust ducts, and overhead light fixtures can be the source of problems. As a result, they must be designed, engineered, and constructed with care.

Dehumidification: It is known now that relative humidity inside a natatorium should be maintained between 50 and 60 percent. This can be done best in most areas with the use of refrigerated dehumidification. Such a design must control the dew point, be operated on a 24-hour basis, control condensation, and control the air velocities in the space along with the fresh air mix for needed ventilation. The creature comfort is most noticeable in this phase of the building system.

Materials and Finishes: Because of the high humidity potential and aggressive conditions that may occur in the natatorium space if mechanical systems are shut down either on purpose or by accident, the material choices are the following: tile, epoxy coated steel (stainless steel used in some swimming pool components), glass, concrete, and anodized aluminum.

Considerations for maintenance tasks are important in the design process. These consist of daily custodial needs, scheduled repair and maintenance, emergency repair and/or replacement, future repair and replacement (pool filters/HVAC/dehumidification).

During the construction process a system of inspections and monitoring should be carried out by the owner or his/her representative, i.e., architect/engineer/consultant. This process is necessary to watch for incorrect installation as well as improper components.

COMMISSIONING

This is the important climax to the entire process that has been executed to date. The general contractor, swimming pool contractor, other contractors, the project architect, respective engineers, and the swimming pool/natatorium consultants will coordinate efforts and put the facility into operation. In this process, notes will be made of any and all problems and/or deficiencies. Responsible contractors will make the proper corrections so that the swimming pool and all related systems for the complex will operate according to design and in compliance with all jurisdictional codes and regulations. Likewise, the mechanical HVAC/DH systems will be commissioned.

Because most contracts call for a one year warranty period, it is recommended that a comprehensive inspection be executed just prior to the expiration of the warranty deadline. It is recommended that an independent and qualified inspector make this audit because often times a swimming pool system or piece of equipment will be operating, but not as it should. Such a situation should be noted, documented, and reported to the owner's representative who will notify the responsible contractor for corrective action under the warranty.

Upon the completion of the construction phase and after a final check out (punch list), an orientation of the organization/owner's management and operations staff should take place. This is a step that often is overlooked or minimized. With a multi million dollar complex it is understandable that a thorough and professional set of instructions, including start up procedures, trouble shooting, and daily operation procedures as well as periodic maintenance tasks, should be provided in a well-documented, written operations manual. In addition, a resource contact should be provided for working with the operator as the owner takes over and puts the new facility into use.

TECHNICAL CONSIDERATIONS

Dimensions: The designer of the swimming pool must select the correct dimensions when creating the bounded water volume of the pool(s). Exact dimensions are required for pools which will be used for swimming and diving competitions. These include:

- length
- width
- depths (minimum and maximum)
- bottom profiles
- tolerances and allowances, i.e., touchpad, construction and bulkhead adjustment
- perimeter overflow tolerance at rim flow. (Figures 4.9a,b.)

There is no exception for these types of pools if they are going to be used for organized competition under the sanction of any one of the rule making entities, i.e., Federation Internationale de Natation Amateur, United States Swimming, United States Diving, United States Synchronized Swimming, United States Water Polo, National Collegiate Athletic Association, and the National Federation of State High School Associations and Swimming/Natation Canada. The

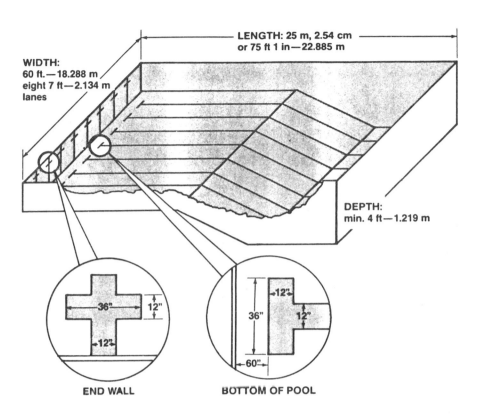

Figure 4.9a. NCAA pool diagram, dimensions and equipment requirements.

following dimensions are provided as an example, however the reader should contact the appropriate association for accurate and updated information prior to finalizing building plans.

Other bodies of water are not as demanding for exact or predetermined measurements, with the exception of health department safety regulations. These consist of minimum depths in shallow water and in diving areas. The degree of slope of the pool bottom in the shallow water and in the deep area usually is dictated by such regulations.

Free form pools are becoming popular in the public sector as "leisure pools" and are appearing at resort hotels, water parks, community aquatic centers, and even schools, colleges, and universities.

Access for the physically disabled has been a design requirement in swimming pools since the 1970s. Methods of egress for the disabled vary. The most popular is the permanent ramp and is used by all attendees whether or not they are disabled. Other systems include portable ramps and stairs plus hydraulic or mechanical lifts. The latter use permanent or temporary anchors in the pool deck. With the creation of new enforcement powers in 1992, more products will become available in years to follow.

INTERIOR FINISHES

Ceramic tile is considered the best choice for the interior of a swimming or diving pool. Its durability, appearance, and

POOL DIMENSIONS AND EQUIPMENT

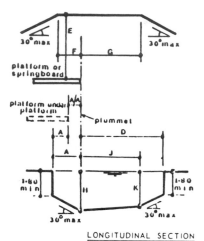

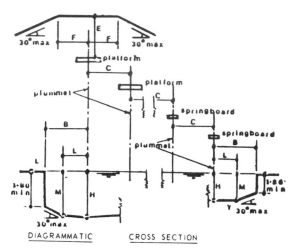

| LONGITUDINAL SECTION | DIAGRAMMATIC | CROSS SECTION |

NCAA Dimensions for Diving Facilities		Dimensions are in Feet	SPRINGBOARD		PLATFORM		
			1 Metre	3 Metres	5 Metres	7.5 Metres	10 Metres
		LENGTH	16'	16'	20'	20'	20'
		WIDTH	1'8"	1'8"	5'	5'	6'7"
		HEIGHT	3'4"	10'	16'5"	24'8"	32'10"
Revised to 1st Jan. 1987			Horiz. Vert.	Horiz. Vert.	Horiz. Vert.	Horiz. Vert.	Horiz. Vert.
A	From plummet BACK TO POOL WALL	Designation	A-1	A-3	A-5	A-7.5	A-10
		Minimum	6'	6'	4'2"	5'	5'
AA	From plummet BACK TO PLATFORM plummet directly below	Designation			AA5/1	AA7.5/3/1	AA10/5/3/1
		Minimum			5'	5'	5'
B	From plummet to POOL WALL AT SIDE	Designation	B-1	B-3	B-5	B-7.5	B-10
		Minimum	8'3"	11'6"	14'	14'10"	17'3"
C	From plummet to ADJACENT PLUMMET	Designation	C-1/1	C-3/3/1	C-5/3/1	C-7.5/5/3/1	C-10/7.5/5/3/1
		Minimum	8'	8'6"	8'6"	8'6"	9'
D	From plummet to POOL WALL AHEAD	Designation	D-1	D-3	D-5	D-7.5	D-10
		Minimum	29'	34'	34'	36'	45'
E	On plummet, from BOARD TO CEILING	Designation	E-1	E-3	E-5	E-7.5	E-10
		Minimum	16'5"	16'5"	11'6"	11'6"	16'5"
F	CLEAR OVERHEAD behind and each side of plummet	Designation	F-1 E-1	F-3 E-3	F-5 E-5	F-7.5 E-7.5	F-10 E-10
		Minimum	8'3" 16'6"	8'3" 16'6"	9' 11'6"	9' 11'6"	9' 16'6"
G	CLEAR OVERHEAD ahead of plummet	Designation	G-1 E-1	G-3 E-3	G-5 E-5	G-7.5 E-7.5	G-10 E-10
		Minimum	16'5" 16'6"	16'5" 16'5"	16'5" 11'6"	16'5" 11'6"	19'8" 16'5"
H	DEPTH OF WATER at plummet	Designation	H-1	H-3	H-5	H-7.5	H-10
		Minimum	11'	12'	14'2"	15'	16'
J-K	DISTANCE AND DEPTH ahead of plummet	Designation	J-1 K-1	J-3 K-3	J-5 K-5	J-7.5 K-7.5	J-10 K-10
		Minimum	16'5" 11'8"	20' 12'2"	20' 12'10"	26'3" 14'6"	36'2" 15'6"
L-M	DISTANCE AND DEPTH each side of plummet	Designation	L-1 M-1	L-3 M-3	L-5 M-5	L-7.5 M-7.5	L-10 M-10
		Minimum	5' 11'2"	6'7" 12'2"	14' 12'10"	14'10" 14'6"	17'2" 15'6"
N	MAXIMUM SLOPE TO REDUCE DIMENSIONS beyond full requirements	Pool depth Ceiling Ht	30 degrees 30 degrees		NOTE: Dimensions C (plummet to adjacent plummet) apply for Platforms with widths as detailed. For wider Platform increase C by half the additional width(s).		

Figure 4.9b. NCAA Pool Dimensions and Equipment Requirements

longevity cannot be matched by the other possibilities. Marble plaster can develop problems on a large pool and/or one which is exposed to construction dust and wind-blown debris. Because plaster should be applied in one continuous process without interruptions, large pools will require large numbers of plaster finishers working simultaneously. Such a large group of skilled craftsmen may not be available in many market areas in North America. (Figure 4.10.)

Another problem that must be solved in the plastering of a large pool is the filling process. For best results, a pool with a green plaster coating should be filled as soon as possible, preferably in 24 hours to 48 hours after the completion of the plastering phase. This water fill should be uninterrupted in order to avoid telltale rings around the pool wall.

A painted pool interior is the least expensive process, but such a finish has a short life. As a result, many painted pool interiors must be repainted every three to five years. In some cases, the repainting is more frequent.

Another problem that sometimes develops is peeling, chipping, or oxidizing which can be unsightly and cause milky water.

GUTTER SYSTEMS (Perimeter overflow recirculation system)

There are numerous gutter configurations used throughout the world. In most cases, the design has been developed by an architect, an engineer, a builder, or a manufacturer. The purpose of the overflow gutter in modern swimming pools is to receive and capture water that flows over the lip. This water then is transferred to the filter plant, usually through a surge chamber which helps stabilize the water displacement in the swimming pool.

The gutter cross section can be created in three basic configurations:

Deep Recessed Gutter

This design often is preferred by competitive swimmers and coaches. The pool deck cantilevers over the gutter trough with the top of the deck being approximately 12 inches to 15 inches above the water. The overhang provides the competitive swimmer with a visual reference plane for the underwater wall. The recessed gutter captures the wave amplitude very effectively and keeps the pool decks relatively dry. The disadvantage is that the high overhang makes egress from the pool rather difficult, and as a result, most people choose to use one of the pool ladders.

Deck Level Gutter

The deck level overflow system features a gutter lip, a flume, and a grate that is

Figure 4.10. Aquatics Center, University of Minnesota--Interior building materials include an epoxy-painted steel structural frame, acoustic metal roof deck, acoustic structural glazed facing tiles, and clear anodized aluminum and stainless steel doors and frames. (Photo by Balthazar Korab, Ltd.)

very close to the elevation of the pool deck. This design enables even the weakest swimmer to egress over the water's edge with little effort. The disadvantage of the deck level configuration is that the decks around this type of pool usually are quite wet. Competitive swimmers often dislike this gutter profile because it is difficult to see a reference point above the water which relates to the pool wall under the water. Frequently a swimmer will misjudge the actual location of the turning surface during a race. Backstroke swimmers, in particular, have problems with this situation.

Roll Out

The third concept is the "roll out" gutter profile. This design combines the features of the fully recessed and the deck level configurations. It consists of a gutter lip and grate or a very shallow flume at the water level. The pool deck is approximately 7 1/2 inches above the water surface, and it forms a curb at the rear of the gutter grate. This curb contains much of the wave action and keeps the pool deck relatively free of water washing up and over the gutter assembly. The low configuration at the water's edge still allows the swimmers to egress easily. A popular concept is the roll out gutter design on the long sides of the pool, with a fully recessed gutter parapet at each end of the race course. This arrangement will provide the competitive swimmers with a good visual reference at the turning walls of the race courses and at the same time provide easy access and egress on the sides of the pool for recreation and student swimmers.

In the case of a separate diving pool, a roll out gutter profile should be featured on all four sides of the diving pool. The curb will contain waves created by activity in the pool plus those created by the bubble sprayer for the platform diving facilities.

A roll out or deck level gutter often is selected for a shallow water recreation pool because of the ease of ingress and egress by the users.

Gutter Construction

Any of the above gutter profiles can be constructed in several different ways:
- cast-in place concrete with tile, paint or plaster finish
- pneumatically applied concrete (gunite or Shotcrete) with tile, plaster or paint finish
- stainless steel fabricated with a grate cover made of stainless steel, fiberglass, high impact plastic, or PVC. This system contains a return water pressure conduit as well as the overflow to the surge tank and/or filter system.

The cast-in-place concrete is a popular method of construction because:
- It is part of the concrete work on the site and is easily included in that section of work.
- A tile finish can produce an attractive appearance.
- It is a long-life material(s) element.

Several other factors should be considered with regard to the cast-in-place system. The gutter flume must feature an outfall system. This can require a periodic gutter drain in the trough or a converter drop at one or more locations in the pool perimeter. The return piping inlet system must be located in the pool walls or in the pool floor.

There are several advantages to a 304 low carbon stainless steel overflow recirculation system:
- The gutter segments are fabricated at the factory and shipped to the site. A few days work by a field welder results in the pool perimeter gutter and return piping system being completely installed. This is beneficial with regard to the scheduling of trades and phases of work.
- If a floor inlet system is omitted, there is no deep buried piping except that for the main drain. In the event the pressure return conduit, which

is part of the gutter assembly, should develop a leak, the water will flow only into the inside of the pool tank. No water will leak into the surrounding soil or into below grade rooms.
- When a stainless steel system is installed, the filter system usually is provided by the same manufacturer or distributor. This creates the desirable situation of having one manufacturer responsible for the entire recirculation system.
- If a movable bulkhead is specified, it usually is provided and installed by the gutter manufacturer. This single source responsibility can be a desirable situation and will avoid disputes which might occur if different contractors are interfacing at the gutter/track.

The stainless steel perimeter overflow system must be approved by local regulatory agencies and be manufactured by a company with experience in similar pool installations. The gutter detail should be a stainless steel prefabricated overflow system featuring a handhold with a gutter profile utilizing a stainless steel, PVC, or fiberglass, grid over the gutter trough. The freeboard on the grid side of the handhold should be 3/4 inches.

The trough of the gutter must have sufficient capacity to meet the requirements of the jurisdictional agencies.

The hydraulics of the recirculation system, regardless of construction materials, shall be such that the gutter trough develops a surge capacity between swimming races when the static surge is non-existent. This is so that the gutter trough subsequently will accommodate the dynamic and static surge during the first length of each race. If a stainless steel perimeter system is selected, two converters should be provided for a 50 meter pool, while one is sufficient for a 25 yard or meter pool.

Parapets and Fully Recessed Gutters

The parapets described above can take many forms. The vertical face toward the race course, however, must provide orientation which will indicate the location of the vertical plane of the race course. Parapets may be temporary or permanent. Parapets result when a fully recessed gutter profile is required to match the above water configuration of the movable bulkhead(s).

SWIMMING POOL MECHANICAL SYSTEMS

Pool Filters

The selection of a filter system is influenced greatly by the limitations created by the volume of waste water that can be removed from the site. The construction of a holding tank is a common solution if sewer capacity is a problem.

Filter Considerations

There are three basic kinds of swimming pool filtration:
- sand filtration
- diatomaceous earth filtration
- cartridge filtration.

Sand Filters

Sand Pressure Systems exist in two forms:
- Rapid sand pressure filtration which operates at flow rate of 3 GPM per square foot of filter area
- High flow (high rate) pressure filtration which operates up to a flow rate of 15 GPM per square foot of filter area.

While many manufacturers rate their system at 20 GPM per square foot, field experience suggests that the lower flow rate results in better water quality. The system must be designed to completely turn over the pool volume as per the requirements of the jurisdictional health department. Some manufacturers produce a high flow sand pressure system which features a multiple cell configuration and operates at approximately 7-1/2 GPM per square foot of filter area. These filters are characterized by longer filter runs.

Sand Vacuum Filter Systems

A recent application of sand filter systems to swimming pool water is the vacuum sand system. These units usually require less space than sand systems.

While sand systems are very popular because of their simple operation, they have one considerable drawback (besides their high installation cost). That is the large water volume that is discharged during backwash. A multi-cell filter, however, can backwash in stages, and thus produce less volume at one time.

Diatomaceous Earth Filters

Pressure diatomaceous earth systems have the same requirement for pressurized backwash as does pressure sand. For this reason, there is not a significant advantage over a pressure sand system with the exception that D-E filters can produce a slightly clearer (polished) water quality.

Vacuum Diatomaceous Earth (D.E.) Filtration with 1-1.5 GPM per square foot of filter area is a viable option. The backwash discharge from the open top filter tank is by gravity, and the filter elements are cleaned by water jet sprays or by manual labor hosing off the elements. As a result, only a little more than the volume of the filter tank needs to be discharged via the sanitary sewer system.

Some jurisdictional authorities require a reclamation tank between the D.E. filter tank and the backwash outfall so that the spent D.E. is captured and not discharged into the sanitary sewer. This understandably increases labor costs.

One important recommendation with a vacuum diatomaceous earth system is that the top of the tank be slightly above the water level of the pool. The pumps and motors must be below water level for a flooded suction situation.

An open topped vacuum system should not be installed in a below grade filter room where the pool water level is above the rim of the filter tank.

There are several quality prefabricated systems available in the marketplace. Several provide the option of fiberglass or stainless steel tanks which is essential. Even when coated with special paint systems, mild carbon steel tanks soon can develop corrosion problems, especially if located in the ground with soil backfilled against the walls.

Another common design is for the filter tank to be part of the concrete surge tank with the pump(s) and face piping in the basement level of the natatorium. Such systems usually feature a two level filter room with open space over both levels.

Cartridge Filter

A third type of filter system is the cartridge filter. It requires virtually no backwash discharge, however, it is very labor intensive when the cartridges are cleaned. Such cleaning probably will occur every three months for an indoor pool. Another disadvantage is that the cartridge life can be 12 months, and the replacement of a set of cartridges is somewhat costly.

Most state health departments require that the selected filter must be listed as approved by the National Sanitation Foundation.

CHEMICAL TREATMENT OF POOL WATER

Swimming pool water must be risk free for the users. This is accomplished by treating the recirculated pool water with a bactericide. Additional treatment is also required to prevent microscopic plant growth such as algae. Algae, if unchecked, can create an environment that will propagate and harbor organisms that can, in varying degrees, be harmful to humans.

The most common bactericide and algaecide is chlorine. This chemical has been used for over a century in the treatment of drinking water by municipal water companies. Its application to swimming pools since the early decades of the 20th century is understandable.

Because chlorine creates hypochlorous acid when mixed with water, the product will kill bacteria, and at the same time it will oxidize organic particulate matter in the swimming pool water.

The most popular form of chlorine treatment for public swimming pools historically has been elemental chlorine, which is in gaseous form when it is released from its storage tank and injected into the swimming pool recirculation system. Because chlorine gas can be hazardous if released into the atmosphere and fatal if inhaled in any significant quantity, there is a definite trend away from gas chlorine and toward chlorine compounds. The most popular for public swimming facilities is sodium hypochlorite, which commonly is called liquid chlorine or bleach.

While liquid chlorine does not create some of the risks the gas chlorine does, it is not without its disadvantages. The main disadvantages are bulk handling, distribution, and storage, plus the tendency to accumulate total dissolved solids in the pool water. This phenomenon can result in water quality problems.

Dry chlorine products are manufactured and sold in the marketplace, however, these products are directed toward the residential pool market, and as a result, the cost of these chemicals is very high. These chemicals usually are impractical for large volume pools, especially for outdoor pools.

Because of the problems and limitations of the chlorine treatment of swimming pool water, a search for an alternative currently is underway in the United States market. The most promising appears to be the corona discharge ozone generation system. Widely used in western Europe and parts of Canada, as well as isolated locations around the world, the process can reduce many of the disadvantages of chlorine treatment. It must be noted that a chlorine system still is required for pools in order to provide a free chlorine residual in the pool water at all times. This residual chlorine is surplus bactericide potential which attacks contaminants and germs that are brought into the water by swimmers. Ozone has many qualities, but it has no sustained residual power after the pool water is treated in the contact chamber.

Another alternative to chlorine treatment is copper and silver ionization. There are at present a number of manufacturers of this in the North American market. This system also must be used with a chlorine system to provide a residual bactericide and algaecide capability.

Both alternative systems, i.e., ozone corona discharge and copper and silver ionization, are in early phases of market penetrations. As a result, the supply and field service after the sale is inconsistent in many locations.

AUTOMATION

Automation has been a part of modern swimming pool design for several decades. The application has focused on two systems. The first is water chemistry, and the second is filtration. (Figure 4.11.)

The water chemistry of the pool is sampled and analyzed electronically by a microprocessor. The analysis is recorded and compared to two set points previously established by the pool operator. One of the set points is the desired level of free chlorine. The other set point is that for pH.

When the analyzer samples the pool water (by means of a sample stream which bypasses part of the recirculation piping), it will compare the result to the set point for the desired level. If the sample shows that the free chlorine level is above the set point of the analyzer, the unit, which is interfaced with the chemical feed pump or a booster pump in the case of chlorine gas, will turn off the chlorine feed pump motor. If the sample reading is below the set point, the analyzer will turn on the feed pump motor if it is off, or it will continue its operation until the pool water in the sample stream reaches the set point level. In the same way, the analyzer will monitor the sample stream for the pH level and then will energize the chemical feed pump that will add the respective buffer agent, i.e., caustic soda or sodium carbonate (soda ash) to raise the pH, or muriatic acid or carbon dioxide to lower the pH.

There are several benefits to an automated water chemistry feed system. The automated system monitors the pool water constantly, as compared to the manual testing by an operator which will take place anywhere from once an hour to once a day. The analyzer will begin and cease the chemical feed system immediately upon demand, as compared to manual adjustments after each manual testing. With manual adjustment, there is no assurance that the change in the rate of feed by the operator will be of sufficient quantity to change the level of chlorine (or pH) to the desired amount. Quite to the contrary, the likelihood is that the chemical level will exceed the desired level before the next manual test is made.

Another benefit of the automatic chemical feed system is the lower chemical cost to the owner. With the constant monitoring of the water and the subsequent activation of the feeders, both on and off, overfeeding is eliminated, and overall chemical costs are lower. This is due to the tendency of a manual set feed system to overfeed the respective chemical until the next manual test is taken, and a new adjustment is made to the feed pump rate of feed setting.

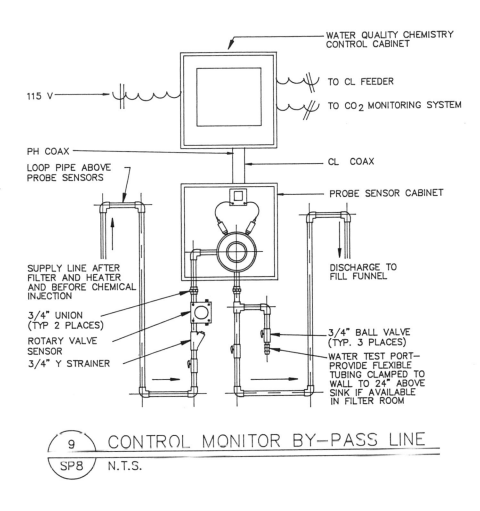

WATER QUALITY CHEMISTRY CONTROL CABINET

115 V

TO CL FEEDER

TO CO_2 MONITORING SYSTEM

PH COAX

CL COAX

LOOP PIPE ABOVE PROBE SENSORS

PROBE SENSOR CABINET

SUPPLY LINE AFTER FILTER AND HEATER AND BEFORE CHEMICAL INJECTION

DISCHARGE TO FILL FUNNEL

3/4" UNION (TYP 2 PLACES)

ROTARY VALVE SENSOR

3/4" Y STRAINER

3/4" BALL VALVE (TYP. 3 PLACES)

WATER TEST PORT—PROVIDE FLEXIBLE TUBING CLAMPED TO WALL TO 24" ABOVE SINK IF AVAILABLE IN FILTER ROOM

$\begin{array}{c} 9 \\ \hline SP8 \end{array}$ CONTROL MONITOR BY-PASS LINE
N.T.S.

Figure 4.11. Control Monitor Bypass Line

Modern automatic water chemistry analyzers can be provided with a remote readout which usually is located in the pool management office. This allows the pool management staff to monitor the water chemistry levels in the pool water without having to walk to the filter room for a visual monitoring of the system. The system also can be interfaced with the building's environmental monitoring and control systems, in which case a PC computer in the pool office can display pool water chemical levels. In addition, a recorder with a tape system will record each reading per minute. This paper tape is stored in the analyzer for review by the operator or maintenance service person. Such data is helpful in understanding the impact of bather loads versus quiescent times in the 24-hour cycle of the pool operations.

MOVABLE BULKHEAD

Movable bulkheads became popular during the late 1970s and have continued through the early 1990s. There are several reasons. The bulkhead, which is usually three or four feet in width, approximately 4-1/2 feet in depth and as long as the pool is wide, can be moved along a horizontal translation.

By moving the bulkhead, a different course length can be created inside of greater course lengths, i.e., with a movable bulkhead, a 50 meter pool can be converted into a 25 yard or 25 meter race course. When two or more bulkheads are used, duplicate or even triplicate courses can be created. In addition to race courses, other aquatic activity areas can be created at the same time, such as synchronized swimming, water polo, instruction classes, or fitness lap swimming.

While United States bulkheads tend to move horizontally over the length of the pool and be stored at the end of the pool when the 50 meter dimension mode is in use, European bulkheads usually move only vertically and they are stored in a floor well when the pool is in the 50 meter mode. The reason for these differences is that the U.S. swimming competition takes place over a several dimensional race course, i.e., 25 yards, 25 meter, and 50 meter, plus other dimensional locations because of activities described above. (Figure 4.12.)

The bulkheads usually are a fiberglass box girder or a stainless steel truss with a skin of PVC or fiberglass grating. The stainless steel truss is designed to accommodate live loading both from above and from the side (laterally). The necessity for these design qualifications is the need to provide a rigid turning surface for the athletes, and in the case of starts from a bulkhead, minimal deflection from the simultaneous thrust from swimmers diving from starting blocks that are mounted on the bulkhead. (It is for this reason that many competitive swimmers prefer starting blocks anchored in the pool deck.)

In recent years, an evolution has occurred in bulkhead design which features a variable buoyancy chamber. This design enables the operator to inflate the chamber, which in turn creates a positive buoyancy in the bulkhead. This situation floats the bulkhead off its resting (bearing points) place on the pool perimeter lip or wall. In this position the bulkhead can be towed to its new

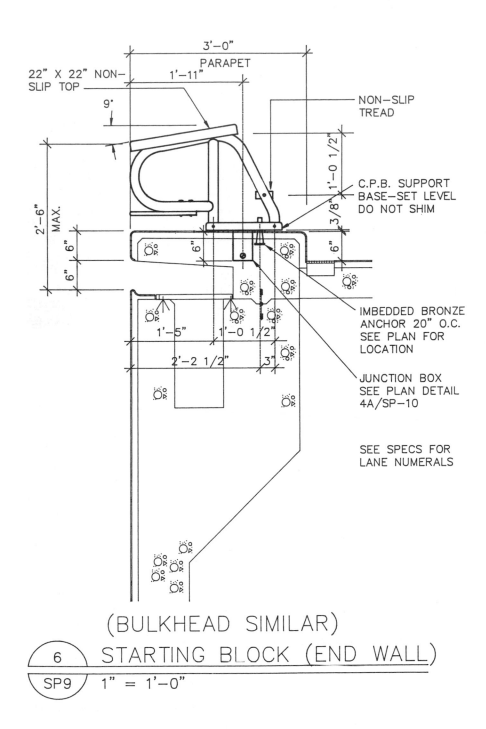

3'-0"
PARAPET
1'-11"

22" X 22" NON-SLIP TOP

9°

NON-SLIP TREAD

1'-0 1/2"

3/8"

C.P.B. SUPPORT BASE—SET LEVEL DO NOT SHIM

2'-6" MAX.

6"

6"

6"

6"

6"

IMBEDDED BRONZE ANCHOR 20" O.C. SEE PLAN FOR LOCATION

1'-5"

1'-0 1/2"

2'-2 1/2"   3"

JUNCTION BOX SEE PLAN DETAIL 4A/SP-10

SEE SPECS FOR LANE NUMERALS

(BULKHEAD SIMILAR)

⑥ STARTING BLOCK (END WALL)

SP9   1" = 1'-0"

Figure 4.12. Bulkhead Diagram

position, deflated, and anchored into the pool perimeter.

Prior to this development, most bulkheads moved on wheels along a track or bearing surface on the pool's perimeter. Difficulty with wheel mechanisms in some bulkheads has resulted in difficulty in moving the units. It is for this reason that the design development is moving toward the variable buoyancy system.

MOVABLE POOL FLOORS

The hydraulic or mechanical driven pool floor has been popular in western Europe for three decades. Originally developed in Germany, it has the ability to create different water depths, which in turn creates conditions for a greater variety of aquatic activities, making it popular especially in indoor natatoria. The floor creates a variety of pool configurations, all under the same roof with the same operational costs. This becomes an impressive comparison when contrasted with building several pools with different depths for different activities. (Figure 4.13.)

The "floors," which usually are installed at the time that the pool is constructed, have been used in competition pools, both long course and short course, as well as rehabilitation centers, wellness centers, and service organizations such as YMCAs and JCCAs.

The majority of movable floors work with hydraulic rams similar to car lifts at an automobile service station. Other systems use scissor mechanisms, cog and chain, or pulley and cable. The latter usually is selected when a below grade walk space is constructed around the pool perimeter. The hydraulic system can work effectively even when the pool shell walls are backfilled.

The approximate maximum size is usually 75 feet-by-42 feet and uses four rams. Such a floor section can be used in a 50 meter-by-25 yard pool and create a functional shallow water area for a number of programs.

Figure 4.13. Movable Pool Floors (Courtesy of AFW of North America)

A frequent addition to the movable floor is a trailing ramp. This is a plane that is hinged to the floor section with the opposite end of the ramp resting on the pool floor with rollers. The ramp extends from pool wall to pool wall and, as such, creates an inclined slope from the edge of the movable floor to the pool bottom. The ramp prevents anyone from swimming underwater beneath the movable floor when it is in a raised position.

The need for movable floors has become more understandable in the past decade because of the requirement or justified rationale to locate starting blocks over deep water. A number of young competitive swimmers have been paralyzed when striking the pool bottom with their head after diving headfirst off a starting platform. If the starting blocks are installed at the deep end of the pool along with the diving board supports, the resulting congestion is not desirable. The historic location of starting platforms at the uncongested shallow end of the pool is hazardous when the starting blocks are used over water five feet deep or less. The movable floor solves these problems by creating an ideal situation for the use of starting blocks, while at the same time avoiding the problems of the combined use of the starting blocks and the diving boards at the deep end of the pool.

DIVING FACILITIES

Diving facilities have endured out of the development and the requirements of competitive springboard and platform diving. The heights of these respective structures have been standardized at 1 meter and 3 meters for springboards and 1, 3, 5, 7.5 and 10 meters for rigid platforms. There are several dimensional requirements, each promulgated by different organizations, i.e., FINA (Federation Internationale De Natation Amateur) and U.S. Diving and National Collegiate Athletic Association (NCAA).

Springboard diving competition has been influenced greatly through the development by one manufacturer of diving boards, i.e., Duraflex International. Since the 1950s, this company has developed three generations of high performance springboards. Using a patented aluminum alloy and design, Duraflex International has developed a conventional diving board, a double tapered board, and a double tapered board with holes across the section of board that lifts the diver and travels the greatest distance through the air of the entire board. As a result, the divers usually are lifted higher in the air, allowing them to execute the complicated dives at a higher elevation with a slightly longer time in the air. Both conditions are advantageous to the competitive diver.

The Duraflex board has a reputation for durability and can last for several decades with intermittent resurfacing by the factory.

Other diving boards are manufactured by different companies and are sold primarily to the residential pool market, semi-public (motel, hotel, condo, apartment), and the public recreation pool market. These boards usually are fiberglass or vinyl-encapsulated wood boards. Other types of diving boards sold to the residential and semi-public market are 100 percent molded fiberglass.

Diving board supports vary, and the difference is reflected in cost. The least expensive are the cast aluminum stand designed and manufactured by Duraflex International, and it is called Durafirm. The 3 meter unit is relatively rigid, is easy to install, requires no underground footing, and needs only a thickened slab beneath the anchored legs.

A more attractive diving board support, in the opinion of many designers and users, is the cantilevered support pedestal with a stainless steel ship's ladder and handrails. The forward leaning profile creates a dramatic appearance and often is used in public pools, clubs, and schools. Because it has more connected parts, it has a tendency to vibrate and rattle if the bolted connectors are not kept tight by the pool operator. If this type of diving board support structure is specified, it is recommended that the pedestal and flanged ends be 304 stainless steel and painted. It is especially important that the flanges and all bolts not be a mild steel because of the predictable corrosion that will occur. This result is a problem for maintenance personnel who must repaint these components frequently.

The third type of diving board support is a cast-in-place concrete structure for both heights, i.e., 1 meter and 3 meters. This structure has no vibration except from the short stand butt plate and fulcrum base assembly. The overall advantage of the concrete support is the monolithic structure which will not shake, vibrate, or loosen component connectors. The result is a firm, stable base for the diving board. Understandably, the solid cast-in-place concrete support costs more than the factory-fabricated metal units. This is a result of the labor and materials required and the stair assembly that usually is a part of the design. Because of the greater cost, the concrete supports usually are designed for universities where the budget will accommodate and the diving program will justify the expense.

With the consideration of diving boards goes the concern with the diving envelope of water into which all divers must dive. The question of water depth relates to safety. Safety for the diver is paramount, which is complicated by the wide ranges of efficiency and skill possessed by different divers. The trained competitive diver consistently will reach a greater depth after entry because of the streamlined body configuration and disciplined movements. Because of his or her experience, injurious impact with the pool bottom is extremely rare. By contrast, the typical recreation diver almost always will enter the water in an inefficient configuration with little or no streamlined characteristics. As a result, this diver will slow body velocity rapidly after entry and will not plunge to the depths that the experienced competitive diver can achieve at will.

While the above describes the typical and common entry of both experienced competitive divers and inexperienced recreation divers, there can be rare exceptions. To anticipate these potential hazardous experiences by divers, the depth and envelope of the water below the diving boards must be adequate. Standards and/or requirements are promulgated by the respective health departments and the governing bodies of competitive diving, i.e., U. S. Diving, NCAA, and FINA. While the competitive rule-making agencies dictate water depths that will accommodate experienced divers, municipal and state regulations allow shallower minimum depths and smaller envelopes. Because there is no way of ascertaining the skill level of a diver before he or she executes a dive, or to know the efficiency with which a dive will be executed, shallower water depths may not be appropriate. Another factor that must be considered is the potential for an original low performance (wood or fiberglass) diving board to be replaced by a high performance aluminum board. When this occurs, a new set of capabilities is created, and new parameters are required.

The different skill levels and body weights of divers and the different lift characteristics of different diving boards suggest that the deeper and larger water envelopes beneath the diving boards (and diving platforms) should be designed for pools which feature regulation aluminum 16 foot diving boards. For this reason, most designers will use the current rules of FINA, U. S. Diving, or the NCAA.

Diving platforms are being built at a noticeable increased rate within new facilities. Most of these are on university campuses and are part of a new 50 meter natatorium. This sudden development has been stimulated by the commencement of platform diving at the NCAA Division I Swimming and Diving Championships in 1988. It is anticipated that platform diving will be added to the order of events at conference meets as more platform towers are built at Division I campuses. The rationale for this development is to better prepare U. S. divers for international competition.

Diving coaches and platform divers are requesting platforms with three center lines instead of the customary two. In the former, the 10 meter, 7-1/2 meter, and SM platforms have separate plummet centerlines so that divers can dive from each platform at the same time without conflict. In the latter, the 10 meter platform is directly above the 5 meter and 1 meter platforms in what is called a stacked configuration. Likewise, the 7.5 meter is stacked above the 3 meter platform. The two centerline design is featured in the great majority of the diving platforms in the world. There are two basic reasons for this. The three centerline structure is difficult to fit into the desired dimensions of a diving pool, and the three centerline structure is more expensive than the two centerline design.

Due to budget constraints, tower assemblies sometimes are designed with fewer than the five levels. When this is done, the option most often selected is a single centerline. Other options include a 5 meter, 7-1/2 meter, and a 10 meter. Sometimes a 1 meter is added, thus omitting only the 3 meter platform.

If a diving tower is specified, the water depth and envelope beneath the tower should meet or exceed the FINA requirements. Diving platforms usually are located over an independent/separate diving pool. This is done for several reasons. The first is to avoid conflict with swimming which would be the case if the water beneath the platforms (landing zone) was part of the bounded water volume of the race course. Such a situation is considered undesirable because of conflict during meets as well as during practice. Another important reason is the desired water temperature by divers, which is warmer than that preferred by competitive swimmers.

When there is a separate diving pool, the bottom sometimes is finished with a dark blue color. The reason is that platform divers find that the dark color helps them with their orientation when spinning and twisting in the execution of their dives.

The deck area that surrounds the swimming and/or diving pool(s) provides the medium of access to the water's edge. This space (and material) is the most important element to the user, other than the pool tanks and their contents. A short observation of a pool in use (especially for recreation free swim) will reveal that the swimmers continually interact with the pool deck and the pool water. As a result, the pool deck takes on a number of important functions:

- The deck is the surface over which all users must travel to reach the water's edge or reach a diving facility and then into the water. Because of this

function, the deck must be smooth enough to be comfortable for bare feet and yet rough enough to prevent slipping when the deck is wet.

- Information must be displayed in the deck surface to advise users of potential hazards. This signage will state water depths, warnings, and instructions.

- Because the swimmers and divers continuously are carrying water out of the pool, which drips and splashes into the deck, a workable deck drainage system must be provided.

There are several basic deck drainage systems that are practical around a swimming pool.

Area Drains: This is the most common. The deck area is divided into sections, and the surface in each section slopes to a low point (usually in the center) where a flush perforated drain fitting is located. This drain is connected to the other drain fittings in the deck, all of which drain the deck surface water to a sanitary sewer.

Slot Drains: There are a number of varieties of the drain configuration. The feature that they all have in common is the concentric location they have with the pool perimeter. Slot drains usually are located approximately three to five feet from the water's edge. Because the deck slopes away from the pool and toward the slot drain, the great majority of the splashed water and the water carried out by the swimmers falls on the upside of the slope from the slot drain and the pool's edge and quickly drains away. The slot in the pool deck can be created in several ways. The primary feature is a conduit that is either level or slopes to an outfall where the deck water that has drained into the slot will flow to the sanitary sewer.

The slot most commonly is created by casting a plastic pipe in the deck slab with the tangent point of the pipe approximately 1-1/2 inches below the top of the concrete deck. After the concrete has been cured, a 1/4 to 3/8-inch saw cut is made along the tangent point which is the valley of the deck. In this way, water falling on both sides of

the slot will drain to the slot and be carried away to waste.

There are other ways of creating the slot which include extruded plastic conduits that are cast into the pool deck. These units usually are covered with a perforated plastic or stainless steel cap. Other designs utilize a stainless steel square conduit with a slot at the top. This unit is cast in the deck with the slot and its stainless steel edges flush with the pool deck. While there are industrial products on the market, many stainless steel systems are custom-fabricated with the necessary outfall fittings at the correct intervals for the sanitary connections. The stainless steel slot, like the saw cut version, is not covered with a grate.

In addition to the cast-in-place plastic conduit with the perforated cap, another version is practical although more costly. That is a depressed flume, approximately four inches wide, cast in the pool deck along the valley. This flume then is covered with a grating of some kind, either extruded PVC, bronze, or stainless steel.

In pools with narrow decks, drainage can occur across the deck to a shallow trough along the natatorium wall, or off the edge of the deck into a French drain if the pool is outdoors.

BUILDING ENVELOPE

A natatorium is a room inside of which is one or more swimming pools. How the room, in its entirety, is constructed is of immense importance. The structural components must be such that they will withstand the normal wear and tear of a public space, plus the unique demands of an enclosed space above (and below) a large body of water which is treated with chemicals and will evaporate tons of water vapor over the period of one year. This, multiplied by 30 or 50 years, underscores the aggression that the building will be subjected to. Mild steel should be avoided where possible and should be limited to large structural components. These components, if exposed to the natatorium environment, should be coated with an industrial grade epoxy. If the roof decking is mild steel or even galvanized, it must be coated in the same way to protect the metal from corrosion. Non-metallic building components must withstand the impact of high humidity and aggressive chemical laced air. For this reason, concrete, plastic, glass, and stainless steel are appropriate.

In considering stainless steel, it is important to understand that stainless steel has many grades and alloys. The 300 series usually is used for swimming pool equipment. Even so, certain environmental conditions can adversely affect stainless steel over a period of time. For this reason, it is unwise to use small and yet strategic components which are put under stress as a structural component, i.e., fasteners that are part of a roof suspension system. Other than pool gutters, bulkhead, and deck equipment, unpainted stainless steel should not be used in natatoria.

The roof sandwich demands scrutiny in its design so as to avoid problems with the air barrier, the vapor retarder, the insulation, and the moisture membrane. The avoidance of thermal bridging is essential, especially in locales with a cold winter climate. Condensation inside the natatorium can cause many problems if not controlled. The most significant is the creation of hydrochloric acid if vapor with chlorine molecules condenses. The same concerns exist for natatorium walls, and design decisions must take the above issues into consideration.

The architectural features in a natatorium may vary depending upon the type of owner, the location, the climate, and the activity program.

FENESTRATION

The decision to use windows in a natatorium will be influenced by the location of the natatorium. If the facility is located in a park setting or has an attractive view, i.e., mountain, ocean, lake, forest, etc., wall windows can be a major feature of the facility. If, on the other hand, the view is an unattractive cityscape such as a parking lot, blank building walls, unattractive streetscape, there is little reason to introduce light through a wall window because of the glare that will likely develop across the surface of the water. This reflected glare can be a distraction to spectators during a swim meet, a safety problem for lifeguards during recreation swimming, a heat loss or heat gain, or/ can create condensation with possible corrosion damage to window casements and walls. All of these problems can be dealt with if justification for the window and natural light can be established.

One means of avoiding many of the negatives named above is the use of translucent skylights. While this technique will avoid many of the negative aspects of wall fenestration, heat gain still can be a problem, but control can reduce greatly the negative effects. Skylights usually will avoid negative glare on the water surface and at the same time reduce the level of needed artificial light. Artificial light is a very important feature in the design of a poolscape, whether it is indoors or outdoors. Indoor light levels are influenced to some degree by standards or rules set forth by the national governing bodies of competitive swimming, diving, synchronized swimming, and water polo. State and local health department agencies frequently will set requirements for outdoor and indoor pools, both for overhead and underwater light sources. A review of the applicable regulations will enable the designer to meet these requirements.

Acoustics is an issue which must be addressed. Often times, acoustics will be overlooked, dismissed, or eliminated because of budget. Reverberating sound is a common problem in natatoria. Sound sources include whistles, gunshots, and diving board impact noises, plus shouts, conversation, and the sounds of splashing. Loudspeakers should be selected and specified by an acoustics and sound consultant. Understandably, the size of the natatorium will influence the acceptable reverberation time in the space.

Outdoor acoustics usually are a factor in the overall design of the poolscape. The pool site can be both a source and a recipient of noise. If the pool is near a residential area or some other land use that should not have excessive sound impact, landscape design can provide buffers. If, on the other hand, off-site noise is produced by an adjacent roadway and/or industrial site, protection must be created for the poolscape.

SUPPORT SPACES

While the bodies of water are the focal point of the facility, the design, arrangement, and adjacencies of the support spaces are factors of the overall design that will influence the efficiency of the operation and the effectiveness of the programs.

The starting point of the adjacency profile is the user's point of entry. A control point must exist at this location. After passing the control point, the user must arrive at the dressing area. The two dressing rooms should have a dry entrance from the control point area and a wet exit to the pool deck. (The reverse applies for users leaving the pool area.)

The pool office should be located with a visual access of the pool deck area and the exits from the dressing rooms onto the pool deck. Other spaces/ rooms can be added to the control area depending upon the size of the pool(s) and programs. The spaces can include an office for lifeguards, a first aid room, and an office for instructors and coaches. Additional spaces may include a swim meet management office, drug testing room(s), and sports technology research offices. If the facility is a university with a physical education major and post graduate studies, other spaces used for research should be considered.

Functional support spaces include filtration and chemical treatment, storage, circulation, and spectator seating.

The issue of spectator seating is somewhat complex. It requires the identification of the type of spectator events that will take place, their frequency, the number of spectators, and the type of facilities that will be provided for the spectators. If there are to be spectator events, is it best to provide permanent or temporary seating? The answer to this question will be influenced not only by the issues listed above, but also by budget, available space, and in some cases, the off-site activities of the owner. The difference of the two basic systems, i.e., permanent and temporary, will be reflected in cost. This applies not only to first costs, but also can influence the construction budget in such areas as exits, stairwells, and even parking spaces. Because of the variables, it is important to have a good understanding (and agreement among the owner's project committee) of the true purpose of the spectator facilities.

Both indoor and outdoor access to the seating area can be an important design problem, and it can affect significantly the total construction cost.

HVAC - DEHUMIDIFICATION

The environment in an indoor pool, i.e., natatorium, can be comfortable to the swimmers and spectators if the relative humidity is controlled and maintained at 50 to 55 percent. An even greater benefit of this range is the lack of aggressive atmospheric conditions relative to the materials in the space. For many years the soaring humidity in a natatorium was controlled by opening the windows and allowing natural ventilation to release the moist atmosphere. In this method the laws of physics replaced that warm moist air with cooler, dryer outside air. Understandably the next improvement

was the introduction of motorized exhaust fans that mechanically maintained a constant air flow out of the natatorium with a controlled and strategically located introduction of fresh air louvers. This system, which still is in use in the 1990s, is effective if the outside air is at the appropriate temperature and relative humidity level. In some climatic areas, the appropriate level for outside air is available much of the time. Most locations, however, have appropriate levels only a small percentage of the time. During the majority of the time, high levels of temperature and humidity in the outside air result in higher temperatures and humidity levels in the natatorium.

During the 1970s, following the fuel crisis and the escalating cost of energy, modifications were made to the conventional mechanical ventilation systems. These modifications captured the heat that previously was exhausted to the outside and used it to raise the heat of the outside air being brought into the natatorium space. Once again, this worked only if the outside weather conditions were correct.

In the late 1970s refrigerated dehumidification was developed. This system is an outgrowth of air conditioning, whereby the warm moist air is mechanically drawn across an evaporator coil. This lowers the temperature of the air and causes it to condense on the cold coil. The dryer air that exits from the other side of the coil has a lower temperature and a lower relative humidity. This air then is reheated and mixes with the natatorium air. In so doing, it stabilizes the temperature in the natatorium at or near the desired level or set point.

Refrigerated systems also use the heat that has been captured and removed from the processed natatorium air to heat the swimming pool water, heat the natatorium space, or even heat the potable shower water. By using the heat that is taken out of the natatorium air as described above, the overall energy costs of the natatorium are much lower.

In spite of a higher first cost for the refrigerated dehumidification, the savings in operating costs create an attractive payback to the owner. This is enhanced if energy costs continue to rise.

Designers must consider the human needs for ventilation and fresh air. While dehumidifiers will control humidity without ventilation, fresh outside air is needed for the occupants of the natatorium. If there is a large number of spectators at special events, i.e., swimming meets, tournaments, water shows, etc., a separate mode will be required to serve this greater demand for outside fresh air. All modes must meet local building codes and the applicable ASHRAE standards (American Society of Heating, Refrigeration and Air Conditioning Engineers).

MAINTENANCE AND REPAIR

In planning a swimming pool and/or a natatorium, consideration must be given to the ongoing cost of custodial care, maintenance, and repair. Often this aspect of swimming pool and natatorium design is overlooked. The result is a higher operating cost for each day the facility is in operation, all the way to the end of the facility's life.

Custodial care often is taken for granted by the project committee, and little thought is given to the daily chores that must take place to keep the pool and its support spaces in a high level of cleanliness. The result is greater labor hours expended, which impacts the annual budget and at the same time may result in a lower level of cleanliness due to a future mandate to cut labor hours because of budget constraints.

Preventive maintenance is always a task that must be executed if the facility is to be maintained as it should. While budget can have an impact on how well preventive maintenance is carried out, the design of the mechanical systems, support components, working space, and ingress and egress from the mechanical spaces can influence the enthusiasm that physical plant staff will have for practicing preventive maintenance.

The repair of components in the pool and support spaces will be less costly in time and material (and down time of the facility) if parts are available as shelf items.

If long lead times are required to obtain some parts, they should be pre-purchased and inventoried before the need occurs. This applies to pumps, motors, impellers, chemical feed pumps, air handling units, blowers, some filter components, etc.

SAFETY FEATURES

Safety is no accident. It must receive careful consideration by planners, architects, and operators of pools. Many people have been confronted with litigation as a result of an accident in their pools. Lawyers inevitably look for areas of negligence in the operation of the pool or for any defect in the pool's design. Listed below are some essential safety principles, procedures, and policies which should be adhered to in designing the pool and in its operation.

- Rules governing pool use must be conspicuously posted at all points of entry to the pool.
- Special rules should be developed and posted for use at such facilities as diving boards, slides, and towers.
- A lifeguard should be on duty at all times that the pool is open.
- In areas of the pool which contain less than 5 feet 0 inches of water, signs and warnings should be placed at the edge (coping) of the pool which state "SHALLOW WATER - NO DIVING." In shallow water training pools on the edge of the pool, signs should be posted stating "DANGER SHALLOW WATER - NO DIVING."
- Where springboards and platform diving is provided, the depth of water and other related measurements must conform to the rules of FINA,

USD, NCAA, or the NFHSAA.
- Starting blocks for competitive swimming should be installed in the deep end of the pools unless the shallow end of the pool is at least 5 feet 0 inches deep.
- Adequate lighting, both underwater and in the pool area, must be provided to assure the safety of users and meet applicable rules, regulations, and codes.
- Clarity of pool water is essential and must meet applicable rules, regulations, and codes.
- Depth markers at least four inches high must be placed in the interior wall of the pool at or above water level. Larger depth markings must be placed on the pool deck as per health department regulations.
- Never consider the minimum standards for pools promulgated by state governments or the pool industry to be the proper level to achieve in planning a pool. Minimums often become obsolete very quickly.
- Ladders which hang on the edge of a pool and extend into the water represent hazards to swimmers. All ladders should be recessed into the pool wall.
- No safety ledge should ever extend into the pool. Instead the ledge should be recessed into the wall at a depth of approximately 4 feet 0 inches.

CHECK LIST FOR USE BY PLANNING COMMITTEE AND OWNER

Planning Factors

1. A clear statement identifies the nature and scope of the program and the special requirements for space, equipment, and facilities dictated by the activities to be conducted.

2. The swimming pool has been planned to meet the requirements of the intended program, as well as less frequent special needs.

3. There are other recreational facilities nearby for the convenience and enjoyment of swimmers.

4. An experienced pool consultant, architect, and/or engineer has been called in to advise on design and equipment.

5. The design of the pool reflects the most current knowledge and experience regarding the technical aspects of swimming pools.

6. The pool plans reflect the needs of physically disabled people.

7. All plans and specifications meet the regulations of both state and local boards of health.

8. Provision for accomodating young children has been considered.

9. Consideration has been given to provide a room or area near the pool suitable for video/TV and lectures.

10. Adequate parking space has been provided.

Design Factors

1. The bathhouse is properly located, with entrance to the pool leading to the shallow end.

2. The locker rooms are large enough to accommodate peak loads and meet jurisdictional regulations.

3. The area for spectators has been separated from the pool area.

4. There is adequate deck space around the pool.

5. The swimming pool manager's or director's office faces the pool and contains a window with a view of the entire pool area.

6. There is a toilet-shower-dressing area next to the office for instructors.

7. The specifications for competitive swimming set forth by ruling groups have been met.

8. If the pool shell has a tile finish, the length of the pool has been increased by three inches over the "official" size in order to permit eventual tiling of the basin without making the pool too short.

9. The width of any movable bulkhead has been considered in calculating total pool length.

10. Consideration has been given to an easy method of moving the bulkhead.

11. All diving standards can be anchored properly.

12. Separate storage spaces have been allocated for maintenance and instructional equipment.

13. A properly constructed overflow gutter extends around the pool perimeter.

14. Where skimmers are used, they are located so that they are not turning walls where competitive swimming is to be conducted.

15. The proper pitch to drains has been allowed in the pool, on the pool deck, in the overflow gutter, and on the floor of shower and dressing rooms as per local jurisdictional regulation.

16. Inlets and outlets are adequate in number and located to ensure effective circulation of water in the pool.

17. There is easy access to the filter room to permit the transport of chemicals and other supplies.

18. The recirculation pump is located below the water level.

19. The recirculation-filtration system has been designed to meet anticipated future pool loads.

20. Underwater lights in end racing walls have been located 3-1/2 feet directly below surface lane line anchors, and they are on a separate circuit.

21. There is adequate acoustical treatment of walls and ceilings of the indoor pool.

22. There is adequate overhead clearance for diving.

23. Reflection of light from the outside has been kept to a minimum by proper location of windows or skylights.

24. All wall electrical receptacles are covered.

25. Proper subsurface drainage has been provided.

26. An area for sunbathing has been provided and oriented for the outdoor pool.

27. Outdoor diving boards or platforms are oriented so that they face north or northeast.

28. The outdoor pool is oriented correctly in relation to the sun.

29. Wind screens have been provided in situations where heavy winds prevail.

30. Lounging for swimmers has been provided for outdoor pools.

Safety and Health

1. The pool layout provides the most efficient control of swimmers from showers and locker rooms to the pool.

2. Toilet facilities are provided for wet swimmers, separate from the dry area.

3. There is an area set aside for eating, apart from the pool deck.

4. There is adequate deep water for diving which meets U.S. diving rules.

5. Required space has been provided between diving boards and between the diving boards and sidewalls.

6. Recessed steps or removable ladders are located on the walls so as not to interfere with competitive swimming turns.

7. There is adequate provision for life-saving equipment and pool cleaning equipment.

8. The proper numbers of lifeguard stands have been provided and properly located.

9. All metal fittings are of noncorrosive material. All metal in the pool area is grounded to a ground-fault interrupter.

10. Provision has been made for underwater lights.

11. The chemical feed systems and containers have been placed in a separate room, accessible from and vented to the outside.

12. A pool heater has been included and properly sized.

13. Automatic controls for water chemistry have been specified.

14. Proper ventilation has been provided in the indoor pool.

15. There is adequate underwater and overhead lighting.

16. There is provision for proper temperature control in the pool room for both water and air.

17. The humidity of the natatorium room can be controlled.

18. A fence has been placed around the outdoor pool to prevent its use when the pool is closed.

19. Rules for use of the pool have been developed and displayed prominently.

20. Warning signs are placed where needed and on such equipment as diving boards and slides.

21. Starting blocks are placed in the deep end of pool (minimum depth five feet).

22. There is a telephone in the pool area with numbers of rescue and emergency agencies.

23. Emergency equipment, including a spineboard, has been provided.

24. The steps leading into the pool have a black edge to make them visible to underwater swimmers.

25. Bottom drain covers are fastened securely to prevent their removal by interlopers.

26. The diving stands are equipped with guardrails which extend at least to the water.

27. The deck is made of nonslip material.

RULING BODIES OF COMPETITIVE SWIMMING AND DIVING

USS (United States Swimming, Inc.)
1750 East Boulder Street
Colorado Springs, CO 80909.

USD (United States Diving, Inc.)
901 West New York Street
Indianapolis, IN 46202.

USWP (United States Water Polo)
1750 East Boulder Street
Colorado Springs, CO 80909.

USSS (United States Synchronized Swimming)
901 West New York Street
Indianapolis, IN 46233.

NCAA (National Collegiate Athletic Association)
P. O. Box 1906
Shawnee Mission, KS 66201.

NFHSAA (National Federation of State High School Athletic Associations)
11724 Plaza Circle
Box 20626
Kansas City, MO 64195

FINA (Federation International De Natation Amateur)
c/o Ross E. Wales
425 Walnut Street, Suite 1610,
Cincinnati, OH 45202.

REFERENCES

Flynn, Richard B. (Ed.) 1985. *Planning Facilities for Athletics, Physical Education and Recreation,* The Athletic Institute and American Alliance for Health, Physical Education, Recreation and Dance.

NCAA Guides. Overland Park, KS: National Collegiate Athletic Association.

ABOUT THE AUTHOR:
D.J. Hunsaker is president of Counsilman/Hunsaker and Associates, Natatorium Planners and Design Consultants in St. Louis, MO.

Chapter 5
LARGE INDOOR SPORTS AND RECREATION FACILITIES
by Todd Seidler

INTRODUCTION

This chapter will present an overview and analysis of field houses, stadiums, arenas, and campus recreation centers. All are large indoor sports or recreation facilities and may have many features in common. Which category a particular building may fall under often is open to debate and may be determined by what the owner decides to call it. In general, stadiums and arenas are spectator facilities, while field houses and campus recreation centers are designed primarily for activity, and spectator seating usually is limited. (Figure 5.1.)

FIELD HOUSES

Field houses were first constructed in the United States to meet storage needs near outdoor sports fields. In inclement weather, it was a natural step to move practice periods for outdoor sports under the roof and onto the dirt floors of the field house. As field houses increased in sophistication, dirt floors became unacceptable, and flooring surfaces were added that included wood, asphalt, synthetic surfaces, and artificial turf. Designers began to include locker and team rooms, full plumbing, offices, and spectator accommodations which provided wider indoor recreational and instructional usage.

Today, the building most commonly referred to as the field house is a structure that encloses large open areas for sports and recreational activities. Some field houses are large enough to contain a full size football field, a 200 meter running track, swimming pools, and a multitude of court setups. In general, low cost construction systems are used in order to achieve a large amount of activity area for a reasonable price.

Time and the development of these low-cost construction techniques has made it difficult to differentiate between the gymnasiums built in recent years and field houses. Historically, the gymnasium was a small enclosed area for indoor sports, usually within a main school building. Today it is generally a large multi-use facility located in a wing of a building or is a separate building. In many cases, the gymnasium and field house have become synonymous.

Activities performed in the field house include instruction in physical education; practice for intercollegiate athletics; intramural, interscholastic, or intercollegiate competition; informal recreation; exhibitions; dances; commencement exercises; registration, and final examinations. Community uses may include concerts, exhibits, various forms of entertainment, recreation, and mass meetings.

Many field houses allow two or more activities to take place at the same time. This usually is accommodated by dividing activity areas with a system of movable nets or curtains that hang from the ceiling.

Figure 5.1. Farley Field House, Bowdoin College (Photo by P. Gobell. Courtesy of Sasaki Associates)

Figure 5.2. National Institute for Fitness and Sport, Indianapolis, IN

Examples

- *Cornell University.* This field house is comprised of two primary areas. These areas include a gymnasium with three full basketball courts and roll out seating for 5,000 and an artificial turf field area. Opened in 1990, it also contains an indoor climbing wall, classrooms, meeting rooms, locker rooms, training facilities, and offices.

-*William Farley Field House.* This 60,000-square-foot field house is a major part of the 100,000-square-foot Bowdoin Athletic Complex at Bowdoin College in Brunswick, Maine. Opened in 1987, the field house contains a six-lane, 200 meter track, a separate free weight area, and 6,500 square feet of translucent panels to allow for natural lighting. The infield consists of four tennis courts with a system of movable nets to divide activity spaces. (Figure 5.1.)

- *Freeman Athletic Center.* Located on the campus of Wesleyan University in Middletown, Connecticut, the field house provides a 60,000-square-foot synthetic surface. It includes a six-

lane 200 meter track, three basketball courts, and four competition and two recreational tennis courts. Opened in 1990, the field house is only a part of a $21 million recreational, intramural, and intercollegiate athletic facility expansion project.

- *National Institute for Fitness and Sport.* This $10.5 million facility is located in Indianapolis, Indiana and was opened in 1987. The activity area of this 120,000-square-foot facility contains a 200 meter running track, aerobic room, weight room, and serves as the training facility for the United States Gymnastics Federation. The 200 meter track is unique in that the curves can be flat or banked and can be adjusted hydraulically. Also included in the facility are a complete exercise testing and research center, exhibit hall, 120 seat auditorium, resource library, offices, and locker rooms. (Figure 5.2.)

Indoor Football Practice Field Houses

Indoor football practice buildings are another version of the field house that is

becoming more common. These structures usually are designed for football to be the primary activity and sometimes the only activity. Other activities occasionally may use the facility, but often no accommodations have been made for these activities. Most often found in colder climates, these field houses usually contain a full size, or near full size artificial turf football field. These football field houses also may contain offices, a weight room, locker rooms, and a synthetic track around the field. Some schools find that having an indoor football facility is as important for recruiting as it is for practice.

Examples

-*University of Michigan.* Opened in 1980, the Indoor Practice Facility was the first field house built primarily for indoor football practice. It contains a 120 yard synthetic turf football field with end zones, two regulation goal posts, and has a 75-foot-high ceiling. Construction cost was $1,800,000.

-*Loftus Sports Center.* Located at the University of Notre Dame, this $6.4 million field house contains a full size football field that is surrounded by a five-laps-per-mile track. A 7,000-square-foot weight room, locker rooms, lecture room, and offices are included in this 135,000-square-foot structure. Opened in 1987, the field can be divided into separate activity areas by a state-of-the-art, computerized netting system. (Figure 5.3.)

-*Kent State University.* Opened in 1989, this $7,000,000 football field house covers 120,000 square feet. It houses a full size football field, a six-lane 320 yard track, a weight room, locker rooms, and offices. An advanced netting system allows for several activities to be conducted simultaneously. Partially funded by student fees, this facility is used by the entire student population.

Figure 5.3. Loftus Center, University of Notre Dame (Photo courtesy of Ellerbe Becket Architects)

INDOOR ICE ARENAS

Ice skating and ice hockey are gaining in popularity with the result that more and more indoor ice rinks are being built. Following is the 1992 NCAA Ice Hockey rink suggested layout (Figure 5.4.). Line drawings and photographs of the National Hockey Center, St. Cloud State University are included in the appendix.

INDOOR STADIUMS

Stadiums usually are built more specifically for exhibition purposes with mass seating. Until recently, stadiums were almost exclusively outdoor facilities, but with the advent of new structural technologies, more indoor stadiums are being built. In addition to competitive athletic events, these structures often are used for such purposes as convocations, concerts, various forms of entertainment, mass meetings, and rallies.

Examples

-Astrodome. The Houston Astrodome was opened in 1965 and was the first of the huge indoor stadiums.

The roof is 642 feet across and is based on the principles of the geodesic dome. It is made up of 4,596 rectangular panels of clear Lucite and originally was designed to allow direct sunshine to enter in order to allow the growth of natural grass. Baseball players found that the resulting glare made catching fly balls too difficult, so the solution was to tint the Lucite gray. The resulting decrease in sunlight was not enough to maintain the grass, and this is what prompted the development of Astroturf. The Astrodome seats 55,000 for baseball and 65,000 for football.

-SkyDome. Located in Toronto, Ontario, SkyDome is presently the only stadium that has a fully retractable roof. Opened in 1989, SkyDome can completely open or close the entire steel trussed roof in 20 minutes. This is accomplished by three movable roof sections, two of which slide and another that rotates. The stadium seats 50,600 for baseball, 53,000 for football, and has different seating arrangements for concerts ranging from 10,000 to 70,000. It also contains 161 luxury SkyBoxes, a 348 room hotel and health club, full broadcast facilities, underground park-

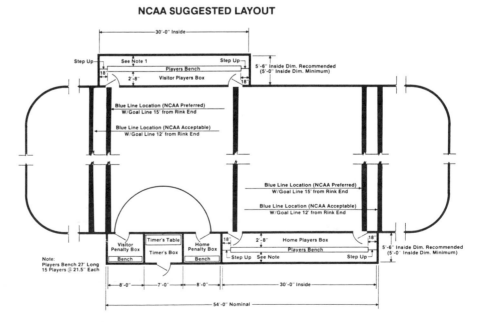

Figure 5.4. Ice Hockey Rink (1992 NCAA Ice Hockey Rules and Interpretations)

Figure 5.5. Skydome (Photo by Ian Steer)

ing, and a 110-by-33 foot state-of-the-art video screen. Original estimates of the cost for SkyDome were $184 million (Canadian) but the final cost was close to $585 million. (Figure 5.5.)

-FARGODOME. Scheduled to open in early 1993, the FARGODOME is located in Fargo, North Dakota. The roof is pre-formed structural steel and rises to a height of 115 feet above the playing surface. This multi-purpose facility will seat 19,300 for football, about 11,000 for basketball, hockey, or tennis, and about 32,000 when set up for concerts. The FARGODOME will contain about 470,000 square feet and should cost close to $43 million.

ARENAS

Arenas generally are large indoor spectator facilities. Often it may be difficult to tell the difference between the large arenas and indoor stadiums. Webster's Dictionary defines a stadium as "a large usually unroofed building with tiers of seats for spectators at sports events" and an arena as "an enclosed area for public entertainment." Both are large enclosed spectator facilities with the main differences being that stadiums tend to have a greater amount of spectator seating and are designed to handle field sports such as football and baseball. Arenas usually tend to be designed more for court type activities such as basketball.

Examples

-University Arena. Located at the University of New Mexico in Albuquerque, the Pit first opened in 1966. It originally was built for the bargain price of $1.4 million dollars and seated 14,800, all of which were ground level or below. Several years later the seating was expanded to 17,100. Over the 25 years of its existence, the Pit has averaged 15,993 fans for UNM basketball games, with the largest single crowd recorded at 19,452. The initial cost of the Pit was kept so low because of the unique construction process used. The walls and roof were erected first, a large hole was then excavated and the concrete for the floor and seating areas was poured. Even as old as it is, the Pit still is considered to be one of the top five spectator arenas in the country.

-Ball State University Arena. Opened in 1991, the Arena is a part of a $29.5 million dollar building project. Designed as a multi-purpose activity center, it features permanent and portable seating for 12,000 spectators, as well as 32 permanent wheelchair positions. Full men's, women's, visiting team, and officials' locker rooms are provided, as well as a full kitchen. In order to enhance television coverage, fixed camera positions with permanent cable runs are provided. (Figure 5.6.)

-America West Arena. Opened in 1992, the America West Arena is located in Phoenix, Arizona and is jointly owned by the City of Phoenix and the Phoenix Suns basketball team. This $89 million multi-purpose arena seats

Figure 5.6. University Arena, Ball State University (Photo by Gregory Murphey Photography. Courtesy of Browning Day Mullins Dierdorf, Inc.)

19,000 for basketball and has 87 luxury suites for lease. Other events scheduled include arena football, concerts, circuses, shows, and exhibitions. Complete ice rink facilities also are included.

-*Jack Breslin Student Events Center.* Completed in 1989, the Breslin Center is located at Michigan State University. This multi-purpose facility was built for a cost of $43 million and can seat 15,138 for basketball. The spectator seating is a combination of bench and chairback seats as well as eight luxury boxes. The Center also contains an 8,000-square-foot auxiliary gym, conference rooms, weight room, locker rooms, press room, training room, and offices. A ramp and tunnel at the south end permit truck access to the arena floor.

Trends in Arena and Stadium Design

Historically, most large arenas and stadiums have been funded by city or state governments, or by colleges and universities. Recently these entities have had tighter budgets, and, more than ever, the emphasis is on making a profit. The current trend is more toward private funding. In order to make such a large investment profitable, every effort must be made to ensure that the facility be able to accommodate as many different events and kinds of activities as possible. Recent design improvements also have focused on being able to change over from one event to another as quickly as possible. Some facilities now schedule from 250 to 600 events per year, including sporting events, concerts, conventions, trade shows, rodeos, monster truck shows, and professional wrestling. Efficient design can allow a crew to change the setup for one kind of event to another in a matter of hours. This means that more than one event can take place in the same day. Several aspects of design that allow a facility to accommodate a wide variety of events and also quickly alter the setup for different events include:

-Versatile lighting and sound systems that can adequately handle the wide variety of events.

-Ramps that allow semi-trucks to back all the way to the floor. Even better, some facilities provide floor access for two or more trucks at a time so that one can be loaded while another is unloaded.

-Heavy-duty lighting grids that can be lowered to the floor in order to enhance the placement of sound and lighting equipment for concerts.

-Fixed, pre-wired camera positions that allow for quick and easy setup for television broadcasts. The Palace of Auburn Hills even has a full television production studio which permits a television network to broadcast a game without bringing in its semitrailers full of production equipment.

-A movable arena floor such as the one in the Target Center in Minneapolis, Minnesota. This floor can be raised and lowered a full five feet in order to maintain good sight lines for either event. For basketball, the floor is in the bottom position, and temporary seating extends all the way down to courtside. When changing over for hockey, some of the temporary seats are removed and the 2.5 million pound, computer-controlled floor is elevated five feet. This eliminates the old problem of having to lay the basketball floor on the larger surface of the hockey rink and then setting up temporary seating around the perimeter of the floor on a flat surface. These seats may be close to the action, but since several rows of seats are on the same level, the sight lines are poor.

Another trend in arena and stadium design is the move toward more upscale facilities and greater service and convenience for the spectators. Some aspects of this trend include:

-More restrooms. In the past, many spectator facilities provided only enough restrooms to satisfy the local code requirements. This often resulted in long lines and frustration on the part of the spectators. Many facilities now are being designed with up to twice as many restrooms as the minimum required. Since some events may draw a disproportionate number of men or women, consideration should be given to designing some restrooms that can serve either sex simply by changing the sign on the door.

-Taking into consideration the requirements of those customers with handicaps is a priority. With the advent of the Americans With Disabilities Act, full accommodation of the needs of the disabled is now federal law.

-The building of larger concourse areas and the addition of separate concourses to serve different levels. Improved access and less crowding makes these areas more attractive. Some concourse areas are being designed to resemble a mini-mall by offering many different choices of food and novelty items.

-One of the most significant trends in stadium and arena design is the addition of luxury boxes or suites. These suites usually are leased to individuals or companies who desire a semi-private lounge area, actually large enough to accommodate about 20 guests. Suites normally are leased on multi-year contracts and are furnished and decorated by the tenant. The prevalence of these luxury suites is growing rapidly primarily because they are such good revenue producers.

The Palace of Auburn Hills is a good example of how important suites have become to the economics of this type of facility. The original plans called for 100 luxury suites to be built as part of the arena. About one-third of the way through construction, all of the suites had been rented. Some quick design changes by the architect added an additional 80 suites, that made for a total of 180. The added suites also were leased by the time The Palace opened. Total construction cost was about $63 million, and the income from the rental of the suites alone is about $11 million per year. Luxury suites have become a significant trend and may make the construction of future arenas and stadiums more economically feasible.

CAMPUS RECREATION CENTERS

Campus recreation centers are one of the fastest growing concepts on college and university campuses today. These centers are not designed along the lines of the typical physical education/ recreation buildings of the past. The "new breed" of rec center often includes not only gyms, pools, weight rooms, racquetball courts, etc. that one expects to find, but also indoor jogging tracks, leisure pools, game rooms, TV rooms, bowling alleys, study rooms, food service, and other areas designed to improve the quality of campus life. (Figure 5.7.) These recreation centers

Figure 5.7. Main Street, Student Recreation Center, Central Michigan University (Photo by Balthazar Korab Ltd. Courtesy of TMP Associates, Inc.)

often are constructed primarily for campus recreation, with an emphasis on social recreation, and may tend to limit use by physical education classes or athletics. They often are designed as a hub of campus social life. (Figure 5.7.)

Trends in Campus Recreation Centers

-Many recreation centers are being built with a large central corridor along which all of the activity areas are located. Typically there are large windows into the various activity spaces. This main street gives the feeling of a shopping mall and allows those not interested in participating in an activity the opportunity to observe others at play or to just hang out.

-Climbing walls are gaining in popularity and may be located either on inside or outside walls. These walls are designed to allow for safe climbing instruction and practice in a controlled setting. Climbing walls can be a cause for concern of liability and should be planned with adequate security precautions in mind.

- Innovations are appearing all the time in campus rec centers. A recent feature found in colder climates is the all-purpose gym that is designed to accommodate floor hockey. These rooms are built with rounded corners and have walls that are designed to withstand the abuses of being hit by flying pucks, sticks, and bodies. This was introduced at Eastern Michigan University in the early 1980s, and similar facilities are located now at the University of Toledo, Central Michigan University, and others. This design increases the usability of the room and does not limit traditional activities such as basketball, volleyball, and aerobic dance from taking place. These rooms have proven to be very popular at the above institutions. (Figure 5.8.)

-Another trend in recreational facilities is the move away from building competitive pools and constructing leisure pools instead. Leisure pools are

Figure 5.8. Multipurpose gym with rounded corners, Central Michigan University (Photo by Balthazar Korab, Ltd. Courtesy of TMP Associates, Inc.)

designed for play and are very different in concept. Typical leisure pool design features include water slides, current channels, wave machines, waterfalls, plunge tanks, and a high percentage of shallow water. (Figure 5.9.) Another common feature is called a zero-depth pool. This consists of a dry deck area that slopes down into the water and gradually increases in depth. This

Figure 5.9. Leisure pool, University of Toledo

simulates a beach area and makes a great area for play or lounging. Usually a large deck area by the pool with spas, saunas, or steam rooms is included to allow for pool parties.

-The variable depth pool floor is becoming more common in recreational facilities. Typically, these floors can be adjusted from a depth of four feet up to deck level or anywhere in between. This allows for tremendous flexibility in use of the pool. At zero depth, wheelchairs can be rolled onto the floor and then lowered to the desired depth. The floor can be set at six inches for water play for infants or to four feet for lap swimming. The initial cost of a variable depth floor is higher than standard pool design, but can increase dramatically the programming possibilities.

-Many recreation centers are providing upscale locker rooms that give more of a feeling of belonging to a private health club. In place of the humid, harsh feeling of the traditional locker room, an effort is being made to transform these areas into a more warm, friendly, and inviting atmosphere. Carpeting, upscale lockers, at least a few private shower stalls, steam rooms or saunas, music, good ventilation, hair dryers, and soft lighting are a few of the amenities sometimes found in these locker rooms. Careful consideration always should be given to security and supervision of locker areas.

-Other features that may help give the feeling of being in a private health club often are included in recreation centers. Many are opening pro shops that sell sports equipment such as balls, racquets, and shoes, along with other supplies and clothing. Juice bars and health food snack bars also are appearing more often in an attempt to make the facility more attractive to the student population.

Examples of Campus Recreation Centers

- *Eastern Michigan University.* The first of the large campus recreation centers that emphasized a health club type atmosphere, this facility opened in 1982. A list of features includes four full basketball courts, a 50 meter pool with one and three-meter boards and five, seven, and 10-meter platforms, a club pool with whirlpool, sauna and two habitat rooms. These are small rooms that allow one or two people to experience music, steam, water sprays, heat, and wind. Four separate weight areas provide a total of 8,700 square feet of area for lifting. Also included within the recreation building are 13 racquetball courts, an aerobics room, batting cage, combatives room, utility gym with rounded corners for floor hockey, a 9.8 laps-per-mile jogging track, pool hall, dining room with food service, and a full service sporting goods shop.

-University of Toledo. Located in Toledo, Ohio, this campus recreation center was opened in 1990. It is truly a multi-purpose recreational activity center that includes a gym with six full basketball courts, an enclosed rounded corner floor hockey room, a 300 meter suspended jogging track, free weight room, machine weight/fitness area, 25 meter-by-25 yard competitive pool, leisure pool with water slide, plunge tank (diving pool), six glass wall racquetball courts, aerobic dance room, snack bar/restaurant, table game area, social lounges, meeting rooms and auditoriums, locker rooms, and offices.

-Vanderbilt University. The Student Recreation Center encompasses 132,000 square feet and was opened in 1990. Located in Nashville, Tennessee, the SRC was built for a cost of $14.2 million. It contains a gymnasium with three full basketball courts, a 9.2 laps-per-mile jogging track, a 33 1/3 meter-by-25 yard pool, six racquetball courts, two squash courts, a 6,000-square-foot weight room, two multi-purpose activity rooms, locker rooms, food services, lounge, and offices. A 28 foot high-by-20 foot wide climbing wall is located just inside the main entrance. The activity spaces are arranged along a 320 foot, two-story corridor from which many of the activities may be viewed.

-Arizona State University. Opened in 1989, the Student Recreation Complex contains 142,000 square feet and was built for a cost of $15.7 million. The facility contains three gyms with two basketball courts each, three multi-purpose/dance rooms, 15 racquetball courts, a 9,000-square-foot fitness/weight room, rehabilitation/weight room, pro shop, locker rooms, and administrative office space. Instead of being confined to just the weight room, a large number of aerobic exercise machines, such as step-climbers and stationary bikes, line the lobbies and corridors and allow for a wide variety of views and locations in which to work out. (Figure 5.10.) Outdoor activity areas include several intramural fields, tennis courts, sand volleyball courts, and a 70 meter-by-25 yard pool with two movable bulkheads.

-Central Michigan University. The Student Activity Center, located in Mt. Pleasant, Michigan, is designed to be the center of campus social life. Most activity areas in the building are located adjacent to a large mall-like concourse that divides the building in half. This 450-by-24 foot corridor provides visual access to most of the activity areas and serves as a place for students to gather and socialize. The facility contains six basketball courts, two floor hockey/multi-purpose rooms with rounded corners, a 25 yard pool with variable depth floor, a 25 seat spa, sauna, a 12 lane handicap accessible bowling alley, a 9,000 square foot fitness room containing aerobic equipment and weight machines, a free weight room, six glass back wall racquetball courts, study areas, food service, and more! This makes the Student Activity Center the focal point for socialization for the entire campus.

GENERAL PLANNING CONSIDERATIONS

In order to ensure that a large sports or recreation facility will meet the present and future needs of the users, a number

Figure 5.10. Aerobic exercise equipment, Arizona State University

of considerations must be addressed during the planning process. A preliminary study must be conducted as a basis for writing the building program. A partial list of factors that should be included in this study are:

- an analysis of the present program
- desired future program changes
- financial considerations
- site availability and adequacy
- local, state, and federal codes and regulations
- aesthetics
- a sound justification for the need for a new facility of this type.

A building committee must be formed and should include a representative from each of the major user groups that the facility will be built to accommodate. The committee itself should be kept to a fairly small and manageable size. If there are too many people involved, it will cause more problems than it will solve. The committee should seek out and welcome input and ideas from any person who is even remotely involved. Great ideas sometimes come from unexpected places. Those asked for input might include current faculty, staff, and students, those at other similar institutions, the general public, facility consultants, and any other group that may use the facility. When an institution has determined that more space is needed for current or projected programs, exploratory meetings are essential for determining what to build and how to build it.

Remember that the technology is available to build whatever can be envisioned and in the early stages, all ideas are valuable.

It is highly recommended that a professional consultant be hired to advise the planning committee. Experienced consultants can save a project many times the amount paid for their salary. The consultant should be brought in on the project as early as possible. A qualified consultant will bring a professional orientation and practical experience in overcoming the problems often encountered in the planning process.

The consultant can help educate the committee about current trends and innovations, making efficient use of space, and may show photo or slide examples of good and bad facilities. Other areas of advice may include recommending experienced architects, helping to select the architect, providing ideas on financing, recommending materials, and acting as a go-between with the planning committee and the architect. A professional consultant is paid only for advice and can be a very valuable asset to the overall project.

Site Selection

Intelligent and imaginative facility site selection and development are significant aspects of the planning process. The site can affect the desired programs, budget, transportation and parking, landscaping, and numerous other program components. A few of the important factors that the site selection process must take into consideration include accessibility, relationship to existing facilities, drainage, aesthetics, climate, topography, property lines and easements, utilities, parking, and security.

A primary requisite for a satisfactory site is adequacy of size. The size of the facility should be determined by careful study of the present and future needs of all programs, existing facilities, and available funds. The site must be large enough to accommodate the desired activities and all support areas such as parking, storage, and room for future expansion. The site should be readily accessible to the primary users. In the case of a college or university campus recreation center, a location near the dormitories and student housing might be desirable. Large spectator facilities should be situated where the public will have easy access and parking. It also may be desirable to separate the facility from other buildings.

Facilities must be located to allow for future expansion. It is much easier and cheaper to plan for growth from the beginning than to try and 'shoehorn' an expansion into an unplanned space. If there is a possiblity that the size of the facility will need to be increased in the foreseeable future, the method of expansion should be predetermined and the necessary details incorporated in the original footings and other construction. As far as possible, the requirements for future expansion should be built into the initial structure.

Adequate parking areas adjacent to the facility, with a paved access roadway leading to the building, are necessary. When admission is charged for parking, a fence with a minimum height of seven feet surrounding the spectator structure and the enclosed field is desirable. Gates are necessary for spectator and service entrances and exits. Admission gates should be located near the parking lots and other main approaches to the structure. The number and size of the entrances depends on the projected and potential attendance. Exits should permit the crowd to vacate the enclosure within 10 minutes. At least one gate 14-feet high and 14-feet wide should be provided to accommodate trucks and buses. Surface drainage of the site and adjacent areas, as well as the subsurface soils and geological formations, must be considered.

Areas with two or more similar organizations or schools may consider the construction of one facility for their combined use. Teams from each school may practice on local fields and play their regular games at the stadium. If possible, the structure should be located on or adjacent to one of the school's sites for reasons of greater accessibility, maximum use, and more efficient maintenance, operation, and super-vision.

An idea that recently has gained favor on some large university campuses is satellite facilities, located at several different areas on campus, usually near dormitories or student housing. This makes recreational areas readily available to the students and eliminates the need for locker room facilities on site. Locating facilities where the students are helps to promote recreational participation and can reduce parking problems at the central facility.

Single Use vs Multi-Purpose Facilities

Building a facility that ideally is suited for a specific purpose means that it is going to be less than ideal for other activities. In order to make a facility adequate for several different events, a number of compromises must be made.

An example is that of one large arena that was built primarily to house a big-time college basketball program. The arena was designed to seat 16,000 fans, and there is not a bad seat in the house. The fixed seating goes right down to courtside so that the usable floor area is limited to the size of a basketball court. It is a great spectator facility for basketball. The problem is that this school has only about 15 home basketball games per year. Other than graduation, a few other varsity contests, and a few concerts a year, the arena sits empty the rest of the time. With only one court, its not even cost efficient to turn on the lights for intramurals or recreation. If the first several rows of seats had been roll-away bleachers, a larger court area would have made the entire facility more functional. There always are trade-offs to consider. In this case the original designers felt that looks and comfort for basketball were more important than multiple function.

Too often, single purpose facilities are not cost efficient, and they become liabilities rather than assets. Many large spaces, constructed primarily to serve an athletic team, become financially self-supporting only by serving a variety of other events. The continual emergence of new synthetic materials, improved building techniques, and changing program needs can complicate the planning of a functional athletic, physical education, and recreation facility. Certainly the trend is to construct multi-purpose facilities with the flexibility to adapt to a number of diverse needs.

Modules

A module is a specified area that makes optimal use of a limited amount of space. One of the most common module sizes is a space 100 feet-by-124 feet. An area this size can accommodate a full size competition basketball or volleyball court, two practice basketball courts, three volleyball courts, or six badminton courts. The two basketball practice courts are each 84 feet-by 50 feet, with eight feet of clear space on each side and between them. The two practice basketball courts will be at right angles to the main court (94 feet-by-50 feet) that will be located in the center of the gym. Decreasing the area of a module would change entirely the number and/or size of the courts that can be accommodated, while minor increases in the size of the module will not result in more courts. Gymnasiums often are referred to by how many modules they contain, i.e., a one module or two module gym. (Figure 5.11.)

Lighting

The use of natural lighting, or fenestration, should be considered in the planning stage. Natural lighting can reduce electric power consumption and also can improve the aesthetics. Natural light may be introduced through the use of windows, skylights, fabric roofs, and clerestories. Windows should be located to prevent the interference of sunlight with player performance or spectator viewing at any time during the day. In general, windows along a north wall will admit the best light and will be easiest to prevent the admittance of direct sunlight.

Artificial lighting may be provided by incandescent, fluorescent, or high intensity discharge (HID) lights which include mercury, metal-halide, and sodium vapor lighting fixtures. Many users prefer metal-halide lighting

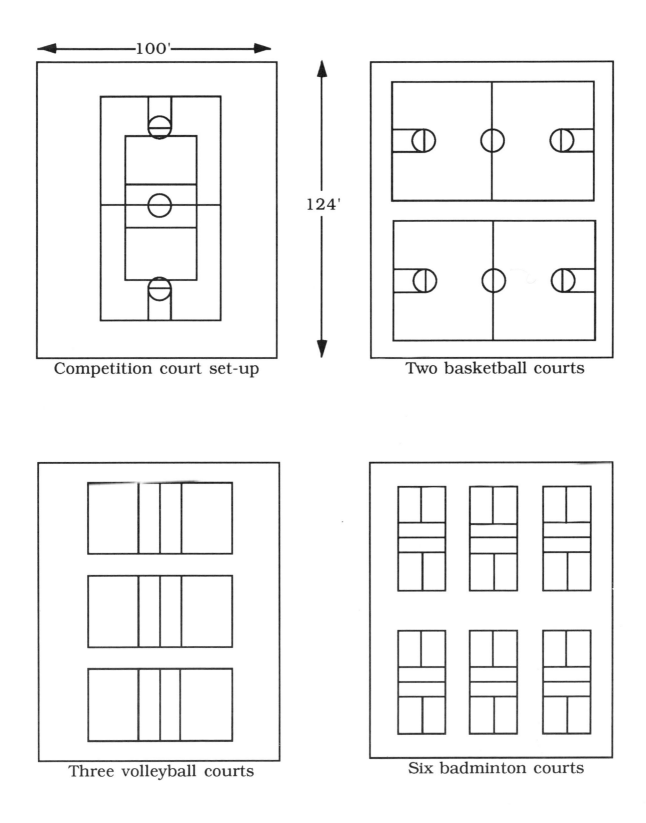

100'

124'

Competition court set-up

Two basketball courts

Three volleyball courts

Six badminton courts

Example of how a general use module 124' X 100'
can accomodate several different court layouts.

Figure 5.11. Alternate court layouts

because it provides excellent color-correct light at a very low operating cost. In order to enhance the lighting system used, light color surface treatments for walls, ceilings, and flooring should be considered. This helps to reflect available light and makes it easier to track balls moving at high speed.

The amount of lighting within different activity areas often is inadequate. Uniform and adequate illumination is necessary for proper judgment of moving objects. As a rule of thumb, the smaller and faster moving the object that must be watched, the more illumination that is required. More light is necessary to safely play racquetball than for weight training or swimming. It is recommended that a minimum of 100 footcandles be available on all courts and gyms. Swimming pools, weight rooms, dance studios, etc. should have at least 50 footcandles and a minimum of 100 footcandles if spectators or television cameras will be present. Careful consideration also must be given to the proper placement and aiming of lights.

It is best to overestimate the lighting needs for each area because illumination systems tend to lose brightness over time. It is not unusual to have a new system that produces 100 footcandles of illumination and have it drop to 75 footcandles after five years of operation. Standards for the design and location of sports lighting are published by the Illuminating Engineering Society of North America.

Controls for gymnasium lighting should be located conveniently. A central control panel within the administrative area that controls all major lighting in the building should be considered. If the controls are to be located at or near the activity area, they should be recessed and keyed. When the lighting system is being planned, the initial costs should be compared with replacement costs and operational or electrical expenses, since some systems are less expensive to install but are very expensive to operate or maintain. Any

lights in an activity area must be enclosed and protected. This usually is accomplished by covering the lamp with a tempered glass lens and then by an acrylic lens and possibly a wire screen. These coverings will not only reduce the chance of breaking the lamp, but also will contain all of the glass and pieces if breakage does occur.

Heating, Ventilation, and Air Conditioning

Another area that will cause many problems if improperly designed or engineered is the heating, ventilation, and air conditioning (HVAC) system. Different areas of the facility have differing requirements for the HVAC system. High ceiling areas need good air circulation in order to keep heat stratification to a minimum. Wet areas such as pools, spas, and shower rooms require dehumidification and a fast turnover rate (10 to 12 air changes per hour) of the air handling system. It is important that the fresh air be introduced into the area so as not to create a draft on the occupants. Enclosed areas that are likely to have occupants who sweat a lot, such as weight rooms and racquetball courts, also need to be able to turn over the air quickly in order to remove odors and humidity. It is recommended that each different area be individually thermostatically controlled if possible.

Where climatic conditions permit, evaporating cooling systems should be considered. These systems can cost up to 80 percent less than mechanical cooling in initial construction costs and also cost less to operate.

Entrances, Exits, and Lobbies

User access should be considered thoroughly during the planning process. Control of all entrance and exit points is important in any kind of sports or recreation facility. For recreational facilities, it is best to have one point that all people must pass through when

entering or leaving the building. This is essential for those that will be charging a fee or checking identifications for admittance to the facility.

Many types of security systems exist to control access through both exterior and interior doors. A central control panel located in the facility management office can be installed to electronically lock or unlock doors throughout the facility. This control panel also may indicate when a door is opened by an unauthorized person so that a facility attendant can be dispatched to investigate.

Some systems use magnetic cards instead of keys to open doors. Controlled by a central computer, records can be kept automatically which document which door was opened, what time it was opened, and whose card was used to open it. This type of system has the advantage of not having to change all of the locks if someone loses a key. Instead, that numbered card is canceled in the computer, which makes the card worthless to anyone that finds it.

Controlling access to recreational sport facilities is a major concern of the facility operator. Systems now exist that can connect either a magnetic strip or barcode card reader to a computer and compare the information on a user's I.D. card with current information in the computer data base. The user passes his/her I.D. card through the card reader at the building control point and is either admitted or turned away from entering. A picture I.D. usually is used, and the picture is compared with the user to confirm that the card has not been borrowed or stolen. This type of system also can be set up to record who, when, and how often an individual is using the facility. This information then can be used to determine both who is using and not using the facility. This type of information can be very valuable for targeting certain individuals or groups in a marketing campaign.

Entrances should be located with reference to parking facilities and traffic approaches. Provisions should be made for a paved access roadway, and at least one entrance should accommodate trucks. Floor materials and wall treatments should be selected for their resistance to punish- ment and ease of maintenance. Handicap accessibility also must be addressed.

A careful analysis of the anticipated pedestrian traffic flow in the building will pay enormous dividends in terms of efficient supervision and lower maintenance costs. All building, health, and fire codes must be considered as a basic guide during the planning process. The architectural style should be designed to conform with the municipal or campus surroundings.

In spectator facilities the lobby should be designed for ticket selling and collecting so that the traffic will flow in as straight a line as possible from the entrances to the ticket windows to the ticket collectors. To avoid congestion, approximately two-thirds of the lobby should be planned for accommodating box offices and ticket purchasers. The remainder should be reserved for ticket holders, who should have direct access to admission gates. The main lobby should be of sufficient size to accommodate anticipated crowds purchasing tickets and entering, particularly in colder climates.

The seating capacity and the number of seats in each section will determine the number of entrances and exits required. It is important that spectators be able to leave quickly. It is highly desirable to have exit ramps leading from stepped aisles. Ramps, stairs, and passageways should be as wide as the deck aisles served.

Good traffic control should permit the efficient movement of users to and from the gymnasium, locker rooms, and other related service areas. All traffic arrangements for spectators should provide direct movement to and from seating with a minimum of foot traffic on gymnasium floors. Spectators should have access to drinking fountains, concession stands, and restrooms without crossing the gymnasium floor. Steep, high stairways should be avoided.

Facility Management Offices

The facility administrative offices serve as the focal point for most business and management functions within the facility. Often the most efficient location for these offices is very near the main entrance. In the case of a facility that allows only limited access, it may be desirable to locate the offices of the facility manager and staff at a point just outside the control point. This allows access to the office by visitors or those with business without having to provide I.D. or to pay.

It may be advantageous to locate assorted building controls in the main office. These controls may include master lighting controls for the entire building, the public address system, a centralized security system, and controls for the heating, ventilation, and air conditioning.

Restrooms

All events that attract spectators require public restroom facilities. Restrooms should be designed for proper light, ventilation, maintenance, sanitation, and for handicapped usage. Separate toilet facilities in sufficient number for men and women spectators also should be provided close to the seating areas and near traffic lanes. Many spectator facilities now are building more womens toilets than mens as a response to complaints. Where large crowds attend games, it is advisable to place supplementary toilet facilities off the main lobby. The number of authorized building users, the capacity of spectator seating, and the state and local building codes will dictate the number and location of toilet facilities.

For spectator facilities that must accommodate large numbers of people simultaneously, consideration should be given to designing rest rooms with a one-way traffic flow. Separate "in" and "out" doors at different ends of the room can ease congestion during rush periods. It also may be beneficial to plan for a section of the restroom to be closed off for smaller crowds. This can greatly reduce cleaning, maintenance, and repair costs when large restrooms are not needed.

Storage

The single most common complaint and the one thing that most sport and recreational facilities have in common is a lack of adequate storage space. These areas usually are the first to be removed from the plans if the budget is tight or often are converted into something else that was neglected during the planning stage. It is essential to have adequate and conveniently placed storage space if the facilities are to be fully usable.

Lockable storage space must be provided for both small and large equipment and supplies. Large equipment such as standards, nets, mats, etc. should never be stored on the floor of an activity area. Equipment that is not properly stored is subject to abuse, theft, and may be a cause of accidental injury. With the prevalence of lawsuits these days, liability is a constant concern.

After a building is completed, it is practically impossible to add storage space unless that space is taken from areas designed for other uses. Realistic planning of storage space should be done while determining total space requirements. Adequate maintenance and control over supplies and equipment is possible only when proper storage space exists.

A large storage room should be located adjacent to the gymnasium floors. Storage areas should be accessible directly to the gym floor through a double door without a threshold or center post. For safety reasons, the doors should open inward and be easily secured. Locks that always re-lock upon closing may be considered. The storage room may contain lockable storage cabinets and deep shelving for storage of smaller, loose equipment. Much of the shelving should be adjustable to best accommodate changing needs.

Spectator Seating

If possible, the seating capacity of a stadium or arena should be sufficient to meet present needs, as well as the needs for the foreseeable future. If building the desired number of seats is not possible, planning for later expansion to satisfy predicted needs for a period of at least 20 years is recommended. The number of seats required will be influenced by the activities offered, enrollment (if planning for a school or college), budget, population and socioeconomic status of the surrounding area, and planned expansion of the program. Providing a greater number of seats than realistically is required can be a financial disaster that can be avoided only by careful planning and research.

Along with the total number of seats, another important question that must be answered is just how to provide those seats. Are all of the seats going to be permanent, or will some or all be supplied by portable bleachers? Portable bleachers usually are not as comfortable as permanent seats, but can be moved to allow for an increase in activity space.

When bleachers are extended, the first row should be a minimum of 10 feet away from the court sidelines and end lines (12 feet for volleyball). The amount of storage space required to store bleacher units varies greatly and should be determined during planning.

Portable bleachers also may be used as movable walls or dividers to separate activity areas.

Sight Lines

Seating facilities should be constructed to provide spectators with a good view of the performance. Nearness and an unobstructed view of the desired points affect the quality of the building as a spectator facility. *A sight line is a straight line from the eyes of the seated spectator, over the heads of others below, to a point on the field or court that represents the spot nearest the structure that should be in the field of vision.*

It is essential to consider sight lines in the planning stages of any spectator facility. One major track and field stadium was built so that over 40 percent of the seats did not have a clear view of the finish line. Many baseball stadiums with high outfield fences limit the sight of the spectators seated beyond the fence. The right field fence at the Metrodome in Minneapolis, Minnesota does not allow many of those in the right field seats to see the outfield areas near the fence.

Recommended focal points for sight lines are as follows:
- for football, the nearest side boundary lines
- for basketball, about knee height of a player along the nearest side or end line
- for baseball, several feet behind the catcher
- for track, about knee-height of the runner in the nearest lane
- for side seating for tennis, four feet in toward the seats from the doubles bound- ary line
- for end seating for tennis, 10 feet behind the base line.

Other Considerations

The height of the ceiling in the main gym should be at least 30 feet clear to accommodate power volleyball and to provide for proper sight lines for all spectators.

Acoustical treatment of ceilings and walls is important where spectators will be present or if teaching is to take place. There are many types of acoustical treatment available, however those that will chip or break when hit with a ball should be avoided.

A first aid room should be considered, especially if this will be a spectator facility. This room also may serve as a training room if desired, but it should be located within easy access of spectator areas.

To determine requirements for ramps, stairs, exits, doors, corridors, and fire alarm systems, planners should consult local, state, and federal laws and the local building, health, safety, and fire codes.

Common Design Errors

A recent informal survey of athletic and recreational building managers found that the most common design errors include the following:
- lack of adequate storage space
- inadequate lighting
- failure to consider operating costs during planning phase
- too much wasted space
- not planning for maintenance
- poor traffic patterns
- assuming that all architects know what is best for you.

It is not uncommon that the architect selected to design an athletic, physical education, or recreation facility has never worked on this type of project before. Also, the primary concern of many architects is to design a pretty building, which may be done at the cost of function. The building managers surveyed stressed that the planning committee should research and feel comfortable with the architect's recommendations and designs.

INNOVATIONS IN TYPES OF CONSTRUCTION

The ability to enclose vast surface areas to accommodate multi-purpose field layouts has created the opportunity to develop a variety of construction techniques. Tension structures, air-supported fabric structures, wooden domes, geodesic domes, and cable domes are examples of building designs that have been used successfully in enclosing large sports facilities.

Geodesic Domes

The geodesic dome offers one of the many options in types of construction. Invented by American architect Buckminster Fuller, a geodesic dome is a framework to enclose space. In technical language, a geodesic dome is the result of a series of physical and complex mathematical properties that create a lightweight, strong, possibly transportable, and economical structure that can be used in a multitude of ways. It is made by precisely interlocking triangles that appear as a series of hexagons on a completed building. Enormous spans and heights can be achieved, including a complete sphere, without the need of inside support walls. The familiar half-sphere shape has given way to many complicated shapes as engineering knowledge and confidence has progressed.

Fabric Structures

A fairly recent development in the area of physical education, recreation, and athletic facilities is the concept of fabric structures. The fabric used most commonly is a Teflon-coated fiberglass material. The fiberglass yarn used to make the material is pound-for-pound stronger than steel and also is less expensive. It can be designed to allow either a large amount or very little natural light to penetrate. The fabric can withstand temperatures of 1300 to 1500 degrees Fahrenheit and is not adversely affected by cold or the ultraviolet rays of the sun. Fabric structures offer a number of possible advantages and disadvantages when compared with standard construction. (Figure 5.12.)

Advantages

- *Lower Initial Cost.* Initial costs usually are lower than with conventional construction. Several factors contribute to this, the primary one being weight. A fabric roof is 1/30 the weight of a conventional steel truss roof. This reduced weight means that the walls, footings, and foundations are not required to be nearly as strong as in a conventional building.
- *Less Construction Time.* The amount of construction time is related directly to the initial cost of the structure. The total time necessary to build a fabric structure is usually less than for a conventional roof.
- *Natural Lighting.* Since the fiberglass fabric material that is used is translucent, it results in a higher amount of interior natural lighting. Without using artificial lights during the day, the light intensity inside can vary anywhere from 100 to 1000 footcandles, depending on the weather conditions, the design, and choice of the fabric. The interior light is considered to be of high quality because it is non-glare and shadow-free.
- *Possibly Lower Energy Costs.* In some climates or regions energy costs may be substantially reduced by the fabric's translucenct characteristics. The large amount of natural light may reduce or eliminate the need for artificial light during the daytime. This also may reduce the need for air conditioning required to overcome the heat generated by the artificial lights.
- *Less Maintenance.* The non-stick characteristics of Teflon allows the fabric to be washed clean each time it rains.
- *Full Utilization of Space.* Depending on the fabric structure's configuration and support, the area that can be enclosed is almost limitless.

Disadvantages

- *Life Span.* The fabric envelope in use today has a life expectancy of up to 25 years, with longer-life materials being tested. All other items such as the foundation, flooring, and mechanical equipment have the life span of a conventional building.
- *Poor Thermal Insulation.* In cold climates there may be an increase in energy cost when compared with conventional construction, due to lower insulating properties of the fabric roof. The insulating value of a typical fabric roof is about R-2 but can be increased substantially. The cost of heating is a significant factor and should be evaluated with that of a conventional building over time. During winter months when the heat is required to melt the snow or to cause it to slide off, a safe level of temperature will have to be maintained at all times at the expense of heating

Figure 5.12. Hoosier Dome (Photo courtesy of Browning Day Mullins Dierdorf, Inc.)

costs. If the bubble is not to be heated during the inactive hours, it will have to be supervised constantly for the dangers of unexpected snowfall. In the summertime the heat gain of the air-supported structure may pose a cooling problem.

- *Acoustic Problem*. The curved shape of the air-supported structure produces a peculiar acoustic environment. This poses limitations on its use for large gatherings and open-plan arrangements for different groups.

- *Restriction Due to Wind*. In winds of hurricane velocity, most codes require that the structure be evacuated.

There are three basic types of fabric structures in use today. These three types are tension structures, air-supported structures, and cable domes. Tension structures are made by stretching fabric between several rigid supports. Air-supported structures are sealed buildings which, through the use of fans, maintain a positive internal air pressure that supports the roof. These structures actually are inflated like a balloon and must maintain the positive air pressure to remain inflated. Cable domes are the newest type of fabric structure. The cable dome actually is a modified tension structure. A complex network of cables and girders is erected to support a fabric roof.

Tension Structures

Some projects lend themselves more naturally to tension structures than to air-supported structures or cable domes. Some of the conditions in which tension structures may be more favorable are as follows:

- Free and open access from the sides is desirable or required.

- A unique design or aesthetics is important.

- The facility will be largely unattended or not monitored.

- Possible deflation of an air structure would constitute a severe operational or safety problem.

- A retrofit to an existing

building or structure, such as a swimming pool or an outdoor stadium, is desired.

Examples

- *Knott Athletic Recreation Convocation Center*. Located at Mount Saint Marys College in Emmitsburg, Maryland, the Knott Center is a unique

combination of standard construction and a fabric tension structure. (Figures 5.13, 5.14.) Completed in 1987, most of the facility is built with standard brick construction, with the tension structure field house connected onto one side of the building. The fabric roof covers 30,000 square feet of activity space including a multiple court set-up and a 10-lap-per-mile running track.

Figure 5.13. Exterior of Knott Center, Mount St. Mary's College (Photo by Matt Wargo. Courtesy of Bohlin, Cywinski, Jackson.)

Figure 5.14. Interior of Knott Center, Mount St. Mary's College (Photo by Matt Wargo. Courtesy of Bohlin, Cywinski, Jackson.)

Rising to a height of 40 feet, the double layered roof provides for almost exclusive use of natural light during the day. Also included within the facility are four racquetball courts, locker rooms, and a 25 yard pool.

- *La Verne College.* La Verne College in La Verne, California contains the first permanent enclosed fiberglass structure in the United States. It was completed in 1973. The tent-like structure covers 1.4 acres, with the fabric roof having been erected in just three days. Called the Campus Center, it contains a gymnasium that seats 900 people, men's and women's locker rooms, offices, the campus bookstore, and lecture areas. A smaller separate tension structure houses the drama department.

- *Hanover Park Recreation Center.* This city-owned community recreation center is located in Hanover Park, Illinois. It houses six tennis courts and a gymnasium. Completed in 1976.

- *Lindsay Park.* The Lindsay Park Sports Centre in Calgary, Alberta, Canada, houses a 50 meter pool, a diving pool, a fully equipped 30,000-square-foot gymnasium, and a 200 meter running track. The roof is unique in that it was designed with insulation that is rated at R-16. This compares with a typical fabric roof that has about an R-2 rating. Despite the great improvement in insulating qualities, the fabric roof still is translucent enough to allow for an interior illumination of about 200 footcandles. Completed in 1983.

- *McClain Athletic Training Facility.* Completed in 1988, this field house is located at the University of Wisconsin at Madison, Wisconsin. Due to site restrictions, this $9.5 million facility contains a 90 yard football field instead of a full size field. Most of the 76,380-square-foot field is covered by a 42,000-square-foot fabric tension roof that admits up to 750 foot candles of natural light into the structure. When comparing the fabric roof to standard construction, it is estimated that the increased cost for heating and the reduced cost for artificial lighting results

in an overall saving of about $21,000 per year. Below the synthetic turf field lies a full 64,320-square-foot basement that contains locker rooms for football, track, and coaches, weight room, training facilities, and therapy pool. The therapy pool is 15-by-40 feet and goes from four to seven feet in depth. Also included in the facility are an auditorium, six meeting rooms, and a film room. (Figure 5.15.)

Air-Supported Structures

There are two basic types of air-supported structures. These include the large permanent structures and smaller, more portable structures.

Air-supported fabric structures are supported by a positive air pressure within a totally enclosed building. This positive air pressure is produced by a group of large fans. In conventional buildings the foundation, walls, and internal columns must support a roof weight of between 10 and 40 pounds per square foot. On the other hand, in air-supported structures, a roof weight of about one pound per square foot is

transmitted directly to the ground by the increased pressure. This increases air pressure of about four or five pounds per square foot greater than ambient pressure and usually is unnoticed by the building's occupants.

Some of the instances when an air structure may be preferable to a tension structure or standard construction are:

- when column-free spans of greater than 150 feet are desired

- when large, column-free spans are desired at a cost that is greatly reduced compared to conventional structures. In fact, cost per unit area usually decreases as the size of the span increases

- when a low silhouette is desired.

In spite of the many advantages of the large air-supported structures, their days may be numbered. The primary disadvantage of air-supported structures is the need for the constant positive air pressure. Since this positive air pressure is what supports the roof, if there is even temporary loss of pressure, the fabric will hang down on the

Figure 5.15. McClain Athletic Training Facility, University of Wisconsin

supporting cables. Although this alone should cause no damage to the facility, this is when the structural system is the most vulnerable. Even light winds, snow, or rain may cause extensive damage to a fabric roof in the deflated position. These facilities must be monitored constantly, and all precautions must be taken to ensure that all systems are functioning properly.

Cable domes appear to have the same advantages as the large air-pressure structures but with fewer problems. It is entirely possible that we have seen the last large air-supported structure that will ever be built. (See section on Cable Domes, page 134.)

Examples

-*Dedmon Center*. Located at Radford University, Radford, Virginia, the Dedmon Center was constructed for a cost of $6,750,000 and opened in 1982. Encompassing 110,000-square-feet, it has 5,000 temporary seats for basketball. Used for physical education, athletics, and recreation, the Center provides five full basketball courts, weight room, pool, locker rooms, and offices. (Figure 5.16.)

- *Thomas E. Leavey Activities Center*. This physical education and athletic complex is located at the University of Santa Clara in Santa Clara, California. It contains a 5,000 seat arena for basketball and volleyball along with racquetball courts, wrestling, gymnastics, weight training and conditioning areas, conference rooms, staff offices, and a 25 meter swimming pool. The pool is covered by a separate air-supported fabric roof that can be removed in the summertime, converting it into an outdoor pool. Completed in 1978.

- *DakotaDome*. Located at the University of South Dakota in Vermillion, South Dakota, the DakotaDome contains five basketball/volleyball courts, two tennis courts, an eight-lane 200 meter track, four racquetball courts, six-lane 25 meter pool, locker rooms, classrooms, and the offices for the athletic department. The main floor is a synthetic surface that is used for most court activities and has an artificial turf football field that can be rolled out for football, soccer, and other field events. When the facility is set up for football, there is seating for 12,000 spectators. The entire facility was built for the bargain price of about $51 per square foot. Completed in 1978.

- *Carrier Dome*. The Carrier Dome, located in Syracuse, New York, is the home of Syracuse University athletics. The stadium seats 50,000 for football and over 30,000 for basketball. Also a great bargain, total construction cost was $27,715,000, which figures out to $554 per seat. This is very inexpensive when compared to conventional covered stadiums. Completed in 1980.

- *Silverdome*. The Silverdome, located in Pontiac, Michigan, has the largest capacity of any indoor stadium in the world. Opened in 1975, the Silverdome has permanent seating for over 80,000 spectators for football and has accommodated over 90,000 for special events. The inflated fabric roof covers an area of 10 acres and is maintained at a height of 202 feet above the playing surface. The Silverdome is owned by the city of Pontiac and currently is the home of the Detroit Lions.

Other Examples:

- *Steve Lacy Field house*. Milligan College, Milligan, Tennessee - 1974.
- *Uni-Dome*, University of Northern Iowa, Cedar Falls, Iowa - 1975.
- *Sun Dome*. University of South Florida, Tampa, Florida - 1981.
- *Metrodome*. Minneapolis, Minnesota - 1982.
- *B.C. Place Amphitheater*. Vancouver, British Columbia, Canada - 1983.
- *Hoosier Dome*. Indianapolis, Indiana - 1984.

Since the concept of fabric structures is still quite new, not all the problems have been resolved. However, each new fabric structure appears to have fewer problems and to be an

Figure 5.16. Dedmon Center, Radford University (Courtesy of Sasaki Associates)

Figure 5.17. Hoosier Dome (Photo by Wilbur Montgomery Photography. Courtesy of Browning Day Mullins Dierdorf, Inc.)

improvement over those built previously. (Figure 5.17.)

Combining Air-Supported and Tension

A recent development in the construction of fabric structures is the idea of combining both an air-supported roof and a tension roof in the same building. An example of this concept is the Stephen C. O'Connell Center. This physical education, recreation, and athletic complex is located at the University of Florida at Gainesville. This was the first structure to combine both air-supported and tension roofs in one building. The center or main arena is covered by a large air-inflated roof, while the outer areas of the building are the tension covered spaces. The main arena has an indoor track and can seat 10,400 spectators for basketball. Located under the tension supported areas are a gymnastics area, dance studio, weight room, locker rooms,

offices, and a 3,000 seat, 50 meter natatorium. Like most fabric structures, this facility was a bargain. The total construction cost was $11,954,418 which comes out to about $49 per square foot. Completed in 1980.

Portable Air Structures

This section will discuss the merits of the smaller and more portable air structures. Air structures work well as environmental covers placed over existing recreational areas and, for many organizations, the 'Bubble' is the answer to an increasing need for large covered activity areas at a nominal cost. Cost savings are in proportion to the size of the space to be covered. Spaces over 300-square-feet usually bring a cost savings when compared to conventional roofing. Because of heat gain, which seems to present a more severe problem than heat loss, the northern areas of the United States seem better suited for environmental covers. There are num-

erous playing fields within communities and around schools and colleges that lend themselves easily to enclosure by a fabric air structure.

Some of the additional advantages and disadvantages of using small air-supported structures are:

Advantages

- *Speed of Erection*. The actual erection of the structure usually takes only one or two days. However, additional time is required for ground work, site services, foundation, anchorage, flooring, and installation of mechanical and electrical equipment. Only minimal field labor is needed.
- *Ease of Deflation, Inflation and Repair*. Deflation and inflation of the fabric envelope usually does not require skilled labor.
- *Portability*. When deflated and packed, the fabric envelope can be stored in a small space or easily transported elsewhere for storage or

use. Depending on the size of the dome, deflation and packing usually requires one or two days.

- Adaptability for Temporary Functions. For temporary use, the air-supported structure has definite physical and financial advantages over a conventional building.

- Long-Span and High Ceiling Features. Clear and unobstructed spaces is an inherent feature of the structure. Conventional long-span and high ceiling structures are much more expensive.

- Integrated Heating, Ventilation, and Air-Pressure System. The integrated heating, ventilation, and air-pressure system is simple and less expensive than conventional systems. Lengthy duct and pipe work is not required.

Examples

- Memorial Stadium. A portable inflatable fabric bubble is used to cover the entire football field at the University of Illinois in the winter. First erected in 1986, it was purchased for $1.5 million. With an average inside winter temperature of 55 degrees, the field is used heavily by several departments across the campus. The concept of a portable dome over the game field adds extra use to a facility that otherwise would sit empty much of the year.

- University of Santa Clara. The swimming pool at the Thomas E. Leavey Center is covered by a portable air structure. It is removed for use as an outdoor pool in the summer months and then re-inflated for the winter to transform the pool for indoor use.

Many public and private tennis complexes, pools, and golf driving ranges are located across the country.

Cable Domes

Cable domes are the most recent innovation in fabric structure technology. Through a complex system of cables and girders, very large spans can be covered inexpensively by a fabric roof without the need for columns or

fans to maintain integrity. Engineers predict that the cable dome concept is feasible for spans of at least 1,000 feet. Cable domes incorporate most of the advantages of fabric structures when compared to standard construction, and fewer of the disadvantages. Many experts in fabric roof technology believe that cable domes will replace the air-supported structure as the design of choice for the future. There probably

will not be any more large air structures built because of the inherent advantages of the cable dome. Some of these advantages are:

- huge column-free spans can be covered
- no need for expensive energy consuming fans
- passive system - no need to constantly monitor facility.
- extremely low silhouette

Figure 5.18. Exterior of Redbird Arena, Illinois State University (Photo by Illinois State University Photo Service)

Figure 5.19. Interior of Redbird Arena, Illinois State University (Photo by Illinois State University Photo Service)

Examples

- *Redbird Arena.* Opened in 1991, Redbird Arena is on the campus of Illinois State University in Bloomington-Normal, Illinois. This multi-purpose arena can seat 10,500 spectators for basketball, with the ability to add an additional 1,500 seats on the floor for concerts or commencement. The lower sections of seats are portable bleachers that can be removed to provide 36,000-square-feet of space on the main floor. Built for a cost of $20 million, Redbird is the first cable dome to be constructed on a college campus, but probably won't be the last. (Figures 5.18., 5.19.)

- *Suncoast Dome.* The Florida Suncoast Dome is located in St. Petersburg, Florida and was opened in 1990. This multi-purpose stadium was designed primarily for baseball, yet with the flexibility to accommodate football, basketball, soccer, and tennis, as well as concerts and trade shows. In addition to 50 private suites, a variety of seating arrangements allow the facility to function as an 18,000 seat arena or a 43,000 seat stadium for baseball. The unique movable grandstands contain built-in concession stands and public toilets. The fabric roof is 688 feet in diameter and was constructed on a tilt of six degrees. This tilt is designed to allow more clearance for the trajectory of fly balls and allows the roof to reach a height of 225 feet in front of home plate. The cable truss roof system is capable of supporting 60 tons of lighting and sound equipment for concerts, yet weighs a mere six pounds per square foot. The Suncoast Dome was built for a cost of $132 million. (Figure 5.20.)

- *Georgia Dome.* Located in downtown Atlanta, Georgia, the Georgia Dome was completed in August, 1992. This $210 million structure is scheduled to be the site of the Super Bowl and the Olympics in 1996. The Teflon-coated fabric roof covers 8.6 acres, weighs 68 tons, and incorporates 11.1 miles of steel support cables. This multi-purpose

Figure 5.20. Suncoast Dome (Photo by George Cott Courtesy of HOK)

facility seats 70,500 for football and is the new home of the Atlanta Falcons. A total of 202 Executive Suites are located on different levels around the stadium. They range in price from $20,000 to $120,000 per year for a 10-year lease. During the planning process it was estimated that changing the design from an open air stadium to a fabric covered dome would increase the cost of the project by only 20 percent or less.

Wooden Domes

Another recent development in the area of encapsulated spaces is the wooden dome. These spherical wooden structures have several advantages over conventional structures. Column-free spans of up to 800 feet are possible, and they generally are easier to build. There are several wooden dome structures around the country, ranging from high school gymnasiums to very large arenas.

Some of the advantages of wooden domes when compared with standard construction may include:

- huge column-free spans can be constructed efficiently
- lower initial cost when compared with conventional construction
- less construction time
- full utilization of space
- good acoustical properties.

Examples

- *Round Valley Ensphere.* Located in Eager, Arizona, this wooden dome is the only high school domed football stadium in the world. Opened in 1991, it was built for a total cost of $11.5 million and is unique in many respects. The 113,000-square-feet of unobstructed floor space provides a full size synthetic turf football field with seating for 5,000, a six-lane 200 meter synthetic surface running track with 100 meter straight-away, seven combination basketball, volleyball, or tennis courts, a softball field, as well as offices, training room and four full locker rooms. The wooden roof is insulated to a value of R-28 and is very energy and acoustically efficient. (Figures 5.21, 5.22.)

One of the most interesting features of the dome is that it contains a large skylight in the center of the roof. This skylight is made of clear Lexan and provides good illumination of the activity areas on even overcast days. At an elevation of over 7,000 feet, the Round Valley area experiences extremes in weather, including snow-packed winters. During these colder months, the skylight also acts as a solar collector, helping to make the Ensphere very energy efficient.

Figure 5.21. Exterior of Round Valley Ensphere (Photo by Mark Boisclair. Courtesy of Rossman, Schneider, Gadbery, Shay)

Figure 5.22. Interior of Round Valley Ensphere (Photo by Mark Boisclair. Courtesy of Rossman, Schneider, Gadbery, Shay)

- *Walkup Skydome*. This laminated wood dome is located at Northern Arizona University in Flagstaff, Arizona. Opened in 1977, the Skydome is 502 feet across and covers 6.2 acres. It contains a full size, roll-up, synthetic football/soccer field, a professional size ice hockey rink, a 1/5 mile running track, a portable wood basketball court, and has seating for more than 15,000 people. The total construction cost was $8.3 million, or about $620 per seat.

- *Tacoma Dome*. The Tacoma Dome in Tacoma, Washington, was opened in 1983. This $44 million multi-purpose complex is 530 feet across and for eight years was the largest wooden dome in the world. It can seat 20,722 for football, 25,138 for basketball, and contains a permanent ice hockey rink.

- *Superior Dome*. Constructed on the campus of Northern Michigan University in Marquette, Michigan, this state-owned, wooden dome was opened in the fall of 1991. With a diameter of 533 feet, this now is the largest wooden dome in the world and is the fourth largest rigid domed stadium in the United States. The 14-story, $21.8 million structure was envisioned in 1985 as an Olympic training center. It has a 200 meter track, a full size football field and is home to the NMU football team with seating for 8,000 spectators. Designed to be constructed in phases as funding becomes available, its plans for the future include an additional 5,000 seats, an ice rink for hockey, speed skating, and figure skating, locker rooms, sports medicine facilities, and public use areas. (Figure 5.23.)

- *WinterGreens Golf Dome* Located in Flint, Michigan, the WinterGreens Golf Dome is a nine hole, par three, pitch and putt golf course that is covered by a fabric air structure. The holes vary in length from 26 to 62 yards. The dome is 55 feet high and covers about an acre. The fabric allows enough natural light inside for real grass to be grown for the playing surface.

REFERENCES

Cohen, A. 1991. Back to the future. *Athletic Business*, 15 (7), pp.31-37.

Dethlefs, D. 1991. Multiple cheers. *College Athletic Management*, 3 (3), pp. 28-33.

Flynn, Richard B. (Ed.). 1985. *Planning Facilities for Athletics, Physical Education and Recreation*, The Athletic Institute and American Alliance for Health, Physical Education, Recreation and Dance.

Figure 5.23. Superior Dome, Northern Michigan University (Photo by Balthazar Korab, Ltd. Courtesy of TMP Associates, Inc.)

Gordon, J. 1990. "The suite smell of success." *Skybox*, 1 (2), pp.6-9.

Johnson, R. 1991. "All in one." *College Athletic Management*, 3 (3), pp. 28-33.

Krenson, F. 1988. "Crowd-pleasing arena design." *Athletic Business*, 12 (9), pp. 66-69.

Maas, G. 1990, April. "Electronic ID Card Check for Facility Access: Gateway for Learning More About Recreational Sports Participants." Paper presented at National Intramural-Recreational Sports Association, Cincinnati, OH.

Meagher, J. 1985. "Eliminating the negative in sports facility design." *Athletic Business*, 9 (1), pp. 32-35.

Miller, J. & Blunck, M. 1991. "Rec centers with personality." *Athletic Business*, 15 (8), pp .51-53.

NCAA Guides. Overland Park, KS: National Collegiate Athletic Association.

Sports Lighting. Illuminating Engineering Society of North America.

Whitney, T. 1992. "A house divided." *Athletic Business*, 16 (3), pp. 44-51.

Wolfe, R. 1987. Designing facilities to meet future needs. "*Athletic Business*, 11 (9), pp. 48-55.

Zepp, L. 1991. "Fargodome construction running on schedule." *Amusement Business*, 103 (13), pp. 11-12.

ABOUT THE AUTHOR:
Todd Seidler serves as coordinator of the graduate Sports Administration Department at Wayne State University.

The information in this chapter is intended to assist planners, designers, and administrators in their efforts to create superior locker rooms, training, administrative, laundry, storage, and maintenance facilities. The guidance offered by this chapter will support, not replace, a normal and rigorous planning and design process.

This chapter will aid the planning and design of ancillary facilities by identifying many of the questions which must be asked, along with the variables which should be considered as the project team responds to the unique circumstances of each project, each site, and each community of users.

Actual design recommendations for specific solutions will be avoided because the professional planning/design team that follows the analytical guidelines and considerations brought out in this chapter will be well prepared to reach their own conclusions. Asking the right questions is an essential part of recognizing the best answers.

Design of ancillary areas will require input from the following specialists:

- owner's project manager
- facility planner
- design architect
- construction cost consultant
- operations consultant
- providers of facility components.

The operations consultant will provide input related to staffing, management, maintenance, marketing, specialized FF&E (fixtures, furnishings, and equipment), and other operational issues that impact design of ancillary areas.

Providers of facility components are the manufacturers of the special products and equipment which will be included in the facility. They are an essential source of information regarding proper application of their products.

For each ancillary area, the following variables will be examined and discussed:

- issues of size, quantity, and dimension
- issues of location and relationship (adjacent/proximate, remote)
- access and circulation considerations for all users--staff, guests, disabled, users and/or members
- matters of style, image, and color
- issues of materials and finishes
- engineering issues regarding lighting, HVAC, and plumbing
- gender-specific requirements and other user needs
- requirements for expansion and adaptability.

The most significant variable affecting ancillary areas is that of facility type. As the title of this book suggests, there are many types (and sub-types) including athletics (sub-types for different sports), physical education (sub-types for different age groups: elementary, junior high, high school, and college), recreation/fitness (sub-types for university, municipal, and private).

In addition, many facilities try to wear two or three hats, that is, their mission is to serve the programming needs of a variety of users, varsity athletics, intramural athletics, and physical education, for example. Proper design for ancillary areas will be driven by the particular needs of the overall facility type. Therefore, this chapter will discuss locker rooms in general, and then distinguish between the design of locker rooms for specific types of facilities.

Clearly, planning and design of locker rooms should vary according to facility type. Similarly, other kinds of ancillary areas will vary in use and function for different facility types. The planning and design of training rooms, administrative offices, laundry facilities, storage rooms and maintenance areas must be viewed in light of their fit to the overall facility mission.

Ancillary, by definition, refers to those functions which are necessary to support the primary program activities for which the facility will be created.

LOCKER ROOMS IN GENERAL

The term "locker room" encompasses a multitude of components and facilities. More than a room of lockers, the modern locker room accommodates a broad range of functions related to dressing, storage, grooming, personal hygiene, therapy, social exchange, information handling, aesthetics, and comfort.

Many aspects of locker room planning and design must be considered in the light of the overall facility type. However, there are some basic principles which apply to all types of locker rooms regardless of the user. These principles are the planning and design considerations which must be addressed in defining the basic components common to all locker rooms: lockers, toilets, showers, amenities, and grooming stations.

Essential to the accommodation of these functions is the proper location of the locker room within the overall facility and the proper relationship of these components within the locker room itself.

Figure 6.1 illustrates the primary relationships which must be considered in properly locating the locker room within the overall facility. Whenever possible, the locker room should be on the same floor as the aquatic facilities.

At least one wall of the locker room block should be an outside wall, located so future expansion can take place. Locker room expansion also can be accommodated by means of internal conversion of "soft" use space which is located deliberately next to the locker room. "Soft" space refers to uses that require little or no special provisions (such as plumbing or expensive finishes), and therefore is easily relocated and the vacated space converted to locker room expansion. Examples of "soft" uses include storage rooms, offices, and meeting rooms.

All but the most primitive locker rooms will have lockers, showers, grooming stations, amenities, and toilet facilities. Figure 6.2 provides a conceptual illustration of the proper relationship of these components. Conventional design wisdom has held that consolidation of plumbing facilities to minimize piping runs is a primary consideration in the layout of locker rooms. In truth, the actual economies are not significant, and the resulting consolidation of plumbing can be quite contrary to the principles of user friendly design. Toilet facilities backed up to showers will save minor quantities of piping, but can result in a mix of wet bare feet from shower traffic with dry street shoes from toilet room users. Lavatory grooming counters near toilets and urinals again will save minor amounts of piping, but may result in a

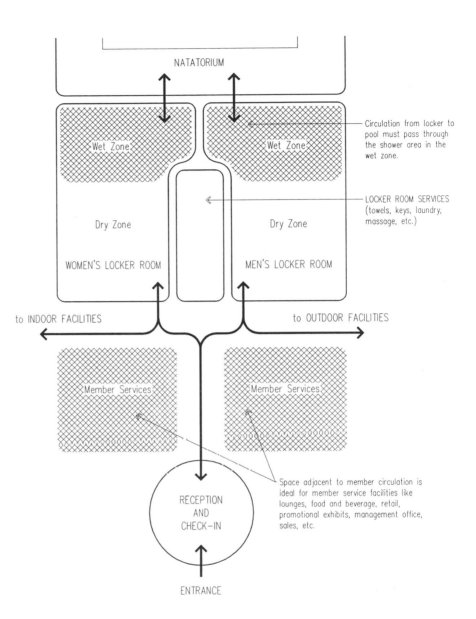

Figure 6.1. Locker location within the facility

loss of privacy for toilet users and a compromised atmosphere for personal grooming functions.

Locker Room Size

The number and size of lockers required will help determine the size of the overall room, as will the inclusion of special amenities such as steam rooms, saunas, jacuzzi, baths, lounges, or massage rooms. A range of 10 to 20-square-feet per locker is possible, depending on locker size and other variables. The best way to program accurately the locker room size that is appropriate for a given facility is to calculate the user capacity of the entire facility during peak usage periods. When an allowance is made for those who are waiting to participate and those who are finished and showering, the total number of occupied lockers can be determined. Estimates of the gender ratio of users

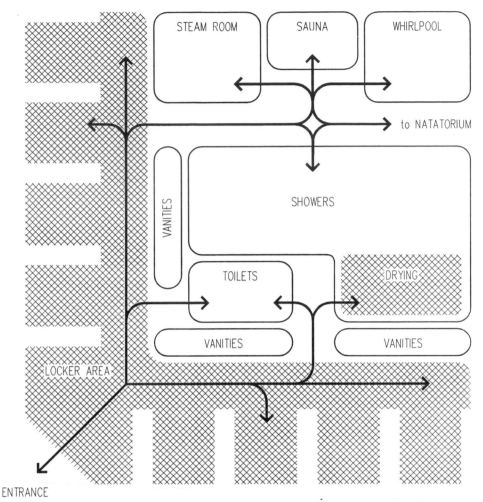

Figure 6.2. Diagrammatic locker area layout

will allow the total locker count to be distributed between men's and women's locker rooms. Unless special circumstances dictate otherwise, the size of locker rooms for men and women should be the same and each locker count equal to 60 percent of the total required number of occupied lockers.

The planning objective is to provide a balance between locker room capacity and the floor capacity of activity areas. An imbalance in this ratio will result in unused capacity in either the locker rooms or the activity areas.

Locker Area

The locker area must provide more than securable storage compartments. A good locker layout will allow for a multitude of functional considerations:

- Seated dressing space removed from main circulation paths.

- At least one private dressing cubicle for users with special privacy needs.

- At least one dressing/locker cubicle equipped for use by the disabled.

- Size and quantities of lockers determined by analysis of anticipated user groups. In most cases, it is appropriate and sometimes required to provide facilities of equal size for men and women.

- Odor control achieved by means of natural or induced locker ventilation. Management procedures which encourage proper care of locker contents by users also will be beneficial. Provision of swimsuit dryers can help prevent odors and locker damage caused

by storing wet suits.

- Efficiency of locker count can be improved by increasing the height of locker tiers, but caution must be exercised to avoid having lockers so high that they are out of reach of the expected user.

Figure 6.3 illustrates a range of possible locker and bench configurations with recommended dimensions.

- When possible, avoid vast and deep maze-like arrays of lockers. Shallow perimeter layouts around three sides of a wet core are more user friendly. This will allow shorter distances between locker and shower. Supervision of locker areas may be an important consideration for some facility types. Avoid hidden alcoves where unobserved behavior can take place.

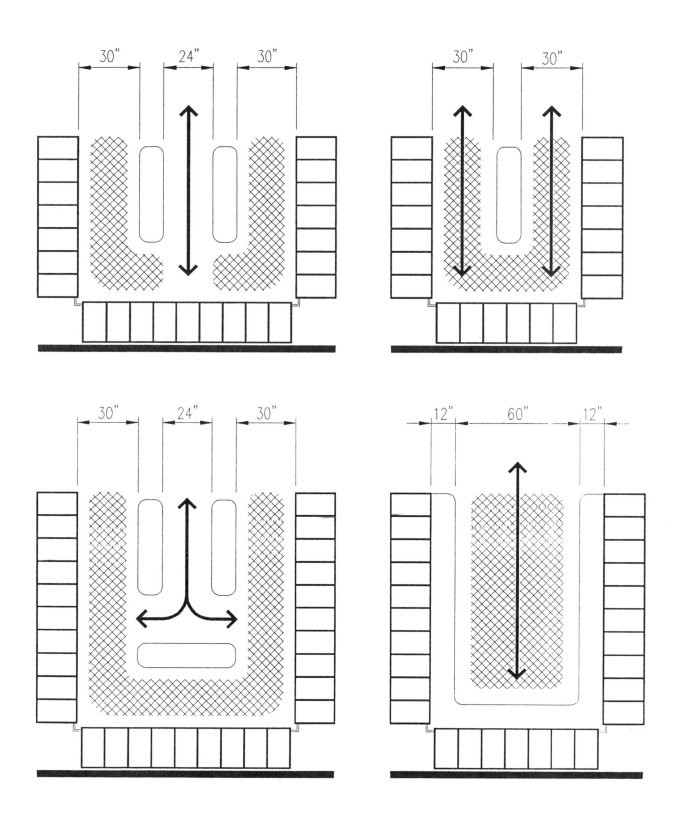

 = DRESSING ZONE

= CIRCULATION ZONE

= LOCKERS

= BENCHES

Figure 6.3. Variations of alcove-type locker arrangements are shown to illustrate the potential conflict between dressing and circulation. Similar concerns apply to locker arrangements with long open-ended rows.

- The main locker room access will need to accommodate heavy two-way traffic from users carrying bags or equipment. Therefore, locker room doors should be avoided, and if required by code, should be held open with code-approved devices connected to the fire alarm system. Doorless locker room entries are a commonplace answer to the need for unobstructed two-way circulation in high volume uses such as stadiums and airports. The necessary visual screening of locker room interiors can be provided easily and should be done even if doors are installed.

- For improved locker room flow, entries should be located so that traffic is divided naturally into two directions upon entry. This minimizes the impact of heavy circulation patterns within the locker room.

- Materials and finishes should be selected with the anticipated maintenance in mind. A variety of impervious floor surfaces is available - ceramic tile, etched terrazzo, vinyl, and synthetics. Consideration should be given to slippery qualities, cleaning techniques, color selection, aesthetics, and cost. If the daily maintenance program will consist of a hosing down or pressure wash, the best choice of flooring is ceramic tile or a liquid-applied synthetic. Such materials should be fully coved at walls.

Other floor material options include wood and carpet. Wood floors have been used successfully as an accent in upscale club locker rooms. Carpet is a good choice for locker room dry areas when a proper maintenance program can be assured. The benefits of carpet (quiet, clean, attractive, durable) will be lost if it is not vacuumed twice daily and shampooed at least four times annually. Odor control of carpet can be enhanced by specifying a factory applied anti-microbial treatment and taking care in planning of wet areas to prevent excessive tracking of water to the carpet.

- Ceilings should provide for good light diffusion and acoustic absorption. Moisture resistance also is important. The aesthetic impact of ceiling treatment should not be overlooked. Consider the possibility of lighting the locker room indirectly by mounting strip light fixtures on top of lockers. Emergency lighting must be provided.

- Natural day lighting by means of skylights or high sidewall windows with glazing will enhance the locker room environment.

Lockers

Locker systems are available in a variety of materials - painted steel, wood, and plastic laminate-faced particle board or fiber-resin board. The selection of locker material and construction is a function of several factors. Considerations include:

- appearance requirements
- resistance to abuse
- resistance to corrosion
- availability of desired size and accessories
- installation requirements.

Wood may be most suitable in applications where a traditional or luxury image is desired, and the risk of vandalism is small. A variety of wood stains and door designs is available.

Painted steel may be most suitable in noncorrosive environments where the desire for upscale image does not exist, and the risk of abusive behavior is present. A variety of standard and custom paint colors is available from most manufacturers. Choice of door styles is somewhat limited, but painted steel lockers have been the standard choice for applications where economy, utility, and durability are the prime concerns. (Figure 6.4.)

Plastic laminate-faced board may be the most suitable choice where economy and upscale design image are both important. A rich variety of colors, textures, and finishes is readily available for door faces. This type of locker may be a good choice for corrosive environments. Many optional accessories such as shelves, hooks, rods, mirrors, and locking systems are available.

Toilets

Careful consideration must be given to location of locker room toilets. Will they be used under wet or dry conditions? Are the locker room toilets intended to serve the natatorium? If so, users will be wet, and toilets must be located in the locker room wet area. In this case, other toilet facilities should be provided for "dry" users in the dry zone of the

Figure 6.4. Functional and attractive locker area

locker room or in a location outside of the locker room. In any case, mixing of dry and wet toilet room traffic should be avoided. Street shoes on wet slippery floors are a hazard, and the presence of bare feet on wet floors that have been soiled by street shoes is unsanitary and unpleasant. Possible solutions are:

- "dry" locker room toilets near the entry and "wet" toilets near the shower area

- "dry" locker room toilets near the entry (for convenience of use from outside of locker room) and wet toilets within the natatorium

- "dry" toilets outside of the locker room and "wet" toilets near the shower area.

Other considerations for planning and designing locker room toilets are:

- Sufficient quantities of fixtures (water closets and urinals) should be provided to meet peak user demand. The unique circumstances of each project must be evaluated in making this determination. Rules of thumb suggest that a ratio of one water closet per 60 lockers is sufficient, but this ratio could be doubled or halved by special circumstances.

- Provide handicapped access space and accessories for at least one toilet stall.

- Careful attention should be paid to toilet partition materials and construction. Problems with rusting, delamination, warping, and vandalism are common. This is not the place to cut quality to reduce cost.

- Lighting of toilet stalls should be placed toward the back of the stall in the form of downlight, wall sconce or valance light. This location will provide the best lighting for cleanliness inspections.

- Maintenance access to piping and valves must be provided. Access panels in plumbing walls are a common solution to this need.

Figure 6.5. Individual showers

Showers

The quantity of showers and the corresponding capacity of hot water generating equipment together are the single most critical component of an athletic facility's ancillary areas. Shortcomings in any other component can be adapted to or in some way tolerated. Cold showers and/or long lines of people waiting for too few showers will create an extremely negative experience for the facility user.

Unfortunately, rules of thumb for shower count are not always reliable. One shower per 20 lockers is a ratio that sometimes is applicable. However, there will be cases when that ratio will result in too many or too few showers. The best approach is for the project planner to conduct an analysis of anticipated overall user capacity in the facility as the basis for predicting the peak shower-taking population at any given time. This projection will, in turn, form the basis of the calculation of flow rate of hot water which must be sustained for showers. (Figure 6.5.)

The selection of a control valve and shower head should be considered carefully to arrive at the balance of shower quality and water economy which is most appropriate for a given

facility and the users it serves. Control valves can be specified for automatic shut-off, automatic temperature control, variable or fixed volume, and vandal resistance. It is absolutely essential that shower piping and valves be accessible for maintenance and repair without destruction of the enclosing wall and finishes. Access panels can be provided easily.

Shower rooms must be ventilated and exhausted to prevent odors and moisture accumulation. Air supply points must be arranged to minimize drafts.

A variety of shower types and layouts is possible and are illustrated in Figure 6.6..

Other general guidelines for shower planning and design include:

- Provide flush type recessed hose bibs for cleaning purposes.

- Walls and floors of the shower enclosure must be completely waterproof.

- Shower heads should be self-cleaning and water-conserving. Adjustability of spray and angle should be considered on a case-by-case basis.

- Shower finishes must be impervious to water and easily cleaned. Ceramic tile, stone, or etched terrazzo are good choices for floors and walls.

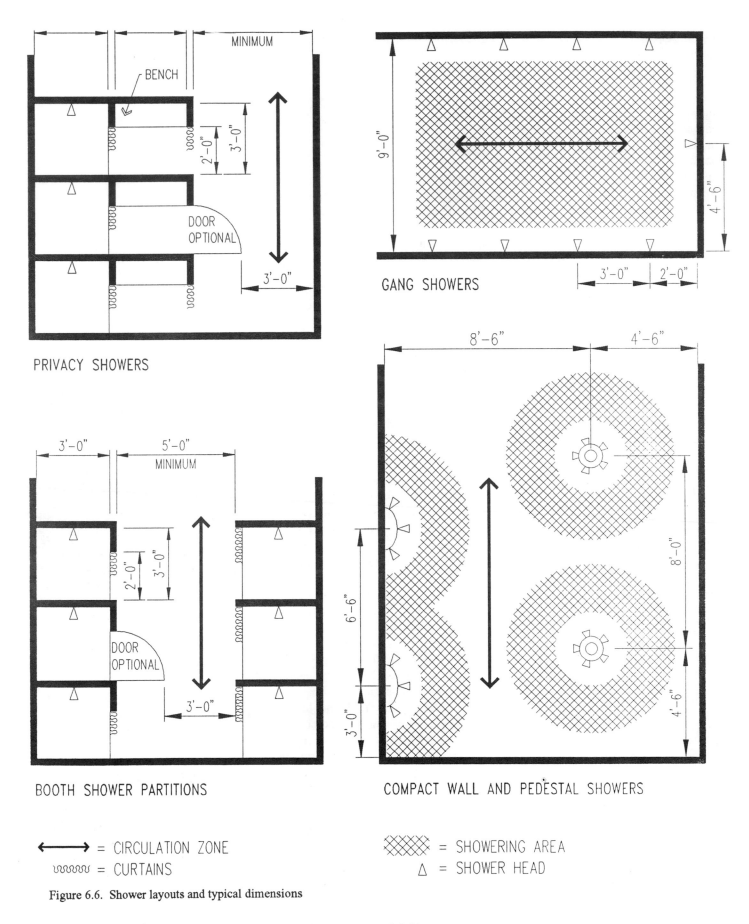

PRIVACY SHOWERS

GANG SHOWERS

BOOTH SHOWER PARTITIONS

COMPACT WALL AND PEDESTAL SHOWERS

⟷ = CIRCULATION ZONE

ᘐᘐᘐᘐ = CURTAINS

▨▨▨ = SHOWERING AREA

△ = SHOWER HEAD

Figure 6.6. Shower layouts and typical dimensions

Ceilings can be finished with ceramic tile or epoxy paint. Use larger size tile whenever possible because difficult-to-clean grout lines will be minimized.

- Minimum spacing for gang showers is 30 inches per occupant capacity. Shower head heights should be set according to anticipated size of users. A variety of heights can be provided if a mix of users is anticipated. Recommended mounting heights for shower heads are:

Men - 6 feet 8 inches
Women - 6 feet 4 inches
Children - 5 feet 6 inches (or adjustable)
Handicapped - 4 feet 0 inches (and adjustable)

Other design issues affecting wet area finishes are:

- Select color of tiles to conceal apparent stains. Large tiles minimize the amount of grout.

- All outside corners should be rounded and joints of walls and floors coved.

- Evaluate slippery qualities of a floor material when wet. Most manufacturers can provide a slip coefficient for their products. Avoid use of curbs as they can be a safety problem.

- Substrata -- a finish material will perform only as well as its underlying support. Of the many options for wet area wall substrata, gypsum board is the least reliable.

- Floor construction of showers and drying areas must be sloped to perimeter or center drains in order to avoid birdbath-like puddles of water on the floor.

- Shower planning also must address the inclusion or exclusion of clean towel distribution, towel hooks, used towel collection, and provision, if any, of soap and shampoo.

- Inclusion of a drying zone between shower and locker is important. This area can be equipped with floor mats and drains to prevent tracking of water onto dry area finishes.

- The shower area often is positioned to serve users of indoor and outdoor aquatic facilities as well as locker room amenities such as steam room, sauna, and jacuzzi bath. Users of these amenities should be encouraged by the layout and flow to shower prior to use.

Amenities

Steam, sauna and jacuzzi are the amenities most often considered for inclusion in an upscale locker room facility. Each of these requires careful attention to a host of planning and design considerations.

Steam Rooms

- As a guideline, sizing should be based on a capacity factor of one person per 12-square-feet.

- Entrance doors to steam rooms will release large quantities of steam and should be located where this vapor-laden air will not damage nearby fittings and finishes.

- Walls, floor, and ceiling of steam rooms must be completely waterproof and finished with nonslip ceramic tile or stone.

- Provision of a glazed door and sidelight will improve supervision and make a more pleasant and open experience for the steam room user.

- Slope the steam room ceiling to a sidewall or uninhabited drip point in order to prevent condensation from dripping on users.

- All components of steam rooms (lights, hinges, frames, fasteners, etc.) must be corrosion resistant. Plastic and aluminum usually are satisfactory. Stainless steel is not a reliable choice. Avoid mild painted steel at all costs.

- Most steam room failures are related to failure of the substrata or wall structures to resist the corrosive effects of the vapor-laden air. Proven steam room construction details are published by the ceramic tile industry and should be followed carefully.

- Maintenance access to the steam generator room should be available from a coed corridor, so that servicing of steam equipment can occur without closing the locker room to use. Steam room controls, other than a thermostatic sensor, should be located in a staff only area.

- The decision to include a steam room must be based on consideration of the operating and maintenance expense, as well as the initial construction cost. Periodic staff supervision also is necessary to prevent misuse.

- Location of steam jets and sensor must be planned and detailed to minimize risk of burns and ensure proper temperature control.

- Accessories usually include thermometer, hose bib, hose, and clock. An overhead shower head sometimes is included.

Sauna

Saunas are designed to provide dry heat at extremely high temperatures. They are less costly to install than steam rooms but often result in maintenance problems that are more difficult to manage. Planning and design considerations follow: (Figure 6.7.)

- Wood-lined walls, floors, and seats are the usual choice, however, tile-lined rooms are easier to maintain and can be used if a means of providing cooled seating and floor surfaces is devised. Use of towels is one answer. The high temperatures involved require that users be protected from contact with metal and other highly conductive materials which could cause burns.

- The main problems with wood surface saunas are the staining which occurs from accumulated sweat and the odors which result. Use of a light colored wood will reduce the unsightliness of the staining problem. The best approach to odor control is to require use of individual towels for seating, along with daily pressure cleaning. For these reasons a sauna may not be suitable for many types of public facilities where towels and multiple daily cleaning are not provided.

Figure 6.7. Sauna

- Glazed doors and sidelights will create a more pleasant and more easily supervised sauna.

- As a guideline, sizing decisions can be based on a capacity factor of one person per 12 square feet.

- Adequate lighting is particularly important for sanitation and maintenance.

- Commonly specified accessories are clock, thermometer, and water supply.

- A floor drain can be provided for ease of cleaning, but it may need to be a self-priming type to prevent the sauna heat from drying out the trap.

Jacuzzi

Also known as a whirlpool bath, this amenity is a communal body of water (104 degrees Fahrenheit) equipped with air and water jets to create a turbulent massaging effect for the immersed user. Pre-packaged units generally are unsuitable for the applications addressed in this book. Water quality control is the single most important issue impacting the planning and design of these facilities. Local health regulations will control many aspects of the water purification system,

as well as pool and deck materials and configuration. Other considerations:

- Capacity factors are in the range of 10 to 15 square feet per person.

- Equipment rooms should be located for coed access.

- Location is important to encourage users to shower before using the jacuzzi.

- Pool basins should be completely tile lined to allow for the

frequent draining and cleaning which is necessary to keep a sanitary and attractive body of water. Plaster-lined pools will be more difficult to clean.

- The vapor-laden air of the jacuzzi area will be made more corrosive by the presence of chlorine. Even stainless steel eventually will succumb to corrosion in this atmosphere. Aluminum, stone, plastic, glass, and ceramic tile will provide more durability.

- It is essential that air-handling systems for the jacuzzi area be designed to produce a negative air pressure relative to surrounding uses. This will prevent the migration of vapor and odor to other parts of the locker room and even other parts of the facility. (Figure 6.8.)

Grooming Stations

Minimal facilities for a wet grooming station are a sink with hot and cold water, a mirror, and a ground fault-protected power source. Minimal facilities for a dry grooming station are a mirror, a power source, and a small shelf. Optional enhancements of grooming provisions can include such niceties as, hand-held hair dryers, wall-mounted dryers, make-up mirrors, stools, soap or lotion dispensers, face

Figure 6.8. Jacuzzi Bath

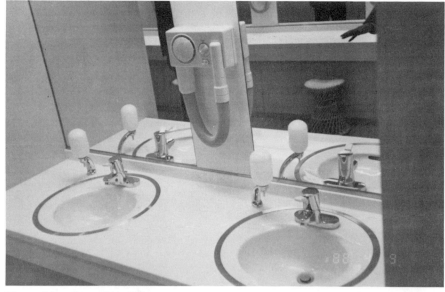

Figure 6.9. Grooming station

clothes, paper towels, waste receptacles, and disposable grooming aids such as razors and combs. Each facility must develop its own policy regarding provision of these necessities. Will they be supplied by building management or by each individual user?

General consideration for planning and design of grooming stations:

- The required number of wet and dry grooming stations needed must be analyzed according to the unique circumstances of each project and gender-specific grooming practices. As a rule of thumb, total grooming stations should be approximately the same or slightly more than the shower count. A 50-50 split between wet and dry grooming stations may be varied by some planners to provide more wet stations for men (shaving) and more dry stations for women (make-up).

- Lighting at mirrors should be arranged to illuminate both sides of a person's face. Provide a color of light that enhances flesh tones, such as incandescent or warm white fluorescent. (Figure 6.9.)

- Avoid locating grooming facilities with toilets or placing them too deeply into wet areas. For convenience of use, they should be located on the seam between the locker

dry zone and the shower wet zone.

- The design image of grooming stations can be used to convey the intended character of a facility. Upscale club environments should have luxurious grooming facilities. Public recreation facilities may want to convey a more modest but functional character.

- A full length mirror should be provided for use along the locker room exit path.

Locker Room Auxiliary Spaces

Special uses sometimes are incorporated into locker room plans to meet particular project needs. The specific requirements of each must be identified. Examples include social lounges, attendant services, shoe shine, laundry service, workout clothing service, massage, tanning, private telephone cubicles, and personal storage lockers of various sizes. The arguments for inclusion or exclusion of each item should be examined by the Planning Team.

Locker Room Accessories

Considerations for a well equipped locker room include an electric water cooler, clock, scale, automatic swimsuit dryer, telephone, emergency call system,

plastic bag dispenser, hair dryers, and vending machines for personal grooming items or beverages.

TRAINING ROOMS IN GENERAL

Ancillary areas which directly treat the health and safety of athletes of all types generally are referred to as training rooms. Regardless of the project type, certain sets of concerns apply to all training rooms.

- *Location*: Training rooms should be located for ease of access from both men and women's locker rooms. Joint use by both men and women is considered acceptable. Ready access to an ambulance loading berth also is important.

- *Finishes*: Floors should be of nonslip impervious material such as vinyl or ceramic tile. Liquid-applied membrane floors also are suitable. Ceiling finishes should have acoustically absorbent characteristics and be at least 10 feet clear.

- *Lighting and Power*: 50 footcandles at four feet above the floor is recommended. Easy access to adequate power outlets of 110 and 220 volts must be provided as required by the equipment layout in the space. Consideration should be given to future needs by building in some excess electrical capacity.

- *HVAC*: The training room must be on a separate control zone with its own thermostat. Vapors from the steam and hydrotherapy equipment will cause discomfort to users if adequate ventilation is not provided. Comfort conditions may be difficult to define for a room where partially dressed athletes will be treated by fully clothed trainers. (Figure 6.10.)

- *Uses*: The training room will need to accommodate a mix of therapeutic and administrative activities including first aid, taping, hydrotherapy, electrotherapy, stress testing, physical examinations, massage therapy, rehabilitation, drug testing, medical

Figure 6.10. Training Room in the University of Virginia Frank McCue Training Center (Photo by Alan Karchmer. Courtesy of HOK Sports Facilities Group)

procedures, trainer's office, and storeroom. There will be a need for some designated rehabilitation equipment. The working style and procedural preferences of each group of trainers can vary. The designer must consider the unique operational requirements of each client in developing the size and layout of the training room. Rules of thumb are unnecessary here. A well-managed dialogue between user and designer is the most reliable approach to arriving at the proper size and layout. The equipment and furnishing program will include taping tables, treatment and exam tables, ice maker, hydrotherapy tanks, electrotherapy equipment, lockers, and a variety of seating. The designer, in responding to staff requirements, should keep in mind that programs change and that required functions are accommodated best in a flexible space that can be adapted easily to the inevitable need for change. This means building as few permanent walls as possible. Privacy and space definition can be accomplished by means other than permanent partitions. Perhaps the only spaces within the training room that would require complete enclosure are the trainer's office and the examination/consultation room.

As athletic and fitness programs become more integrated into an overall health maintenance concept with an emphasis on sports medicine, the need will develop to provide medical examination and treatment space within the traditional training room environment. Planners and designers will need to understand stress testing, X-rays, blood and urine testing, lung, and vision and hearing evaluation as part of a complete physical examination.

ADMINISTRATIVE OFFICES IN GENERAL

Staff offices must be barrier free to disabled job candidates and equally accessible to men and women. Staff offices generally fall into two categories of space.

1. Back office space is required for staff who have little or no regular contact with active facility users. Examples include: accounting, administration, and marketing staff.

2. Front office space is required for staff with supervisory responsibilities and regular contact with active facility users:

- Reception and check in for the facility at large

- Supervision stations for natatorium, fitness floor, gymnasium, racquet sports

- Faculty/coaches/instructors' offices.

The size, quantity, and furnishings required by each of these staff offices must be determined by the planner in dialogue with department heads and user representatives. Questions to be considered include:

1. What are the expected number of full- and part-time staff? What are their titles and work descriptions?

2. Which staff members require enclosed private offices? Open but private work stations? Shared work stations (concurrently or alternately)?

3. Which staff members require frequent contact with each other? With certain activity areas? With certain users?

With answers to these questions in hand, the designer can begin preparation of a space plan for administrative offices. Design considerations include:

- anticipated traffic patterns
- type of partition and extent of glass, if any, in walls and doors
- need for acoustic privacy
- lighting system for both ambient and task lighting
- provision of adequate power, communication, and computer hookups
- provision of year-round heating and cooling
- need for natural daylight or outside view.

Office uses require supplemental spaces which can accommodate the functions necessary to support the working station. The design process should bring these questions to the table for discussion by all appropriate parties. Such spaces include:

- utility area for facsimile machines, copiers, office supplies, and storage
- employee kitchen area with coffee maker, microwave, refrigerator, dishwasher, and storage, sometimes included as part of a lunch room or staff lounge
- conference rooms
- coat closets or employee security lockers
- designated and specially ventilated smoker's rooms if operating policies will allow staff smoking on premises
- staff-only restrooms and shower/locker rooms may be desired

- location and type of central telephone reception and distribution must be determined. Many multi-feature phone systems are available.

- Mail and message handling system should be planned into the administrative component. Voice-mail phone capabilities are becoming more affordable.

- The passage of recent legislation ensuring the rights of the disabled will require that all spaces, even administrative offices, be designed to be barrier free to all disabled persons.

LAUNDRY

Planning and design of laundry facilities is predicated upon the workload. Just as kitchen design is based on the menu, so laundry design is based on quantity and type of articles to be processed. Towels and athletic clothing are the most common articles needing to be laundered in a recreation facility. The unit of measure applicable to laundry equipment is the pound. Therefore it is necessary to translate the laundry workload from quantity of articles to their weight in pounds, which must be processed per hour. This is a measure of the actual dry weight of articles to be washed. Without reliable information on weight, quantity, and use rates of laundered articles, the planning of laundry facilities is pure guesswork.

Most equipment cycles allow two loads per hour. Thus it is possible to arrive at a calculation of required laundry capacity by establishing with the facility operator how many hours per day the laundry will be staffed and running. Certainly a double shift operation will get more production from a given quantity of equipment than a single eight-hour work shift, but a double shift may not be practical for other reasons. Once the workload is determined, the size and quantity of washers and dryers can be set. It generally is advisable to select machine sizes that allow at least two washing units and two drying units. In this way,

a malfunction in one machine will not shut down completely the laundry operation. (Figure 6.11.)

The location of laundry facilities is of great importance. The best locations are close to the storage/ distribution place for cleaned articles or the collection point for soiled articles. A ground level, grade-supported floor slab is preferred for ease of plumbing and control of vibrations from the equipment. Commercial washer extractors work at very high RPM which can generate destructive vibrations. Most units must be bolted securely into a 24-inch thick grade-supported concrete slab in order to control vibration. If an on-grade location is not possible, it will be necessary to specify an extraction machine with a built-in vibrations dampening system. Most manufacturers offer such a unit as an option.

Other factors to consider in selecting a laundry location are:

- The need for an outside combustion air supply for gas fired dryers may suggest a location along an outside wall.

- The need for an exhaust flue for both gas and electric dryers may suggest a single story location with a roof surface immediately overhead.

- The high volume of waste water discharge for most commercial washers requires a high capacity trench drain recessed into the floor. Such a drain can be installed most easily at grade level.

- Consideration should be given to how equipment can be moved into and out of the laundry space. Equipment sizes should be researched carefully prior to sizing and locating access doorways.

- Accessibility by both men and women staff is needed.

The laundry planner must consider how and by what route both soiled and cleaned articles will arrive at their proper destinations. If carts are used, space must be allocated for storage or holding of extra carts at points of collection, cleaning, and distribution. Folding and sorting of laundered articles is a very labor intensive process. Use of mechanical towel folders is becoming more common in high volume athletic facilities.

Other planning and design considerations for laundry facilities:

- Confirm that adequate utility capacities exist for electric power, water supply, water temperature, sanitary waste, and gas.

- Domestic washer/dryers will prove unsuitable for all but the most incidental, low volume laundry operation.

- Placement of washers and dryers should be conducive to a logical and efficient work flow.

- Extractor type washers use centrifugal force to wring maximum moisture from wet articles prior to drying. This will conserve dryer energy and save time in the drying process.

- Laundry room floors, walls, and ceilings should be finished with a smooth, easily cleaned impervious coating that will not catch dust and lint.

- Dryers typically have a greater weight capacity than a corresponding washer. A 35 pound washer normally will be paired up with a 50 pound dryer.

- The laundry room must include space for chemical storage, carts, folding counters, a two or three compartment sink, and adequate service access space around the equipment.

The final pieces of the laundry puzzle are the washer and dryer themselves. Numerous manufacturers offer commercial units varying in size, power, quality, durability, design, and cost. Selection of the best manufacturers (washers and dryers are not necessarily made by the same company) requires diligent comparisons of actual cylinder sizes, types of motor control capabilities, and physical construction.

STORAGE FACILITIES

Of course, storage rooms should be sized and shaped to accommodate the items to be stored. However, it is not always possible to predict, over the life

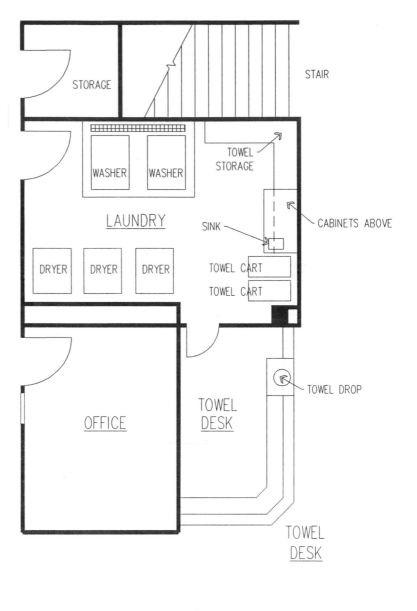

Figure 6.11. An example of a laundry room layout.

of a facility, how much and what kinds of things will need to be stored. Therefore, when it comes to sizing storage rooms, it is best to err on the side of accommodation and provide at least 20 percent more storage space than can be justified by actual measurement of volume of articles to be stored.

Designers frequently assign the storage function to odd shaped leftover spaces which are not necessarily conducive to efficient storage. There are a few simple planning and design guidelines for storage rooms.

- Within the storage room allow for a circulation way - preferably double loaded - between actual storage space. It is the depth of the storage space which must be appropriate to the item stored so that it may be retrieved without repositioning of intervening stored items.

- Storage room doors should open out and swing flat against adjacent walls. Double wide doors should be considered wherever bulky items will be stored.

- Access to storage rooms should be configured so that large, long articles such as ladders can be maneuvered in and out of the room.

- Adequate, though utilitarian, lighting is a must.

- All storage rooms should be ventilated.

- Provisions must be made for storage of outside field equipment so that access to storage does not result in unnecessary soiling of interior walkways.

- Code restrictions may impose limits on storage room locations. Many codes, for instance, do not allow use of the dead space under stairway enclosures for storage.

In general, storage rooms should be located close to the point of use for items being stored. The matter of maintaining storage security and limiting access to authorized persons deserves careful consideration by the design team. The use of motion detection security devices may be appropriate for storage of high cost items such as audio-visual equipment.

MAINTENANCE FACILITIES

In general, there are two types of assets which require maintenance programs: (1) Buildings and Landscaping, and (2) Fixtures, Furniture and Equipment (FF&E). The value represented by these assets is integral to the overall facility mission. No matter how perfectly they are planned and designed, these assets will require a continuing and well managed maintenance program to sustain their value. The conduct of this maintenance program will require space allocation and support provisions such as power, lighting, water supply, communications, waste handling, access, FF&E, storage, and safety devices.

An ongoing maintenance program occasionally will require cross-gender access to locker rooms. Planners can anticipate this need and provide subdividable locker rooms that don't need to be completely shut down to allow cross-gender access to a repair site. In addition, planners should not assume that all maintenance staff will be male and must plan accordingly when locating equipment rooms and maintenance access points.

Prerequisite to making a space allocation for a maintenance workshop is the planning exercise of itemizing the assets to be maintained, the procedures to be followed, and the equipment required. The following checklist of components will serve as a basic agenda for the dialogue which should take place between the planning/design team and the operations and maintenance director who will have responsibility for the finished assets.

BUILDING COMPONENTS

Exterior

- landscape improvements
- plant materials (trees, shrubs, flowers, grass)
- pavement (sweeping and snow removal)
- roofing and walls
- window and door openings
- signage and lighting
- irrigation and drainage
- recreational surfaces
- fencing
- pools and fountains
- waste handling equipment
- safety devices

Interior

- floor finishes
- wall and ceiling finishes
- lighting and power
- plumbing
- HVAC
- a variety of fixed/built-in equipment
- built-in accessories
- built-in waste handling equipment
- glass
- elevator
- built-in life and fire safety devices

FF&E COMPONENTS

- furniture
- exercise equipment
- laundry equipment
- food and beverage equipment
- audiovisual equipment
- communication equipment
- accessories
- waste handling
- signage
- life and fire safety devices

Custodial rooms holding supplies and equipment for cleaning should be located conveniently throughout the facility. There should be about 50-square-feet of such rooms for every 10,000-square-feet of floor space. At least one such room should be provided on each floor.

Proper attention to maintenance and housekeeping facilities during the planning and design process will pay dividends for the life of the building.

The remainder of this chapter will examine the ways in which ancillary facilities in general should be customized to meet the unique requirements of each project type: athletic facilities, physical education facilities, and recreation/fitness facilities.

ATHLETIC FACILITIES

These are the buildings and fields used by educational institutions to conduct competitive, inter-school athletic programs and include facilities for both training and performance. It normally is only at the collegiate level that designated facilities are provided for the exclusive use of the intercollegiate athletic program. High school athletic facilities generally are shared with physical education uses.

Requirements for the ancillary areas of intercollegiate athletic facilities include recognition of the important role such facilities play in recruiting top level athletes and the maintenance of a successful competitive record.

Locker Rooms

Size, quantity, type, and location of team locker rooms will be determined by the number and size of active sports teams, the timing of practice and competitive seasons, the timing of daily practice sessions, and the location of practice and competition facilities. Other design and planning considerations for team locker rooms:

- Visiting team locker rooms must be provided for competitive events. Planners must analyze scheduling patterns for all sports with overlapping seasons to determine the number of visiting team locker rooms needed. Security of this area is of utmost importance.

- Locker sizes for athletics will be determined by the equipment required for a given sport. Of course, football and hockey lockers will be larger than basketball and track lockers. The amount of dressing space allowed also should increase as locker sizes increase to accommodate more equipment. Sports with non-overlapping practice and competition seasons can share the same locker space.

- Direct outside access to practice and/or game fields may be desirable for sports such as football,

soccer, lacrosse, and baseball. The soiling of interior hallways thus can be minimized.

- Planning efforts must ensure that locker room facilities provide equal opportunities for both men and women.

- Game day locker facilities also should be provided for coaches and officials.

- Proper locker ventilation for drying stored articles is extremely important in preventing the build-up of unpleasant odors.

- Competitive sports will require team meetings and "chalk talks" which can be conducted in one or more lecture rooms ideally located close to the locker rooms. Such rooms should be equipped with chalkboards and audio-visual equipment.

Administrative Offices

The need for staff work stations for athletic team programs can be quite extensive. This is particularly true for the high profile competitive sports programs found in Division I and II universities. Each case must be analyzed for its own unique set of requirements, but it is not unusual for multi-sport programs to require defined working quarters for such staff positions as athletic director and assistants, head coaches and assistants, public relations and media coordinators, fund-raising and alumni relations director(s), facilities manager, ticket sales staff, recruiting and scholarship coordinator, accounting staff, student advisors, chaplain, transportation coordinator, equipment and supply manager, director of security, secretarial and clerical aides, audio-visual personnel, and part-time or seasonal employees. Allowances should be made for anticipated growth in the scale of the athletic program and the staff to support it.

The planning process must identify all positions requiring a work station, and itemize the needs of each in a written document that will be approved by the controlling authority prior to the

start of the facility design work. In developing a layout of staff offices, the designer will confront the issue of centralized vs. decentralized administrative offices. This matter is best resolved with input from the owner's project coordinator.

Laundry

Requirements for laundry services to athletic team programs goes beyond the provision of clean towels. The laundry service must deal with the program's need for clean and sanitary towels, practice and game uniforms, protective equipment (shoulder pads, headgear, etc.) personal wear and miscellaneous items such as floor mats, foul weather gear, equipment bags, footwear, and utility items. The laundry is best located at the distribution/collection point for all materials to be supplied by the institution. If the laundry is to be a large central plant shared with other institutional users, a remote location may be required. However, a convenient and secure distribution center then should be created for the team sports facility.

The use of individual mesh laundry bags is an effective way to simplify handling of personal items. Each bag carries an identification tag and can be filled with soiled personal wear, turned in, washed, dried, and held for later retrieval by the user. A numbered storage rack will be helpful in keeping the bags arranged for speedy retrieval.

Storage and Maintenance

Off-season handling of reusable sports equipment must be provided. Planning and design considerations include:

- Adequate space for storage includes shelving and/or racks appropriate for the items being stored. Helmets and shoulder pads, for example, will have a longer useful life if properly racked instead of being dumped into a bulk storage bin. Provide for receiving incoming equipment and issuing outgoing equipment.

- Adequate space for repair of items before being stored is important. This procedure will allow non-repairable inventory to be identified, discarded, and reordered prior to the next season.

- For team sports, the security of stored items is particularly important. Designers must address the issue of lock keying and access control in coordination with the facility manager.

- Storage areas should be kept ventilated and dry to prevent mildew and other deteriorating forces.

PHYSICAL EDUCATION FACILITIES

These are the buildings and fields used by institutions of learning in the conduct of physical education programs for all ages. Such programs commonly are provided for students of elementary, middle, junior high, and high schools, as well as at the university undergraduate level. Programming of physical education generally is organized in a class format with one or more instructors. A wide variety of skill development activities must be accommodated. Special considerations for the planning and design of the ancillary facilities which support the physical education program follow.

Locker Rooms

Because of the scheduled class format, physical education locker rooms must be able to accommodate large influxes of user groups occupying and quickly vacating lockers, toilets, showers, and grooming facilities. Planners must analyze these use patterns in terms of class size, class duration, age, gender-mix, duration of changeover time between classes, and types of activities being conducted. This analysis will guide determinations such as number and size of lockers, number of toilets,

showers and lavatories, types of locker room accessories provided, and types of finishes to be used throughout. Designers will reference the same analysis as they create and select provisions for towels, workout clothing, locker security, soap handling, energy conservation, grooming aids, handling of refuse, and control of facility abuse. The design strategy for dealing with each of these issues should be developed out of the dialogue among planners, designers, managers, faculty, and users.

Other planning and design considerations unique to physical education locker rooms include:

- Height of locker benches, lockers, and locker security devices should be studied carefully, relative to the average height, reach, and eye level of the typical user. This also applies to heights of water coolers, lavatories, toilets, urinals, and counter tops. In case of a wide mix of users, the design orientation should favor the least able user or provide a mix of accom-modations.

- Many schools have after-hours programs for community use by both adults and children. If the overall facility is going to offer such programs, the locker room should have the capability to accommodate these people.

- Locker systems must be customized to meet the special needs of the physical education program being served. The dressing locker and box storage system frequently is used. In this system, a series of small storage lockers is located near a larger dressing locker. Security of the storage locker is accomplished with a combination padlock, which is transferred to the dressing locker along with all the contents of the storage locker when the student is in class. Many variations of locker systems have been developed to meet the special needs of physical education facilities. The designer must analyze the unique circumstances of each application before selecting the most appropriate system for a given project.

- Because these locker rooms may play host to large groups of unsupervised adolescents, the design of all components and finishes should be as abuse-resistant as practical. Avoid creating hidden alcoves where unsupervised behavior could lead to facility damage or personal safety problems.

- The need for visual inspection by facility managers of locker contents may exist. If this is the case, the use of an expanded mesh locker construction may be the best choice.

Training Room

A conventional training facility as usually provided for an athletic team facility is not needed for most physical education programs. However the need does exist for a first aid treatment room to deal with medical emergencies and sports injuries. Planners should designate access routes for emergency vehicles and make certain that all activity areas and locker rooms are reachable by stretcher or gurney.

Staff Offices

The need for physical education staff work stations is limited primarily to faculty office space. The relationship of these offices to those of the athletic teams and administration is the subject of much discussion in schools with both programs. In general, administrative units requiring little or no contact with students may not benefit from close proximity to those with regular involvement with large numbers of students. However, in some cases, interaction and good communication between these groups of staff may produce beneficial results. This is another planning question that defies universal resolution. It must be resolved as a matter of policy, on a case-by-case basis, by each institution.

Laundry

Options for handling the laundry needs of physical education students are:

1. Students are responsible for personal laundry needs including towels and/or gym uniforms.

2. School maintains a laundry facility on the premises for towels and/or gym uniforms.

3. School contracts to an outside service for towel laundry and/or gym uniforms.

Potential benefits of a school laundry are improved health, reduction of odors, and cleaner uniforms. The feasibility of an on-site laundry must be demonstrated on a case-by-case basis by analysis of all factors of cost such as staff, equipment, floor space, maintenance, utility connections, operating costs, and supplies.

RECREATION/ FITNESS FACILITIES

This section addresses those buildings and fields created by universities, municipalities, and a variety of private clubs to serve the recreational/fitness needs of their respective constituencies. These constituencies include: student intramural programs, public recreation programs, and individual fee paying user/members. The basic motivation underlying the purpose of these facilities is enjoyment of sporting activities and/or desire for self-improvement and health maintenance through fitness. To be successful, this type of facility must serve the needs of its user/members who are not obligated to participate or who can elect to take their business elsewhere. This service orientation can exist on many levels of quality, image, and cost, but it is clearly an orientation which must be reflected in the substance and style of a facility's ancillary areas. The following summary of special planning and design considerations is directed toward the ancillary areas of recreation/fitness facilities.

Locker Rooms

Comfort, style, and service are matters of concern in recreation/fitness locker rooms. These concerns do not override the basic functional requirements of locker rooms discussed earlier. Depending on the target market of the facility and the operational economics which are driven by price and volume of user/members, the level of comfort, style, and service must be set by the planning/design team.

The level of comfort is affected by number, size, and spacing of lockers, lavatories, and showers. It also is affected by spaciousness and the kind of seating provided in dressing areas, the lighting, the quality of the heating and cooling systems, and the acoustical ambiance of the space. (Figure 6.12.)

The style and image of the locker room is influenced by color, texture, finish materials, and furnishings. These must be selected to ensure compatibility with the overall facility mission and maintain the consistency of the aesthetic statement being made throughout the building. Whether this statement is spartan and utilitarian, luxurious and rich, or high tech and polished, the choices made send a message to the user/member. The designer's challenge is to fit that message to the market place.

The service level of the recreation/fitness locker room is conveyed by the choices made regarding the means of providing locker security, the system for collecting and distributing towels, the availability of soap, shampoo, lotions and grooming aids, the means of drying hair, and the availability of such amenities as steam, sauna and jacuzzi, telephone, and shoe shine.

Attention to the details of providing comfort, style and service at a level appropriate to the target market is the key to creating a successful recreation/fitness locker room. Other planning and design considerations

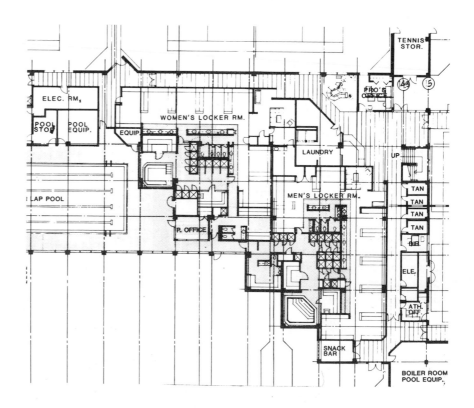

Figure 6.12. An example of an ancillary area layout

unique to locker rooms of this facility type follow.

- Private shower booths with doors or curtains may be provided.

- It generally is impractical to offer a permanent full-size private locker to each member. Consider offering a mix of small size private rental lockers as an extra cost option and providing a full-size dressing locker to each member for day use.

- A ratio of one full-size day locker per 10 members will be sufficient for facilities with average rates of utilization by its members. Adjustment of this ratio up or down can be made by planning on a case-by-case basis to respond to special circumstances.

Training Room

Although a recreation/fitness facility does not need a training room such as the traditional athletic team type, there is good reason for operators and planners to consider including any or all of a full menu of medically related services such as:

- a physical therapy practice
- sports medicine practice
- weight control/nutrition clinic
- orthopedic practice
- cardiac rehab center
- health evaluation/lifestyle counseling service
- massage therapy

The planning and design requirements can be derived from interviews with providers of these services. The most common arrangement for including them is by lease agreement. At a minimum, all recreation/fitness facilities should include an emergency first aid room and appropriately trained personnel.

Administrative Offices

In general, the administrative departments of a recreation/fitness facility will include the following units: membership sales, management, recreation/fitness programming, acc-

ounting, maintenance/housekeeping, personnel, food/beverage, and front desk/check-in. There is little benefit to consolidating these offices into a single administrative block. Management and sales offices should be located near the front desk check-in point. Recreation/fitness programming staff should be located close to the activity areas they serve. Accounting, maintenance/housekeeping, and personnel can be placed in a more remote back office location because they have little need for direct member contact. The food and beverage office should be included within the restaurant bar area if provided. The front desk reception station must be equipped to confirm validity of arriving members, control access to the facility, handle telephone reception and routing, confirm activity programming and court reservations, handle all public inquiries and member service requests. The front desk also may be the best place from which to control lighting throughout the facility and to conduct announcements over the public address system. It is essential that the front desk be positioned to provide clear control of the line separating the public/free access zone of the facility from the member-only zones. This control of access will preserve the value of membership by preventing guests and non-members from using the facilities without proper payment.

MULTI-PURPOSE FACILITIES

It is not uncommon for a sports facility to be an intercollegiate athletic team center serving student athletics, a physical education center serving all students, and a center for recreation and fitness serving dues-paying alumni and faculty, as well as the student intramural sports system.

Facilities which attempt to accommodate a variety of uses must be planned accordingly. With so many diverse groups competing for space and time, conflicts are inevitable. The

economic benefits are obvious. Multi-purpose facilities are utilized more fully by avoiding duplication of facilities which may sit idle most of the day. However, scheduling compromises may reduce access by certain user groups to unacceptable low levels. Institutions without the financial resources to fund independent facilities for athletics, physical education, and recreation/fitness may elect to undertake the planning challenges of a multi-purpose facility. These challenges involve facility planning, curriculum planning, and schedule planning to accommodate as effectively as possible the needs of each constituency.

Special considerations for the ancillary areas of multi-purpose facilities are primarily applicable to locker rooms. Multiple locker rooms will be needed to allow separate accommodations for disparate user groups as they cycle into and out of shared athletic facilities. Gymnasium space, for example, might be scheduled for early afternoon physical education classes, late afternoon varsity basketball practice and evening student intramural games. It is unlikely that all of these users could be supported by a single pair of locker rooms. Once established, an array of multiple locker rooms could be used with great flexibility to accommodate a broad spectrum of user groups such as men or women's varsity athletic teams, men or women's varsity athletic teams, physical education classes, intramural sports teams, individual member users, and user groups having access rights by special contract, such as gymnastic classes, martial arts schools, and community youth programs.

CONCLUSION

In general, the key to creating superior ancillary facilities is found in a design process that invites input from users, managers, staff, design specialists, and component providers. Such a process always will examine comparable design solutions with a critical eye in a diligent effort to avoid repeating past mistakes and to learn from past successes. It is the mix of solid experience and open-minded inventiveness that produces successful design solutions.

REFERENCES

Flynn, Richard B. (Ed.) 1985. *Planning Facilities for Athletics, Physical Education and Recreation,* The Athletic Institute and American Alliance for Health, Physical Education, Recreation and Dance.

ABOUT THE AUTHOR:
Hervey LaVoie is principal and president of Ohlson LaVoie Corporation, Architecture and Planning, Denver, CO.

Chapter 7
RECREATION, PARKS, AND CAMPING
by Edsel Buchanan

The focus of this chapter is on planning facilities to support recreational activities conducted in a selected variety of green spaces within the "great out-of-doors" (often referred to as green belts/open spaces/parks). The chapter also reviews selected facilities and camps typically associated with green spaces. Preceding chapters have focused on the planning process (Chapter 1) and indoor and outdoor facilities (Chapters 2 and 3). Each of the three chapters also discusses a variety of standards and specifications. Those aspects are not duplicated within this chapter. A few aspects are re-emphasized briefly due to the uniqueness of the recreational characteristics of the area and/or facility.

PLANNING, ACQUISITION, AND DESIGN

At present, and for decades to come, the significance of thorough planning, timely acquisition, and appropriate design will dominate the actions of leaders as they try to serve their publics. Perhaps no other areas are so diverse as are those within recreation and leisure. Many events from the 1980s have set clearly the patterns for practices of the 1990s. Several practices and expectations continue, such as:

- Doing more with fewer resources has not necessarily worked, but doing your best with fewer resources is typically expected.

- Turmoil within political environments continues, and being politically astute is essential.

- Regional and world economies are changing, and the impacts penetrate every level.

- The electronic media dominates the information age, and the impact of computers continues to grow rapidly.

- Innovation continues in the design and utility of leisure.

- Medical care is experiencing dramatic advances, yet millions have no provisions for medical care.

- The family unit is changing drastically with both parents working, or with the single parent as the sole provider, or with the inclusion of the "significant other."

- Change in employment and unemployment is dramatic in the workplace, and gender issues dominate.

- Recreation and leisure are becoming accepted as essential parts of an individual's lifestyle.

Recreation and leisure lifestyles have fully incorporated leisure activity as a part of the daily American routine. In accommodating this contemporary routine, facility and space planning must accommodate these continuing practices and expectations.

Critical to all planning is 1) representation of highly diverse publics and 2) the development of a comprehensive master plan. Chapter 1 contains the details of general master planning.

Master plans for recreation facilities and space within urban areas require several special considerations. Green space is typically at a premium or simply not available. Inner city residents typically face problems due to insufficient economic resources, deteriorating housing and business, high population density, inadequate or no transportation, no health care, high crime rates, and lack of representation within most urban planning units.

Maximum efficient accommodation of inner city residents will require some unique practices. Suggestions include recreational use of public housing facilities; social, educational, and health programs within community recreation centers; and expanded roles for fire and police stations and other such facilities operated by local government. Parking lots and building roofs are excellent for recreation activity during off time business hours. Plans must consider accessibility for residents without transportation and for the disabled. Maximum use of facilities and areas must be a priority with 24-hour usage whenever possible and/or appropriate.

Standards

Well-conceived professional standards exist for most outdoor and indoor spaces and facilities (National Recreation and Park Association, American Institute of Architects, American Camping Association, Illuminating Engineering Society, and others). Many agencies within the American government also set standards, some with the force of law. The U.S. Consumer Products Safety Commission (USCPSC) and the American Society for Testing and Materials (ASTM) also make recommendations which often become legal standards via litigation. Standards on size, location, number required, use, carrying capacity, engineering, and design are readily available. Standards provide a basis for the intelligent development of local plans. The appraisal of standards for recreational areas and facilities often requires change when warranted by program needs.

The proposal of at least one acre of green/open/park space for every 100 of the present and estimated future population is widely accepted (*Recreation, Park and Open Space Standards and Guidelines*). Facility experts suggest an upward adjustment of this general standard. Some municipal planning officials believe that the development of large outlying properties owned by the city will help meet the recognized deficiency in the inner city. This proposal is a substitute indicative not just of need, but also of feasibility.

OUTDOOR FACILITIES AND GREEN SPACE

Park and Recreation Areas

The types of parks and recreation areas described represent a variety of service units used in programs controlled by schools and community agencies. Program needs and other local conditions will dictate selections in any given place. Different combinations of facilities will emerge as the solution to the problem of meeting the needs and interests of a particular area.

There is some controversy over parkland aesthetics as defined by the terms active and passive recreation. Many individuals with an inherent interest in recreational pursuits associated with nature denounce the intrusion into parklands by tennis buffs or ball players. Obviously, these two groups have different attitudes about the character of parklands. Parklands are provided for active or passive use, or both, and without destroying aesthetic values. The use of parklands should

Figure 7.1. Merrill Park, Altamonte Springs, Florida (Photo courtesy of HNTB)

reflect the meeting of needs for the most people and the protection of the health, well-being, and safety of the users.

Abandoned industrial sites, such as strip mines, waste disposal areas, and sand/gravel pits, offer exceptional possibilities for parks and other recreational development. Often, recreational use is not only the most helpful, but the most economic use of such sites. The recreation planner must not overlook the chance of getting such sites for public use. Through early cooperative planning with site owners and operators, the landscape features become more appealing for recreational use. Utility rights-of-way offer excellent areas for recreation and are attainable via the securement of easements.

Mini-Parks and Playlots: Size, Location, Features

The mini-park or playlot is a small recreational area (less than one acre) designed for the safe play of pre-school children or for adult relaxation. As an independent unit, the mini-park/playlot best serves large housing projects or densely populated urban areas. More often, the unit exists as a feature of a larger recreation area. If a community can operate a neighborhood playground

within a one-quarter mile zone of every home, playlots should be a unit of the playground site. A location near a playground entrance, close to restrooms and away from active game areas, is ideal.

The ideal mini-park/playlot design features enclosures such as a low fence or solid planting to help supervisors in safeguarding children. Another design feature which also aids supervision involves placement of benches, both with and without shade. A drinking fountain with a step helps service both children and adults.

The design and placement of correctly sized equipment (age appropriate) within the mini-park/playlot will facilitate play by pre-school age children. The setting will combine both traditional and creative play apparatus. Traditional favorites such as the strap, bucket, or glider swing, six-foot slide, and small merry-go-round are standard. Equipment should conform to current Consumer Product Safety Commission standards. Such features as a simulated train, boat, airplane, or playhouse and fiberglass or concrete animals stimulate hours of creative play. A small climbing structure and facilities for sand play are ideal. Whenever possible, water play also should be available.

Play Structures and Areas

Where children play is a critical consideration for any community. Community playground environments are abundant, but are they safe and developmentally sound? Professionals within the American Alliance for Health, Physical Education, Recreation, and Dance (AAHPERD, Committee On Play) have raised serious questions about both safety and developmental appropriateness within America's playgrounds.

The traditional playground (most are several decades old) fails to provide "arousal-seeking" experiences. Fixed, non-manipulative, non-complex equipment (slides, monkey bars, swings) simply do not sustain children's interest. Modern playgrounds must receive proper planning, design, and placement of areas and equipment to create a play environment which will emphasize exploration, investigation, and complexity. There is a pressing need to develop play environments which also meet the needs of the disabled. Accessible playgrounds for the disabled simply do not exist in most American communities.

Experienced professionals whose careers focus on children's play recognize that play is the child's method of learning. Play is a complex, intimate process through which children explore, manipulate, develop, and become socialized. The richness of the child's environment determines the quality of the child's physical and social development. The planning, design, and supervision of play environments is critical. Designers of play must follow the most sound principles and practices in order to create safe, appropriate play. Professionals in children's play have identified the following principles about play:

- Children learn through play. Quality play significantly impacts development.
- Play value (type, quality, complexity, diversity, frequency) directly affects quality of development.
- Supervision and/or leadership is critical to learning and development. Trained leaders and/or staff are a prerequisite to quality development.
- Disabled/handicapped children (mental, emotional, physical, social, economic) have an equal right to play opportunities.
- The Americans with Disabilities Act re-emphasizes the significance of integration of the disabled. Accessibility must apply to programmatic, physical, and social environments. Attitude and awareness development are critical.
- Risk management is mandatory. Litigation can be reduced when play environments have quality planning, design, supervision, and maintenance. Most of today's playgrounds have shortcomings which encourage lawsuits.

It is urgent that all play structures and play areas/surfaces conform with Consumer Product Safety Commission Guidelines. Play structures and apparatus also must be age-appropriate, with the play area design and layout receiving careful attention. The design of playground equipment and play areas can affect significantly children's psychomotor, effective, and cognitive development. To meet psychomotor needs, equipment should be age-specific to better stimulate locomotor, non-locomotor, and manipulative actions. Equipment should elicit repetitive responses as well as increasingly new complex responses. Some equipment should be permanent and stable to stimulate the child to move. Children also should be able to move some pieces from place to place. Modular wooden structures are ideal for providing variable environments and are modified readily by professional personnel. Many play equipment manufacturers carry a full line of modular equipment, both wood and metal. Equipment must be installed according to manufacturer's specifications. Appropriate surfacing beneath equipment helps maximize safety, especially when falls from the equipment are possible.

Younger children need opportunities to create, build, and manipulate the environment. Older children need play settings which stimulate multiple responses -- more than one way to move from one piece of equipment to another. To meet cognitive needs of children, provide equipment which is multi-purpose in design. Equipment should whet children's curiosity, stimulate exploration, and elicit a variety of responses. Children use a variety of bases of support, direction, and range of movement on different pieces of equipment. No one piece provides adequate variety for all children. A broad selection of equipment often is necessary. Playgrounds and their equipment should be age-specific so children are using equipment appropriate to their age, size, and psychomotor development. Older playgrounds typically try to accommodate all age groups and sizes of children by having an assortment of equipment. They do not meet individual needs well, nor do they provide for maximum safety.

Needs are met effectively by varying the shapes of pieces such as squares, circles, and rectangles. Varying spaces will increase a variety of responses. Some should be narrow, wide, large, small, high, and low. Some pieces should be thick (planks), while others should be thin (bars). Sculptured animals and natural objects, such as tree trunks, are ideal. Textures should vary from loose, soft, and smooth such as sand, bark, and wood chips to hard, shiny, dull, and rough such as metal, wood, plastic, fiberglass, and concrete. Colors impregnated in plastic and cement prevent frequent painting. The color of the equipment should be in contrast to the surfacing beneath. Some equipment and areas should encourage social play while others should provide for quiet contemplation. Play apparatus, such as interconnected equipment, should sustain the interest of individuals.

Other pieces of equipment should appeal as unpredictable and challenging. (Figure 7.2.)

Equipment chosen for outdoor areas should be consistent with materials used indoors. This will illustrate a coordinated curricular philosophy of recreation interests. Equipment should be easy to use in physical education classes as well as at recess. Equipment must be durable, safe, and sanitary. Some pieces should be resilient. All pieces requiring cement footings are to be kept covered by dirt or a softer ground cover. Footings should be deep enough to maintain stability. Metal pieces may need shade to keep them cool. Paint on equipment prevents rust and makes the piece cleanable. Moving parts are to be lubricated regularly. Nuts and bolts are to be tightened frequently. Equipment requiring low maintenance is advisable. As stated earlier, equipment and installation must meet Consumer Product Safety Commission standards.

The surface treatment under apparatus equipment is extremely important. Better materials include sand, pea gravel, wood chips, synthetic fibers, shredded tires, and a variety of synthetic surfaces. Grass, packed dirt, asphalt, and concrete do not provide the safest surfaces. The use of asphalt covered with a synthetic material has been gaining in popularity. Safety and aesthetic aspects are good, but the initial cost is higher. The level surface of the asphalt and synthetic covering is safer. Water puddles do not appear under swings, and surface maintenance is minimal. Unfortunately, the safest surfaces (sand, pea gravel, wood chips, shredded tires, synthetic fibers) typically have high maintenance costs. According to the Consumer Product Safety Commission, falls constitute about 70 percent of all playground accidents. It is clearly in the interest of children's safety to use surface materials which maximize safety.

Enclosing play areas may be appropriate to help prevent nuisance legal problems. A perimeter definition helps age-appropriate usage. If equip-

Figure 7.2. A typical elementary school playground

ment requires adult supervision, a fence with a lock is needed.

Although homemade equipment may be durable and cost less initially, legal concerns may warrant the purchase of commercial equipment. Comparative shopping may reduce the cost of commercially-made pieces by as much as 50 percent.

Play area design requires consultation with educational consultants, landscape architects, or commercial planners. Locating pieces of equipment for age groups is important. Equipment placement should stimulate movement from one piece to another. Moving parts require spaces for a range of movements. Equipment location needs to provide for ease of supervision and safe traffic patterns. The movement of modular wooded structures and free standing equipment helps provide children with new opportunities to explore the environment. Play areas throughout the community should reflect variety.

Small Activities/Games Courts

The mini-park or playlot also may include courts and areas for such activities as hopscotch, rope jumping, marbles, and ring toss. Most activity areas are multi-purpose. Neighborhood parks and schools offer most of the areas for small games and activities. The areas and courts are used for both

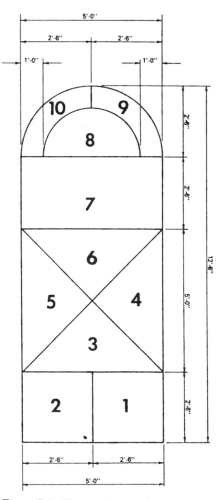

Figure 7.3. Hopscotch court layout

class instruction and recreation programs.

Small activities need a minimum area of 25-by-25 feet, next to a crafts-and-apparatus area. Good drainage is needed. The area needs to be surrounded by a fence or shrubbery barrier for maximum safety and control. The surface may be of sandy loam, asphalt, or concrete.

Hopscotch is popular with children. A special court needs to be provided in one section of the activities area. (Figure 7.3.)

The Neighborhood Park

In many communities the neighborhood park is connected to an elementary school (park-school concept). The neighborhood park is green space set aside primarily for both active and passive recreation. Ideally, it gives the impression of being rural in its character. It emphasizes horticultural features, with spacious turf areas bordered by trees, shrubs, and sometimes floral arrangements. The neighborhood park is considered a must in densely populated areas.

A separately located neighborhood park normally requires three to five acres. As a measure of expediency, an isolated area as small as one or two acres is adequate. Sometimes the functions of a neighborhood park are served by a community or a city-wide park. The neighborhood park plays an important role in setting standards for community aesthetics. Therefore, it should include open green space and walks. Aesthetic requirements also may be met through sculpture forms, pools, and fountains for ornamentation. Creative planning will employ contouring, contrasting surfaces, masonry, and other modern techniques to provide both eye appeal and utility.

Community Parks and Playfields

This type of recreational area serves a community where it is not possible to develop a community park-school. The typical area serviced by a secondary (junior/senior high) school is the entire community in which the students reside. The community park and playfield, like the neighborhood playground, provides facilities for a variety of organized recreational activities. It will have the characteristics of a landscaped park and serve as the playground for children living in the immediate neighborhood. Its primary service, however, is to a much wider age group. Thus, it supplies a greater variety of facilities and more extensive services than the neighborhood playground. The school child, teenager, young adult, hobbyist, senior citizen, and family group all find attractive facilities at a well-developed community park and playfield. When there is no school building at this area, some type of indoor facility will be found. Often a multi-purpose recreation building meets this need.

Fitness Trails

The continuing physical fitness boom of the 1980s and early 1990s has inspired the development of outdoor facilities for total body conditioning programs, typically named fitness/exercise trails. Such facilities are marketed commercially under a variety of names including Fitness Trail, Fit-Trail, Lifecourse, and Parcourse. All combine features designed to help improve cardiovascular fitness, agility, flexibility, strength, and endurance. The fitness/exercise trail consists of several exercise stations located at various lengths along a walking or jogging course. A typical trail could have a 1.5 mile distance with 13 exercise stations. The running intervals and exercises help give a balanced program of overall fitness. (Figure 7.4.)

Golf Courses

The design, construction, operation, and maintenance of golf courses is too extensive a subject for a complete presentation within this chapter. For information and guidance about this complex facility, contact the U.S. Golf Association. Address: Liberty Corner Road, Far Hills, NJ 07931.

Assuming the available land is suitable for construction of a golf course, the following space requirements exist:

- For a standard 18-hole course -- 120 to 160 acres
- For a standard 9-hole course -- 70 to 90 acres
- For a 9-hole, par three course (including two par four holes) -- 45 to 60 acres

Planning also should provide for an administrative clubhouse, a locker room area, a practice putting green, a practice driving range, adequate parking, concession areas, drinking fountains, restrooms, and maintenance support areas.

Marinas

Americans love water. The plethora of inland lakes, rivers, and streams, and the thousands of miles of coastline help satisfy their consummate desire to take advantage of these natural resources. Boating commands more of the recreational dollar than does baseball, fishing, golf, or any other single aquatic activity. There is a need for efficient, realistic, and functional planning for facilities to accommodate the ever-growing desire for water-based activities.

The launching, mooring, and storage of powerboats, sailboats, rowboats, and other watercraft are the function of a marina. Marina planning will involve knowledgeable and experienced personnel. These experts will survey the number, types, and sizes of existing watercraft in the area, the number and size of existing berthing facilities, and the condition of such existing facilities. The survey also should include the demographics of the surrounding area to help determine and project the aquatic demands for both the present and future.

An accurate and comprehensive assessment is the first step in planning a marina. The survey data will help determine the basic consideration in laying out the marina and choosing the correct number of slips for each size required. Marinas vary in their design, function, location, and capacity. It is very difficult to arrive at standard conclusions and judgments concerning a model marina. Each planner will be able to apply the general principles to his unique circumstances. From that point, however, one must adapt the marina to the peculiar needs and characteristics of the community. (Figure 7.5.)

Performing Arts Areas

A significant aspect of the growth of outdoor recreation is the demand for suitable outdoor facilities. Americans continue to push for outdoor areas/facilities for operas, plays, band, and orchestral concerts, pageants, festivals, holiday programs, and civic celebrations. When performed outdoors, such activities usually require a stage or band shell with an adjoining amphitheater capable of accommodating many spectators.

Selection of the proper site for an outdoor theater is essential. It must have good acoustical properties. The site must be located in a quiet place away from the noise of traffic or of groups at play. A natural bowl or depression on a hillside with a slope of 10 to 20 degrees, preferably bordered by slopes or densely wooded areas, provides a fine location.

At some outdoor theaters, people sit on the slope of the amphitheater. At others there are permanent seats. Terraced areas with a turf surface are too difficult to maintain. Enough level space is needed at the rear of the seating area for the circulation of spectators. Aisles should be wide enough to ease the seating of large numbers in a short time. Public comfort stations and refreshment facilities are needed near the entrance to the amphitheater. Provision for the nearby parking of automobiles is essential. Vehicles should be parked in areas where noises and car lights do not disturb the stage action.

The dimensions of the stage vary with the proposed usage. Rarely should a stage be less than 50 feet in width or 30 feet in depth. The rear of the stage may be a wall or high hedge, or even a planting of trees. The wings

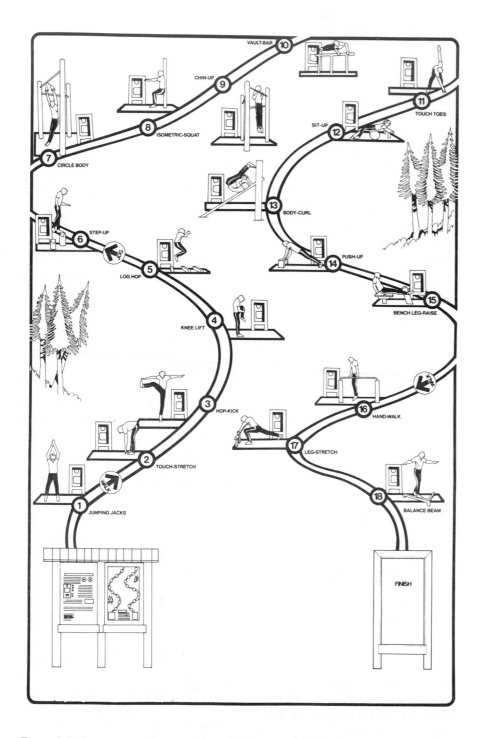

Figure 7.4. Parcourse outdoor exercise trail (Courtesy PARCOURSE Ltd.)

Figure 7.5. Baylor University Marina is used for instruction during the day and is open for recreational use in the afternoon and evening.

often are formed by natural plant materials. The band or music shell, however, is more satisfactory for projecting voices and sound that is free from echoes and interference. A vertical rear wall with inclined ceiling is not only the simplest and most economical to construct, but affords excellent acoustical qualities.

The band shell usually contains dressing rooms, toilets, storage space, and control centers for sound amplification and lighting equipment. Separate structures near the back of the stage also may be used for such facilities. The orchestra pit will be placed between the auditorium and the stage.

Mobile units with self-contained lighting and acoustical systems have become very popular. They are used to serve many parks instead of restricting programs to one permanent location. Mobile units equipped to serve as a band shell, stage, puppet theater, or platform for other performing arts bring productions to audiences not exposed before to such activities. Excellent units are available at a cost less than that required for a permanent band shell.

Target Archery

Archery appeals to a sizable group in most communities. Ample range space helps provide for the safety and enjoyment of the participants. For target archery, the range should provide shooting distances of 100, 80, 60, 50, 40, and 30 yards. For junior use, target ranges can be from 10 to 50 yards. Targets are 48 inches wide and should be at least 15 feet apart. Most ranges provide a fixed target line with variable shooting lines. Most side boundaries extend 10 yards to either side of the range target and shooting lines. The safe range provides additional space beyond the target, free from stones and other substances that might cause the breakage of arrows errant of their mark. This additional space usually is supported by an earth bunker or bales of hay and straw piled up to the top of the target.

The target archery range should be fairly level. Orientation should be north and south so archers will not be facing the sun. A fence enclosure is desirable, but not essential. Planned control of shooters not on line and of spectators will avoid potential safety threats caused by those who would walk through the range. Storage sheds for the target butts and other equipment are sometimes a part of the archery range. Some ranges place storage rooms within the earth bunker behind the targets.

In providing for the use of the range by the disabled, it is desirable to provide a four-foot wide, ground level, hard surface walk for wheelchair use along the shooting lines. Another walk could extend to the target line (preferably down the center), with perhaps another walkway behind the targets to provide access for extracting arrows. Such walks reduce interference from inclement weather, increase the use of the range, and reduce maintenance costs.

Nature Centers

The nature center is a particular type of development that aids learning in the outdoors. Centers also assist the growth of recreational interests. The establishing of nature centers is promoted extensively by science and nature-related organizations. Children's museums are a part of this development, although many such museums lack adjacent lands for outdoor education.

The proper facility design for the nature center will permit expansion as the program grows and as more funds become available. In its initial stage, the building should contain a minimum space of 2,500 square feet. This is enough space to contain one class adequately. The building design also must meet the needs set by the program. The minimum design provides for the following:
- Office for staff.
- Toilet facilities, with access provided from the outside and interior of the building.
- Large meeting room, with useable wall space for exhibits. The provision of low cabinets along the walls for storage of educational aids; long counter (on top of the cabinets) to provide work and display space.
- At least two classrooms so a class may be broken up into smaller groups when necessary.

- A workroom for constructing displays and for arts and crafts.
- Science laboratory. A room equipped with microscopes, soil and mineral-testing equipment, and other materials necessary for scientific studies.
- Library. The largest meeting room could house the library, which could occupy one section of the room. The library should contain reference material, field guides, magazines, and novels concerned with the outdoors.
- Storage room. Adequate space for storage of the many pieces of instructional and janitorial equipment that will collect over the years.

Interpretive Centers

Interpretive centers offer a specific service to the public and, in some cases, to school groups. The National Park Service has the most extensive development of such centers. State and metropolitan parks have been expanding the number of their interpretive centers. The U.S. Forest Service is beginning to develop information centers that are essentially interpretive centers.

The primary purpose of interpretive centers is to help visitors understand and appreciate the natural, historical, or archeological features of the areas which the centers represent. Since the problems of interpretation for each area are different, facility developments will vary.

Interpretive centers frequently contain a trailside museum or interpretive center building. This may vary in size from 10-by-20 feet to a large, multi-roomed structure. The size of the center depends on the nature of the visiting groups, the interpretive materials available, and the types of programs expected. A large center may contain all the following:
- display rooms with habitat cases and other exhibits
- office space for staff
- a laboratory for research and the preparation of display materials

- meeting rooms for lectures, slides, or movies
- lavatories and toilets
- a counter for the sale of books and the distribution of pamphlets
- an outdoor amphitheater or campfire area for lectures and movies
- trails to points of interest (often self-guiding nature trails)
- parapets or other special observation points, often including mounted telescopes and pointers to places of interest
- interpretive devices at points of interest, including bulletin boards, maps, diagrams, and displays
- parking areas.

School groups often visit interpretive centers, usually by bus/van on a one-day basis. Picnic areas are desirable for such groups. Work space, where children can work on projects at the center, is a desirable feature.

Camp, School, and Community Gardens and Farms

Gardens, farms, and forests provide direct experiences with growing plants and with domestic animals. Camps, schools, park and recreation agencies, and a few private agencies have developed such facilities. Even when such facilities operate under the jurisdiction of park, recreation, or private agencies, there is some direct relationship with schools. The facilities of the agency and the instructional program of the schools complement each other.

Tract Gardens

The most common type of camp, school, or community garden is the tract garden. Land ranging in size from one to 10 acres will be divided into small tracts for garden use by individuals. A typical plot size may be 10-by-20 feet, but adults and families can use larger plots. One-fourth acre of land will support 25 tract gardens, although more space is desirable. Four acres of land can hold

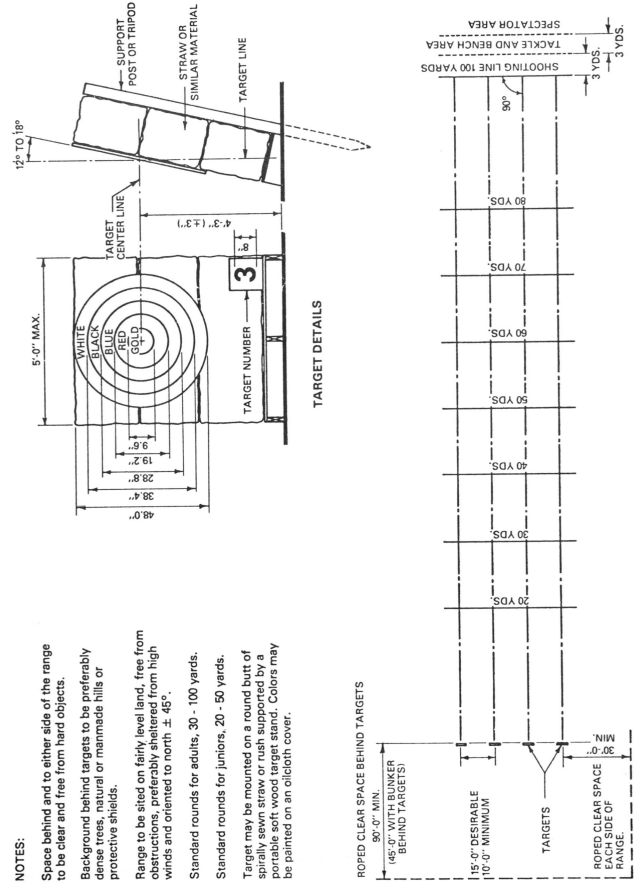

NOTES:

Space behind and to either side of the range to be clear and free from hard objects.

Background behind targets to be preferably dense trees, natural or manmade hills or protective shields.

Range to be sited on fairly level land, free from obstructions, preferably sheltered from high winds and oriented to north ± 45°.

Standard rounds for adults, 30 - 100 yards.

Standard rounds for juniors, 20 - 50 yards.

Target may be mounted on a round butt of spirally sewn straw or rush supported by a portable soft wood target stand. Colors may be painted on an oilcloth cover.

Figure 7.6. Archery Range Layout

TARGET DETAILS

SUPPORT POST OR TRIPOD

STRAW OR SIMILAR MATERIAL

TARGET LINE

TARGET CENTER LINE

12° TO 18°

4'-3'' (±3'')

5'-0'' MAX.

WHITE
BLACK
BLUE
RED
GOLD

9.6''
19.2''
28.8''
38.4''
48.0''

8''

TARGET NUMBER

SPECTATOR AREA

TACKLE AND BENCH AREA

SHOOTING LINE 100 YARDS

3 YDS.
3 YDS.
3 YDS.

90°

80 YDS.

70 YDS.

60 YDS.

50 YDS.

40 YDS.

30 YDS.

20 YDS.

ROPED CLEAR SPACE BEHIND TARGETS

90'-0'' MIN.
(45'-0'' WITH BUNKER BEHIND TARGETS)

15'-0'' DESIRABLE
10'-0'' MINIMUM

TARGETS

ROPED CLEAR SPACE EACH SIDE OF RANGE.

30'-0'' MIN.

100 gardeners with plots of varied size and community crops. This size allows space for a service building and activity area. It should be on rich, well-drained soil with water available.

Garden programs may involve instruction, environmental projects, field trips, and science activities. Community projects may include novelty crops such as a pumpkin patch, gourds, Indian corn, and a Christmas tree farm. Gardening appeals to all ages and is an excellent program for families.

Some of the desirable features of the tract garden are:

- storage building, adequate for the storage of tools and equipment or large enough for class meetings and indoor activities during inclement weather

- toilet facilities adequate to care for the maximum number of participants expected on the garden plot at one time

- greenhouse for plant propagation

- ready access to water, with spigots and hoses available for irrigation

- fencing for protection of the garden

- pathways and walkways to provide easy access to all plots

- a demonstration home yard, with grass, flowers, and shrubs

- good landscaping

- within walking distance for the participants.

Tract gardens for adults and families are set up as a social service in some communities. These gardens make it possible for people living in crowded urban centers or apartments to be able to garden. Often, these gardens are some distance from home. Transportation must be provided by the individuals concerned.

Other Outdoor Areas/Facilities

Information pertinent to sports fields and courts in outdoor areas/facilities is available in Chapter 3.

ORGANIZED CAMPING

Organized camping is a major industry within America. It encompasses a wide range of types of camps associated with programs for children, adults, and families. Some programs may be delivered by using only open spaces, however, most programs use both outdoor areas and facilities. Typical designations for sites involving organized camping are: day camps, resident camps, family camps, wilderness camps, school camps, trip and travel camps. Camps are developed by many public agencies at all levels of government. Private independent camps typically operate on a year-round basis and serve a select clientele. Most organized camping occurs on agency-owned or private property; however, public land is becoming increasingly involved.

Public land is often a major resource for school camps and for school outdoor education programs. Schools may use the facilities/areas during the school year, and park and recreation agencies use them during summers. The goals of outdoor education are basically the same whether sponsored by park and recreation departments or by schools. Cooperative planning is needed to attain the most from the community dollar. Such planning helps to assure that suitable lands and sites are available. If adequate space and facilities are to be available to meet the needs of organized camping, plans must be made for year-round use of facilities.

Facilities and Areas for Camp Programming

The highlight of organized camping is its programming activity. The following is a sampling of the areas and facilities used for programming.

Aquatic activities are extremely popular during summer camps. They also lend themselves to year-round programming associated with fishing, boating, canoeing, skiing, snorkeling, scuba, and many other water-related activities.

Streams, ponds, lakes, bays, and inlets offer a wide range of recreational and outdoor education opportunities. Safety must be a primary factor associated with aquatic activity. We must see that these special facilities receive careful study about depths, slopes, currents, eddies, undertows, shoreline characteristics, debris, and other water-related factors.

Canoeing, power boating, sailing, and skiing are typical aquatic activities. The aquatic area should have the appropriate accessory facilities for complementing the activity. Such accessories include docks, floats, markers, buoys, and possibly a marina. Different aquatic activities and events require different sizes of bodies of water. Canoe races, for example, typically have courses for competition in races of 100, 200, 440, 880 yards and even one mile. Small craft, power boats, and sailboards typically require a larger body of water. This is due to a variety of factors specific to each activity, such as wind factors, course requirements, boat size, speed, separation of events, and spectator viewing.

Simulation is common for fly and rod-and-reel casting when actual facilities are not present, or with unskilled participants. Practice casting on a playing field or within a gymnasium makes year-round practice possible. When ponds or lakes are near, a shoreline or dock may provide an excellent facility for casting. Casting requires an area about 100-by-300 feet to conduct all phases of instruction. It is easy to construct casting targets from a variety of materials or props. Ten targets size 30 inches in diameter will accommodate a normal size class or group. Water targets also should be 30 inches in diameter and should float. Hollow tubing which will float, yet anchor easily, may be used for target construction.

The diversity of camp programming facilities is large. Typical examples not mentioned previously include campfire circles, amphitheaters, council rings, corrals, craft centers, covered pavilions, firing ranges, archery ranges, and ropes/confidence courses. Highly specialized camps with a focus on one activity typically have highly specialized facilities and areas. A horsemanship camp and a tennis camp are but two examples.

Day Camps

The day camp involves space and facilities intended to provide a program of activities similar to that for a resident camp. The day camp staff and campers sleep at home. Many of the considerations of planning for resident camps apply to day camps. Operating problems (staffing and all services) are simpler because day campers sleep at home and usually eat only their lunch at camp. Many day camps will have the campers bring their lunch (brown bag) and provide campers with only snacks. Provisions, however simple, must consider water, toilets, inclement weather, eating and cooking, refrigeration, first aid, and program supplies. The focus of this section is that of selecting an appropriate day camp site/facility.

Enough acreage to support the anticipated programming is necessary, especially when the program focus is on outdoor-related activities. A remote and not readily accessible area with a varied topography supportive of outdoor program skills is highly desirable. Natural parks, park-school areas, and community forests often have the desired characteristics for day camp sites. Some communities have developed special day camp areas; others make appropriate park and recreation areas available for day camp use.

It is typical to use vans and buses to transport campers to the day camp. The use of more than one-half hour in transporting campers each way will alter the effectiveness of the program.

The control of day camps and camper groups should be according to recognized standards such as those of the American Camping Association. Ratios of counselors to campers may vary from one to six to as many as one to 20. This variable relates to the age of the campers with younger campers requiring the smaller ratio. Many day camps provide basic, simple facilities such as fire sites for cooking and eating and storage facilities. They may serve a daily meal in a central dining hall. This practice ends the need for fire sites and satellite eating areas.

Food, equipment, and program supplies require storage areas. Some day camps use vans, trucks, or other vehicles for storage as well as for

Figure 7.7a. Combination community center and day camp, Jewish Community Center Family Campus, Wilmington, DE (Courtesy of Tetra Tech Richardson, Inc.)

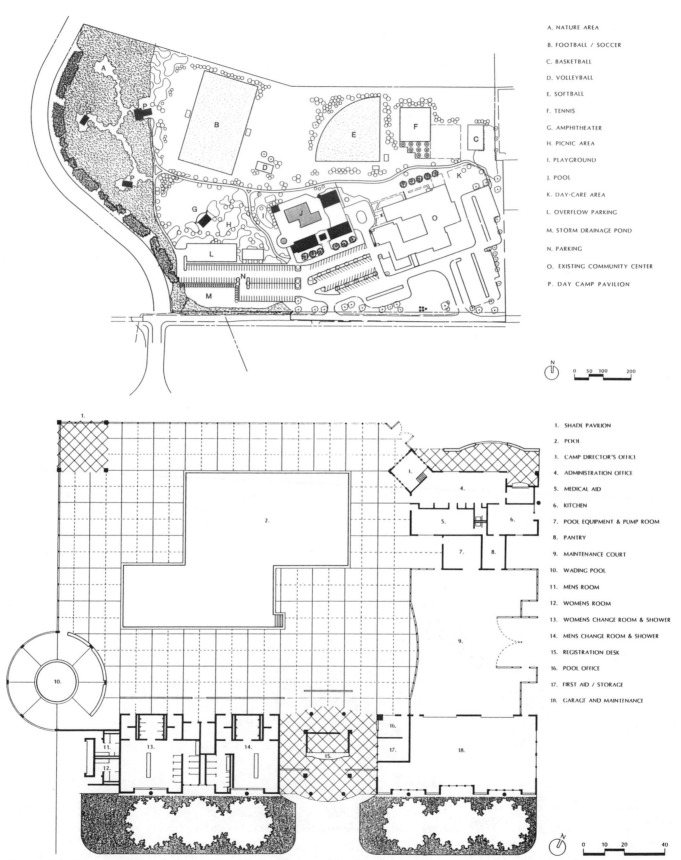

A. NATURE AREA
B. FOOTBALL / SOCCER
C. BASKETBALL
D. VOLLEYBALL
E. SOFTBALL
F. TENNIS
G. AMPHITHEATER
H. PICNIC AREA
I. PLAYGROUND
J. POOL
K. DAY-CARE AREA
L. OVERFLOW PARKING
M. STORM DRAINAGE POND
N. PARKING
O. EXISTING COMMUNITY CENTER
P. DAY CAMP PAVILION

1. SHADE PAVILION
2. POOL
3. CAMP DIRECTOR'S OFFICE
4. ADMINISTRATION OFFICE
5. MEDICAL AID
6. KITCHEN
7. POOL EQUIPMENT & PUMP ROOM
8. PANTRY
9. MAINTENANCE COURT
10. WADING POOL
11. MENS ROOM
12. WOMENS ROOM
13. WOMENS CHANGE ROOM & SHOWER
14. MENS CHANGE ROOM & SHOWER
15. REGISTRATION DESK
16. POOL OFFICE
17. FIRST AID / STORAGE
18. GARAGE AND MAINTENANCE

Figures 7.7b, 7.7c. Combination community center and day camp, Jewish Community Center Family Campus, Wilmington, DE. (Courtesy of Tetra Tech Richardson, Inc.)

transporting such items to and from camp each day. A well-equipped first aid station and a rest area facility are essential.

Resident Camps

The resident camp offers perhaps the broadest program of activities for all groups of campers. Resident camp sessions range from as few as two days and one night to as much as an entire season encompassing about 12 weeks. There are about 8,000 camps within the United States, and most are day camps. The American Camping Association reports that most camps which operate year-round are resident camps. The American Camping Association accredits annually about 2,500 camps.

The resident camp experience is a 24-hour experience for both campers and staff. Campers literally live at the camp and participate in a wide range of activities. Programming includes swimming, horseback riding, shooting sports, small aquatic craft, arts and crafts, pioneer skills, archery, fishing, outdoor living skills, sports of all types, hiking, outdoor education, dramatics, orienteering, and more. Resident camps range in size from 200 to 500-plus acres and have permanent facilities and structures. Campers may sleep in tents, covered wagons, tepees, cabins, and multi-unit dormitories. Food services typically are available indoors, with outdoor cooking offered as an educational experience and opportunity. Both indoor and outdoor program activities place an emphasis on lifetime skill development for the campers. The better resident camps are truly an enriched version of home away from home. Members of the camp staff are surrogate parents who make every effort to offer a safe living and learning setting for the campers.

The typical resident camp will have many permanent, year-round facilities. These include offices, buildings for sleeping, eating, health care, activity instruction, and arts and crafts. There are swimming pools, specialized sport areas, horseback riding and horsemanship training areas, game rooms, and other facilities and spaces indigenous to the particular camp. Many schools use both private and agency resident camps for outdoor education programming. Very few American schools own camps.

School Camps

School camps typically meet the standards for accreditation by the American Camping Association. In doing so, they are not significantly different from most accredited day or resident camps; however, their goals for the campers/students are different. School camp goals are curriculum-oriented with an outdoor education/laboratory focus.

Few school systems own and operate a camp. Of those which do have camps, many have operated them for decades. Some were founded as early as the 1930s. The Tyler, Texas schools have one of the oldest and better known school camps in America. Most schools deliver their outdoor education curriculum to students in the fifth and sixth grades. Non-school camps are used for the delivery of most school-based outdoor education curricula. Many 4-H camps in America incorporate outdoor education as a regular program activity.

Conference/Retreat Centers

The use of camps for conferences or retreats is common. Such camps often have special areas/facilities which are multi-purpose in design and lend themselves to supporting a wide range of activity. Other special facilities are available with design characteristics specifically for conference activities. Whether a camp or a special facility, most will operate on a year-round basis. Since most conferences or retreats involve the mature adult, conference centers usually are designed with special facility considerations for adults. Many such centers will have a resort atmosphere. The American Camping Association (ACA) is developing accreditation standards for conference/retreat centers (1993), and they have had standards for camps for many years. The standards will focus on the following areas: site and facilities, food service, administration and hospitality, transportation and vehicles, personnel, recreation and leisure services, health care, aquatic activities, and horseback riding. Conference/retreat centers typically are comprehensive in their nature and services and are similar to hotels and motor inns. Function and comfort are essential aspects of a conference/retreat center, especially when used for more than one day.

Meeting rooms/areas are at the heart of the conference/retreat center and should provide the following: space for flexible chair and table arrangements, controllable lighting, ventilation and temperature control, and abundant electrical power outlets. They also will provide audio-visual equipment and sound control for multi-group speaking conditions. For extensive detail about facility design and construction, refer to Chapters 2 and 3.

Outdoor Education/Recreation

As predicted during the 1970s and 1980s, the outdoors has vaulted into prominence as a significant place for both education and recreation. There has been a growth of all types of outdoor activities causing the acquisition of land areas and facilities for outdoor education. There is a continuing awareness that the current generation and those to come are likely to lose touch with the land and the rural life of their forebearers. School age children and many adults know little about the outdoors. The lack of such knowledge requires specific efforts to educate them in, about, and for the outdoors.

Outdoor education involves learning activities in, about, and for the outdoors. The provision of learning activities for outdoor education is needed in the curricula of schools, colleges, and universities. The need also exists for programs of community recreation agencies and camps. It is a means of curriculum extension and enrichment through outdoor experiences, not a separate discipline with prescribed goals, such as science and mathematics. It is a learning climate offering opportunities for direct laboratory experiences in identifying and resolving real-life problems. It provides for gaining skills with which to enjoy an enriched life and helps build a concern about man and his natural environment. Outdoor education allows individuals to get back in touch with those aspects of living where roots were once firm and deep.

CONSIDERATIONS IN SELECTING A SITE FOR OUTDOOR EDUCATION AND RECREATION

Size

The type of program planned should determine the size of the site. Site size alone does not mean much. It does affect the numbers of certain species of wildlife that might live in the area. A large area may not have a diversity of physical features. It may just be level land, harboring only a few species of trees, with no particularly outstanding features. Nevertheless, such an area could be highly interesting from an educational viewpoint, provided good leadership is available.

Many schools, recreation departments, and community agencies already have school sites, parks, and recreational areas suitable for outdoor programs. Schools, as well as other agencies in some sections in the country, also have forest lands which are very suitable for use in a broad educational and recreational program. Again,

planners and programmers for outdoor education should not overlook the multi-purpose, multi-function capabilities of established camps.

Site Characteristics

The type of program planned influences the characteristics required of a site. If planning for the site involves daily use only, fewer requirements must be met. Many characteristics are required if the land and facilities are to support all aspects of the educational curriculum. This is very true if there is to be a special emphasis on science, conservation, and outdoor skills. Desired site characteristics are:

- a location favoring safety, privacy, and solitude
- year-round access by road
- a minimum of natural and man-made hazards
- interesting geological features, such as rock outcroppings, open field flat terrain, and a variety of soil types
- a variety of native vegetation, including woods
- a sustainable wildlife base
- a pond, stream, sea, or large body of water
- demonstration areas for conservation practices
- woods for practicing outdoor skills and use of native materials
- sanitary facilities, including good drainage and good drinking water
- simple shelters for inclement weather
- proximity to adequate medical and hospital services

INDOOR RECREATIONAL SPACES and FACILITIES (Public)

Buildings for General Recreation

Multi-function, multi-purpose recreational buildings will meet most needs

and interests of residents within specific neighborhoods or communities. Neither buildings nor programs should discriminate in any manner, especially on meeting requirements of the Americans With Disabilities Act. General recreation buildings should provide a safe, healthful, and attractive atmosphere. Good buildings allow every person in the community or neighborhood to enjoy his/her leisure by participating in activities of a social, inspirational, cultural, or physical nature. Both buildings and programs must focus on the broad concept of wellness.

Recreational buildings may range from the simple picnic shelter to the complex community recreation building designed to facilitate a wide range of programs and activities. Designs may range from the rustic to the contemporary. As emphasized throughout this text, present-day structures must provide for diversity and multiple use. There are needs for single-purpose buildings, however, they have the potential to serve significantly fewer people. The multi-function/multi-purpose concept has stimulated the development of a variety of recreational buildings.

Neighborhood Recreation Centers

The one facility which is, perhaps, closest to the grass roots service level is the neighborhood recreation center. Neighborhood recreation centers service an area of about 8,000 people. Planners define a typical neighborhood as an area served by one to three elementary schools. The neighborhood recreation center encloses 15,000 to 25,000 square feet. The size also will depend on whether the building is a single structure or part of a park-school complex where additional facilities are available in the school.

The neighborhood recreation center typically includes the following facilities:

Figure 7.8. Artist's rendering of the Student Recreation Center, University of Toledo (Courtesy of Hastings and Chivetta)

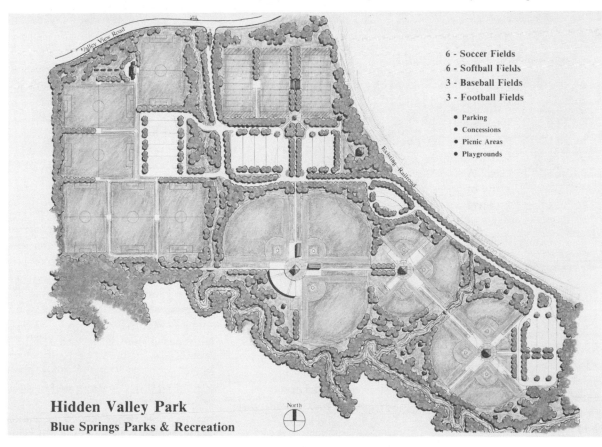

6 - Soccer Fields
6 - Softball Fields
3 - Baseball Fields
3 - Football Fields

- Parking
- Concessions
- Picnic Areas
- Playgrounds

Hidden Valley Park
Blue Springs Parks & Recreation

North

Figure 7.9. Hidden Valley Park, Blue Springs Parks and Recreation (Courtesy of HNTB)

Figure 7.10. Livermore Recreational Community Center, Livermore, CA (Courtesy of Roland/Miller/Associates)

- multi-purpose room or rooms
- gymnasium (if not available in neighborhood school)
- shower and locker rooms, when a gymnasium is provided
- arts and crafts room
- game room
- kitchen
- restrooms
- lounge and lobby
- office
- large storage areas

Community Recreation Centers

A community recreation center functions beyond the primary purpose of serving a neighborhood. Community recreation centers service a population typically served by one high school. Such centers help meet the complete recreational needs of most people within that community. Within large cities having more than one public high school, the typical community recreation center may service a population larger than that served by one high school.

The building size will vary by the number of people served and the projected program plan. Size also varies when the center is a part of a park-school site or a separate building. The community recreation center usually contains 30,000 to 40,000 square feet of space. Major recreation areas such as park-school sites or community parks typically serve as ideal locations for community centers.

Community recreation centers typically include the following facilities:
- multi-purpose rooms
- gymnasium
- shower and locker rooms
- swimming pool (natatorium)
- stage and auditorium (sometimes combined with gymnasium)

- rooms for programs in the arts (art, dance, music, drama)
- game room
- kitchen
- restrooms
- foyer, lobby, and lounge
- staff offices
- large storage areas
- classrooms for instruction
- specialized areas as program dictates (racquet courts, gymnastics, weight and exercise room, photography workshop, and so on). (Figure 7.10.)

Some of the above facility features are special. They are considered special because many recreational buildings do not have such facilities (gymnasium, swimming pool, photo room, etc.). This text discusses such special facilities in detail within other chapters. There are a few "select facilities," however, worthy of discussion here.

HIGHLY SPECIALIZED RECREATION FACILITIES

Art Center, Community Playhouse, Children's Museum, Zoo

Many communities either provide or support recreation programs that require highly specialized facilities. Examples are an art center, a community playhouse for performing arts, a children's museum, an ice rink, a shooting range, tennis center, and a zoo. There are, of course, other specialized facilities, however, there are too many to mention.

Planning for such highly specialized facilities must be exceptionally thorough. Good planning will provide for maximum year-round use. Carefully locating such a facility helps the delivery of services to all potential users. Architects and contractors creating such facilities should have ample experience specific to such facilities. Experienced personnel offer greater assurance of compliance with all design and construction standards and specifications. Several other chapters within this text address the essential exacting requirements for such specialized facilities.

SUMMARY

Parks and open green spaces are widely recognized as being an important component in contemporary living. These spaces allow for recreation and leisure activities in many forms to address a wide range of interests. They can include large parks and recreation areas, playgrounds, fitness trails, golf courses, marinas, outdoor performing arts areas, and other sites. Camps, nature centers and community gardens are examples of how these spaces can provide access to both leisure and educational pursuits. Planning for parks and open green spaces must address programming, equipment, facilities, activity areas, and staffing.

SELECTED REFERENCES/ BIBLIOGRAPHY

A Handbook for Public Playground Safety. Volume I: General Guidelines for New and Existing Playgrounds. 1986. Washington, D.C.: U.S. Consumer Product Safety Commission.

A Handbook for Public Playground Safety. Volume II: Technical Guidelines for Equipment and Surfacing. Washington, D.C.: U.S. Consumer Product Safety Commission, 1986.

A Model Playground for the Multiply Handicapped. 1982. Urbana/Champaign: University of Illinois, William W. Fox Developmental Center, Office of Recreation and Park Resources.

Bowers, Louis. February, 1983. "Tomorrow's Play." *Journal of Physical Education, Recreation and Dance,* 54:pp. 40,41. Reston, VA: American Alliance for Health, Physical Education, Recreation and Dance.

Bruya, Lawrence. February, 1983. "Playing the American Dream." *Journal of Physical Education, Recreation and Dance,* 54:p. 38. Reston, VA: American Alliance for Health, Physical Education, Recreation and Dance.

Bruya, Lawrence and Langendorfer, Steve. 1988. *Where Our Children Play: Elementary School Playground Equipment, Volume I,* Reston, VA: American Association for Recreation and Leisure.

Bruya, Lawrence. 1988. *Play Spaces for Children: A New Beginning. Volume II,* Reston, VA: American Association for Leisure and Recreation.

Camp Sites and Facilities. 1988. Irving, Texas: Boy Scouts of America.

Chamberlain, Clinton. 1985. *Marinas: Recommendations for Design, Construction, and Management, Volume 1.* Chicago: National Marine Manufacturers Association.

Coastal Marinas Assessment Guidance Handbook. 1984. Atlanta, GA: U.S. Environmental Protection Agency.

Coppa and Avery Consultants. November, 1980. "Adaptation and Design of Parks and Recreational Facilities for the Handicapped." *Vance Bibliographies.*

Cordell, Ken and Hendee, John. 1982. *Renewable Resources for Recreation in the United States: Supply, Demand, and Critical Policy Issues.* Washington, D.C.: American Forestry Association.

Crossley, John. 1986. *Public-Commercial Cooperation In Parks and Recreation.* Columbus, Ohio: Publishing Horizons.

Encyclopedia of Associations. 1992. Detroit, MI: Gale Research Company.

Fitness Systems by Landscape Structures, Incorporated: Healthbeat, Wheel Course, Vita Course, Fitcore. 1984. Delano, MN: Landscape Structures, Inc.

Fitzgerald, Sharon. January/February, 1983. "Will-A-Way: Georgia's Unique Facility for the Handicapped." *CEFP Journal* 21 , pp. 8-9.

Flynn, Richard B. (Ed.). 1985. *Planning Facilities for Athletics, Physical Education, and Recreation.* Athletic Institute of America and American Alliance for Health, Physical Education, Recreation, and Dance.

Frakt, Arthur and Rankin, Janna. 1982. *The Law of Parks, Recreation Resources, and Leisure Services.* Columbus, OH: Publishing Horizons.

Frost, Joe and Klein, Barry. 1983. *Children's Play and Playgrounds.* Austin, TX: Playscapes International.

Gill, Don. 1986. *A Guide to Building Fitness Trails.* Columbus, Ohio: Publishing Horizons.

Godbey, Geoffrey. 1980. *Leisure in Your Life: An Exploration.* Philadelphia: W.B. Saunders.

Gold, Seymour. August, 1991. "Inspecting Playgrounds for Hazards." *Parks and Recreation,* 26, pp. 32-37.

Hasegaqa, Sandra and Elliot, Steve. May, 1983. "Public Spaces by Private Enterprise." *Urban Land* 42, pp. 12-15.

Handbook for Public Playground Safety. November, 1991. Washington, D.C.: U.S. Consumer Product Safety Commission.

Hogan, Paul. February, 1983. "Working for Play." *Journal of Physical Education, Recreation and Dance,* 54, p. 39. Reston, VA: American Alliance for Health, Physical Education, Recreation and Dance.

_____. 1988. *The Playground Safety Checker,* Phoenixville, PA.

Hospitality: The Key To Success (Student Toolbook). 1989. Reston, VA: National Campground Owners Association.

Hospitality: The Key To Success (Trainer's Guide). 1989. Reston, VA: National Campground Owners Association.

Jambor, Tom and Palmer, Donald. 1991. *Playground Safety Manual.* Birmingham, AL: University of Alabama.

Knudson, Douglas. 1984. *Outdoor Recreation.* New York: Macmillan.

Kraus, Richard. 1984. Recreation and Leisure in Modern Society. Glenview, Illinois: Scott, Foresman and Company.

Lehew, Edward and Lehew, Shirley. January/February, 1983. "White Oak Village Offers Wide Variety of Recreational Facilities for the Handicapped." *CEFP Journal* 21, pp. 9-11.

Leisure and Life 2000. 1988. San Jose, CA: Department of Recreation, Parks and Community Services.

Lopez, Stephen. January, 1983. "Preserving Open Space via Community Stewardship." *Parks and Recreation* 17, pp. 66-69.

Maguire, Meg. November, 1982. "An Open Letter to Park and Recreation Advocates." *Parks and Recreation* 17, pp. 44-52.

Meier, Joel. 1980. *High Adventure Outdoor Pursuits: Organization and Leadership.* Columbus, OH: Publishing Horizons.

Meier, Joel and Mitchell, Viola. 1986. *Camp Counseling: Leadership and Programming for the Organized Camp.* Sixth Edition, Philadelphia, PA: W.B. Saunders.

Nationwide Recreation Survey (1982-83). 1984. Washington, D.C.: Bureau of the Census, Government Printing Office.

Nelson, Charles and Leroy, Lawrence. January, 1983. "County Parks - State of the Art Today." *Parks and Recreation* 17, pp. 84-86.

Peterson, James. 1987. *Risk Management for Park, Recreation, and Leisure Services.* Champaign, IL: Management Learning Laboratories.

Play For All Guidelines: Planning, Design and Management of Outdoor Play Settings for All Children. 1987. Berkeley, CA: MIG Communications.

Playrights. Raleigh, NC: International Association for the Child's Right To Play (IPA), quarterly.

Pohndorf, Richard. 1960. *Camp Waterfront Programs and Management.* New York: Association Press.

Rea, Phillip and Warren, Roger. 1986. *Recreation Management of Water Resources,* Columbus, OH: Publishing Horizons, Inc.

Recreation Innovations - Abroad. 1980. Washington, D.C.: Heritage Conservation and Recreation Service, Technical Notes.

Recreation, Park, and Open Space Standards and Guidelines. 1983. Arlington, VA: National Recreation and Park Association.

Sandman, Peter. June, 1983. "Green Acres in the 80's." New Jersey County and Municipal Government Study Commission.

Shedlock, Robert. March 17, 1983. "Water-Play Parks on Public Land: A Revenue Source and a Public Benefit." *Parks and Recreation.* pp. 38-40.

Standards for Day and Resident Camps. 1990. Martinsville, Indiana: American Camping Association.

Standards for Conference/ Retreat Centers (draft). November, 1991. Martinsville, IN: American Camping Association.

Sternloff, Robert and Warren, Roger. 1984. *Park and Recreation Maintenance Management.* New York: Macmillan Publishing Company.

Suggestions for Waterpark Signs. 1990. Alexandria, VA: World Waterpark Association and International Association of Amusement Parks and Attractions.

Thompson, Donna. Nov./Dec. 1991. "Safe Playground Surfaces: What Should Be Used Under Playground Equipment?". *Journal of Physical Education, Recreation and Dance.,* pp. 74-75. Reston, VA: American Alliance for Health, Physical Education, Recreation and Dance.

Thompson, Donna and Bowers, Louis. 1989. *Where Our Children Play: Community Park Playground Equipment.* Reston, VA: American Association for Leisure and Recreation.

Urban Parks and Recreation: A Trends/Analysis Report. August, 1980. U.S. Department of the Interior.

U.S. Coast Guard. 1984. *Boating Safety Manual.* Washington, D.C.: U.S. Department of Transportation.

U.S. Department of Agriculture. 1981. *1981 Program Report and Environmental Impact Statement.* Washington, D.C.

U.S. Department of Housing and Urban Development. 1980. *Private and Volunteer Sector Involvement in Urban Recreation: An Information Bulletin of the Community and Economic Development Task Force of the Urban Consortium.*

Wallach, Frances. April, 1992. "Playground Safety: What Did We Do Wrong?". *Park and Recreation Magazine,* pp. 52-57, 83.

Warren, Roger. 1989. *Management of Aquatic Recreation Resources.* Columbus, OH: Publishing Horizons.

_____. 1986. *Recreation Management of Water Resources.* New York: Macmillan Publishing.

Warren, Roger and Rea, Phillip. 1985. *Swimming Pool Management.* Columbus, OH: Publishing Horizons.

Waterpark Signs. 1990. Lenexa, Kansas: World Waterpark Association and International Association of Amusement Parks and Attractions, Alexandria, VA.

Weiskopf, Donald. 1982. *Recreation and Leisure: Improving the Quality of Life.* Second Edition. Rockleigh, NJ: Allyn and Bacon.

Wolfram, Gary. August, 1981. "The Sale of Development Rights and Zoning in the Preservation of Open Space." *Land Economics* 57, pp. 398-413.

Wortham, Sue and Frost, Joe. 1990. *Playgrounds for Young Children: National Survey and Perspectives.* Reston, VA: American Association for Leisure and Recreation.

Zito, Anthony. July, 1983. "Park Board Members: What Do They Want To Know?" *Parks and Recreation* 18, pp. 54-55, 68.

ABOUT THE AUTHOR:
Edsel Buchanan is a retired professor and former coordinator of the Recreation and Leisure Studies Program at the University of Nebraska at Omaha.

Chapter 8
RISK MANAGEMENT: PURPOSE AND VALUE OF RISK MANAGEMENT

by Marc Rabinoff

Risk management can be defined best as the systematic analysis of facilities and programs in an effort to identify potential risk situations and thus to minimize injuries, accidents, and the potential for costly and long-term law suits.

In risk management one must analyze the existing facilities and then evaluate the goals and objectives of the facilities in terms of the activities that are offered and the personnel needed to conduct such activities, as well as supervise and instruct the participants. Future needs also can be established through risk management. The best way to look at risk analysis is to look at it in terms of raising the level of awareness of staff personnel, as well as that of the participant, based on the limits of the facilities in terms of the activities offered within that facility.

A sound risk management program can prevent damage to the facility as well as to individuals and can work on the growth components of a program considering what works and what doesn't work within the facility. Risk management acts as a motivator because staff will be working together to offer the best, most efficient, effective, and safe programs as possible within the facility. Risk management can provide essential documentation that a concerned staff is interested in providing the most state-of-the-art facility for the participant. This alone can be of great value if a law suit should arise, or it may serve to convince insurance carriers to lower or reduce the premiums because a risk management program is in place.

COMPONENTS OF RISK MANAGEMENT

There are four basic components for an appropriate risk management program.

Analysis of Existing Program

The first component is an analysis of what exists in the facility, including an examination of the overall scope of the program, a review of types of programs or activities offered, and a discussion of how they will be conducted in the facility. Do these programs or activities require any medical backgrounds on participants? Are there written procedures regarding proper supervision of programs, as well as of various types of equipment used? In terms of the programs offered in the facility, are the hiring qualifications and procedures for evaluating the staff of the facility on file? The frequency and nature of all staff meetings required, safety guidelines, other injury prevention techniques, and first aid concepts must be evaluated. All present consent and waiver forms should be reviewed.

A study of the history of any prior claims, accidents, or law suits should be conducted. All injury reporting procedures need to be reviewed on an ongoing basis, especially with legal counsel and/or insurance representatives, as well as the accident investigation procedures should an accident happen. The facility inspection procedures should be set up for the different teaching or activity stations which can include such areas as

weight training rooms or machinery, tennis courts, racquetball courts, swimming pools, running surfaces, outdoor and indoor facilities, dance studios, etc.

The equipment also must be evaluated as it exists at the time and should include the maintenance schedules. Information from this initial phase will give the facility and the risk management person an overall picture of what exists at that moment and will provide a starting point to develop the risk management program and analysis.

Educate Personnel

The second basic component of a risk management plan would be to educate the staff, faculty, and supervisory personnel of the facility in terms of various components of liability. These components include a discussion of basic legal terms, types of liability, basic working knowledge of the anatomy of a law suit, and some concepts dealing with the standard of care in the athletics, physical education, and recreation profession.

There are three basic sub-categories of types of liability: participant liability, facility liability, and product liability. These types of liability form the basis for a discussion of the "business" of operating facilities for athletics, physical education, and recreation. Basic to the business concept are procedures for hiring, advertising, establishing credibility of programs, and certification of programs. Issues dealing with insurance, how to select insurance, and how to work with insurance carriers are critical to proper coverage for the facility. The "failure to warn" concept and warning signage issues must be covered. All of the above will be covered later in this chapter in greater detail.

The Risk Analysis Survey

The third component of an effective risk management plan is the actual inspection, also known as the "risk analysis survey." The risk analysis survey should be a complete risk management instrument which includes a checkoff list covering every aspect of the facility, equipment analysis, maintenance schedules, policy and procedures, job descriptions, and operations items specific to the facility. The survey should be done on a regular basis whether it be weekly or monthly according to the needs and the size of the facility.

The survey will cover generally five major areas: 1) personnel, 2) equipment, 3) facilities, 4) training procedures, 5) business practices. The appendix includes a checklist for a "Risk Analysis Survey."

Under personnel, there should be a complete review of the resumes of employees, including formal education, certifications, and relevant work experience. There should be an interview of all employees. Employees should be observed working with trainees. A complete personnel evaluation checklist should be available to evaluate the personnel on an ongoing, regular basis. Under equipment there should be a complete checklist. Items under equipment can include welds, bolts, nuts, screws, and basic machine design. There should be a review and ongoing evaluation of all adjustable equipment, including seats, cables, springs, rollers, sprockets, pulleys, etc. The weight stacks in the weight rooms should be checked daily. Appropriate size limits should be evaluated on an ongoing basis in terms of the number of people at a teaching station and/or

activity station. The manufacturer of the equipment should be reputable and available for questions, should the facility need information relating to that particular piece of equipment. The space and location of equipment must be considered in terms of traffic flow for the efficient and effective operation of that facility.

These are just some overall examples under the equipment checklist category. This text provides information regarding standards that are needed for the varied facilities in the area of athletics, physical education, and recreation. Therefore, the other chapters should be reviewed and the appropriate associations/organizations that are named should be contacted for standards applicable to a checklist for a specific facility.

The third area, facilities, should include a general overview of the facility operations. This can include prior notices of problems, claims, law suits, or notices of any defects. It should include records and reports of any potential incidents. This must be recorded properly and maintained and should include a complete review of any documents that clearly place the operators on notice of problems. Also, an overall general view of the facility should include surfaces of all the courts (indoors and outdoors), lighting, fire exits, mirrors, signs, storage areas, and walls (especially those with glass and mirrors). Total environment should be reviewed. Environment includes sound system, temperature, air exchanges, air quality, lighting, and electrical appliances.

The fourth area, training procedures, should include an examination of what the participant is doing in the facility in terms of his/her activities, to see if these activities are recommended by qualified or recognized authorities. If the training routines or activities are customized for an individual, then proper supervision must be provided for that individual within the facility.

The last area of the "risk analysis survey" is that of the business practices, a complete review of contracts, i.e., sales and membership, statutory requirements for operations, and professional standards of care, such as those established within this text. There should be an income expense review in terms of budgeting and sales and marketing techniques. Ethics codes might be included in terms of putting together a sound risk management program under the area of business management.

Follow-up Report

The fourth component of the risk management program is a follow-up report, which should include a complete summary of the present programs and facilities and an analysis of where, under present legal climate, the facility may be at risk. This follow-up report should provide the written guidelines, objectives, goals, and procedures which will allow the facility to identify potential risk areas and act in compliance with its legal responsibilities.

Some examples of the information that can be contained in such a follow-up report are legally enforceable waivers and consents and suggested procedures and forms for record keeping, ranging from medical histories to equipment and facilities maintenance. There should be detailed procedures to document accidents and subsequent investigations so as to provide the best defense in the event of litigation. An analysis is needed of the staffing patterns to make sure that the people who are operating the facility are qualified to provide such supervision and/or instruction. Maintenance of equipment schedules and qualifications of the maintenance staff for the overall facility must be analyzed so that each participant is given the assurance that he/she is doing the activity in a facility that is efficient, effective, and safe.

Any risk management plan is not static in nature. It is dynamic. It always is changing. There must be flexibility built into every risk management plan. Since programs will change, as needs change or as a facility design changes, so must the risk management plans change. Therefore, this review must be analyzed on an ongoing basis and must be changed as the facility changes.

Once these four components are completed in a risk management plan, there are three basic steps for implementation of the risk management plan.

1. The first step involves the identification of risks as determined from the overall four-component program.

2. The second is to evaluate the extent and potential impact of these risks on the participant and on the physical plant itself.

3. The third step is to devise and establish all of the operational procedures to minimize the risks that were identified and to begin implementing processes and controls to minimize the risks.

One important point to remember at this time is that anyone can be sued by anybody at any time for anything, anywhere and that a facility and its management cannot waive its liability. What this basically means is that injuries will occur, especially in the area of athletics, physical education, and recreation because of the nature of these activities. However, even though we know injuries can and will occur, it is the responsibility of the facility, its staff, its instructors and management to provide the safest, most effective, and efficient activity area in which to conduct these kinds of events.

Over the years we have seen many litigations in the courts concerning facilities, equipment, staffing, supervision, warnings, and the general overall operations of activities for athletics, physical education, and recreation. A selected list of some litigations that occurred between 1977 and 1991 is included in the appendix.

WORKING DEFINITIONS

Knowing that lawsuits occur is not enough for the staff of a facility to understand totally how and why risk management must be in place, implemented, or reviewed on an ongoing basis. Therefore, in order to better understand the concepts of risk management, we should look at some terms that are used in just about every litigation involving athletics, physical education, and recreation facilities. Although we can't cover every term used by the legal community, some key terms should be understood.

ACT OF GOD (PROVIDENCE)
Manifestation of the forces of nature which are unpredictable and difficult to anticipate; the result of the direct, immediate, and exclusive operation of the forces of nature, uncontrolled or uninfluenced by the power of man and without human intervention, which is of such character that it could not have been prevented or avoided by foresight or prudence. Examples are floods, lightning, earthquakes, and a sudden illness or death of a person.

ASSUMPTION OF THE RISK
In torts, an affirmative defense used by the defendant to a negligence suit in which it is claimed that plaintiff had knowledge of a condition or situation obviously dangerous to himself, and yet voluntarily exposed himself to the hazard created by defendant, who is thereby relieved of legal responsibility for any resulting injury.

ATTRACTIVE NUISANCE
The doctrine in tort law which holds that one who maintains a dangerous instrument on his premises which is likely to attract children, is under a duty to reasonably protect those children against the dangers of that attraction.

CLAIM
The assertion of a right to money or property, the aggregate of operative facts giving rise to a right enforceable in the courts.

DAMAGES
Monetary compensation which the law awards to one who has been injured by the action of another.

Actual Damages - Those losses which readily can be proven to have been sustained, and for which the injured party should be compensated as a matter of right.

Exemplary (Punitive) Damages - Compensation in excess of actual damages; a form of punishment to the wrongdoers and excess enhancement to the injured; nominal or actual damages must exist before exemplary damages will be found, and then they will be awarded only in rare instances of malicious or wanton and willful misconduct.

DEFENSE
A denial, answer, or plea opposing truth or validity of plaintiff's case. It often is done by introduction of evidence designed to refute all or part of the allegations of the plaintiff's case.

FORESEEABILITY
The facility and/or instructor knows or could have known of an existing condition.

IN LOCO PARENTS
In the place of a parent; according to its generally accepted common law meaning, refers to a person who has put himself in the situation of a legal parent by assuming the same obligations as the parent without being formally responsible as in legal adoption.

LIABILITY
An obligation to do or refrain from doing something; a duty which eventually must be performed; an obligation to pay money; one's responsibility for his conduct, such as

contractual liability, tort liability, criminal liability.

NEGLIGENCE
Failure to exercise that degree of care which a person of ordinary prudence (a reasonable person) would exercise under the same and similar circumstances. The term refers to conduct which falls below the standard established by law (or standards set by professional learned societies) for the protection of others against unreasonable risk of harm.

PLAINTIFF
The one who initially brings the suit and personal action, seeks a remedy in a court of justice for an injury or other abridgment of his rights.

PRODUCT LIABILITY
Dictates that a manufacturer is strictly liable in tort when a product it places in the market (that it is to be used without inspection for defects) proves to have a defect that causes injury to the user.

STATUTE
An act of the legislature, adopted pursuant to its constitutional authority, by prescribed means and in certain form such that it becomes the law governing conduct within its scope.

STANDARD OF CARE
That care which has been established by professional organizations and/or statute which all professionals must follow to provide safe and reasonable facilities for participants. The person who is given the responsibility for supervising or instructing is charged with having and using that degree of knowledge, skill and care that is required and used by similar professionals in the same field of practice and who are practicing in the same or similar locality at the same time.

SUIT
Any proceeding in a court of justice by

which an individual pursues that remedy which the law affords.

TORT
A civil wrong; a private or civil wrong or injury independent of contract, resulting from a breach of a legal duty.

WAIVER
An intentional and voluntary giving up relinquishment, or surrender of some known right.

ANATOMY OF A LAWSUIT

Once the professional has a good working understanding of these terms that will show up in every type of litigation, the person also must understand the anatomy of a lawsuit. Every state has statutory laws governing the torts liability within that state. A tort, as we defined, is a civil wrong and comes under the civil court system. All states must follow what is known as "rules of civil procedure." Under these rules of civil procedure, the following general actions will occur:

1. There is a filing of a complaint. The complaint basically is the legal document that sets forth to the court what the plaintiff (the person who has been injured) believes the facility or individuals named did to cause the injury. An example of such a complaint can be found in the appendix in the litigation, Jacqueline Jacobson v. Holiday Health Club, Inc., Case No. A 85 CV 1249, Division 7, District Court, Arapahoe County, State of Colorado. This litigation was tried; the jury verdict was for Jacqueline Jacobson for over $90,000 and was appealed to the Appellate Court. The Appellate Court upheld the jury verdict, and this litigation now is completed.

The reader should become very aware of the types of arguments that the plaintiff is making in the 20 claims for relief as stated in this document. Although this was a health club litigation, these same types of arguments

can be held against any facility in an athletics, physical education, or recreation setting.

2. Summons to be served. The court cannot do anything until the defendant gets the summons.

3. "Theory of Liability" must occur at this point in all cases. Under this theory of liability, there are four basic concepts that must be shown to the court. These also are known as legal tests of a tortious act: a) the existence of a legal duty of one person to another, b) a breach of that duty, c) a causal link between the breach and distress of the injured party, and d) there must be damages. When examining the legal test of a tortious act, the court must be shown that there was at least one of the three dimensions of a tortious act in order for them to continue the case. These dimensions are: a) misfeasance - the improper performance of a legal act, b) malfeasance - the commission of an unlawful act and c) nonfeasance - the omission to perform a required duty. These must exist in order for the court to allow the litigation to go forward.

4. The injunction process. At this point, in order for either the plaintiff or the defendant to stop the action, there must be an injunction ordered by the court to stop the procedure. If there is none, the action proceeds.

5. The discovery part of the litigation begins. Under discovery, the first component is to have the plaintiff supply the defendant with interrogatories. Interrogatories are questions given to the defendant as to the setting of the accident or injury, as to their answers the way they see it, as to how the injury occurred, and possibly whom they thought was liable and why.

6. Answers by the defendant come back to the plaintiff, and the plaintiff's attorney will continue to review the litigation.

7. There can be counter claims or cross claims filed by multiple defendants as to who is to be blamed at this point. There can be multiple defendants in a litigation, known as joint and several liability. Other parties

can be brought into the litigation at this point.

8. Depositions are testimony given under oath, taken down by a court reporter in the presence of both plaintiff and defense attorneys by either eye witnesses or expert witnesses, who will render personal or professional opinions based upon statutory laws and/or professional organizational standards, such as set forth by AAHPERD and other organizations, which we will examine later in this chapter.

9. Request to search for documents. During this request the plaintiff and defense attorneys will ask each other to submit documents that they believe would be pertinent to their case in proving their side of the argument. Prior to being set for trial, usually the defense side (the side representing the facility) will ask for a motion for summary judgment. This means that the judge will be asked to throw the case out of court as all of the previous concepts were not proven to the court. The plaintiff attorney will submit arguments against the summary judgment. If the summary judgment is affirmed, the case is thrown out of court. If it is denied, then the case could be scheduled for court and move along the process.

10. Trial time. Should the case go to trial, both plaintiff and defense should be ready to defend their clients. After the trial and a verdict is rendered, there is always the appeal process to the Appellate Court and to the Supreme Court, as well as Federal courts, depending upon the statutory nature of the litigation. The facility management should be in direct contact with their legal counsel during this entire procedure to get proper legal advice in terms of appeals and in moving the litigation forward to its conclusion.

Although risk management is conducted by the professionals in the field at the facility, at no time should any professional practice law or render legal advice to anyone. This should be done only by an attorney who is licensed to practice law in the jurisdiction where where the facility exists. Remember, no risk management document is necessarily a legal instrument. It is a tool to document what the facility has been doing and will be doing.

FACILITIES AND CONTROL OF ACTIVITIES

Once the types of claims that the plaintiff will be making against a facility designed for athletics, physical education, and recreation activities and the basic concepts of a risk management program, including a working knowledge of basic definitions, are understood, the need to examine the types of facilities both indoor and outdoor that require a risk analysis survey should begin.

These facilities include all of the area covered in the previous chapters in this text. In operating these facilities, there are control issues such as crowd control, spectator liability, and state and national codes, as well as design construction that must be considered when operating risk management programs. The chapters in this text clearly illustrate the design construction standards as established by AAHPERD in terms of designing the facility. Whenever a new facility is being designed, or additions to existing facilities are being considered and implemented, all state and national codes for construction must be considered. Architectural firms, as well as construction companies, etc., must be skilled in the area of these standards.

In terms of crowd control and spectator liability, one always must be cognizant of the fact that when one pays admission to a facility, he/she is given a safe place in which to observe and enjoy the activity. The facility is responsible for the safety of all spectators as well as the athletes.

LITIGATION CLAIMS

When considering this type of liability, there are basically three areas of concern that show up in every litigation. The first area of concern is lack of supervision, either direct or specific, general, or transitional and roving. The second area is poor instruction. The third area is failure to warn, which involves the assumption of risk doctrine.

Proper Supervision

In examining these three areas, 80 percent of litigations will involve the lack of supervision issue. Proper supervision is critical to the safe, effective, and efficient operations of all athletic, physical education, and recreation activities. The type of supervision for each activity must be determined by the professional standards of organizations that set up the standards in which the professional will operate. Some selected professional organizations' standards of care include AAHPERD, ACSM - American College of Sports Medicine, NSCA - National Strength and Conditioning Association, NHCA - National Health Club Association, IDEA - International Dance Education Association, which has now changed its name to the American Council on Exercise - ACE, NATA - National Athletic Trainers Association, APTA - American Physical Therapy Association, AMA - American Medical Association, YMCA, YMHA and the ACC - American College of Cardiology. These are some of the more prevalent national organizations that have position papers and standards of care that involve athletics, physical education and recreational activities. Although no one manager, whether it be a risk manager or a supervisor of a facility, can possibly know and belong to all these organizations, it behooves the professionals conducting activities within these facilities to have knowledge of these organizations.

The purpose for knowing these organizations and their standards is that as an activity begins in a facility, the person directly responsible for conducting that activity must be familiar with one or more of these organizations. This responsible member or active participant should receive journals and other publications illustrating the standards of care by which the facility must abide.

Poor Instruction

The second area of concern, that of poor instruction, deals with how the facility is being used in an instructional setting. For schools, colleges, and universities, as well as some recreational facilities, the instructor is critical to the safe, effective, and efficient operations for the participant to learn the activity that he/she is studying at the time. For example, AAHPERD, through its subsidiary, NASPE, has a standard of care for preparing professionals in the adult fitness field. AAHPERD has national standards for preparing K-12 physical educators, as well as graduate programs in all aspects of physical education and athletics. These programs and/or degrees, whether they be two-year associate programs, four-year undergraduate or graduate degrees, have standards that must be met by the student before graduation. When teaching and instructing, these standards must be followed and can be viewed through lesson plans and unit plans that are supplied by the instructor to the supervisors.

Failure to Warn

The third area, failure to warn, deals with the legal doctrine that in order for a participant to assume his/her own risk, the participant must understand and appreciate that risk and have knowledge of the risk of the activity prior to participating in the activity. Therefore, it behooves the instructor, the supervisor, and the facility (via posters, warning statements, directional placards, etc.) to educate the consumer about any of the risks inherent in the activity so that the consumer can assume his/her own responsibilities when choosing to participate in the activity.

WARNINGS AND INSTRUCTIONAL SIGNAGE

Not only should a facility have directional signs and warning signs posted, but it also must understand the concepts of warnings in general. In just about every litigation the plaintiff attempts to make a case that there was a duty to warn and that no warning was given or that the warning was inadequate and that the injury that was sustained was a direct cause of the lack or inadequacy of the warning. In Muncy v. Magnolia Chemical Company, 437SW2D15, the legal requirements were set forth as a warning that would be reasonably expected to catch the attention of a reasonably prudent person under the same or similar circumstances of use. It would be implied in the warnings that there is a duty to warn with a degree of intensity that would cause a reasonable person to exercise caution commensurate with the potential danger and that the warning must be comprehensible to a reasonable person. One must remember that the reason and value of a warning is to affect the behavior of the user or consumer to avoid potential bodily damage when doing the activity.

Human factors experts have set standards for the types of warnings, as well as the design of warnings. Included in these standards and factors are the colors of the warnings, the size of the warnings, the shape of the warnings, whether pictures or drawings or just words are used, where they are attached to the facility or to the piece of equipment, whether it is written in English or in a foreign language, depending on the type of consumer that is using the facility. A warning is of no value unless it is in the zone of danger itself. The warning must be visible to all who are in that zone of danger. The warning must reflect the level of danger, and it must attract immediate attention. If the warning is not strong enough, the warning will not be successful. An example of a warning, waiver, consent form is included in the appendix.

In choosing the verbiage for warning signs, there are basically three terms that are used in proper warning signs - caution - warning - danger. Caution is used if personal injury may occur. Warning is used if personal injury could occur, and serious personal injury or death can occur. Danger is used when an immediate hazard, if not avoided, will result in severe injury or death.

Remember, even using the words "caution," "warning," or "danger" is not enough, as the warning also must illustrate how to avoid such dangers.

In terms of instructional signs, the basic concepts involved in setting up these signs is that the least amount of verbiage is most appropriate. Do not use abstract terms or cliches that some people may not understand. Be brief in terms of the instructional placard.

THE RISK MANAGER AND SAFETY COMMITTEE

The risk manager is a critical component of any facility. Some facilities have specific risk managers. Other facilities rely on the supervisors and administrators to do the risk analysis, who, in turn, rely on their staff, both professional and administrative, to assist in the risk management of a facility. Remember, the risk manager is not a safety director. The risk manager is a person who is concerned with the overall operations of a facility. Many facilities have risk management teams and/or committees. These committees may consist of the director of athletics, physical education, or human performance, sport and leisure studies departments, and directors of recreation or leisure studies programs. The equipment managers of all three types of facilities, including intramural, sports, and athletics personnel, should be invited to be part of a safety committee.

The safety committee should meet on an ongoing, regular basis to discuss all aspects of the operations of a facility. Although the safety risk management committee will be meeting on an ongoing basis, they are only as good as the feedback they receive from all staff personnel who are operating within the facility. That is why all staff personnel must have a solid working knowledge of the issues of liability and risk management for the facility in which they work.

INSURANCE COVERAGE

Recreational Resources Magazine (1991) reports that a recent survey found 96 percent of the people surveyed who were asked the question, ''Are liability concerns more or less important to your organization now than they were five years ago?'' indicated that they are more important now and only four percent mentioned that they are less important now. This type of survey clearly indicates that many people in the athletic, physical education, and recreation field still do not totally understand risk management or liability. This is a critical deficit for our industry today more than ever, according to this article. Insurance companies will view this deficit in terms of their needs and require that a facility offer a sound program of risk management.

The trend of the insurance industry is to demand more risk management of athletic, physical education, and recreational facilities. Litigations seem to be on an upward spiral, and insurance companies now are doing more close evaluations of

facilities before they issue coverage. Once coverage is issued, insurance companies are now doing more complex site inspections and often order a risk analysis survey by independent, trained risk management experts. These specialists can verify how a facility is managing its risks and where the potential problems are.

When architects design a facility for athletic, physical education, or recreation, one concept under a risk management program that must be considered is that of liability insurance. All organizations should provide proper coverage as there is always the chance of someone being injured, and this injury may result in a lawsuit. Liability insurance coverage basically ensures that the facility is covered against claims for negligence while allowing the activities or services to continue. This is basic protection for the organization from mistakes and errors in judgment of its staff, as well as supervisory and instructional personnel.

The facility and/or institution management personnel should shop around and obtain a number of estimates and quotes regarding coverage. It should compare companies involved, and should feel comfortable dealing with the agent or the broker. The best rating of ''A'' is recommended for facility coverage. To check for this rating, it is best to talk with your State Insurance Commission to see whether that carrier has good standing with the state officials or that any claims or judgments have been brought against the carrier for not fulfilling its policies as set forth in the policy document.

The facility management must understand the policy so they will know what is covered and what is not covered, especially when it comes to catastrophic injuries which have occurred in athletics, physical education, and recreational activities. These policies should include provisions for the issues discussed previously in this chapter, mainly the lack of supervision, poor instruction, and failure to warn issues, as well as for the structural facility itself. Everyone

involved in a facility for athletics, physical education, and recreation has a duty to cooperate completely with the insurance carrier providing the coverage for that facility.

Remember, the carrier will demand and require that appropriate personnel be available and take an active part in putting together any reports or information that can be used in the defense when the carrier is defending the facility. The facility is obligated to assist a carrier in providing these necessary defenses and to work with the carrier as the legal system proceeds.

The bottom line is to understand your insurance policy. You should know its inclusions and exclusions and have a good working relationship with your agent or broker who can answer any specific questions pertaining to the policy.

We have examined the purpose and value of risk management, the working definitions of terms in risk management, and liability. We have explained the basic steps of a law suit, and described basic management as it relates to facilities, equipment, crowd control, the safety committee, concepts of warning, and standards of care from selected professional organizations. Also presented were some basic concepts in dealing with insurance. We are now at the stage of examining one more facet that involves risk management in facilities of athletics, physical education, and recreation. That facet is key legislation that affects the operations of facilities in our discipline.

KEY LEGISLATIVE ACTIVITIES

Key legislative statutes include:

1. *Occupational Safety and Health Act* (OSHA enacted in 1970) requires safety in the equipment installation, maintenance, and construction of all facilities.

2. *Title IX*. This is the 1972

amendment to the U.S. Constitution that basically says one cannot discriminate on the basis of sex in terms of activities that are federally funded. Much has been written about Title IX since 1972, and this definitely will affect the operations and activities that are offered for athletics, physical education, and recreation.

3. *Public Law 94-142 and Section 504 of the Rehabilitation Act of 1973* basically indicates that all handicapped children have available a free reasonable public education and that they are to be educated to the degree that reflects the least restrictive environment of their education. This includes the concept of mainstreaming the handicapped person into the regular physical education class.

4. *Amateur Sports Act of 1978* basically says that each governing body must provide education for all of the athletes registered under that governing body. For example, The United States Gymnastics Federation, the governing body for the sport of gymnastics, has produced the first issue of the Gymnastics Safety Certification Manual written in 1985, updated in 1990, as well as a certification program for all gymnastics instructors. The trend is that most governing bodies in the other sports will be establishing such manuals and standards of care within their sport activities.

5. *Americans with Disabilities Act of 1992.* All institutions that offer athletics, physical education, and recreation will be affected, as well as many businesses, health and fitness facilities, and employee recreation organizations, as this act becomes effective on July 26, 1992. Basically the Disabilities Act (ADA) will require employers to provide reasonable accommodations for the disabled. Under this act it will be illegal for employers who are covered under the act to discriminate in employment against qualified individuals who have disabilities. Furthermore, all reasonable accommodations must be made for the disabled person unless the employer can show that doing such would cause

the employer extreme hardship in the hiring of this person with such a disability.

Since this law defines "disabled," it behooves the management of facilities for athletics, physical education, and recreation to become very aware of this definition and understand this act as completely as possible. This act gives the Attorney General the power to initiate legal actions. The sections within the act provide for any prevailing party, except the United States government, to collect attorney fees, including litigation expenses and costs. Therefore, people who have disabilities who file a lawsuit probably will have no problem finding attorneys to represent them. This act, therefore, makes it mandatory that facilities for athletics, physical education, and recreation have wheelchair accessibilities to all facilities and training rooms and training settings. Sport leagues will have to be open to the disabled as well. Basically then, each disabled person must be considered individually and must have the opportunity to make his or her own informed decision on participation. Any denial of this individual for participation must be well reasoned, justified, and the proper documents must be filled out and signed.

SUMMARY

In summary, life is a risk. That is a given. However, in the disciplines of athletics, physical education, and recreation, the risks are greater and more prevalent than in most other activities. With this understanding, appropriate planning can provide for properly operated facilities, newly constructed facilities, and renovated facilities that will hopefully prevent injuries, minimize the damages, and cut down the number and costs of law suits in the future.

It should be noted, that according to the "Verdict Research, Inc." *Special Research 4.49, 1989*, plaintiffs recovered 55 percent in all

claims of sports related liability, ranging from a high of 88 percent recovery for plaintiffs of jogging and track injuries to a low of 23 percent recovery for plaintiffs of skiing injuries. This would indicate clearly that plaintiff attorneys have found the world of athletics, physical education, and recreation to be fertile ground for law suits.

During the same period of time "Verdict Research, Inc." reported that sports related accidents range from a low of $50 to a high of $6.5 million. Risk management is, therefore, the best method in which a facility designed for athletics, physical education, and recreation can operate in our modern world in a way that is profitable and enjoyable for the participant and the professional alike.

SELECTED REFERENCES

Acknowledgement, Assumption, Consent, Waiver Release Form. 1990. Denver, CO: Fitness Risk Management, Inc.

Adams, S., Adrian, M., Bayles, M. 1987. *Catastrophic Injury in Sports Avoidance Strategies,.* Indianapolis, IN: Benchmark Press, Inc.

American College of Sports Medicine. 1991. *Guidelines for Exercise Testing and Prescriptions, 4th Edition.* Philadelphia, PA: Lea & Febiger.

Appenzeller, Herb. 1985. *Sports and Law Contemporary Issues.* Charlottesville, VA: The Miche Company.

Appenzeller, Herb. 1983. *The Right To Participate*, Charlottesville, VA: The Miche Company.

Bailey, James and Mathews, Davis. 1984. *Law and Liability in Athletics, Physical Education and Recreation.* Boston, MA: Allyn and Bacon, Inc.

Bartlett, Cody B. April, 1991. "Standards of Care," *Journal of The National Employee Services & Recreation Association*, p. 34.

Bartlett, Cody B. July, 1990. "Stop Taking Chances on Volunteer Liability," *Journal of The National Employee Services & Recreation Association*, p. 9.

Bartlett, Cody B. and Rabinoff, Marc. September, 1990. "Dealer Sued by Consumer," *Fitness Equipment Dealer Magazine*, p. 36.

Bartlett, Cody B. 1990. "Recent Legal Liability Developments," *National Strength and Conditioning Journal*. Vol 12 No 2, p. 28.

Bartlett, Cody B. 1991. *The Handbook of Safety for Health, Fitness, Sports and Fitness Recreation Facilities*. Denver, CO: Fitness Risk Management, Inc.

Bartlett, Cody B. July, 1991. "Liability Insurance," *Journal of The National Employee Services and Recreation Association*.

Black's Law Dictionary, 4th Edition. 1968. St. Paul, MN: West Publishing Company.

Fitness Risk Management, Inc. 1990. "Safety Audit Summary Package," *Fitness Risk Management* Denver, CO.

Hall, Gerald. 1986. *The Failure to Warn Handbook*, Hanrow Press Nuts and Bolts Series.

Horine, Larry. 1991. *The Administration of Physical Education and Sports Programs, 2nd Edition*, William C. Brown Publishers.
The Journal of Fitness Risk Management, Vol 1, February, 1991.

Jury Verdict Research, Inc. 1989. "Sports Liability Plaintiff Recovery Rates," Solon, OH 44139-2291.

Nyggard, G. and T.H. Boone. 1985. *Coaches Guide to Sport Law,* Champaign, IL, Human Kinetics Publishers.

Rabinoff, Marc. January, 1986. "Size Up Your Programs Safety Factors," *Sports Fitness Magazine*, p. 27.

Rabinoff, Marc and Shaw, Cindy. March, 1987. "The Weight Room: Don't Leave It Alone," *Looking Fit,* p. 88.

Rabinoff, Marc. March, 1987. "Who Can Stop The High Cost of Insurance?" *Looking Fit*, p. 33.

Rabinoff, Marc and Bartlett, Cody. February, 1991. "Americans with Disabilities Act" *Journal of The National Employees Services and Recreation Association*.

Rabinoff, Marc and Bartlett, Cody. May-June, 1991. "Safety Audits and Risk Management," *Journal of The National Employees Services and Recreation Association*.

Rabinoff, Marc. May, 1988. "An Examination of Four Recent Cases Against Fitness Instructors," *The Exercise Standards and Malpractice Reporter*, Vol 2 No 3.

Rabinoff, Marc. *Required Readings in Liability Issues for Athletics Physical Education*, Vol 1-9. 1982-1992. Metropolitan State College of Denver.

Rabinoff, Marc. *Required Readings Anthologies in Sports and Adult Fitness.* Vol 1-6. 1988-1992. Metropolitan State College of Denver.

Rabinoff, Marc. June, 1991. "A Conversation with A Liability Expert," *Aqua Magazine*, pp. 14-15.

Recreational Resources Magazine. May-June, 1991. "Trends: The Liability Issue Have Things Improved."

Schubert, George, Smith, Rodney and Trentadue, Jessie. 1986. *Sports Law*. St. Paul, MN: West Publishing Co.

Stotlar, David. 1986. "Applying Legal Concepts in Strength & Conditioning Programs," *National Strength and Conditioning Association Journal*, pp. 77-88.

vanderSmissen, Betty. 1990. *Legal Liability and Risk Management for Public and Private Entities.* Cincinnati, OH: Anderson Publishing Co.

Weistart, J.C. and C.H. Lowell. 1979. *The Law of Sports*, Charlottesville, VA: The Bobs Merrill Co., Inc..

SELECTED JOURNALS

The Exercise Standards and Malpractice Reporter, Canton, OH: Professional Reports Corporation.

The Journal of Fitness Risk Management, 1256 W. Bayaud, Suite 160, Denver, CO.

ABOUT THE AUTHOR:
Marc Rabinoff is a professor for the School of Professional Studies, Metropolitan State College of Denver, CO.

Chapter 9
TRENDS IN FACILITY DESIGN
by David Miller

THE FORCES OF CHANGE

There are several trends in facility design and equipment which have been crystallizing during the past five to 10 years. And as important as these trends are the forces of change which caused them to happen. At the forefront of these catalysts are the interests and demographics of the user groups, the shift in the entities responsible for delivering programs and facilities, and the source of money financing facilities.

USER GROUPS

Exercise and fitness has become an important and enduring change in the life styles of Americans. Over 100 million people now participate in sports and recreation activities. These participants are as varied in demographics and interests as the United States itself. From infants in tot swim classes to senior citizens using fitness walking tracks, all age groups are participating in recreational activities requiring proper facilities.

Twenty years ago the biggest drawing card for the leisure business was competition. Of the most popular sports today, there clearly is an increase in interest for individual and non-competitive sports. Swimming is still the most popular sport in the United States, followed by exercise walking. The move toward fitness-related activities is happening for several reasons.

1. Teams once were used as a means of bonding for participants. Today both men and women, particularly on the college campus, seem to be more individualistic than team-oriented.

2. Participants no longer are willing to make long-term commitments (for eight to 10 week tournaments) like participants 20 years ago. Drop-in activities apparently are more appealing to the individual.

3. Participants seem to be more health conscious and select activities which best contribute to physical fitness.

4. Self image as it applies to physical appearance has become paramount to our society. Thus, more than ever, participants are selecting activities which best affect their physical appearance.

OWNERS/OPERATORS

With the demand for facilities on the rise, they are being funded and built by colleges, universities, communities, and private institutions. Colleges and universities are finding themselves competing for a smaller pool of traditional applicants. As the high school age population continues to decline, administrators are looking towards sports and recreation facilities to attract new students. Communities again are building community centers on the demand of their citizens. Generally, facilities are rising up in suburban and rural communities as a focal point and image maker for the town. Once one community has a facility, adjoining towns or other towns in the area are pressed to develop similar facilities.

Where facilities are not provided by the public sector, private clubs have constructed facilities for participants willing to pay a premium. Because the demand for facility space outweighs the capabilities of most public agencies, health clubs are springing up rapidly around the country. To meet the needs of those unable to afford private clubs, construction of YMCAs also is on the rise.

Hospitals are finding that wellness centers which combine fitness with rehabilitation are self-supporting. Physicians can prescribe exercise for cardiac patients, while recreational users have the convenience of on-site medical staff to assess fitness and treat injuries which may occur. (Figure 9.2.)

Employers are investing in fitness centers for their employees because of the return on investment.

MOST POPULAR SPORTS

1. Swimming
2. Exercise Walking
3. Bicycle Riding
4. Camping
5. Fishing
6. Bowling
7. Exercising with Equipment
8. Aerobic Exercising
9. Basketball
10. Running/Jogging

Figure 9.1. Most Popular Sports (Based on the National Sporting Goods Association Survey, 1990)

Figure 9.2. Hospital-based wellness centers combine medicine with fitness (Photo by Beth Singer. Courtesy of Hastings and Chivetta)

Money which is spent to provide facilities and programs is being justified by decreased absenteeism and increased productivity.

FINANCING FACILITIES

Economic factors have become the driving force behind obtaining new facilities. The financing and operation of sports and fitness facilities has changed in the past 10 years from traditional public sources to a "pay as you play" concept.

Public and non-public organizations have considerably more options available for funding. Gifts and donations from individuals can take many forms. The pledge of a cash donation is the most common in fund-raising drives. Prospective contributors are very receptive to the idea of having their name displayed in the building in return for a gift. However, donations may be something other than cash. Land, for example, commonly is donated. Grants from both governmental agencies and private foundations represent another significant source of funds for new projects. The Land and Water Conservation Fund, for example, still has available funds for projects which meet specific requirements. Another source of funds is the nation's more than 21,000 private foundations. Identifying the most appropriate foundations is the first step in acquiring their support. *The Foundation Center National Date Book* and *The Foundation Directory* are available in most libraries and list the names of various foundations and provide information on asset size and interest. In-kind contributions represent a way of reducing overall project costs through community involvement. For example, local suppliers and contractors can donate materials and services in exchange for the tax write-off.

Another development in financing mechanisms is the creation of state bonding authorities to issue tax-exempt bonds for hospitals and public institutions. The tax-exempt status of the bonds means that a lower interest rate is possible without diminishing their salability in the bond institution which must repay the bondholders. The bond debt usually is retired by assessing a fee or special tax on the population for whom the facility is built.

Perhaps the most common source of funding is some combination of the above. With available funds growing increasingly scarce, multiple financing mechanisms are now commonplace. More often than ever, facilities are being developed through some sort of "joint venture" arrangement. Southeast Missouri State University recently completed its Show Me Center and Student Recreation Center in a joint venture between the University, the State of Missouri, and the City of Cape Girardeau. Students assessed themselves an extra fee to raise construction funds, the city instituted

Figure 9.3. Exercise Area, Wisconsin Electric Power Company, Milwaukee, WI (Photo courtesy of Flad and Associates)

Figure 9.4. The Show Me Center at Southeast Missouri State University was funded through state funds, a student referendum, and an entertainment tax in the community. (Courtesy of Hastings and Chivetta)

an entertainment tax on restaurants and motels, and the state appropriated capitol development funds.

MACRO TRENDS INFLUENCING FACILITY DESIGN

In light of the aforementioned shift in demographics, changing interests, and increased budgetary pressure, how are planners responding in terms of facility design? There are at least four "macro" trends in facility design which have emerged during the past five to 10 years:

    1. greater emphasis placed on open, drop-in recreation

    2. centralization of facilities

    3. development of multiple-use buildings

    4. adaptive re-use of aging facilities.

EMPHASIS ON DROP-IN RECREATION

The interest in drop-in recreation and individual sports is here to stay. However, sport and fitness facilities traditionally have been designed with team sports and scheduled programs in mind. Unfortunately, these facilities do not lend themselves well to drop-in users. Accommodating a multitude of spectators requires that much of the square footage of a building is unusable to the drop-in recreator. While spectator facilities are continuing to be built, accommodating the recreational user is at the forefront of facility trends.

    On the college campus, larger institutions are building facilities for the sole use of students to play. Large multi-purpose gymnasiums continue to be built, yet other facility components which accommodate individual sports are increasing in number and size.

Jogging, swimming, aerobics, and weight training are examples of areas which now are typically assigned more square footage than ever before to satisfy the drop-in user. Smaller campuses are building multiple-use facilities for both varsity sports and recreation. In the past, use of facilities designated for athletics by the general student population was not allowed. Today, use by the general student population is given at least equal consideration. In communities where facilities are scarce, a greater number of people are accommodated through highly structured leagues. Yet community centers built within the past 10 years are distinctively marked by their dedication to drop-in recreational users. Once passing a control point where a fee is paid or identification checked, participants choose from a smorgasbord of activities in the building. Open gyms, weight training rooms, and warm-water "leisure pools" which simulate beaches are now common amenities found in community centers across the United States.

CENTRALIZATION OF FACILITIES

Campuses and communities alike now are centralizing their facilities for a wide variety of reasons. Paramount in their reasoning is the significant savings incurred when the duplication of facilities is avoided. Rather than several disconnected facilities each with their own lockers, showers, and staff, many institutions are creating a cluster of facilities which can share support spaces. This phenomenon, coupled with a marked decrease in the availability of suitable land, has led to the development of a new field of expertise: sports and recreation master planning. Through careful master planning, administrators can determine the maximum use of

Figure 9.5. Spaces which accommodate individual sports, such as aerobics, are increasing in number and size. (Photo by Sam Fentress. Courtesy of Hastings and Chivetta)

existing facilities, anticipate the direction of future growth, and develop long-term plans for sport and recreation complexes. (Figure 9.6.)

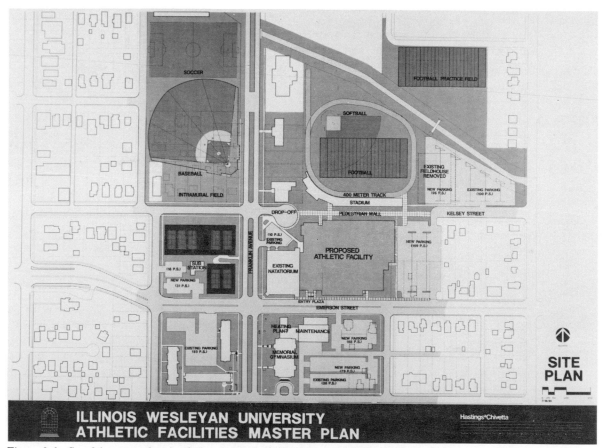

Figure 9.6. Careful master planning helps to avoid duplication of facilities and gives direction for future growth, Illinois Wesleyan University (Courtesy of Hastings and Chivetta)

DEVELOPMENT OF MULTIPLE-USE BUILDINGS

Participants are coming to sports and recreation facilities to do much more than just "work out." These buildings have become the focal point for socialization, studying, eating, and even doing business. As an example, the new Student Services Building at Carson-Newman College in Jefferson, Tennessee houses a wide variety of activities and departments. The 100,000-square-foot facility includes a gymnasium, jogging track, pool, weight room, racquetball courts, wellness lab, bookstore, post office, and a restaurant.

Accordingly, it is not un-common for facilities to include all or a combination of the following spaces:

- restaurant
- bookstore
- library
- proshop
- theater
- academic classroom
- arts and crafts
- conference/banquet center
- juice bar and lounge
- baby sitting

As the nature and purpose of these facilities evolves, spaces which typically are not found in sports and recreation buildings are becoming more commonplace.

ADAPTIVE RE-USE OF AGING FACILITIES

As baby boomers from the post-World War II period entered college or the work force, campuses expanded at an unprecedented rate to meet the demand. Many of the facilities built during that era are now 25 to 30 years old. Coupled with the heavy use they have been subjected to, the buildings are showing signs of wear and tear.

Renovating facilities can offer several advantages when compared to new construction. Other than the

Figure 9.7. Social pool at Tulane University's Reily Student Recreation Center (Photo by Jerry Ward. Courtesy of HOK Sports Facilities Group)

obvious monetary savings reaped from utilizing existing structural systems and walls, some advantages are not as self-evident. The historical and sentimental value of older buildings cannot always be measured monetarily. Further, land quickly is becoming a scarce commodity for some institutions. Renovation often allows for facilities to be sited at a more centrally accessible location.

While some facilities will not lend themselves easily to new building programs, previously under-utilized spaces sometimes can be recaptured for new uses. Spaces under permanent bleachers, basement areas, and rooms with unnecessarily high ceilings can be renovated for a wide variety of uses. For example, the University of

Nebraska's Coliseum contained a large stage loft that was recaptured to house three levels of racquetball courts. (Figure 9.8.)

MICRO TRENDS INFLUENCING FACILITY DESIGN

Other than the major trends driven by user interests and economics, several "micro" trends influencing facility design have emerged during the past decade. These catalysts for change include legal requirements and litigation, energy conservation, aesthetics, technical innovations, and planning principles.

Figure 9.8. The stage loft in the University of Nebraska-Lincoln was converted to house three levels of racquetball courts. (Courtesy of Hastings and Chivetta)

LEGAL REQUIREMENTS AND LITIGATION

It is no secret that we have a litigious society. Liability has become a significant influence in facility design. The rising cost of liability insurance and the fear of being sued has lead to institutions taking steps to protect themselves. Rarely are high diving boards still found at public swimming pools; slides are being removed from parks; wet areas are being designed with slip-proof floors; balcony areas no longer have handrails that are climbable by children; and attendant stations now are designed into weight rooms. All of these trends are occurring to avoid litigation and the high cost of insurance.

The legal requirements for facilities have been emerging for more than 20 years. In 1970, the Occupational Safety and Health Act required safety in construction, maintenance, and equipment installation. In 1972 Title IX of the Education Amendment Act was enacted to end sex discrimination in American education. The act requires that educational institutions receiving federal funds take measures to provide equal facilities for all programs.

Perhaps the most important legislation relative to facilities passed in recent years is the Americans With Disabilities Act (ADA) of 1992. Not only will the ADA guarantee equal access to disabled individuals who wish to participate in sports and recreation activities, but it also requires that public and private providers of these activities give equal consideration to disabled persons when hiring staff. Under Title I, employers are required to make "reasonable accommodations" for disabled individuals unless it can be demonstrated that the accommodations impose "undue hardship" on the employer. Reasonable accommodations include installing ramps, reassigning employees, and purchasing equipment which will facilitate the performance of required duties.

More importantly, the ADA expands the definition of a disability. Examples of impairments which are included are visual, speech, and hearing, HIV infection, cancer, heart disease, and emotional or mental illness. These impairments are regarded as disabilities when they substantially limit a major life activity such as walking, seeing, hearing, speaking, breathing, and working. How and if this expansion of the definition of a disability affects facility design remains to be seen as the statute is tested and interpreted.

Title III prohibits discrimination against persons with disabilities with regard to full and equal enjoyment of facilities open to the public. Also, any building constructed after January 26, 1993 cannot provide goods and services to disabled persons that are different or segregated from those offered to the general public, unless doing so is necessary to provide equal benefits. For example, arenas cannot restrict disabled persons to a designated section, but designated restrooms are allowable because they may be necessary to provide an equal benefit.

See Chapter 8 for a more comprehensive discussion of risk management and legal requirements related to facilities.

ENERGY CONSERVATION

Energy conserving features have become the norm in modern sports and recreation facilities. As energy costs continue to rise, new and innovative means of lowering operating costs are being developed. The most common measures being taken are found in the air handling, natatorium, and electrical systems in facilities.

Air Handling Systems

Exhaust systems in restrooms, locker rooms, storage rooms, and shower facilities should utilize the air already available within the building. This allows air which has already been heated or cooled to be recirculated, thus outside air is used several times to eliminate excessive energy use. (Figure 9.9.)

In non-air conditioned gymnasiums, variable air flow rates can be used to ventilate and cool spaces. During summer months, outdoor air louvers on exterior walls allow for increased air flow through the building. When air movement is kept within 8'-0" of playing surface, it provides an evaporating cooling process to participants. Since winter months require less air flow than summer months, variable speed drives are helpful to control motor speeds and the amount of air delivered. Also, inlet vanes on constant speed fans and two speed motors help to control air flow rates.

Ice storage systems are feasible to air condition a facility if off-peak rates are discounted enough. Typically, ice is created and stored during the late night hours when billing rates drop. During the day when utility prices are higher, water is circulated through the

ice storage, which then is used to cool the facility. However, these systems usually are designed as a supplementary system in order to lower the design requirement of traditional systems.

Energy monitoring systems (not to be confused with energy management systems) help to control building systems. These systems are used to document operating conditions, run times of equipment, and start/stop functions of equipment. This information can be used to analyze energy conservation opportunities, determine equipment malfunctions, develop preventive maintenance schedules, and document energy use. Energy monitoring systems typically are pneumatic or electronic and are tied back to a central monitoring station. This station can be a panel, data logger, or a personal computer.

Natatorium Systems

Natatorium systems recently have come to the forefront of design concerns for a new facility. These systems remove warm, moist, chemical-laden air which is harmful to typical building components. Recent events have shown that if systems are not designed properly, natatorium conditions and air can be extremely harmful to the building and the participants.

Specially designed dehumidification systems are available which have built-in energy conservation features. Heat reclaim for pool and domestic hot water, economize cycles,

and high efficiency refrigeration cycles are quickly becoming standard. Typically, heat from the refrigeration condenser cycle is diverted to heat pool and domestic water. Also, special condensation pans allow the water vapor lost in the evaporation cycle to be diverted back to the pool water make-up. Phone modem connections allow dehumidifying systems to be monitored remotely.

Also, air-to-air heat exchange can be used to reclaim waste heat from exhaust systems. A heat wheel is used to warm outdoor air into air handling units to reduce energy input. (Figure 9.10.)

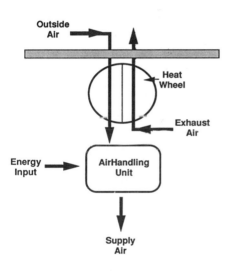

Figure 9.10. A heat wheel warms air from the outside for use inside.

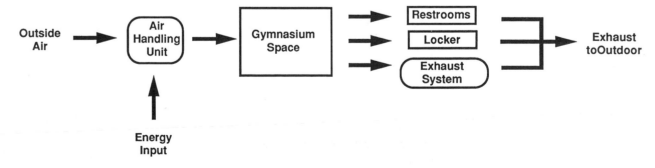

Figure 9.9. Air which has been heated or cooled can be used more than once before it is exhausted.

Electrical Systems

Lighting controls should be centralized. A control panel at the entry desk allows lights to be turned on and off as participants enter and leave areas. This allows better control and reduces electrical consumption when areas are not in use. (Figure 9.11.)

Skylights allow natural lighting into large playing areas. With skylights accounting for three to five percent of roof areas, the participant areas can be lighted with minimal use of fixtures.

Lighting systems should have variable lighting levels built in. This allows reduced lighting levels to service non-competitive events or supplement natural lighting. For example, use two 400 watt fixtures instead of one 800 watt fixture. By switching fixtures separately, a pick-up game of basketball can be lit with one 400 watt fixture or 50 footcandles, while an intercollegiate game requires two 400 watt fixtures or 100 footcandles.

Infrared or sensor type lighting controls switch on and off automatically. When a person walks in a room, the light comes on; when they leave, the light turns off. Considerable care should be taken when deciding where to install automatic lighting controls because if there is no movement in the room, the lights will shut off after a few minutes. Typically these switches are used in offices, storage rooms, mechanical rooms, and restrooms.

AESTHETICS

"Less is more." This quote of Ludwig Mies van der Rohe, the famed German architect, captures the attitude that planners and administrators once had towards aesthetics. Generally speaking, aesthetics were sacrificed in order to focus construction dollars on increasing functional space. Carried to the extreme, the result was a wave of spartan, utilitarian structures which were functional, yet drab.

Figure 9.11. A central control panel for lighting and climate controls allows electrical consumption to be reduced when areas are not in use, University of Nebraska-Lincoln. (Courtesy of Hastings and Chivetta)

In recent years a shift has occurred away from an aesthetic minimalism towards facilities which are designed to promote an image of fun, warmth, and an inviting atmosphere. The challenge is to design a facility which enhances its surroundings and creates an attractive environment in the most efficient and economic manner. (Figure 9.12.)

Bright colors and health club aesthetics are more popular than ever. Sports and fitness facilities have promoted a more festive look with the introduction of social gathering spots and natural lighting. Color plays a major role in creating an atmosphere conducive to participation. Bright colors tend to excite the senses, while cooler colors tend to have a relaxing effect.

Figure 9.12. Facilities are being designed to promote an image of fun and warmth, University of Toledo. (Photo by David Hollman. Courtesy of Hastings and Chivetta)

Locker rooms are no longer dark and dreary and often include health club type amenities such as saunas, whirlpools, and steam rooms. Social gathering spots and eating places allow people to watch other participants. The "open plan" gymnasium allows for the view of several activities at once, thus adding to the festive atmosphere. Natural lighting provides a soft, pleasant light while minimizing glare and providing ample insulation.

While budget constraints most often will dictate the level of aesthetics in a facility, it has become increasingly more apparent that "less" is, more often than not, less.

Figure 9.13. Open plan allows several activities to be viewed simultaneously, Burger Recreation Center, Lafayette, CO. (Photo by Jerry Butts. Courtesy of Barker Rinker Seacat and Partners Architects)

TECHNICAL INNOVATIONS

The rate of evolution for technological advancement in the sport and fitness industry is astounding. State-of-the-art equipment from as recently as five years ago has become antiquated compared to new developments. The following are ideas and innovations that reflect current trends and technology.

- *Identification/Entry Card* - Scanning an I.D. card through a slot which reads a code to allow entry. The technology already has been developed for scanners to actually read thumb prints to allow access.

- *Simulated Golf* - These rooms have improved dramatically to allow the golfer to view each hole on a large screen television which tracks the ball flight and simulates the golf flight. There are even instructional modes which offer video tips to help participants improve their game.

- *Hydraulic Sport Floors* - Floors can be raised or lowered to accommodate

Figure 9.14. Card scanners at entry points allow for added control of a facility, Vanderbilt University. (Photo courtesy of Parkin Architects)

different site lines and to increase or decrease seating capacity.

- *Computerized Circuit and Weight Training* - Individuals enter their personal code, and the exercise machine adjusts to a pre-programmed resistance level. These circuit machines also coach the users through a voice simulator.

- *Lightning Deflector* - A pocket-sized optical sensing unit can detect dangerously electrified clouds 15 to 20 minutes before they produce ground strikes.

- *Hydraulic Wheelchair Lift* - A wheelchair-sized lift allows disabled spectators to rise above people who stand up in front of them.

- *Retractable Arena Seating* - Fold up seating is no longer limited to bleacher style seats. Full armchair seating is available in retractable style. (Figure 9.15.)

- *Ozone Water Purification Systems* - Already popular in Europe, these systems are coming into wider use due to their gentler effect as an irritant.

- *Glass Treatment* - New glass technology allows the use of more glass without sacrificing R-ratings, glare, or harmful ray protection. (Figure 9.16.)

- *Inflatable Pool Covers* - The pool bottom is actually a PVC channel system which, when filled with air, floats to the surface and becomes the pool cover.

- *Movable Pool Bulkheads* - These bulkheads allow a pool to switch easily from 25 yard to 25 meter lengths. Most are air-inflated and are manually operated. (Figure 9.17.)

- *Synthetic Ice* - Plastic ice offers a low-cost alternative for facilities unable to afford a rink. No refrigeration is required, and maintenance consists of occasionally spraying with a lubricant.

- *Climbing Walls* - As climbing walls become more common, several manufacturers have developed systems which allow for interchangeable holds. By changing and adjusting the holds, skill levels are altered, and memorization of climbing routes is avoided.

- *Removable Synthetic Turf* - Through the use of air jets or large rolls,

Figure 9.15. Retractable seating is now available in arm chairs rather than bleachers, University of California at Irvine. (Photo courtesy of Parkin Architects)

Figure 9.16. Heat mirrored insulated glass offers superior insulation properties, prevents fogging, and keeps out ultraviolet rays. (Photo by Jerry Butts. Courtesy of Barker Rinker Seacat and Partners Architects)

Figure 9.17. Moveable bulkheads in swimming pools allow for lap distances to vary as well as simultaneous events, Edora Pool and Ice Center, Fort Collins, CO. (Courtesy of Hastings and Chivetta)

an area can be converted to a turf field in a matter of minutes. Seams are fastened with Velcro or zippers.

Figure 9.18. Natatoriums are being designed with a wide range of amenities, including water slides, University of Toledo. (Photo by David Hollman. Courtesy of Hartings and Chivetta)

- Convertible Roofs - Swimming pools and stadiums recently have been designed which have roofs that roll back to produce an outdoor environment.

- Illuminated Game Lines - Through the use of fiber optics, game lines can be lit to aid participants with deciphering the maze of lines typically on a multi-purpose floor.

- "Invisible" Shot Clocks - Through the use of holographs, shot clocks can appear on glass backboards. Nothing else is visible except a digital display on a corner of the glass.

- Spectacular Water Slides - High, long, and imaginative slides are being designed for both inside and outdoor pools. (Figure 9.18.)

- Wave Pools - Communities which are not near large bodies of water are bringing the beach to their area through indoor and outdoor wave-simulating pools.

- Telescoping Volleyball Standards - Volleyball and other net standards can be recessed in sleeves beneath the floor. When needed, a sleeve cap is opened and the standards pulled.

- Central Control Panels - Control panels for lights, HVAC systems, divider curtains, and backboard winches can help to control an entire facility from a central location.

- Sophisticated Divider Curtains - Through automated winch systems, divider (or "drop") curtains can allow for physical and visual separation of activities. (Figure 9.19.)

- Convertible Racquetball Courts - Moveable backwalls and removable telltales allow both racquetball and squash to be played on the same court.

- Silk Trees - Silk trees and plants are remarkably similar to the real thing and enhance the atmosphere of a building without having to worry about watering and sunshine.

PLANNING IDEAS

Architects and planners have become increasingly more specialized. Therefore, those who have concentrated on sports-related facilities have developed a level of sophistication never realized before. Many of the points listed below reflect a widespread application of simply "good ideas" that have burgeoned during the past few years.

- *Family Changing Rooms* - Private changing and shower closets which allow parents to assist small children have been common in Europe for years. These areas also are ideal for wheelchair-bound users.

- *Parking Garages* - Taking a cue from office developments, sports facilities are being designed with parking garages underneath. (Figure 9.20.)

- *Single Access and Control* - In order to monitor a large complex and maintain security, control desks adjacent to the entrance area allow staff members to check identification and issue equipment.

- *Elevated Jogging Track* - Elevated or suspended tracks allow for increased use of a volume of space. (Figure 9.21.)

- *Leisure Pools* - Free form pools with zero-depth, simulated beaches, slides, bubble makers, and flow channels are attracting users of all ages. (Figure 9.22.)

- *On-Site Sports Medicine Offices*- These offices treat injuries and prescribe exercise. Once available only to collegiate and professional athletes, they now are available to all.

- *Multi-use Facilities* - Different from multi-purpose facilities, multi-use buildings reach differing age groups as well as activities. For example, a new high school physical education wing becomes a recreation center after school hours. Seniors use the cafeteria and lounge during the day and tutor students. The students run a baby sitting service in the child development area.

- *A Return to Wood* - After the development of synthetic, rubber, and carpet surfaces, wood again has gained in popularity as the surface of choice for gymnasiums and other multi-purpose areas.

- *Open-Plan Facilities* - Buildings which are self-merchandising allow users to enter a facility and literally see all the activities going on from a single vantage point.

Figure 9.19. Divider curtains isolate courts and allow several different activities to occur simultaneously, Southern Illinois University-Carbondale. (Photo by Sam Fentress. Courtesy of Hastings and Chivetta)

Figure 9.20. Loyola University's Recreational Sports Complex sits on top of a four story parking garage. (Photo by Timothy Hursley. Courtesy of Hastings and Chivetta)

Figure 9.21. Elevated jogging tracks allow for increased use of a space without increasing the building volume, Commerce City Recreation Center, CO. (Photo by Jerry Butts. Courtesy of Barker Rinker Seacat Partners, Architects)

Figure 9.22. Corridors are eliminated by having users pass through a fitness room to enter into a gym and racquetball area. (Photo by Jerry Butts. Courtesy of Barker Rinker Seacat Partners, Architects)

- Phased Construction Planning - When money is not readily available to fund a facility which meets program requirements, the building can be constructed in steps, or phases. Careful planning also takes into consideration future expansion for unforeseen future needs.

- Elimination of Corridors - Unnecessary corridors can be avoided by having users pass through fitness rooms or lounge areas to enter a gymnasium or racquetball area. (Figure 9.23.)

- Pace Clock Circuits - Any clocks which need to be synchronized for pacing need to be on the same electrical circuit.

- Non-Regulation Dimensions - If a space is going to be used for recreational purposes, the dimensions do not have to adhere to regulations. Many gymnasiums have been planned with "short" courts to help keep construction costs down.

- Locker Room Adjacent Facilities - Adjacent locker rooms ensure the locker/shower area is accessible to the pool or desired activity area without forcing participants to walk down corridors or through other spaces.

- Mini Health Clubs - Small health clubs are being designed in office buildings. Typically they are about 20,000-square-feet with no pool, basketball, or racquetball.

SUMMARY

Trends in facility design begin with the forces of change which caused them to happen. At the forefront of these catalysts are: the interests and demographics of the user groups; the entities responsible for delivering programs and facilities; and the funding sources to finance these facilities. From infants in tot swim classes to senior citizens using fitness walking tracks, all age groups are using facilities. These participants seem to be more interested in individual and non-competitive sports. In terms of funding, colleges, universities, communities, and private institutions are utilizing the "pay as you play" concept for buildings and programs. All these forces of change are reflected in four "macro" trends in facility design. These trends are: (1) greater emphasis placed on open, drop-in recreation; (2) a centralization of facilities; (3) development of multiple use buildings; and (4) the adaptive re-use of aging facilities. In addition to the major trends driven by user interests and economics, several "micro" trends influencing facility design have emerged including legal requirements and litigation, energy conservation, aesthetics, technical innovations, and planning principles. These catalysts for change have produced an astounding rate of evolution in technological advancements in the sport and fitness industry.

REFERENCES

Flynn, Richard B. (Ed.). 1985. *Planning Facilities for Athletics, Physical Education and Recreation,* The Athletic Institute and American Alliance for Health, Physical Education, Recreation and Dance.

The author would like to acknowledge the contributions and assistance of the following individuals:

David Body, Parkin Architects; Kurt Carmen, University of Toledo; Christopher Chivetta, Hastings & Chivetta; William McMinn, Southern Illinois University--Carbondale; Betty Montgomery, Hastings & Chivetta; Ron Rinker, Barker Rinker Seacat Partners, Architects; Ron Zwierlein, Bowling Green State University.

ABOUT THE AUTHOR:
David Miller is the Sports and Recreation Specialist for Hastings and Chivetta Architects in St. Louis, MO.

APPENDIX A
GENERAL RESOURCES FOR PLANNING FACILITIES

BOOKS AND GUIDES

Council of Educational Facility Planners (CEFP), International. 1985. *Guide for Planning Educational Facilities*, Columbus, OH: Council of Educational Facility Planners.

DeChiara, J. and Callendar, J.H. 1990. *Time-Saver Standards for Building Types* (3rd ed.), New York: McGraw-Hill.

Gillis, John (Editor). 1992. *National Federation Court and Field Diagram Guide*, Kansas City, MO: National Federation of State High School Associations.

Gonsoulin, Sid (Editor). 1988. *Outstanding Sports Facilities*, Corvallis, OR: National Intramural-Recreational Sports Association.

National Collegiate Athletic Association Rules and Interpretations Guides, Overland Park KS:
- Baseball
- Basketball
- Illustrated Basketball
- Football
- Ice Hockey
- LaCrosse
- Rifle
- Skiing
- Soccer
- Swimming & Diving
- Track & Field/Cross Country
- Water Polo
- Wrestling

Sol, Neil and Foster, Carl (Editors). 1992. The American College of Sport Medicine's *Health/Fitness Facility Standards and Guidelines*, Champaign, IL: Human Kinetics Books.

PERIODICALS

Athletic Business. Published monthly by Athletic Business Publications, 1842 Hoffman Street, Suite 201, Madison, WI 53704, (608) 249-0186.

Athletic Management. Published bimonthly by College Athletic Administrator, Inc., 438 West State Street, Ithaca, NY 14850, (607) 272-0265.

Club Industry. Published monthly by Sportscape Inc., Framingham Corporate Center, 492 Old Connecticut Path, Third Floor, Framingham, MA 01701, (508) 872-2021.

Fitness Management. Published monthly by Leisure Publications, Inc., 3923 West 6th Street, Los Angeles, CA 90020, (213) 385-3926.

Journal of Physical Education, Recreation and Dance. Published monthly except in July by American Alliance for Health, Physical Education, Recreation and Dance, 1900 Association Drive, Reston, VA 22091, (703) 476-3400.

Parks and Recreation. Published monthly by National Recreation and Parks Association, 3101 Park Center Drive, Alexandria, VA 22302, (703) 820-4940.

The Physician and Sports Medicine. Published monthly by McGraw-Hill Co., 4530 W. 77th Street, Minneapolis, MN 55435, (612) 835-3222.

Recreation Resources. Published monthly by Lakewood Publications, 50 South Ninth Street, Minneapolis, MN 55402, (612) 333-0471.

Sports Medicine Digest. Published monthly by PM, Inc., P.O. Box 10172, Van Nuys, CA 91410, (818) 997-8011.

Tennis Industry. Published monthly by Sterling Southeast Inc., 3230 West Commercial Blvd., Fort Lauderdale, FL 33309, (305) 731-0000.

APPENDIX B
ASSOCIATIONS PERTINENT TO PLANNING RECREATION, ATHLETIC, AND PHYSICAL EDUCATION FACILITIES

Aerobics & Fitness Association of America.
15250 Ventura, Suite 310
Sherman Oaks, CA 91403, (818) 905-0040

American Alliance for Health, Physical Education, Recreation and Dance (AAHPERD)
1900 Association Drive
Reston, VA 22091, (703) 476-3400

American Amateur Racquetball Association
815 North Weber, Suite 101
Colorado Springs, CO 80903, (719) 635-5396

American Association of Cardiovascular and Pulmonary Rehabilitation
7611 Elmwood Avenue, Suite 201
Middleton, WI 53562, (608) 831-6989

American Athletic Trainers Association and Certification Board, Inc.
660 W. Duarte Road
Arcada, CA 91006, (818) 445-1978

American College of Sports Medicine
P.O. Box 1440
Indianapolis, IN 46206-1440, (317) 637-9200

American Council on Exercise
6190 Cornerstone Court East, Suite 202
San Diego, CA 92121

American Heart Association
7320 Greenville Avenue
Dallas, TX 75231, (214) 373-6300

American Massage Therapy Association
1130 West North Shore Drive
Chicago, IL 60626

Association for Fitness in Business
310 N. Alabama, Suite A100
Indianapolis, IN 46204, (317) 636-6621

Athletic Institute
200 Castlewood Drive
North Palm Beach, FL 33408, (408) 842-3600

Illuminating Engineering Society of North America
345 E. 47th Street
New York, NY 10017, (212) 705-7926

International Council for Health, Physical Education and Recreation (ICHPER)
1900 Association Drive
Reston, VA 22091, (703) 476-3400

International Dance Exercise Association (IDEA)
6190 Cornerstone Court East, Suite 204
San Diego, CA 92121, (800) 999-IDEA

International Racquet Sports Association
253 Summer Street
Boston, MA 02210, (800) 228-4772

Maple Flooring Manufacturers Association
60 Revere Drive, Suite 500
Northbrook, IL 60062, (708) 480-9138

National Archery Association
1750 East Boulder Street
Colorado Springs, CO 80909, (719) 578-4576

National Association of Concessionaires
35 East Wacker Drive, #1545
Chicago, IL 60601, (312) 236-3858

National Collegiate Athletic Association
6501 College Blvd
Overland Park, KS 66211-2422, (913) 339-1906

National Employee Services and Recreation Association
2400 S. Downing Avenue
Westchester, IL 60154, (708) 562-8130

National Institute for Occupational Safety and Health.
944 Chestnut Ridge Road
Morgantown, WV 26505

National Intramural-Recreation Sports Association
850 Southwest 15th Street
Corvallis, OR 97333-4145 (503) 737-2088

National Recreation & Park Association
3101 Park Center Drive
Alexandria, VA 22302 (703) 820-4940

National Rifle Association
1600 Rhode Island Avenue, N.W.
Washington, DC 20036 (202) 828-6000

National Strength & Conditioning Association
P.O. Box 81410
Lincoln, NE 68501 (402) 472-3000

National Swimming Pool Foundation
10803 Golfdale, Suite 300
San Antonio, TX 78216 (512) 525-1227

National Wellness Association
University of Wisconsin
Stevens Point, WI 54481

President's Council on Physical Fitness and Sports
450 5th Street, N.W., Suite 7103
Washington, D.C. 20001 (202) 272-3421.

Sporting Goods Manufacturers Association
200 Castlewood Drive
North Palm Beach, FL 33408 (407) 842-4100

United States Badminton Association
920 "O" Street, Fourth Floor
Lincoln, NE 68508 (402) 438-2473

United States Fencing Association
1750 East Boulder Street
Colorado Springs, CO 80909 (719) 632-5737

U.S. Golf Association
P.O. Box 708
Far Hills, NJ 07931 (201) 234-2300

U.S. Gymnastics Federation
Pan American Plaza, Suite 300
201 South Capitol Avenue
Indianapolis, IN 46225 (317) 237-5050

U.S. Handball Association
930 North Benton Avenue
Tucson, AZ 85711 (602) 795-0434

U.S. Squash Racquets Association
P.O. Box 1216
Bala-Cynwyd, PA 19004 (215) 667-4006

U.S. Tennis Court and Track Builders Association
720 Light Street
Baltimore, MD 21230 (301) 752-3500

U.S. Volleyball Association
3595 East Fountain, Suite 1-2
Colorado Springs, CO 80910-1740 (719) 637-8300

Wellness Council of America
7101 Newport Avenue
Omaha, NE 68152 (402) 572-3590

YMCA of the USA
726 Broadway, 5th Floor
New York, NY 10003 (212) 614-2827

YWCA of the USA
101 North Wacker Drive
Chicago, IL 60606 (312) 977-0031

APPENDIX C
ASSOCIATIONS PERTINENT TO PLANNING FOR ACCESSIBILITY

American Coalition of Citizens with Disabilities
1346 Connecticut Avenue, NW, Room 814
Washington, DC 20036
(chapters in states)

American Council of the Blind
1211 Connecticut Avenue NW, Suite 506
Washington, DC 20036
(chapters in states)

Arthritis Foundation
1212 Avenue of the Americas
New York, NY 10036

Association for the Aid of Crippled Children
345 East 46th Street
New York, NY 10017

Disabled American Veterans
3725 Alexandria Pike
Cold Spring, KY 41076
(state and local units)

International Society for the Rehabilitation of the Disabled
219 East 44th Street
New York 10017

Muscular Dystrophy Association of America
1790 Broadway
New York, NY 10019

National Association of the Deaf
814 Thayer Avenue
Silver Spring, MD 20910
(local chapters)

National Association of the Physically Handicapped
76 Elm Street
London, OH 43140
(local chapters)

National Congress of Organizations of the Physically Handicapped
6106 North 30th Street
Arlington, VA 22207

National Easter Seal Society for Crippled Children and Adults
2023 West Ogden Avenue
Chicago, IL 60612

National Foundation for Neuromuscular Diseases
250 West 57th Street
New York, NY 10019

National Multiple Sclerosis Society
257 Park Avenue South
New York, NY 10010

National Paraplegia Foundation
333 North Michigan Avenue
Chicago, IL 60601
(state and local chapters)

Paralyzed Veterans of America
4330 East West Highway, Suite 300
Washington, DC 20014
(state and local chapters)

United Cerebral Palsy Association, Inc.
66 East 34th Street
New York, NY 10016

APPENDIX D

ATHLETIC BUSINESS MAGAZINE'S TOP ATHLETIC AND RECREATIONAL FACILITIES

ATHLETIC BUSINESS MAGAZINE'S TOP ATHLETIC AND RECREATIONAL FACILITIES 1987-1991

YEAR	FACILITY	ARCHITECTS	COST	SQUARE FEET	OCCUPANCY
(1991)	Student Activity Center Central Michigan University Mt. Pleasant, MI	**Architect:** TMP Associates, Inc. Bloomfield Hills, MI **Consultant:** APER Consulting Danville, CA	$14.2 Million	179,800	September 1990
(1991)	Courts Plus Athletic Pavilion Elmhurst Park District Elmhurst, IL	**Architect:** Holabird & Root Chicago, IL **Pool Consultant:** Counsilman/Hunsaker & Associates St. Louis, MO	$ 4.4 Million	46,600	September 1990
(1991)	Student Recreation Center The University of Arizona Tucson, AZ	**Architect:** Parkin Architects Los Angeles, CA **Associated Firm:** The IEF Group Tucson, AZ	$11.7 Million	126,500	August 1990
(1991)	State College Area High School Addition and Alteration State College, PA	**Architect:** Breslin Ridyard Fadero Architects Allentown, PA	$ 6.4 Million	64,000	January 1990
(1991)	Aquatic Center University of Minnesota-Twin Cities Minneapolis, MN	**Architect:** Stageberg Partners/Ralph Rapson Architects Minneapolis, MN **Consultant:** Counsilman/Hunsaker & Associates St. Louis, MO **Engineering Consultant:** Toltz, King, Duvall and Anderson (TKDA) St. Paul, MN	$11.0 Million	73,500	June 1990
(1991)	John Wesley Chandler Athletic Center Williams College Williamstown, MA	**Architect:** Cambridge Seven Associates Inc. Cambridge, MA	$10.5 Million (New Construction)	103,100 (New Construction)	January 1988

YEAR	FACILITY	ARCHITECTS	COST	SQUARE FEET	OCCUPANCY
(1991)	Freeman Athletic Center Wesleyan University Middletown, CT	Architect: Herbert S. Newman and Partners, P.C. New Haven, CT Pool Consultant: Counsilman/Hunsaker & Associates St. Louis, MO Athletic Facilities Planning Consultant: Robert J. Johnston & Associates Victoria, British Columbia	$21.5 Million	150,000 (New and Renovated)	June 1990
(1991)	Target Center Minneapolis, MN	Architect: KMR Architects Ltd. Minneapolis, MN Consultant: HOK Sports Facilities Group Kansas City, MO	$85.0 Million	830,000	October 1990
(1991)	Lawrence Joel Veterans Memorial Coliseum Winston-Salem, NC	Architect: Ellerbe Becket Inc. Minneapolis, MN	$23.8 Million	247,675	August 1989
(1991)	Student Recreation Center Vanderbilt University Nashville, TN	Architect: Street Dixon Street, Architects Nashville, TN Associated Firm: Parkin Architects Los Angeles, CA	$14.2 Million	132,434	January 1990
(1990)	Student Recreation Complex Arizona State University Tempe, AZ	Architect: Parkin/Lorant Architects Los Angeles, CA/Phoenix, AZ	$15.7 Million	142,000	August 1989
(1990)	The John W. Berry Sports Center Dartmouth College Hanover, NH	Architect: Gwathmey Siegel & Associates Architects New York, NY	$ 7.25 Million	69,000 (New Addition)	May 1987
(1990)	Concourse Athletic Club Atlanta, GA	Architect: Ohlson Lavole Corporation Denver, CO	$ 9.1 Million	80,600	June 1989
(1990)	Silvio O. Conte Forum Boston College Chestnut Hill, MA	Architect: Sasaki Associates Inc. Watertown, MA	$28.0 Million	250,000	September 1988
(1990)	Barbee Center The Woodberry Forest School Woodberry Forest, VA	Architect: Tully Associates Melrose, MA	$ 4.6 Million	75,600	September 1987
(1990)	Student Recreation Center University of Missouri Columbia, MO	Architect: RDG Bussard Dikis Des Moines, IA Associated Firm: Gastinger Rees Walker Architects Kansas City, MO	$ 4.9 Million	49,000 (New) 17,000 (Remodeled)	February 1989

YEAR	FACILITY	ARCHITECTS	COST	SQUARE FEET	OCCUPANCY
(1990)	McClain Athletic Training Facility, University of Wisconsin, Madison, WI	Architect: Bowen Williamson Zimmerman, Madison, WI; Consultant: HNTB Sports Architecture Group, Kansas City, MO	$ 8.2 Million	146,000	September 1989
(1990)	Holiday Fitness Center, Atlanta, GA	Architect: Brosso, Wilhelm & McWilliams Inc. Baltimore, MD	$ 3.5 Million	37,500	June 1989
(1990)	Lakewood High School Natatorium, Lakewood, OH	Architect: Lesko Associates Inc. Architects - Planners, Cleveland, OH	$ 2.4 Million	26,122	February 1989
(1990)	Recreation and Special Events Center, Babson College, Wellesley, MA	Architect: Ellenzweig Associates Inc. Cambridge, MA; Consultant: Athletic Facilities Planning Consulting, Cambridge, MA	$ 9.7 Million	85,000 (New) 25,000 (Renovation)	September 1989
(1989)	Reily Student Recreation Center, Tulane University, New Orleans, LA	Architect: S. Stewart Farnet, AIA, Architect and Associates Inc. New Orleans, LA; Associate Architect: HOK Sports Facilities Group, Kansas City, MO	$10.9 Million	150,000	January 1989
(1989)	Bren Events Center, University of California-Irvine, Irvine, CA	Architect: Parkin Architects, Los Angeles, CA	$10.1 Million	84,500	January 1987
(1989)	Hatfield-Chilson Recreation Center, Loveland, CO	Architect: Barker-Rinker-Seacat & Partners, Architects, P.C. Denver, CO	$ 4.9 Million	67,000	December 1987
(1989)	Pilot Field, Buffalo, NY	Architect: HOK Sports Facilities Group, Kansas City, MO	$42.0 Million	19,500 (Seats)	April 1988
(1989)	Paul Bailey Pizzitola Memorial Sports Center, Brown University, Providence, RI	Architect: The Eggers Group P.C. New York, NY; Consultant: Geiger Engineers, New York, NY	$ 7.5 Million	106,000	March 1989
(1989)	Loftus Sports Center, University of Notre Dame, Notre Dame, IN	Architect: Ellerbe Becket, Bloomington, MN	$ 6.4 Million	135,000	October 1987

YEAR	FACILITY	ARCHITECTS		COST	SQUARE FEET	OCCUPANCY
(1989)	Henry Crown Sports Pavilion/ Dellora A. and Lester J. Norris Aquatics Center Northwestern University Evanston, IL	Architect:	Holabird & Root Chicago, IL	$16.9 Million	117,000	November 1987
(1989)	The Palace of Auburn Hills Auburn Hills, MI	Architect: Arena Design Consultant:	Rossetti Associates/Architects Planners Detroit, MI Sink Combs Dethlefs Denver, CO	$62.0 Million	480,000	August 1988
(1989)	Newell Boat House Harvard University Cambridge, MA	Architect: Consultant: Consultant:	Harvard University Planning Group Cambridge, MA Boston Building Consultants Boston, MA Douglas Okun & Associates Cambridge, MA	$ 1.0 Million	N/A	September 1988
(1989)	Knott Athletic Recreation Convocation Complex Mount Saint Mary's College Emmitsburg, MD	Architect:	Bohlin Powell Larkin Cywinski Philadelphia, PA	$ 9.2 Million	105,500	September 1987
(1988)	Joe Robbie Stadium Miami, FL	Architect:	HOK Sports Facilities Group Kansas City, MO	$84.0 Million	73,000 (Seating Capacity)	August 1987
(1988)	Westminster Recreation Center Westminster, CO	Architect:	Barker-Rinker-Seacat & Partners, Architects, P.C. Denver, CO	$ 8.1 Million	62,000	November 1986
(1988)	Show Me Center and Student Recreation Center Southeast Missouri State University Cape Girardeau, MO	Architect: Consultant:	Hastings & Chivetta Architects Inc. St. Louis, MO Ellerbe Becket Inc. Minneapolis, MN	$11.9 Million	170,000	July 1987
(1988)	Autodie Corporation Fitness Center Grand Rapids, MI	Architect: Consultant:	The WBDC Group Grand Rapids, MI Comprehensive Fitness Systems Grand Rapids, MI	$ 2.85 Million	38,000	June 1987

YEAR	FACILITY	ARCHITECTS	COST	SQUARE FEET	OCCUPANCY
(1986)	The International Athletic Club of North Dallas Dallas, TX	Architect: C.W. Fentress & Associates (Sports Facilities Group) Denver, Co Terry Richards Project Architect Consultant: Bill L. Walters Co. Englewood, CO Design Consultant: Rick Herbert International Athletic Clubs of America Englewood, CO	$ 8.9 Million	63,000 (Indoors) 15,000 (Outdoor Deck/Pool)	February 1985
(1986)	The Santa Clara Golf and Tennis Club Santa Clara, CA	Architect: Ellerbe Becket Inc. Offices Nationwide Associate: Warren Gilbert Associates San Jose, CA	$ 2.3 Million	9,085	April 1987
(1986)	Swinney Recreation Center University of Missouri at Kansas City Kansas City, MO	Architect: Abend Singleton Associates Inc. Kansas City, MO Consultant: Richard Flynn Omaha, NE	$10.1 Million	123,500	March 1988
(1986)	Johnson Wax Aquatic Center Racine, WI	Architect: Architectural Associates Ltd. of Wisconsin Racine, WI	$ 4.0 Million	53,000	September 1987
(1986)	Commerce City Recreation Center Commerce City, CO	Architect: Barker-Rinker-Seacat & Partners Architects, P.C. Denver, CO	$ 4.8 Million	49,000	February 1987
(1986)	Field House Remodeling University of Iowa Iowa City, IA	Architect: Bussard/Dikis Associates Ltd. Des Moines, IA	$ 5.6 Million	186,000	January 1985
(1987)	Town of Addison Athletic Club Addison, TX	Architect: The Benham Group Tulsa, OK	$ 3.25 Million	45,000	March 1987
(1987)	Boston College Alumni Stadium and Parking Facility Boston College Chestnut Hill, MA	Architect: Sasaki Associates Watertown, MA	$ 7.0 Million	4,700 (New Seats) 400 (Additional Parking Spaces) 320 (Private Boxes)	June 1986

YEAR	FACILITY	ARCHITECTS		COST	SQUARE FEET	OCCUPANCY
(1987)	The Center Club Alexandria, VA	Architect:	Pace Design/RWK McLean, VA	$ 8.0 Million	47,000	May 1987
(1987)	Cibik Auxiliary Physical Education Center & Stadium Baldwin-Whitehall School District Pittsburgh, PA	Architect:	Akers, Erwin & Gasparella Pittsburgh, PA	$ 3.2 Million	4,000 (Seats)	August 1985
(1987)	Edora Pool & Ice Center (EPIC) Fort Collins, CO	Architect:	Hastings & Chivetta Inc. St. Louis	$ 6.4 Million	83,300	December 1986
(1987)	Carmichael Gymnasium Addition North Carolina State University Raleigh, NC	Architect:	Dellinger/Lee Associates Charlotte, NC	$10.0 Million	154,000	February 1987
(1987)	Western Montana Sports Medicine & Fitness Center Missoula, MT	Architect:	Kessler, Merci & Associates Chicago, IL	$ 4.6 Million	50,000	June 1987
(1987)	Olympic Oval Calgary, Alberta	Architect:	Graham McCourt Calgary, Alberta	$27.8 Million (Canadian)	Skating Oval: 196 Meters Long 89 Meters Wide Seats: 4,000	April 1987
(1987)	Green River Recreation Center Green River, WY	Architect:	NBBB Boulder, CO	$ 4.9 Million	54,000	December 1986
(1987)	Seattle Seahawks Headquarters Kirkland, WA	Architect:	The Callison Partnership Seattle, WA	$ 3.5 Million	37,000	June 1986
(1987)	Physical Education Building Expansion University of Calgary Calgary, Alberta	Architect: Sports Consultant:	Wright Dobell Architects Ltd. Calgary, Alberta Robert J. Johnston University of Calgary Calgary, Alberta	$20.0 Million (Canadian)	231,500	June 1987
(1987)	Boys and Girls Club of Billings & Yellowstone County Billings, MT	Architect:	Johnson-Graham Associates Billings, MT	$ 1.3 Million	N/A	February 1986
(1987)	Malkin Athletic Center Harvard University Cambridge, MA	Architect:	Douglas Okun and Associates Cambridge, MA	$ 4.0 Million	4,000 (New) 2,000 (Renovated)	September 1985
(1987)	Ocean Center Daytona Beach, FL	Architect:	Ellerbe Associates Inc. Minneapolis, MN	$22.0 Million	225,000	September 1985

YEAR	FACILITY	ARCHITECTS		COST	SQUARE FEET	OCCUPANCY
(1987)	W.C. Blair Recreation Center Langley, British Columbia	Architect:	Davies & Smith Architects Victoria, British Columbia	$ 3.8 Million (Canadian)	N/A	December 1986

APPENDIX E

HEALTH, FITNESS, SPORTS AND RECREATION SITE INSPECTION FACILITY SAFETY CHECKLIST AND RISK ANALYSIS

NHCA Member Number: _____

Club Name: _____

Location: _____

Policy Number: _____

Inspector: _____

Date: _____

I. PURPOSE AND INTRODUCTION

A facilities checklist is a simple mechanism for helping to ensure that safe, adequate and usable facilities are maintained for recreational and instructional purposes. These facilities are usually so extensive that if appropriate personnel do not have some organized, relatively fast and simple method for keeping informed about the status of their facilities, the likelihood of unsafe, unusable facilities, as well as potentially litigious situations arising, is greatly increased. Therefore, personnel have an obligation to themselves, the users of the facilities and the firm owning the facilities to ensure that they are regularly inspected and maintained.

Any checklist developed for an organization must not be viewed as being complete and final at any given time. Organizations are dynamic and constantly changing and so their checklists should be continually reviewed and modified. Facilities can be enlarged or reduced. New equipment can be added, old equipment removed. Checklists will have to be periodically updated to accommodate these changes.

With this checklist the attempt is to be simple, while being as comprehensive as possible. The checklist items are written so that the inspector may simply check "yes," "no" or not applicable ("N/A").

II. DEFINITIONS

1. **Undamaged** - when equipment is in operable condition or where only minimal damage has been done.
2. **Secured** - equipment is to be locked or stored away to prevent any unnecessary misfortune or loss.
3. **Standing liquid** - liquids accumulating in an area which could be dangerous; meaning water from rain, showers, or outside conditions being brought inside.
4. **Functioning** - the normal operation for which the equipment component was designed to do.
5. **Debris** - excess trash, dirt, accumulated dust, personal belongings.
6. **Uncluttered** - neat, clean, organized, orderly, uncrowded to where movement would not be inhibited.
7. **Unobstructed** - free from blockage or passage.
8. **Visible** - plain to see and unobstructed.
9. **Recommendations** - changes the facility should make.
10. **Requirements** - changes the facility must make.

III. INSTRUCTIONS TO INSPECTOR

Attach:
1) brochures
2) equipment schedule
3) monthly activity report
4) outside photos
5) inside photos (especially any hazardous areas; and
6) other pertinent material, if available.

In "comments" following each section please comment where further explanation is necessary and write the appropriate number and/or letter for the section which is applicable for the comment. Please make additional or general comments at the end of the document on the space provided.

MOST IMPORTANT: On the last two pages, list the (1) recommended changes and (2) the required changes which are essential to this facility and attach relevant photos, where applicable. Remember, RECOMMENDATIONS are those changes, in your opinion, which the facility should make and REQUIREMENTS are changes, in your opinion, which the facility must make.

Checklist must be signed and dated by inspector.

Signature _____

Date _____

IV. GENERAL INTRODUCTORY

Full corporate name _____

Current number of members _____

Number of full-time employees _____

Number of part-time employees _____

Gross receipts _____

Are instructors sub-contracted: Yes _____ No _____

What are your days and hours of operation?

M - F _____ a.m. _____ p.m.

Saturday _____ a.m. _____ p.m.

Sunday _____ a.m. _____ p.m.

Check the following which are offered at your club:

_____ Aerobic classes   How many per day? _____

_____ Free weights   Square footage of area _____

_____ Circuit training   How many machines? _____

_____ Cardiovascular machines   How many? _____

_____ Sauna _____ Steam room _____ Showers _____ Hot tub

_____ Locker rooms _____ Cold plunge _____ Whirlpool

_____ Body toning machines How many?

_____ Tanning beds   How many? _____

_____ Racquetball courts   How many? _____

_____ Handball courts   How many? _____

_____ Tennis courts   How many indoor? _____

How many outdoor? _____

_____ Basketball courts   How many indoor? _____

How many outdoor? _____

_____ Jogging indoor track

_____ Jogging outdoor track

_____ Swimming pool(s) Indoor _____ Outdoor _____

What is the depth _____ ft.

Is pool area monitored? Yes _____ No _____

Is pool area highly visible?   Yes _____ No _____

Is there a diving board?   Yes _____ No _____

Lifeguards?   Yes _____ No _____

_____ Day nursery/babysitting?

_____ Masseuse

_____ Beauty salon

_____ Gymnastics

_____ Trampolines

_____ Karate/martial arts

_____ Pro Shop

_____ Restaurant

_____ Bar/lounge

_____ Alcoholic beverages (sold or permitted)

_____ Nutrition center (or health food)

_____ Special events, i.e., adventure excursions, dances, picnics, etc.

Specify: _____

_____

_____

COMMENTS: (Cont'd.) _____

_____

	YES	NO	NA

F. <u>WEIGHT ROOM</u>

1. Entry/exit visible, marked and unobstructed   _____   _____   _____

2. Lights functioning and air temperature
     controlled   _____   _____   _____

3. Mirrors secured and unbroken   _____   _____   _____

4. Mirrors proper height from floor, i.e., more
     than 35 inches   _____   _____   _____

5. Does ventilation appear adequate   _____   _____   _____

6. Signs and rules visible, legible and
     undamaged   _____   _____   _____

7. Weight machines, weight racks--cables   _____   _____   _____

     a) Cables do not appear to be frayed   _____   _____   _____

     b) No excessive stress on pulleys and
        attachment points   _____   _____   _____

     c) Lubricated   _____   _____   _____

     d) Securely anchored to wall/floor   _____   _____   _____

     e) Corrosion free   _____   _____   _____

     f) Free of cracked welds   _____   _____   _____

     g) Safety stops not bent   _____   _____   _____

     h) Are foot pedals covered with
        non-slip material?   _____   _____   _____

     i) Hooks on cables/pulleys closed   _____   _____   _____

8. Weight machines spaced properly   _____   _____   _____

APPENDIX F

SELECTED SAMPLE LITIGATIONS IN ATHLETICS, PHYSICAL EDUCATION, RECREATION AND FITNESS BETWEEN 1977-1991

CASE NAME & NUMBER	STATUS OR RESULTS	PLACE	INJURY YEAR	ISSUE
1. Whitlock v. The University of Denver; 79CV7008	Jury verdict of $5.0 million in 1981. Colorado Supreme Court reversed lower court 1987	Denver, CO	1977	Trampoline usage in recreational setting on college campus
2. Lopez v. University of Colorado; 81CV1992 (Defense)	Settled out of court	Boulder, CO	1982	Mini-trampoline use in coaching
3. Schlesinger v. School Dist. RE-2;	Settled out of court	Boulder, CO	1982	Liability of the use of horizontal bar in high school athletics
4. Ross Vogt v. Bd. of Education District 11; 82CV2467	Jury verdict for defendant	Colorado Springs, CO	1983	Trampoline use in physical education class
5. Buchanan v. CNA Insurance, et al; 81CV546A	Jury verdict for defendant	Janesville, WI	1983	Backyard trampoline and product liability
6. Julianne Ekern v. Univ. of of Wisconsin; 79CV99 (Defense)	Settled out of court	Madison, WI	1983	Trampoline use in a varsity setting
7. Hogan v. Alex & Walters Gym; WECO 71401	Settled out of court	Los Angeles, CA	1983	Equipment and instruction issues, health club setting
8. Bruno v. Univ. of Colorado; 83CV1446	Settled out of court	Boulder, CO	1983	Boxing/intramural injury

1

STATUS OR RESULTS	CASE NAME & NUMBER	PLACE	INJURY YEAR	ISSUE
9. Settled out of court April 1990	Theodore v. Sears & Muskin; 88DR404337	Richland County, SC	1983	Above-ground pool diving injury
10. Jury verdict $60,000 to plaintiff, no liability on coach / 20% for plaintiff, 80% for University December 29, 1989	Lennon v. Arizona Board of Regents; C608232	Phoenix, AZ	1984	Conditioning with weights for women's track team
11. Settled out of court August 30, 1990, ($1.3 million)	Platt v. Sears & Muskin, Inc.; 85C341	Montana	1984	Above-ground swimming pool\ diving injury
12. Jury verdict for defendant health club April 1988. Settled prior to appeal	Schaum v. Jack La Lanne; 451711	Orange City, CA	1984	Heart attack in health club, CPR & staffing qualifications
13. Settled out of court	Gary Geurink v. Greeley Gymnastics Center; (Defense)	Greeley, CO	1984	Gymnastics spotting pits
14. Settled out of court	Paone v. Feigley's School of Gymnastics; W-003493-87	South Plainfield, NJ	1984	Gymnastic's club injury
15. Settled out of court	Brandi LeCara v. School District; 84CV77	Lamar, CO	1984	Gymnastic class supervision in public school setting
16. Settled out of court	Montalbo v. AMF; 84CV3562	El Paso County, CO	1985	Backyard trampoline
17. Settled out of court	Lujan v. Tramp	Denver, CO	1985	Backyard trampoline
18. Jury verdict for defendant athletic club August 1988	Peck v. Evergreen Athletic Club; 87CV441	Evergreen, CO	1985	Inversion boot injury, staff qualifications product liability

2

	STATUS OR RESULTS		CASE NAME & NUMBER	PLACE	INJURY YEAR	ISSUE
19.	Jury verdict $800,000 to plaintiff, $740,000 for punitive damages against defendant health club, March 13, 1990		Forrest v. Holiday Health Club; A86CV39, Div. 4	Denver, CO	1985	Weight machine injury
20.	Settled out of court		Sosa v. Jack La Lanne; C339856	Los Angeles, CA	1985	Incorrect prescription of exercises
21.	Settled out of court		Hehr v. Strafford Health Club CV81197255S	Fairfield, CT	1985	Heart attack on weight training machine
22.	Jury verdict for defendant health club April 1990 Verdict upheld by Colo Court of Appeals Oct 1991		Woolsey v. Holiday Health Club; 85CV795	Denver, CO	1985	Hot tub death; lack of supervision
23.	Settled out of court (7/91)		Stephanie Clark v. Manhattan, Kansas School District; 88C197	Manhattan, KS	1985	High school varsity gymnastic practice injury
24.	Settled out of court (4/91)		Perfecto v. Houston Health	Houston, TX	1985	Weight machine injury Club; 8703037
25.	Settled out of court (1/23/91)		Fernicola v. Edison Health Club; W-022476-88	East Brunswick, NJ	1985	Hot tub death; lack of supervision
26.	Settled out of court		Moore v. Bd. of County Commissioners; 85CV109?	Larimer County, CO	1985	Recreational facilities usage
27.	Settled out of court		Blea v. Mesa College; (Defense)	Grand Junction, CO	1986	Safety in gymnasiums and intramural sports in college setting
28.	Settled out of court		Jerve v. Family Fitness Centers; 576456	San Diego, CA	1986	Weight machine injury, product liability, poor design
29.	Settled out of court		Savage v. University of Montana;	Montana	1986	Weight machine injury

3

	CASE NAME & NUMBER	PLACE	INJURY YEAR	ISSUE	STATUS OR RESULTS
30.	Jacobson v. Holiday Health Club; A-85CV1249	Denver, CO	1986	Weight machine injury	Jury verdict for Jacobson $84,000 (11/87) (Upheld by Appeals Court, 7/89)
31.	Battaglia v. Holiday Health Club; 86CV9489	Denver, CO	1986	Weight machine injury	Settled out of court
32.	Johannigmeier v. The Gym; 84CV8468	Denver, CO	1986	Weight machine injury	Settled out of court
33.	Hill v. The Pines Health Club; C88565	Oklahoma City, OK	1986	Swimming pool drowning; lack of supervision	Settled out of court
34.	Smith v. Virginia Board of Regents	West Virginia	1986	Safety at college setting P.E. major's gymnastics class	Settled out of court
35.	Paquin v. BrieTung Township Schools; D-86-5423-NO	Iron River, MI	1986	Gymnastics	Settled out of court December 1988
36.	Savage v. Eagle Performance Systems, Inc., a foreign corporation, & the state of Montana; CDV-85-919	Montana	1986	Groin injury - leg extension machine	Settled out of court
37.	Zawadski v. Palm Beach County School Board; 86-6272	Palm Beach, FL	1987	Trampolines in high school setting	Settled out of court
38.	Theodore v. Sears; 88DR404337	Richland, SC	1987	Backyard above-ground pool diving injury	Settled out of court May 1990
39.	Jones v. JayFro Co. (case citation unavailable)	Staten Island, NY	1987	Tumbling injury and mat equipment	Settled out of court
40.	Guest v. Club La Maison; 87-10033	Media, PA	1987	Weight machine injury	Settled out of court

4

	STATUS OR RESULTS	CASE NAME & NUMBER	PLACE	INJURY YEAR	ISSUE
41.	Jury verdict for defendant health club March 13, 1990	Rivera v. Holiday Health Club; 88CV308	Denver, CO	1987	Weight machine injury
42.	Settled out of court March 1990	Prike v. Cockelbur Country Club; 89CV1307-3	Boulder, CO	1987	Swimming and diving injury at lake front
43.	In litigation	Fink v. Holiday Health Club; (no citation available)	Rochester, NY	1987	Health club weight machine injury
44.	In litigation (Arbitration Hearing 11/13/89 liability found on manufacturer and club owner, awarded damages, not satisfactory to Plaintiff. Testified at trial, 10/3/90)	Little v. Health Works; 89CV1020	Larimer County, CO	1987	Athletic flooring design failure
45.	Jury verdict for Vic Tanny January 18, 1991	Hitzemann v. Vic Tanry; 90CV1056	Racine, WI	1987	Health club weight machine injury
46.	Jury verdict of $21,000 to plaintiff for damages against defendant health club - April 20, 1990	Hellman v. Holiday Health Club; 89CV0443	Westminster, CO	1988	Weight machine injury
47.	In litigation	Kathleen Buell v. Cherry Creek School District; A86CV1115	Denver, CO	1988	Diving in P.E. class setting
48.	Settled out of court	Monte Ballew v. Lamar School District RE 2; 87CV202	Lamar, CO	1988	High school track injury

5

	STATUS OR RESULTS	CASE NAME & NUMBER	PLACE	INJURY YEAR	ISSUE
49.	Settled out of court	Chad Wymer v. John Kreusch, School District; 87CV1157	Denver, CO	1988	High school varsity wrestling practice injury and supervision issue
50.	In litigation	Reed v. Paradise Valley Unified School District CV90-24043 (defense)	Phoenix, AZ	1988	High school football practice death
51.	In litigation	Davis v. Universal Gym 89-9133 DIV.C	New Orleans, LA	1988	Weight machine injury
52.	Settled out of court	Watkins v. Roman Health Spa 90-006944	Harris County, TX	1988	Hot tub injury
53.	Jury verdict for plaintiff - $2.6 million	Perez v. Muskin Pools; 88CV1681	Denver, CO	1989	Backyard above-ground swimming pool diving injury
54.	Litigation dropped December 1989	Babalmorad v. Lakewood Country Club; (no citation available)	Lakewood, CO	1989	Country club facility lake drowning
55.	Settled out of court	Elsea v. Commonwealth of Virginia Attorney General; 161CL87000391 (Defense)	Virginia	1989	Gymnastics injury college P.E. class
56.	Court dismissed	Denver Technical College v. several plaintiffs; (Defense)	Colorado Springs, CO	1989	Curriculum and professional staffing issues at college level
57.	In litigation	Hendricks vs. Greeley School District;	Greeley, CO	1989	Physical Education class injury
58.	Settled out of court	Stratton v. Vail Associates, Inc., et al.; 90-F-1074	Boulder, CO	1989	Ski accident

6

	STATUS OR RESULTS	CASE NAME & NUMBER	PLACE	INJURY YEAR	ISSUE
59.	Settled out of court (11/91)	Ostrosky v. Universal Gym Equipment, Inc.; 90-386148	Novi, MI	1989	Health club weight machine injury
60.	In litigation	Leisner v. Weslo, Inc.	Maryland	1989	Backyard trampoline injury
61.	In litigation	Brooke Gibson, et al v. Jumpking;	Greenville, SC	1990	Backyard trampoline injury
62.	Settled out of court (9/91)	Alex Renes v. Aurora	Aurora, CO Athletic Club; 90CV2797	1990	Child care supervision and facility storage
63.	Jury verdict for defendant (1/92)	Garland v. Burkhardt 90CD-23-4545	Greenville, SC	1989	Backyard trampoline
64.	In litigation	Banks v. Weslo, Inc 91-4996	Dallas, TX	1989	Treadmill injury
65.	In litigation	Dale Jones v. YMCA of Metropolitan Denver (Defense)	Jefferson County, CO	1990	Basketball injury in recreation setting
66.	In litigation	Wade v. Bryd 91CV1346	El Paso County, CO	1990	Backyard trampoline injury
67.	In litigation	Kantor v. Scandinavian Health Club	Akron, OH	1990	Weight machine injuries Instructor qualifications
68.	In litigation	Universal Gym Equipment v. Vic Tanny Health Club	Detroit, MI	1990	Health Club Operations standards of care

rev. 2/5/92

7

APPENDIX G
COMPLAINT FILING --
JACOBSON V. HOLIDAY HEALTH CLUB

DISTRICT COURT, ARAPAHOE COUNTY, STATE OF COLORADO

Case No. A 85 CV 1249, Division 7

SECOND AMENDED COMPLAINT

JACQUELINE JACOBSON
Plaintiff,

v.

HOLIDAY HEALTH CLUB, INC.
Defendant

NOW COMES the Plaintiff Jacqueline Jacobson by and through her attorneys Beam, Raymond & Holmes and for her Second Amended Complaint against defendant states as follows:

FIRST CLAIM FOR RELIEF

1. At all times material herein, Defendant Holiday Health Club, Inc. was the owner and/or operator of a health club known as the Holiday Club and Fitness Center located at 13801 E. Exposition in Aurora, Colorado.

2. At all times material herein, Plaintiff Jacqueline Jacobson ("Plaintiff Jacobson") was a member of the Holiday Health Club and Fitness Center.

3. On or about January 4, 1985, Plaintiff Jacobson was using the exercise facilities at defendant's health club.

4. At said time and place, Plaintiff Jacobson relied upon the expert skills of Defendant Holiday Health Club, Inc. to maintain the weight machine equipment in a proper and safe working condition.

5. At said time and place a weight machine commonly referred to as a "squat machine" was improperly adjusted so as to present a forseeable danger to plaintiff.

6. At said time and place Plaintiff Jacobson went to utilize the "squat machine" and while adjusting the weight level a metal bar on the "squat machine" fell upon her.

7. At all times herein mentioned, Defendant Holiday Health Club, Inc. had the duty to maintain the weight equipment in reasonably safe condition for Plaintiff Jacobson. In particular, Defendant Holiday Health Club, Inc. owed a duty to Plaintiff Jacobson to prevent a dangerous condition unknown to Plaintiff Jacobson to be created or to exist and owed a duty to Plaintiff Jacobson to warn her of the existence of any such dangerous condition.

8. Defendant Holiday Health Club, Inc. breached its duty to Plaintiff Jacobson in the following respects:

a. Defendant negligently and carelessly failed to determine, prior to Plaintiff Jacobson's use of the "squat machine", whether the machine was properly set and safe for its intended use.

b. Defendant negligently and carelessly failed to adjust the "squat machine", prior to Plaintiff Jacobson's use, in a safe and reasonable working condition.

c. Defendant negligently and carelessly failed to warn Plaintiff of the existence of said dangerous condition of the "squat machine".

d. Defendant negligently and carelessly failed to properly train Plaintiff Jacobson and other users of the "squat machine".

e. Defendant negligently and carelessly failed to supervise the use of the "squat machine" so as to create a dangerous condition.

9. As a direct and proximate result of Defendant Holiday Health Club, Inc.'s negligence, Plaintiff Jacobson suffered damages including, but not limited to, medical expenses, lost wages, partial, permanent disability; aggravation of a pre-existing condition; physical pain and suffering; severe emotional distress and loss of enjoyment of life.

SECOND CLAIM FOR RELIEF
(Negligent Misrepresentation)

10. Plaintiff Jacobson incorporates by reference as though set forth at length herein, Paragraphs 1 through 8 of the First Claim for Relief.

11. That at various times and specifically on February 27, 1984 at 13801 E. Exposition in Aurora, Colorado which is the location of defendant's health club and fitness center defendant by and through its employees negligently misrepresented to plaintiff that the defendant had qualified instructors which would properly train plaintiff and others as to the safe and proper use of the exercise equipment and health facilities located at the health club.

12. That the aforesaid representations were false and were then and there known by defendant to be false; that in truth and fact, the defendant did not provide plaintiff and others with qualified instructors to properly train plaintiff and others as to the safe and proper use of the exercise equipment and health facilities.,

13. That plaintiff believed and relied upon the aforesaid representations and was thereby induced to become a member of defendant's health club and to utilize the exercise equipment (specifically utilize the aforementioned squat machine) without proper training and instruction and thereafter was injured and damaged.

14. That by reason of the aforesaid misrepresentations made by defendant to plaintiff, plaintiff has been damaged as more fully set forth in Paragraph 9 of this Complaint.

THIRD CLAIM FOR RELIEF

15. Plaintiff Jacobson incorporates by reference, as though set forth at length herein, Paragraphs 1 through 14 of the First and Second Claim for Relief.

16. Defendant Holiday Health Club, Inc. had knowledge of prior similar accidents with regard to the "squat machine".

17. Defendant Holiday Health Club, Inc. committed acts of misrepresentation more fully set forth in Plaintiff's Second Claim for Relief.

18. The acts and omissions of Defendant Holiday Health Club, Inc. were attended by circumstances of a wanton and reckless disregard for the rights and feelings of Plaintiff Jacobson.

19. As a direct and proximate result of the acts and omissions of Defendant Holiday Health Club, Inc., Plaintiff Jacobson suffered the above described damages (see Paragraph 9).

20. Defendant Holiday Health Club, Inc.'s conduct constitutes a cause of action for punitive damages.

WHEREFORE, Plaintiff Jacqueline Jacobson prays for judgment in her favor and against Defendant Holiday Health Club, Inc. for compensatory damages in an amount deemed reasonable by the Court plus punitive damages in the amount of Two Hundred and Fifty Thousand Dollars ($250,000); prejudgment interest from January 4, 1985; post judgment interest; attorney's fees; expert witness fees; costs; and such other and further relief as the Court deems just and proper.

PLAINTIFF DEMANDS TRIAL TO A JURY OF SIX

DATED this 29th day of October, 1986

APPENDIX H
ACKNOWLEDGEMENT, ASSUMPTION, CONSENT, WAIVER, RELEASE FORM

I acknowledge the risks inherent in the activities that I am about to enter and for this facility and location where the activities take place. All of these risks have been carefully explained to and understood by me.

I hereby assume those risks. I hereby acknowledge that I will be voluntarily engaging in an activity or activities involving a risk of harm to me and others. I know and fully understand the risk of harm, and I hereby accept that risk.

I voluntarily assume the known and appreciated risks involved.

I knowingly and voluntarily accept these risks of harm. I understand and appreciate the risks involved and accept those risks as an inherent condition of the various activities in which I will be engaged.

I hereby consent to these activities and to the risks inherent therein.

I have also been advised of my right to, and, in fact, urged to have a complete physical examination, including but not limited to a stress test and blood work-up. Further, I acknowledge that I have been advised to have a physical examination at least annually and not to embark on any strenuous exercise program without a complete physical examination. Any medical information that I wish to have brought to the attention of instructors and operators of this program are attached to this form, initialled and dated by me, and hereby incorporated by reference. I hereby waive any claims against anyone involved in performing this contract for any disease, illness or injury that would have been preventable by the disclosure of a physical examination. I hereby waive any and all claims against the other party or parties to this contract.

I understand and expressly assume all dangers of these activities, the facility, and location. I waive all claims arising out of the activities and from the location and facility, whether caused by negligence, breach of contract, or otherwise, and whether for bodily injury, property damage, or loss or otherwise.

To the maximum extent permitted by law, I hereby release all other parties, their employees and agents, from any liability for any of their actions or inactions.

I hereby expressly and without reservation intend to and, in fact, do accept total responsibility for my actions or inactions which result in damages of any kind to me or to anyone else involved.

In consideration of being allowed to participate, I hereby agree to indemnify and hold harmless those other persons involved with me in this activity and program.

I fully intend that this agreement shall bind me, my heirs, distributees, assigns, and anyone claiming any interest through me. My rights have been fully explained to me, and I hereby enter into this agreement to induce the other party or parties to enter into it and to provide the goods or services to me as contemplated by our various agreements.

_____   _____

Witness   Date   Enrollee   Date

8/1/90 CBB Final

APPENDIX I
SAFETY CERTIFICATION FOR GYMNASTICS

MEMO

To: Mens Program Committee, Junior Olympic Program Committee, US Elite Coaches Association/Men, National Association of Collegiate Gymnastics Coaches/Men

From: Robert Cowan, Men's Program Administrator, United States Gymnastics Federation

Date: 23 May, 1991

Re: Safety Certification

Just a reminder that in 1992, Safety Certification for all coaches and all judges will be required for participation in all National and International level USGF events, both Junior and Senior.

This includes Junior Olympic National Championships, US National Championships and Winter Nationals. In addition, any trips taken out of the United States by coaches and judges at the Junior and Senior level will require Safety Certification of these personnel.

In 1993, Safety Certification will be required to receive a Professional membership with the USGF and will be associated with Coaches Accreditation.

Thank you for your attention to this detail.

APPENDIX J
SUPPLEMENTAL ARCHITECTURAL MATERIALS

Reily Center, Tulane University

National Hockey Center, St. Cloud State University

Hindman-Hobbs Center, Morningside College

Ryder Center, Saginaw Valley State University

Freeman Athletic Center, Wesleyan University

Donald B. Canham Natatorium, University of Michigan

Cheel Campus Center, Clarkson University

Harry Barbee, Jr. Center, Woodberry Forest School

REILY STUDENT RECREATION CENTER
TULANE UNIVERSITY
NEW ORLEANS, LOUISIANA

Square Footage: 150,000; Cost: $10.9 million; Primary Architect: Farnet Architect and
Associates, Inc.; Associate Architect: HOK Sports Facilities Group;
Completion Date: January 1989

Photo by Alan Karchmer

Photo by Jerry Ward

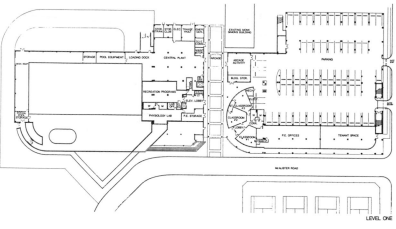

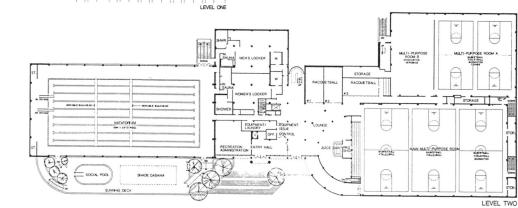

Snack bar area (photo by Alan Karchmer)

Elevated jogging track (photo by Alan Karchmer)

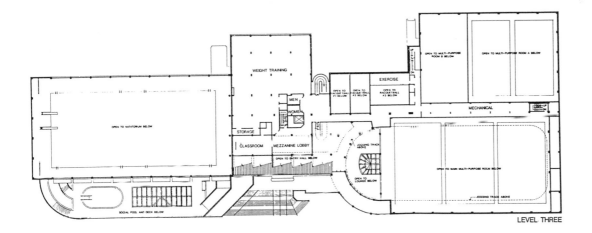

LEVEL THREE

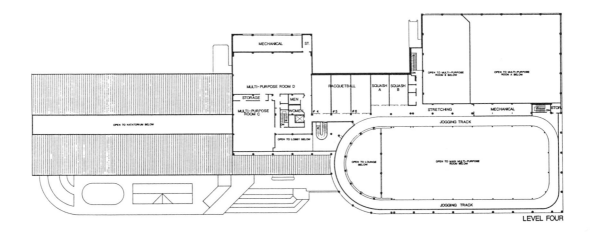

LEVEL FOUR

NATIONAL HOCKEY CENTER
ST. CLOUD STATE UNIVERSITY
ST. CLOUD, MINNESOTA

Square Footage: 135,000; Cost: $9.5 million; Primary Architect: Ellerbe Becket; Completion Date: December 1989

Locker Room

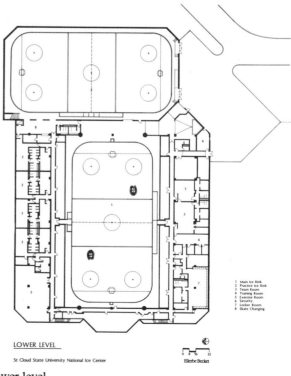

LOWER LEVEL

St Cloud State University National Ice Center

Ellerbe Becket

Lower level

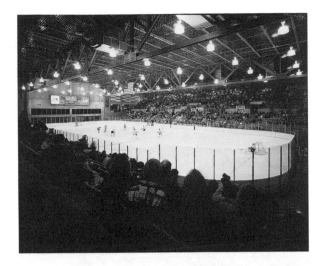

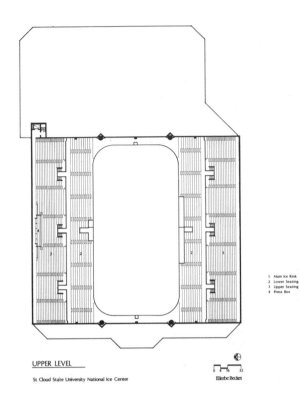

Upper level

UPPER LEVEL

St Cloud State University National Ice Center

1 Main Ice Rink
2 Lower Seating
3 Upper Seating
4 Press Box

Ellerbe Becket

Upper level

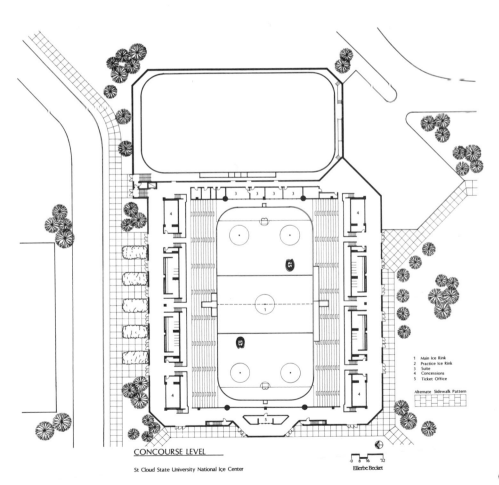

CONCOURSE LEVEL

St Cloud State University National Ice Center

1 Main Ice Rink
2 Practice Ice Rink
3 Suite
4 Concessions
5 Ticket Office

Alternate Sidewalk Pattern

0 8 16   32

Ellerbe Becket

Concourse level

HINDMAN-HOBBS CENTER FOR HEALTH, PHYSICAL EDUCATION, RECREATION
MORNINGSIDE COLLEGE
SIOUX CITY, IOWA

Square Footage: 71,000; Cost: $5.1 million; Primary Architect: Leo A. Daly; Completion Date: September 1989

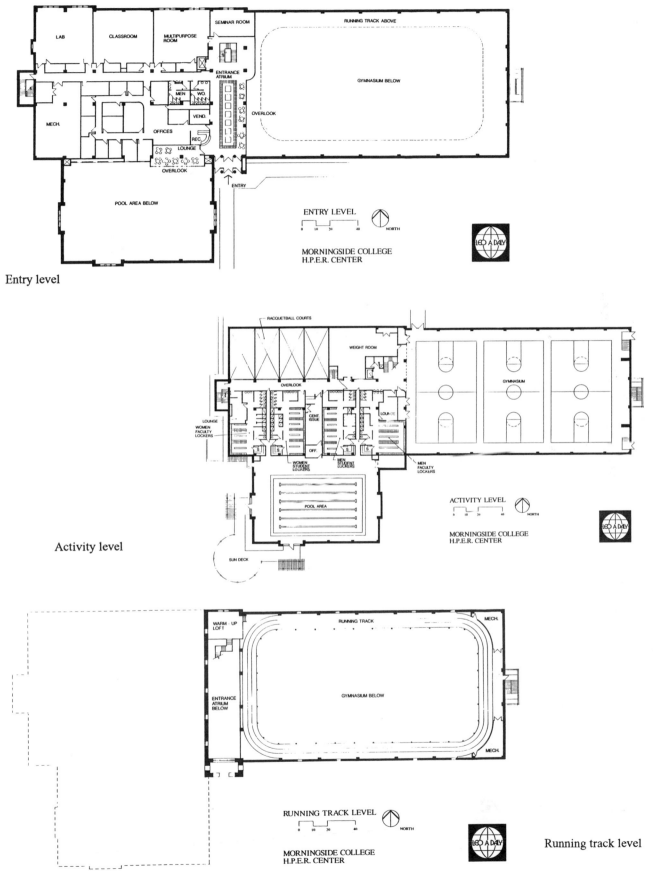

Entry level

ENTRY LEVEL

MORNINGSIDE COLLEGE
H.P.E.R. CENTER

Activity level

ACTIVITY LEVEL

MORNINGSIDE COLLEGE
H.P.E.R. CENTER

Running track level

RUNNING TRACK LEVEL

MORNINGSIDE COLLEGE
H.P.E.R. CENTER

RYDER CENTER FOR HEALTH AND PHYSICAL EDUCATION
SAGINAW VALLEY STATE UNIVERSITY
UNIVERSITY CENTER, MICHIGAN

Square Footage: 203,000; Cost: $16.2 million (building), $3 million (field); Primary Architect: Giffels Hoyem Basso, Inc.; Completion Date: July 1989

Photos by Daniel Bartush

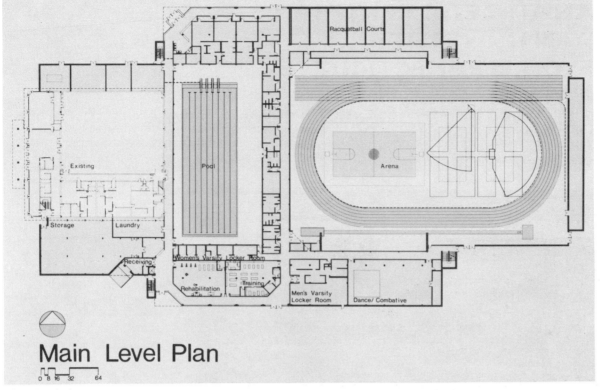

Main Level Plan

0 8 16 32 64

Main level plan

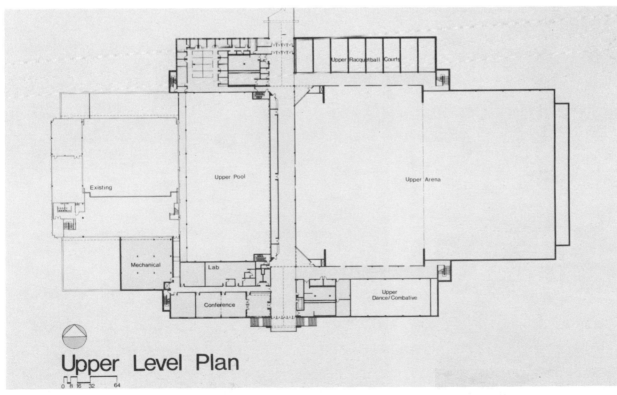

Upper Level Plan

0 8 16 32 64

Upper level plan

FREEMAN ATHLETIC CENTER
WESLEYAN UNIVERSITY
MIDDLETON, CONNECTICUT

Square Footage: 150,000 (new space); **Cost:** $15 million; **Primary Architect:** Herbert S. Newman and Partners; **Completion Date:** 1990

Photos by Nick Wheeler/
Wheeler Photographics
c 1990

Natatorium

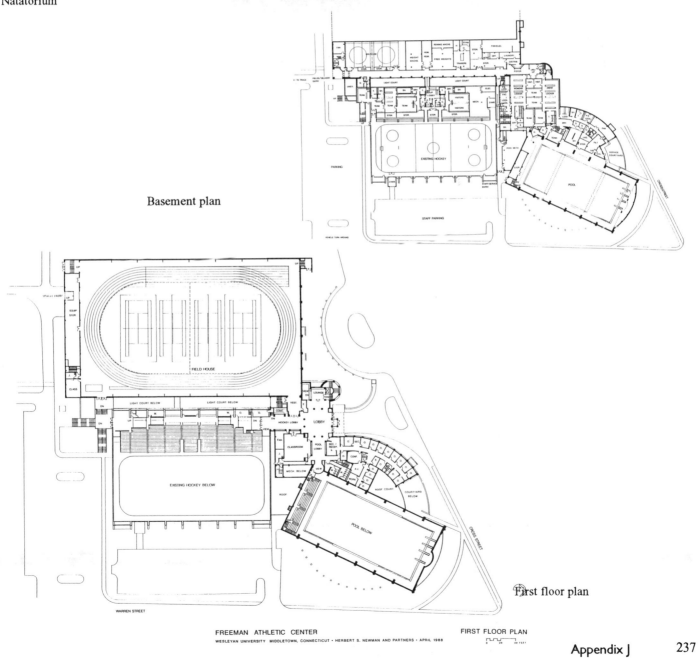

Basement plan

First floor plan

FREEMAN ATHLETIC CENTER
WESLEYAN UNIVERSITY MIDDLETOWN, CONNECTICUT · HERBERT S. NEWMAN AND PARTNERS · APRIL 1988

FIRST FLOOR PLAN

DONALD B. CANHAM NATATORIUM
UNIVERSITY OF MICHIGAN
ANN ARBOR, MICHIGAN

Square Footage: 75,275; Cost: $7.4 million; Primary Architect: Hobbs & Black Associates, Inc.; Completion Date: August 1988

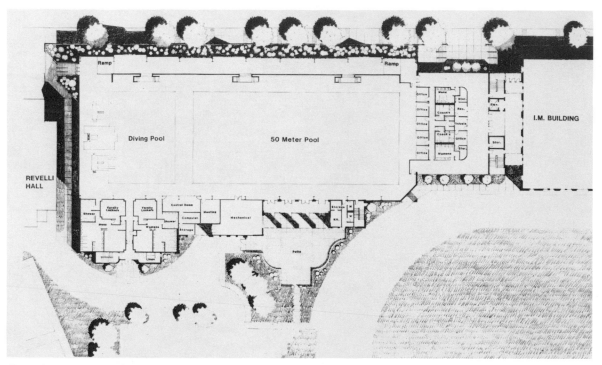

Ground level plan

Photos by Chris Lark,
Lark and Associates, Inc.

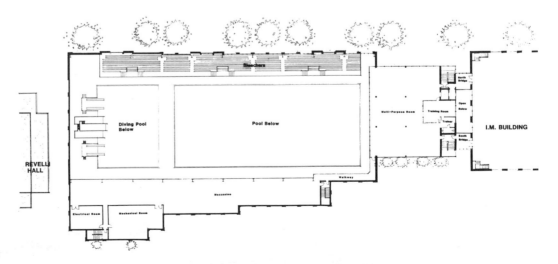

Mezzanine plan

CHEEL CAMPUS CENTER
CLARKSON UNIVERSITY
POTSDAM, NEW YORK

Square Footage: 110,000; **Cost:** $11.5 million; **Primary Architect:** Tully Associates, Inc.; **Completion Date:** September 1991

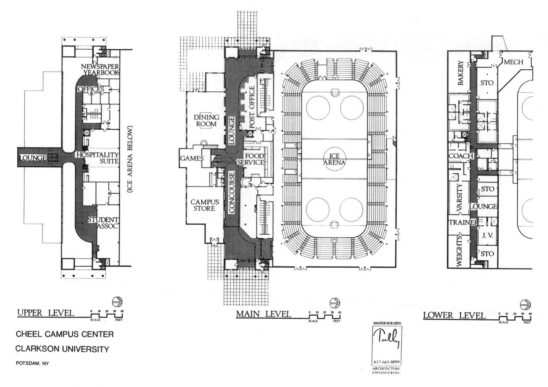

UPPER LEVEL

CHEEL CAMPUS CENTER
CLARKSON UNIVERSITY
POTSDAM, NY

MAIN LEVEL

MASTER BUILDERS
Tully
617-665-0099
ARCHITECTURE
ENGINEERING

LOWER LEVEL

Upper, main, lower levels

Photos by Wayne Soverns, Jr.

HARRY BARBEE, JR. CENTER
WOODBERRY FOREST SCHOOL
WOODBERRY FOREST, VIRGINIA

**Square Footage: 75,606; Cost: $4.6 million; Primary Architect: Tully Associates, Inc.
Completion Date: 1987**

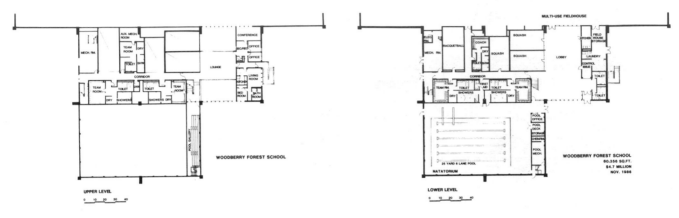

Upper level

Lower level natatorium, courts, ancillary

Lower level field house

Photos by Wayne Soverns, Jr.

APPENDIX K
METRIC CONVERSION FORMULAS

Converting from Metric to English:

To Obtain	Multiply	By
Inches	Centimeters	0.3937007874
Feet	Meters	3.280839895
Yards	Meters	1.093613298
Miles	Kilometers	0.6213711922

Converting from English to Metric:

To Obtain	Multiply	By
Centimeters	Inches	2.54
Meters	Feet	0.3048
Meters	Yards	0.9144
Kilometers	Miles	1.609344

INDEX

247